Studies in General Linguistics and Language Structure

Sound and Meaning

The Roman Jakobson Series in Linguistics and Poetics

C. H. van Schooneveld, Series Editor

N.S. TRUBETZKOY

STUDIES IN GENERAL LINGUISTICS

AND LANGUAGE STRUCTURE

Edited, and with an introduction by Anatoly Liberman

Translated by Marvin Taylor and Anatoly Liberman

DUKE UNIVERSITY PRESS Durham and London 2001

© 2001 Duke University Press

Printed in the United States of America on acid-free paper ∞

Typeset in Stone Serif by Tseng Information Systems, Inc.

Library of Congress Cataloging-in-Publication Data appear on the last printed page of this book.

Contents

Preface

When a scholar discovers an important law or initiates a new trend, his other achievements are apt to be forgotten. N. S. Trubetzkoy is famous for his works on phonology. The concept of the phoneme goes back to Baudouin de Courtenay, but phonology as a science was created by Trubetzkoy. He set its goals, formulated its problems, and offered answers to all the questions his research raised. Although since the 1930s these goals have been partly redefined, his analyses often remain the best ever proposed. Trubetzkoy's momentous achievement—the creation of phonology—overshadowed everything else he did. As a matter of curiosity, it can be mentioned that Trubetzkoy was a popular figure among Russian emigrés (he left Russia soon after the revolution, first settled in Bulgaria, and then moved to Vienna), who knew him mainly as the founder of the so-called Eurasian doctrine. Those interested in Trubetzkoy's contribution to history and political science will find them in *The Legacy of Genghis-Khan* (Trubetzkoy 1991). In his capacity as professor of Slavic at the University of Vienna, Trubetzkoy also taught literature, and some of his works on modern and medieval Russian authors are original and brilliant (see Trubetzkoy 1990, which contains a detailed bibliography). It is natural that Trubetzkoy the student of politics, history, and literature does not enjoy the prestige of Trubetzkoy the phonologist and structuralist. It is equally natural that his essays on Indo-European, Slavic, Finno-Ugric, and Caucasian philology appeal first and foremost to specialists in these areas; yet they also bear the imprint of his genius and deserve much greater exposure. Each of the "specific" works in part II of this book is a study in the general laws of language to the same extent as are the works in part I.

From his emigration in 1919 until his death in 1938, Trubetzkoy wrote mainly in German. But a few articles appeared in French, and the works on Eurasian problems were published in Russian. Language barriers are no less strong among linguists than elsewhere, and at present those wishing to make an impact on linguistic theory have to use English, for German and French have lost their status as the main vehicles of international culture, while Russian has always been a secret language outside Slavistic scholarly circles. The other barrier between Trubetzkoy and the linguistic world has been noted above: it is the material he discussed. Few people other than specialists will take the trouble to read long articles devoted to Balto-Slavic accents or Russian-

Belorussian isoglosses on the off chance of learning something interesting about general prosody or the theory of sound change.

The purpose of this volume is threefold: (1) It is a reminder that Trubetzkoy produced important linguistic works not dealing specifically with phonology. (2) It broadens Trubetzkoy's audience. Slavic scholars will continue to discuss Trubetzkoy's reconstructions for their own sake, while general linguists will now be able to mine his articles for methodological approaches. (3) It presents Trubetzkoy's phonology in a new light. The *Grundzüge der Phonologie* (1939; Principles of phonology) is a posthumous book, a summary of his late views on the linguistic function of speech sounds, but his preliminary, much more detailed discussions of oppositions, length, and other topics clarify his conclusions as they appear in the *Grundzüge* and allow us to follow the development of his thought.

Despite the tremendous growth of published production characteristic of our time, works on the history of scholarship enjoy considerable popularity. Trends come and go, but definitive solutions, some of which seemed to be within reach so few decades ago, keep escaping us, and more and more scholars are realizing that a close look at their predecessors' search for the truth is as important as knowledge of their conclusions and recommendations. No longer optimistic about reaching the promised land, we have come to relish wandering in the desert.

That is why this volume includes not only early articles on phonology but also excerpts from Trubetzkoy's correspondence. Before fleeing from Czechoslovakia in 1939, Roman Jakobson gave Bohumil Trnka a package of letters that he had received from Trubetzkoy between 1920 and 1938. The letters were returned to their addressee after the war and were published with an excellent commentary (Trubetzkoy 1975). But they have not been translated from the original Russian, which explains why they have passed unnoticed by general linguists despite many laudatory reviews.

Had Trubetzkoy not emigrated, he would have taught Indo-European linguistics, Sanskrit, and Avestan. Nothing would have prevented him from developing his phonological ideas, but he hardly would have concentrated on Slavic philology. True, he made a name for himself among Moscow linguists as a critic of Šaxmatov's approach to the genesis of the Russian language and planned writing a book on the subject (see his first letters to Jakobson), but he did not know enough to go beyond a general challenge to Šaxmatov. At Vienna, his duties included teaching the history of all the Slavic languages, and he became one of the principal experts in the field. Superior knowledge bred greater caution. A series of articles appeared in journals, but the book was never written. A very early, lengthy draft of the book perished in Rostov.

Trubetzkoy's correspondence testifies to his mastery of Indo-European linguistics, so his articles on Greek and Latin do not come as a surprise. What always surprises those for whom Trubetzkoy is only the author of the *Grundzüge der Phonologie* is his lifelong interest in diachronic linguistics. Slavic scholars know better, but Germanic, Romance, and other language historians have overlooked this part of his heritage. His earliest works deal with the history of culture, literature (especially folklore), and language. He always looked for the inner logic of evolution. First, he searched for this logic in the laws of linguistic geography and relative chronology. Later, when sound change appeared to him as the history of phonemic oppositions, he detected new principles of evolution, and, had he not died at the age of forty-eight, he would most probably have written *The Principles of Historical Phonology*. His letters show how far advanced he was in this area, how many pitfalls he instinctively avoided, and how early on he reached conclusions that did not become common knowledge until the 1950s.

This volume can cover with any thoroughness only Trubetzkoy's work on general and Indo-European linguistics. Nevertheless, the pieces on the Caucasian languages, together with the excerpts from his letters, give some idea of the breadth of his involvement with Caucasian philology. The same holds for the Finno-Ugric family. A scholar of Trubetzkoy's caliber needs a multivolume set of selected writings, like the one Roman Jakobson took care to provide for himself. Until Trubetzkoy is accorded such an honor, the reader will have to make do with the present collection, two other anthologies (Trubetzkoy 1987, 1988), neither in English, his posthumous books (Trubetzkoy 1950, 1954, 1956, 1964, 1973, 1975, 1990, 1991), and the editions of the *Grundzüge der Phonologie* in various languages.

In producing an English version of Trubetzkoy's prose, we strove to achieve a stylistic unity lacking in the originals, which appeared in three languages. Trubetzkoy knew German and French very well, but neither was his mother tongue, and he often wrote his texts in Russian and then translated them. Whenever possible, his articles have been checked against his letters, and the Russian terms were given the deciding vote in doubtful cases. For example, while discussing Balto-Slavic prosody, Trubetzkoy refers in French to *intonations,* in German (as a rule) to *Akzente,* and in Russian (also as a rule) to *akcenty.* For this reason, the word *accent(s)* has been chosen in English, even in the translations from the French. In only a few exceptional cases has deviation from Trubetzkoy's terminology been considered desirable. For example, Trubetzkoy speaks of *velikorusskij jazyk* '(the) Great Russian (language)' and *malorusskij jazyk* '(the) Small Russian (language),' but in English we have normally used the familiar names *Russian* and *Ukrainian.*

The members of the Prague Circle attempted to find English equivalents of the terms coined by Trubetzkoy and Jakobson in German and Russian, but their efforts were not wholly successful, and Christiane A. M. Baltaxe, the translator of the *Grundzüge der Phonologie* into English, faced a formidable task. She solved many problems admirably, and, to ensure continuity for English readers, the terms used in this volume are generally the same as in *Principles of Phonology*. But when those terms could be improved (without introducing anachronisms), they were. The same is true for the names of "exotic" languages.

Readers who compare our translations with the originals will also observe that we have reworded and streamlined bulky passages, frequently eliminating rhetorical phrases of the type *thus we see, it goes without saying, we may conclude that, in other words,* and so on, relics of the (Russian) academic style of Trubetzkoy's generation. Logical changes, however, were strictly avoided.

Trubetzkoy naturally did not follow any of the style sheets familiar to us, and in his letters (never meant for publication) references were given in full only when he thought Jakobson would need them. Later, Jakobson and his team supplied the volume of Trubetzkoy's correspondence with full bibliographic apparatus, which is of inestimable value. For this edition, the titles occurring in Trubetzkoy's articles and Jakobson's notes to the letters have been verified, often expanded, and in several cases corrected. All the linguistic forms cited by Trubetzkoy have likewise been checked and glosses to them added. Only a few examples from the Caucasian languages appear below unverified. Obvious misprints in the originals have been silently corrected.

The articles selected for this book have been translated by Marvin Taylor, who also compiled the indexes except for the index of subjects. Anatoly Liberman translated the letters from the Russian and checked or supplied glosses for most of the words in languages other than German and French. All the translations have been read and edited by both collaborators. The editor turned several times for help to Dr. Jurij A. Kleiner (of St. Petersburg University), Professor Tadao Shimomiya (of Gakushuin University), and Professors William Miranda and Robert Sonkowsky (both of the University of Minnesota). Our gratitude is due to them and to the Roman Jakobson Trust for permission to publish excerpts from Trubetzkoy's correspondence free of charge.

A few final remarks are in order. Under no circumstances should this volume be looked on as a memorial to Trubetzkoy or as an object of only historical interest. What Trubetzkoy has to say never sounds outdated, whether we agree with him or not, and the problems that he attacked remain at the center of present-day linguistics. In dealing with the formation of language unions, the origin of the Indo-Europeans, Balto-Slavic accentuation, the Latin subjunctive, and so forth (let alone the uses of phonology), modern scholarship has either developed in the direction indicated by Trubetzkoy or attempted to shake off his influence. No one can ignore his views.

It would have been presumptuous on the editor's part to pass judgment on Trubetzkoy's solutions even when he was competent to do so. A fairly recent annotated edition (Trubetzkoy 1987) of Trubetzkoy's contributions to philology (literature/folklore as well as linguistics) quotes extensively from his correspondence and offers some discussion of the problems touched on by him. The selection of Trubetzkoy's letters translated here performs a similar function. Beyond that, only monographs with titles like *Trubetzkoy as a Language Historian, Trubetzkoy and Caucasian Linguistics,* or *The Trubetzkoy-Benveniste Theory of the* a-*Subjunctive,* some of which already exist, will be able to do justice to Trubetzkoy's work. If the present book happens to stimulate a deeper study of Trubetzkoy's legacy and of the problems that interested him and succeeds in introducing his ideas to general linguists not fully aware of their significance, its purpose will have been fulfilled.

A Note on Transcription

The linguistic material in this book appears as it did in Trubetzkoy's original writings. The modern convention of placing phonetic transcriptions within square brackets and phonemic transcriptions within slashes is not used; the material is printed in italics, and the transcriptions are sometimes broader, sometimes narrower, as Trubetzkoy saw fit to make them. Nor have we normalized the phonetic symbols that Trubetzkoy employed, the conventions of which differ according to the language under study; exceptions were made only when linguistic material from one and the same language had been presented in slightly different phonetic alphabets in different articles. Words in Cyrillic alphabets have been transliterated according to the system followed by *The Slavic and Eastern European Journal* and other standard publications. Cyrillic spellings were retained only when information would have been lost by transliterating them, especially in connection with historical forms.

Abbreviations

abl.	ablative	Mordv.	Mordvin
acc.	accusative	n.	noun
adj.	adjective	nom.	nominative
adv.	adverb	nt.	neuter
Avest.	Avestan	OCS	Old Church Slavonic
Beloruss.	Belorussian	OIr.	Old Irish
Bulg.	Bulgarian	OLat.	Old Latin
Čak.	Čakavian	OPr.	Old Prussian
Cher.	Cheremis	opt.	optative
Circ.	Circassian	ORuss.	Old Russian
Cz.	Czech	Osc.	Oscan
dat.	dative	p.	person
dial.	dialectal	part.	participle
e.	eastern	pass.	passive
Engl.	English	perf.	perfect
f.	feminine	pl.	plural
Finn.	Finnish	Pol.	Polish
Fr.	French	pres.	present
fut.	future	pret.	preterite
g.	genitive	Russ.	Russian
Ger.	German	sect.	section
Gmc.	Germanic	Serb.	Serbian
Goth.	Gothic	Serbo-Cr.	Serbo-Croatian
Gk.	Greek	sg.	singular
Gr.Russ.	Great Russian	Skt.	Sanskrit
imper.	imperative	Slav.	Slavic
indic.	indicative	Sloven.	Slovenian
inf.	infinitive	Sorb.	Sorbian
instr.	instrumental	Štok.	Štokavian
interj.	interjection	subj.	subjunctive
intr.	intransitive	Ukr.	Ukrainian
Kab.	Kabardian	Umbr.	Umbrian
Lat.	Latin	v.	verb
Latv.	Latvian	voc.	vocative
Lith.	Lithuanian	w.	western
loc.	locative	WFinn.	West Finnic
m.	masculine		

Studies in General Linguistics and Language Structure

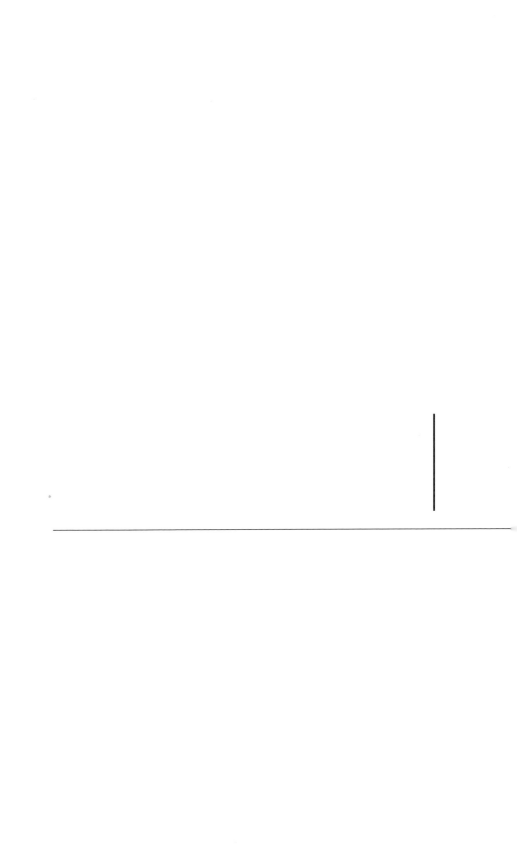

1. Phonological Systems Considered in Themselves and in Relation to General Language Structure

Descriptions of the phonological systems of all the languages of the world are urgently needed. To be successful, however, they must be carried out in a uniform way and organized internationally. Therefore, it is absolutely necessary to create an international association for phonology.

Phonology is concerned not with the sounds of speech as physical, physiological, or psychophysiological phenomena but rather with phonemes, the sound intentions present in the linguistic consciousness and realized in speech. Only sound distinctions capable of differentiating meaning are phonologically relevant, since, from the standpoint of the language structure, only they are intentional. The phonological system of a language is the embodiment of the sound intentions endowed with distinctive function in that language. The study of such systems has shown that the relations among their elements are of many different types: some are bound by common features more closely, others less so. It follows that the phonological systems of different languages display their own, individual structures. Research has also shown that the number of possible structural types is not infinite: certain combinations never occur, while others are restricted to definite conditions. In other words, we must recognize the existence of structural laws for phonological systems.

Phonology sets out not only to identify the content of the phoneme inventory and the structure of the phonological system of a given language but also to investigate the combinations of phonemes that are possible and that actually occur in the language, their relative frequency, and the extent to which they are employed for semantic purposes. This research, which requires various methods, including statistics, illuminates the individual character of the language in question. Here, too, the number of possible types is not infinite, and comparative study reveals the existence of general laws. Since phonology investigates the sound intentions that distinguish meaning, it may be subdivided according to the types of meaning expressed linguistically: general, or lexical, phonology; morphological phonology (or morphonology, for short), which is concerned with the morphological application of phonological distinctions; and syntactic phonology, which investigates phonological phenomena having a syntactic function. The search for general laws is characteristic of all branches of phonology.

The phonological approach can be applied to the functioning of languages in time and space. Important results emerge when the geographic distribution of phonological features and structural types is examined both within the borders of a language and over multilingual geographic areas. The ranges of the features and types often cross language boundaries, and neighboring but genetically unrelated languages frequently belong to the same type. In historical linguistics, too, the phonological approach opens up new perspectives. Since the content of a phoneme is indivisibly linked to its position within the phonological system, change in a phoneme implies change in the structure of the phonological system, and change in the system implies change in the content of the individual phonemes. This new, holistic view of language history contrasts sharply with the older, atomistic approach: language history acquires the inner logic it had lacked. And, since the concept of the phoneme as sound intention and means of semantic differentiation implies purpose, historical phonology becomes, for the first time, a teleological discipline.

The phonological view also gives the reconstruction of older languages a new direction. Inasmuch as the phonological systems of existing languages follow certain principles of structural organization, we may not reconstruct combinations that contradict these principles. The degree of arbitrariness of scholars' reconstructions is thereby reduced and their probability increased. Special questions, as yet uninvestigated but of great importance, emerge where the geographic and chronological lines of perspective on the growth and functioning of languages intersect.

Phonology opens up new vistas for the study of language not only in time and space but also in its social functions. This is especially true of standard and literary languages. The way in which the phonological system of the standard language diverges from the systems of dialects and of the language of the so-called common people brings the goal-oriented aspect of the phonological side of language into sharp relief. And phonology provides a solution to many problems in the study of literary artistic expression that had been either ignored or addressed with a notorious lack of success from the atomistic-phonetic point of view.

The relation between language and writing is illuminated with particular clarity from the phonological perspective. The purpose of a practical writing system is to reproduce not all the sounds that are spoken but only those oppositions with phonological value. We write not what we actually pronounce but rather what we mean or intend to say. This has methodological consequences for the study of dead languages. If a sound system is to be reconstructed on the basis of a preserved alphabet, one may not—as has frequently been done—draw direct conclusions from the writing system about the phonetic value of the sounds. The discrepancy between the preserved writing system and the reconstructed sound system cannot be explained by ostensible faults or imperfections in the alphabet: we must always remember that writing reproduces only the phonological, not the phonetic, system of the language and that these are different things. The conclusions that have been drawn from the orthography of and errors in old inscriptions and manuscripts will have to be thoroughly revised from the phonological standpoint.

In addition to answering academic questions such as these, phonology sheds new light on a number of practical matters. Most important is the creation of new alphabets for languages that have heretofore lacked writing; many linguists have come to phonology from just this area. Closely related, of course, is the task of reforming existing alphabets that are ill suited to their purpose. The reform of stenographic systems could also be mentioned. Finally, elementary school instruction presents the linguist with problems that can be solved systematically only through the consistent application of the phonological point of view.

This brief overview shows that the phonological study of the sounds of human language brings with it profound changes in several important areas of linguistics. Although phonology is an empirical science, it also strives to identify general laws, and the laws thus discovered are much more powerful and far-reaching than those formulated in older linguistics. The two sides of phonology, that looking toward individual languages and that looking toward general laws, are so closely linked as to be inseparable. The general phonological principles are empirical generalizations that can stand only on the basis of the phonological study of all the languages of the world, insofar as this is possible. On the other hand, the idiosyncrasies of the phonological system of a given language can be isolated and analyzed correctly only if one disregards everything in the system stemming from general phonological principles— and this requires knowledge of these principles. The phonological study of all the world's languages must be carried out in a parallel, coordinated fashion. The organization of phonological research is thus a matter of life and death for phonology.

The phonological conference held in Prague in 1930, the proceedings of which will be familiar to participants in the Second International Congress of Linguists, resolved to found an international association for phonology, whose task it will be to support phonological research by means of mutual communication and consultation. The conference also delegated me to request the moral support of the Second International Congress of Linguists for the association. I permit myself, therefore, on behalf of the 1930 conference, to offer the proposition presented above for the consideration of the Second International Congress of Linguists.

2. Phonology versus Phonetics

It was understood long ago that a great difference exists between sound intentions (phonemes) and the sounds actually pronounced, but this fact has been lost on the majority of linguists. Only a very few have made occasional use of it. The distinction was worked out systematically in the school of Baudouin de Courtenay, but this school remained on the periphery of language science until very recently; only since the World War has the pendulum begun to swing back. Independently, and from various quarters, scholars are recognizing that the study of sound intentions, or sound concepts, may be more important for linguistics than the investigation of physiological articulatory processes and acoustic sound values. A fundamental distinction between two disciplines, phonetics and phonology, is emerging.

Phonology is concerned with phonemes, that is, with the sound intentions (or, to put it more simply, sound concepts) employed in a given language to distinguish meaning. A sound contains a whole complex of phonetic features, and the phonetician must investigate all of them. For the differentiation of meaning in a given language, however, only a few features of the sound are employed; the others are irrelevant. Phonology is interested only in the sound concepts abstracted from the features relevant for distinguishing meaning; it looks at their content and mutual relations. Phonologists understand that in speech these concepts become intentions that are realized in objectively perceptible sounds and that these sounds naturally display a number of phonologically irrelevant features in addition to the relevant ones, but they leave the investigation of these sounds or phonetic realizations to the phonetician, whose scope of interests and approach are different. The phonologist also knows that the realization of a phoneme depends on its position and other external factors; a single phoneme can sometimes be realized as a combination of sounds, a phoneme combination sometimes as a single sound. To the phonologist, this merely proves how different the objects of phonological and phonetic study are. The phonetician wants to discover sound distinctions that speakers do not notice in their mother tongue. The phonologist, on the other hand, is interested only in distinctions that speakers *must* notice in their mother tongue because they determine the meaning of words and sentences. The phonetician wants to penetrate the organs of speech and investigate every detail of their operation as if they were a machine, while the phonologist wants to penetrate the linguistic consciousness and study the content of the individual sound concepts that make up the words and sentences of a given language.

This fundamental distinction between the phonetic and the phonological standpoint cannot be emphasized enough. Phonology must never invoke or seek refuge in experimental phonetics. Phonetics can discover every feature of a sound, but it cannot determine which of them are distinctive. Therefore, I would like to warn strongly against Professor De Groot's (1933, 113) recommendation that the results of acoustic-phonetic studies of vowels be carried over into the realm of phonology. A system of sound concepts is something fundamentally different from a table giving the difference between upper and lower formant frequencies according to precise measurements. Professor Bauer (1933) observes correctly that the three vowel phonemes of Arabic are realized differently according to the phonetic environment. If we investigated Arabic vowels with the methods of experimental phonetics, as De Groot recommends, we would have to measure the upper and lower formants for every vowel nuance and enter them all into the formant table. We would then have not three but a much greater number of points, and who can say whether they would form a triangle or a quadrangle? From the phonetic point of view, this would be a graphic representation of the Arabic vowels, but from the phonological standpoint, the picture would be decidedly incorrect, for the phonological system of Arabic has only three vowel phonemes. The Arabic writing system, with its three vowel characters, reflects the phonological state of affairs exactly.

This case is not unique; phonology can learn infinitely more from the analysis of a good writing system (one that was created for the language in question and has proved itself over time) than from detailed acoustic measurements and experiments. A good, practical alphabet represents not the sounds but rather the sound concepts that differentiate meaning in the language, and this is precisely the focus of phonological study. And, if a good writing system can be of great service to phonology, the converse is also true: phonology facilitates the creation of such systems. Many languages are now in the process of romanizing their old national alphabets or otherwise reforming their writing systems, and new alphabets are being introduced for peoples previously without writing. The scholarly literature on this subject shows that those involved are guided not by phonetic but by phonological considerations. A prime example of the significance of phonology in the creation of a practical writing system is the present Japanese roman alphabet. Up to now, Europeans and Americans have transcribed Japanese names and words with a roman transcription (the so-called Hepburn system) that reproduced only the phonetic value of the sounds, without paying attention to the phonological aspect of the language. When the Japanese themselves decided to replace their old writing system with a roman alphabet, it turned out that the phonetically oriented Hepburn system was unacceptable to their linguistic consciousness. Certain sound distinctions marked in this system were irrelevant. In Japanese, *ts* occurs only before *u*, and *t* only before *a, o,* and *e*. Thus, *ts* and *t* always occur in different environments and cannot distinguish meaning; they are not kept apart in the Japanese linguistic consciousness and must be written in the practical alphabet with a single letter, just as, in German, palatal *k* and velar *k* are written with the same letter.

The distinction between phonetics and phonology consists not only in their domains (and thus their methods) but also in their attitudes toward their subject matter. Phonetics is normally isolating and atomistic. A speech sound can be studied phonetically in complete disregard of the other sounds of the language; in phonology, such a procedure is impossible. Since phonology deals with the sound concepts that differentiate meaning, a phoneme is always examined in contrast to other phonemes of the same system, never in isolation. The primary object of phonological study is, in fact, the types of sound opposition that can create distinctions in meaning. The phonological content of a phoneme depends on the oppositions in which it participates, that is, on its relations to other phonemes, its position within the system. And this creates a deep cleft between the methods of phonetics and those of phonology: the atomistically oriented science of phonetics investigates sounds and sound phenomena in isolation; the holistically oriented science of phonology takes the phonological system as a unit to be analyzed into its constituent parts. It frequently happens that a sound opposition distinguishes meaning only in certain positions; it follows that position can affect the content of individual phonemes. The phonologist must investigate not only the content of all phonemes in all positions but also all possible phoneme combinations and describe their distribution and function.

There is a certain similarity between phonology and grammar. Phonemes are conventional signs from which words are constructed, so the phonological system is a sign system, and the phonologist studies the content (the mutual relations) of the signs and their permissible combinations. The grammarian does the same with grammatical forms, which, after all, are merely signs for formal categories. To be sure, there is a considerable inner difference, but the external similarity is unmistakable, and Sechehaye is therefore correct in calling phonology a "grammar of phonemes" (1933, 119). This is a fruitful thought, one that can be developed further and should be of value for the methods of both phonology and grammar.

Since phonemes serve the purpose of sense differentiation, it is appropriate to ask what kinds of distinctions phonological oppositions create. Phonemes and phoneme combinations can be endowed with morphological function:

some combinations, for example, are excluded from the root and can occur only when an affix is attached to it, and these combinations therefore mark the morpheme boundary. Phonological phenomena can also exercise syntactic functions, such as marking word boundaries or lending emphasis to a word. In Czech, for example, word stress is irrelevant for sense differentiation, for it always falls on the first syllable, but in larger syntactic units it marks word boundaries and words that are to receive special emphasis. Still other phonological phenomena, such as intonation, distinguish certain sentence types. The phonological system is thus closely intertwined with the grammatical structure of language, and Karcevskij (1933) is justified in calling for the subdivision of phonology into general phonology, word phonology, morphological phonology, syntactic phonology, and lexical phonology.

The importance of the phonological approach to the study of sounds is not restricted to synchronic, or descriptive, linguistics. It can be of considerable value for diachronic, or historical, linguistics as well, for it is a part of the new structural linguistics that, in the words of Mathesius (1933, 145), should form a synthesis of the Humboldt and the Bopp schools in the study of language. The prevailing, phonetically oriented approach to the history of sounds was necessarily isolating. Scholars wrote the history of individual sounds, not of the system, and some handbooks even presented the history of the sounds in alphabetical order. Historical phonologists, however, see the development of sounds as a restructuring of the phonological system; they ask how the system was affected by each sound change. The consistent application of this principle lends new and sometimes unexpected facets to the history of sounds. The inner logic of sound changes, their meaning, is laid bare—something seldom possible without phonology.

If the phonological system is a meaningful whole, if it is so closely related to grammar and so clearly reveals the individual character of each language, are grammatical and phonological structure connected? The organizing committee put this question on the agenda of the present congress. Charles Bally (1933) answered it by using the examples of French, German, and Latin to sketch out a proof of the connection between the phonic and the conceptual aspect of language. Bally's perceptive remarks are most interesting; here I emphasize only methodological considerations. Most important, Bally's comments show that investigations of this kind require the typological, not genetic, comparison of a number of languages. But one may also ask whether the results are not influenced by the choice of languages to be compared. Bally characterized French by juxtaposing it to German and Latin, but what if he had taken Italian or a non-Indo-European language such as Japanese instead of German? The picture of French that he obtained would surely have been somewhat different. But if the solution to the problem requires comparison with other languages, and if the choice of languages influences the results, then an objective solution is possible only if the given language is compared with all other languages of the world. This will become possible only when the grammatical and phonological systems of all languages have been studied and classified on typological principles.

Here I return to the thought that I expressed in my answer to the question proposed by the organizing committee [chap. 1 in this volume]. The grammatical systems of the world's languages have been described in considerable detail, but we are infinitely worse informed about the various phonological systems. The detailed study and typological classification of these systems represent one of the most pressing tasks in modern linguistics. In the contribution just mentioned, I addressed the significance of a phonological research program of this kind. But this work can be successful only if it is coordinated internationally. To this end, the International Phonological Conference held last year in Prague resolved to found an international association for phonology; this group now asks for the moral support of the Second International Congress of Linguists. We urge every congress participant interested in phonology to join our association, and we propose the following resolution:

The CIPL [Comité International Permanent de Linguistes] *should enter into friendly and official relations with the International Association for Phonology.*

3. The Systematic Phonological Representation of Languages

The comparative phonology of all the languages of the world now has a firm place on our research agenda. Its necessity is obvious and needs no further argument. But a prerequisite for it is the description of phonological systems according to a uniform plan.

The description of the phonological system of a language comprises *word phonology*—divided into *lexical* and *morphological* phonology—and *sentence phonology*. Research programs applicable to the "morphonology" and sentence phonology of all languages (to the extent that it is possible to draft such programs) were proposed by S. Karcevskij and myself at the Prague Phonological Conference and published in its proceedings (Karcevskij 1931; Trubetzkoy 1931a [chap. 11 in this volume]). To be complete, lexical, or general, word phonology must include the following aspects: (1) inventory of the phonemic system and study of its structure; (2) study of the rules governing the distribution of phonemes and phoneme combinations; (3) statistical investigation of the semantic yield of individual phonological oppositions; and (4) statistical investigation of the frequency of individual phonemes and phoneme combinations. I have addressed the structure of phonemic systems elsewhere (Trubetzkoy 1929c, 1931d) and can add nothing to those earlier treatments here. The methodological questions attendant to the statistical aspects of word phonology are not yet ready for definitive discussion. Therefore, I shall speak today only about the distribution rules.

The occurrence and use of phonemes and phoneme combinations are almost always restricted by certain *phonological rules,* which differ from one language to another. The restrictions may be of three types—according to whether they apply to a *phoneme combination,* an isolated *phoneme,* or a *phonological opposition*—and these types have different phonological consequences. The absolute or conditioned prohibition of a phoneme combination affects neither the total number of phonemes nor their phonological content; it limits only *the number of possible combinations.* The prohibition of an individual phoneme in a certain position (e.g., German *ŋ* initially and after a consonant) reduces both the number of combinations and the number of phonemes for the position in question, while their content remains unchanged: if we set up an inventory of the phonemes occurring in the position, it will contain fewer items than the overall phoneme inventory of the language, but the items will be the same. Finally, the neutralization of a phonological opposition alters not only the number of combinations and of phonemes but also the *phonological content of the phonemes* in the position in question.

In many languages, for example, the opposition between voiced and voiceless obstruents is phonologically valid before vowels and sonorants, while before another obstruent it is purely mechanical: only a voiceless obstruent may precede a voiced one, and vice versa. In the latter position, it is irrelevant whether the sound is voiced; the opposition is *neutralized,* and voice is deleted from the content of the phonemes involved. In most such cases, correlational features are neutralized: voiced-voiceless, aspirated-nonaspirated, long-short, rising-falling, and so on. But disjunct features may be neutralized as well. In many languages, for example, the place of articulation of the nasals is phonologically distinctive only before vowels, whereas before consonants it is mechanically accommodated to the following sound—so that here the nasal is conceived of without any feature of place.

The dissolution (neutralization) of phonological oppositions is the most important kind of restriction of the use of phonemes. The resulting neutralized phonemes are treated by the linguistic consciousness as special phonemes and are represented in many writing systems by special characters.[1] This perception of neutralized phonemes is sometimes expressed in their phonetic realization as well, so that they are pronounced as intermediate sounds between the two poles of the correlation.[2] But irrespective of their phonetic realization, they have a special status from the phonological point of view, so they must be treated separately in phonological statistics and must not be confused with the unmarked element of a correlation; there is a fundamental difference between the absence of a feature and its outright prohibition.

The phonological rules affecting the occurrence and use of phonemes must be investigated with respect to *range, direction,* and *targets.*

The *range* of a sound rule is the extent to which it restricts the use of a phoneme or combination or the existence of a phonological opposition. Usually, this can be expressed numerically as a percentage. The rule that German η may occur only after *u, ü, i, e, a,* for example, has a range of 84.4 percent since η is excluded after 84.4 percent of all German phonemes. It is harder to calculate the range of rules that neutralize a phonological opposition in certain positions, but here, too, a formula can generally be found. Numerical expressions of the range of a phonological rule may be called *range exponents.* If the use of a phoneme (or combination or opposition) is restricted by more than one rule, the sum of the range exponents of the rules will represent a mathematical expression for the range of the phoneme. Naturally, these numbers and percentages apply to the *possible* use of the phoneme, but they are also important for the statistical aspects of word phonology in which the actual exploitation of theoretical possibilities is investigated.

Classified according to the *direction* in which they operate, sound rules can be *progressive, regressive,* or oriented *in both directions.* A rule is progressive if it makes the occurrence or nonoccurrence of a phoneme (or combination or opposition) dependent on the following phoneme or word boundary: in German, for example, *v* cannot stand before consonants or word finally (i.e., before the word boundary). Conversely, the rule that German *ŋ* may appear only after *u, ü, i, e,* or *a* is regressive. Rules oriented in both directions are relatively rare.

It is most important for the typology of a language to establish whether progressive or regressive sound rules predominate in it and which kind has the broader range. There are languages in which all rules are progressive, others in which regressive ones predominate. Russian, for example, belongs to the first group, Mordvin to the second; this difference between the two languages is especially striking since their phoneme inventories are almost identical (see Trubetzkoy 1932 [chap. 25 in this volume]).

By the *target* of a sound rule I mean the position in which it operates (before consonants, between vowels, word initially, and so on). The same position can serve as the target for several rules. The more rules that share a given target point, the fewer phonemes that can occur in that position. In this way, positions of *minimal* and *maximal phoneme differentiation* can be identified for most languages. Indeed, *local phoneme inventories* can be drawn up for every position that serves as the target for at least one rule. The distribution of the rules may be such that the individual phoneme inventories do not correspond (e.g., those of word-initial and word-final position) and there is no position in which all phonemes of the language occur, so it is sometimes advisable to dispense with a general phoneme inventory and work only with local ones.

The positions serving as targets for phonological rules differ considerably among languages. It is not even necessary for them to correspond to phonetic reality: thus, it is well known that many sound rules target the word boundary, which is phonetically nonexistent in fluent speech. A similar function can be fulfilled by a morpheme boundary within a word. This is the case in German, for example, in which sound rules operate within the boundaries of the morpheme, not the word. This fact is characteristic of German phonology. It is very important for linguistic typology to establish which positions serve as the targets of phonological rules and which ones seem to be preferred in this respect.

4. A Theory of Phonological Oppositions

1

Modern phonology has so many points of contact with psychology and philosophy that scholars in these areas have been attracted to it from the beginning. I do not feel competent to judge to what extent phonology in its present state can be useful to psychologists and philosophers, but I can state with confidence that these disciplines have already rendered great services to phonology. The articles of Čyževskyj (1931) and Pos (1933) have contributed to the development of our science, and Bühler, especially, in two exemplary articles (1931, 1933) and his remarkable book *Sprachtheorie* (1934), has shed light on its theoretical foundations. A number of scholars interested in general linguistics have been inspired by the example of professional philosophers to reflect on the main concepts of phonology. The resulting series of interesting and, in almost every case, valuable contributions is documented in the *Bulletins d'information* numbers 1 and 2 of the International Association for Phonology (Association Internationale pour les Études Phonologiques 1932, 1935), to which should be added Twaddell's book *On Defining the Phoneme* (1935) and the judicious reviews of it by Swadesh (1935) and Trnka (1935a).

The effort that has so far been expended on delimiting the fields of phonology and phonetics and on defining *phoneme* and *linguistic function* has been worthwhile, and this work will continue. But such problems are hardly the most important ones facing phonologists. Whatever formula one accepts for the definition of the phoneme, all phonologists know very well what must be done in order to isolate the phonemes and establish the phoneme inventory of a given language. In practice, difficulties are presented not by the distinction between phonemes and phonetic variants but by questions such as whether the initial affricate of German *Zahn* 'tooth' is to be considered a single-consonant phoneme or a cluster (*ts*). Problems like this, of a more or less technical type, are ignored by scholarship devoted to the cognitive bases of phonology. But given the current state of the discipline, it is just such questions that are most in need of clear, definitive solutions.

Does it follow, then, that psychologists and philosophers have contributed all they can to the development of phonology and that their help is no longer needed? On the contrary, it is probably needed now more than ever. What I would like to put before them here is not the definition of the phoneme, or the boundary between phonetics and phonology, but a series of other problems.

However one defines the phoneme, one cannot do without the *opposition*. The phoneme is a term of an opposition that cannot be reduced to smaller and simpler phonological units (cf. "Projet de terminologie phonologique standardisée" 1931, 311). Therefore, a phonemic system presupposes a system of oppositions, and the classification of phonemes presupposes a classification of oppositions. But *opposition* is not exclusively a phonological concept, it is a logical one, and the role it plays in phonology is strongly reminiscent of its role in psychology. It is impossible to study phonological oppositions (of which phonemes are only the terms) without analyzing the concept of the opposition from the points of view of psychology and logic. Here, the collaboration of psychologists and philosophers would be particularly useful.

For some years I have been working on a theory of phonological systems, and I have continually run up against the same problem: the lack of a satisfactory theory of oppositions. Perhaps this lack is illusory and due only to my ignorance in the areas of psychology and philosophy; but whatever the reason, I have not been able to find a generally accepted terminology for the different kinds of oppositions encountered in phonology. In an article on "current phonology" (Trubetzkoy 1933, esp. 234–39), I presented to the readers of the *Journal de psychologie* some results of my research on oppositions. Here, I propose to discuss the subject in greater detail, on the assumption that it will attract the attention of psychologists. I must admit that my motivation is not entirely selfless: I am writing not only to inform psychologists of results that may interest them but also to request their help.

The first distinction to be observed is that between *bilateral* (one-dimensional) and *multilateral* (multidimensional) *oppositions*. Each opposition presupposes the existence of a certain number of features common to both its terms. If these common features are shared only by the two terms of the given opposition, the opposition is bilateral. But if they all occur in other members of the same system as well, the opposition is multilateral. In French, for example, the opposition *t-d* is bilateral because these phonemes are the only apical (dental) stop consonants without nasalization in the phonological system of the language, but the opposition *p-t* is multilateral because the features common to the two phonemes (occlusion and absence of voice) occur also in another French phoneme, namely, *k*.

The distinction between bilateral and multilateral oppositions is not unique to phonology; it may be found in any system of oppositions, notably in all systems of signs (since these are always terms of oppositions). For example, in the system of capital letters of the roman alphabet, the opposition *E-F* is bilateral since the features common to the two letters (the two short horizontal bars attached to the right side of the vertical bar at its upper extremity and its midpoint) do not co-occur in any other letter, but the opposition *X-Z* is multilateral since the only feature common to the two letters (the diagonal bar from the upper right to the lower left) also occurs in other letters of the same alphabet (*A, V,* etc.).

Every system contains a greater number of multilateral than of bilateral oppositions. Of the oppositions into which each member of a phonological system enters, only a small number are bilateral, and some phonemes enter only into multilateral oppositions (e.g., German *h*). But the bilateral oppositions are the most important ones for the structure of the phonemic system; their terms are linked much more closely than those of multilateral oppositions.

4

Consistent observance of the distinction between bilateral and multilateral oppositions will require certain changes in the definitions of phonological oppositions and combinatory variants proposed in the "Projet de terminologie phonologique standardisée" (1931). It will now be necessary to distinguish between *directly* and *indirectly distinctive oppositions*. The phonological opposition is defined in the "Projet" as a "phonic difference capable of distinguishing meaning in a given language." This definition remains valid for the oppositions that I propose to call *directly distinctive*. A phonic opposition is directly distinctive if both its terms can occur in the given language in the same environment in such a way that they alone distinguish meaning. These oppositions can be bilateral (e.g., French *t–d* in *toit* 'roof' – *doit* '[he] must') or multilateral (e.g., French *p–t* in *pousser* 'push' – *tousser* 'cough').

It may happen that the terms of an opposition never appear in the same environment; then there are two possibilities. The terms of a multilateral opposition are the realizations of different phonemes only if the sum of the features shared by them recurs in other sounds that form directly distinctive oppositions with the two terms in question. Thus, in German, although *h* and the guttural nasal *ŋ* never occur in the same environment, they are realizations of different phonemes since their only common feature is their consonantal function, a feature shared by all German consonants, most of which enter into directly distinctive oppositions with *h* and *ŋ* (e.g., *p, tz:* cf. *hacken-packen-Zacken* 'hack, pack [v.], tines,' *Ringe-Rippe-Ritze* 'rings, rib, chink'). For such cases, I propose the designation *indirectly distinctive opposition*.

Any other opposition between sounds that do not occur in the same environment is extraphonological, and its terms are combinatory variants of the same phoneme. In German, prepalatal *k* before *i* and postpalatal, labialized *k* before *u* constitute a multilateral opposition because their common features (dorsal articulation, muscular tension, aspiration, absence of voice) also occur in other realizations of German *k* (before *a,* after *e* word finally, etc.); but, since none of these other realizations forms a directly distinctive opposition with either prepalatal or labialized *k,* all of them are combinatory variants of a single phoneme *k.* In French, where voiceless *l* occurs word finally after *k, p, f,* and voiced *l* in all other positions, the two *l*'s form a bilateral opposition and never occur in the same environment, so they must be treated as combinatory variants of one phoneme *l.*

As we see, directly and indirectly distinctive oppositions cannot be differentiated unless one differentiates between bilateral and multilateral oppositions.[1]

5

Just as important for phonology is the distinction between *proportional* and *isolated* oppositions. An opposition is proportional if the relation between its terms is identical with that between the terms of other oppositions in the system; it is isolated if the relation between its terms is unique. These types of opposition may be bilateral as well as multilateral. In French, the opposition *t–d* is bilateral and proportional ($t–d = p–b = k–g = s–z = š–ž = f–v$), the opposition *p–t* is multilateral and proportional ($p–t = b–d = m–n$), the opposition *r–l* is bilateral and isolated (because *r* and *l* are the only two resonants in the French phonemic system), and the opposition *f–z* is multilateral (because its terms share only the feature of being fricatives, which unites them with *s, š, v,* and *ž*) and isolated.

Like the distinction between bilateral and multilateral oppositions, the distinction between proportional and isolated ones is not specific to phonology and can be applied to other sign systems. Among the roman minuscules, for example, the opposition *b–q* is proportional because the same relation of inversion recurs in other oppositions in the alphabet (*d–p, n–u*), while the opposition *t–l* is isolated.

In all phonological systems, proportional oppositions are in the minority, but the numerical relation varies considerably from one language to another. In the system of German consonants, proportional oppositions make up only 10.5 percent of all possible oppositions; for French consonants, the figure is 26.6 percent. For the structure of the system, the most important oppositions are the proportional ones: the distinctive features of each term of an opposition are thrown into particular relief if the same relation between two terms is repeated in other oppositions. And this circumstance facilitates the "phonological decomposition" of such a phoneme, that is, its analysis as the sum of phonological features.

6

As shown above, a bilateral opposition is phonologically distinctive only insofar as its terms occur in the same environment and differentiate meaning. If they do not occur in the same environment, they are variants of the same phoneme, and the opposition is purely phonetic. But it frequently happens that the terms of an opposition can both occur only in a limited number of environments, while in other positions only one of them is permitted. An opposition of this type is phonologically distinctive only in environments in which both terms can occur; everywhere else, its phonological function is neutralized.

Among distinctive bilateral oppositions, therefore, it is important to differentiate between those that are *neutralizable* and those that are *constant.* In French, the opposition between *e* and *ε* is neutralizable because its terms assume distinctive function only in open final syllables (*porter* 'carry' [inf.] – *portait* '[he] carried,' *les* 'the' [pl.] – *lait* 'milk,' *fée* 'fairy' – *fait* '[he] makes,' etc.), while in all other positions the choice is regulated automatically by the well-known formula: *e* in open syllables, *ε* in closed syllables. The opposition *i–e,* on the other hand, is constant because both its terms occur with distinctive function in all imaginable environments: *irriter* 'irritate' – *hériter* 'inherit,' *crie* '(I) shout' – *crée* '(I) create,' *lycée* 'high school' – *laisser* 'let,' and *piste* 'trail' – *peste* 'plague.'

These French examples show the great psychological difference between neutralizable and constant oppositions. From a phonetic point of view, the difference between *i* and *e* is no greater than that between *e* and *ε*. Nevertheless, *e* and *ε* are perceived to be more closely related than *i* and *e*—a subjective judgment stemming from the fact that the opposition *e-ε* is neutralizable while the opposition *i-e* is not. The reason for this psychological difference is not far to seek. The terms of a neutralizable opposition are separate phonemes only in environments in which their difference is phonologically distinctive; elsewhere, they are merely combinatory variants of an "archiphoneme," that is, a phoneme whose phonological content is reduced to the features shared by the two terms. Thus, each term of a neutralizable opposition has two different phonological contents, according to its position in the word. In some environments, all its features are phonologically distinctive. In others, some features have no distinctive function; that is, they are redundant. A consequence of this "double life" is that, even where all their features are distinctive, the terms of a neutralizable opposition can be analyzed phonologically into "archiphoneme + specific feature." In the terms of a constant opposition, on the other hand, all features retain their distinctive function in all positions, with the result that isolating the archiphoneme (i.e., the features shared by the two terms) is more difficult.

The distinction between bilateral neutralizable oppositions and constant oppositions (which is not unique to phonology and may be observed in other sign systems)[2] is of primary importance for the structure of phonological systems. Some languages possess only constant oppositions. In others, all bilateral oppositions are neutralizable. Most phonological systems display constant and neutralizable oppositions in unequal proportions: thus, neutralizable oppositions make up 71 percent of all bilateral oppositions in French, for example, but 58 percent in German.

7

The logical relations between the two terms of a bilateral opposition are just as diverse.

An opposition is *privative* if one of its terms possesses a feature the other lacks. In French, the opposition between nasal and oral vowels is privative (*bon* 'good' – *beau* 'beautiful,' *main* 'hand' – *met* '[he] puts,' *un* 'one' – *eux* 'them' [m.], and *sang* 'blood' – *ça* 'that') because nasalization is a feature only of the nasal vowels, not the oral ones. An opposition is *gradual* if its terms show different degrees of the same feature. The French opposition *i–e* is gradual because the two vowels differ in aperture. An opposition is *equipollent* if each of its terms is characterized by a specific feature. The French opposition *s–š* is equipollent (*sang* 'blood' – *champ* 'field,' *casser* 'break' – *cacher* 'hide,' and *Perse* 'Persian' – *perche* 'perch [fish]') because, from the point of view of French, "hissing" and "hushing" are different features in sibilants; they can be imagined neither as two degrees of a feature nor as the positive and negative value of a feature.

The difference between privative and equipollent oppositions depends to some extent on one's perspective. The voiced stops (*b, d, g*) display vocal cord vibration, which is lacking in the voiceless stops (*p, t, k*), but the latter are characterized by a muscular tension lacking in the voiced stops, so, from a phonetic point of view, the opposition between voiced and voiceless stops is equipollent. But if we disregard either voice or muscular tension, it becomes privative. The same is true for most privative oppositions: they are privative only insofar as certain features of one of the terms are left out of consideration. The difference between privative and gradual oppositions also depends on the point of view. The opposition between short and long vowels would have to be treated as gradual if it were a question of two degrees of length. But if we consider the duration of short vowels as a minimum, the opposition between short and long becomes privative: long vowels possess the feature of exceeding the minimum duration, a feature lacking in the short vowels. Finally, in certain cases, equipollent oppositions can be transformed into gradual ones, and vice versa: if French possessed a cacuminal (retroflex) sibilant in addition to s (apical) and š (palatal), as many languages of India do, the opposition s–š, cited above as equipollent, would have to be treated as gradual.

Although the distinction between privative, gradual, and equipollent oppositions depends on one's point of view, it is neither subjective nor arbitrary, for the point of view is implied by the system. As we have seen, where a term of a neutralizable opposition is the only one permitted, it is identified with the archiphoneme of the opposition. Its distinctive features lose their phonological value and are disregarded; consequently, the other term appears as the only bearer of a feature lacking in its counterpart, and the opposition becomes unambiguously privative. Thus, in Russian, where the opposition between b, d, g and p, t, k is neutralized word finally, with the result that only p, t, k are permitted, the muscular tension characteristic of the voiceless stops is disregarded, and the opposition b, d, g – p, t, k is treated as privative, with voice being its sole distinctive mark. This is a typical case: for an opposition to be clearly privative, it must be neutralizable.

A gradual opposition, on the other hand, is perceived as such only insofar as the phonological system contains a phoneme possessing the same feature as the two terms of the opposition but to a greater or lesser degree. That is why the opposition between long and short vowels is never gradual: as I have attempted to demonstrate elsewhere [chaps. 7 and 8 in this volume], no phonological system distinguishes more than two degrees of quantity. An opposition of the type i–e as in French is gradual because the phonological system contains a phoneme (a) with greater aperture of the mouth than that characteristic of e.

Finally, it is necessary to consider the case of parallelism among various oppositions, which are then seen as proportional. In Japanese, the opposition between "hissing" and "hushing" sibilants is neutralizable before front vowels (e, i): only "hushing" sibilants are permitted before i, only "hissing" ones before e. Exactly the same relation exists between palatal and velar stops, between the palatal spirant (corresponding to the German ich sound) and h, between tš, dž and t, d, and between palatalized and nonpalatalized labials. The parallelism shows that the only relevant distinction between the members of each pair is that of timbre, and the opposition between "hissing" and "hushing" sounds in Japanese can therefore be reduced to a privative opposition between palatalized and nonpalatalized sibilants.

Where the conditions indicated above are not met, the opposition remains equipollent. Thus, although the German opposition between *š* and *s* is neutralizable (before consonants, *š* is permitted only root initially, *s* only root medially),[3] it is nevertheless equipollent. Constant oppositions that are not gradual are also equipollent. One is frequently tempted to consider them as privative, but, as long as this interpretation is not confirmed by the phonological system, it cannot be phonologically correct even if it makes logical sense. In this case, one could speak of equipollent, potentially privative oppositions.

The discussion presented above of privative, gradual, and equipollent oppositions applies only to bilateral oppositions. The logical relations between the terms of multilateral oppositions are more complex but also less important for the study of phonological systems. For this reason, I have not found it necessary to expound on that subject here.[4]

8

The theory of phonological oppositions sketched here is the result of practical work. The study of a large number of phonological systems of the most diverse languages has led me to the conviction that it is impossible to group all phonological oppositions into only two classes (correlations and disjunctions), as phonologists have done up to now, and I have considered it necessary to replace this division with a more complex typology.[5] Bilateral, proportional, neutralizable, privative oppositions, on the one hand, and multilateral, isolated oppositions, on the other, are the two extremes; between them fall types combining various principles of my classification. The degree of coherence, symmetry, and equilibrium of a phonological system depends on the numerical distribution of the different types of opposition that it contains.

In bringing my theory of phonological oppositions to the attention of psychologists and logicians, I would like to take the liberty of expressing the hope that their support will prove as useful to phonologists in this area as it already has been in other areas of phonology.

5. On a New Critique of the Concept of the Phoneme

1

The new direction in linguistics known as phonology was first made public at the International Congress of Linguists in the Hague in 1928.[1] From the start, the general reaction to the theory was surprisingly positive: it was hardly criticized, let alone contested. Most critics were concerned only with the question of priority and attempted to prove that they or their teachers had formulated similar ideas many years ago; they raised no objections to phonological theory itself. Another, much smaller group consisted of certain authors of chronicle notes in academic journals who made no criticism of substance but expressed their skepticism by ironic or disparaging gestures (by setting the words *phonology* and *phoneme* in quotation marks, by adding parenthetical exclamation points, question marks, *sic,* and so on). At most, they pronounced general negative judgments without giving reasons.[2] Few opponents of the young discipline have ventured to attack it; their objections either addressed insignificant details or were so poorly argued that they convinced no one, which made refutation by phonologists unnecessary.

Only recently has there appeared a long article by the Erlangen Indo-Europeanist Alfred Schmitt with the title "The Sound Gestures of Language" (1936), the greater part of which is devoted to the refutation of phonology. The work had been complete in manuscript for some time, but, since the author had previously supported phonology and been a member of the International Phonological Working Group, he wanted to test his new position before going to press. "At first," Schmitt concedes, "I was myself skeptical of the results of my investigation. But, since the writing of the first draft about two years ago, each reexamination has led me to the same conclusion, so I believe that I may now present my work to the public without laying myself open to the charge of undue haste" (p. 57).

Schmitt's article differs from other antiphonological writings primarily in its seriousness and attention to detail, which circumstance alone justifies a response from phonologists. In addition, it is perhaps not inappropriate to take this opportunity to bring up certain important questions of linguistic theory. Schmitt deserves full credit for the sense of responsibility and the self-control that led him to wait so long before publishing his work. Nevertheless, it is regrettable that he did not find the chance to contact phonologists directly in the years following the completion of his manuscript. In conversation or correspondence, a number of apparent disagreements could have been shown to stem from misunderstandings.

2

In the introduction to the article, Schmitt says that his work has led him "to reject the phonological school's concept of the phoneme" (1936, 57). One would now expect to read a critique of the idea of the phoneme as formulated in the writings of the "phonological school." A definition of the phoneme was accepted by the Prague Phonological Conference in 1930 and appeared in the "Projet de terminologie phonologique standardisée" (1931, 311). As the only more or less official definition, this ought to be the starting point for criticism of "the phonological school's concept of the phoneme." But Schmitt does not even mention, let alone discuss, it. He says only that phonologists describe the nature of the phoneme in different ways (1936, sec. 70).

Under these circumstances, it is not clear what "concept of the phoneme" Schmitt finds untenable; the reader can only extrapolate from Schmitt's objections, in much the same way as theological historians reconstruct early Christian heresies from the church fathers' refutations. It turns out that the definition rejected by Schmitt is most similar to one given by Jones (1931, 74). This definition has not been accepted by other phonologists, however, for the simple reason that it quite obviously was created solely for purposes of transcription, as Jones (1931, 78) admitted. (Incidentally, Jones himself has since abandoned it.) [3] It is no wonder that Schmitt criticizes such a conception of the phoneme as an unjustifiable transference of the principles of writing to the description of speech. "If we treat . . . the phoneme as the sum of everything that can be expressed in a given language with the same letter" (1936, p. 92, sec. 70), then, indeed, such a notion makes sense only for writing. But this is not at all "the phonological school's concept of the phoneme"! Schmitt has created a concept of his own and demonstrated its unacceptability; the "phonological school," however, bears no responsibility for this artifact and is in no way harmed by its rejection.

Are Schmitt's arguments applicable to the phonological school's concept of the phoneme? To answer this, we must look more closely at the "official" definition of the phoneme as given in the "Projet de terminologie phonologique standardisée" (see also Trubetzkoy 1935, p. 7, sec. 1). This definition reads, "The phoneme is a *phonological unit* that cannot be divided into (successive) [4] smaller units," and it is supplemented by two others: "A *phonological unit* is a member of a phonological opposition," and "a *phonological opposition* is a sound opposition that can differentiate meaning in a given language."

What is Schmitt's objection to this, the phonological school's concept of

the phoneme? According to Schmitt, different words must also sound differently (except in the very rare case of homophony). "No matter how long a
sound sequence shared by different words may be, at some point a difference
will appear, for otherwise the individual speech gestures could not be kept
apart." One can "identify large or small segments common to a given series of
words" (1936, p. 86, sec. 61), but the remaining parts make it possible to distinguish the words (which otherwise "could not be kept apart"); that is, they
are *phonological units* according to the definition of the phonological school.
So Schmitt, too, acknowledges the existence of phonological units.

Predictably, the length of such units can vary. Also, just as in words, identical and nonidentical sequences can be discovered in larger phonological
units, too, so that in every larger phonological unit elements remain that constitute smaller phonological units. From the German word pair *Biene* 'bee' –
Fahne 'flag' we derive the differentiating elements *bī* and *fā*. Comparison of
Biene with *Bohne* 'bean' and *diene* '(I) serve' allows us to segment the larger
phonological unit *bī* into two smaller ones, *b* and *ī*. But these cannot be segmented further into smaller phonological units; that is, no word pair in German is differentiated by only a part of *b* or of *ī*, as Schmitt will have to agree.
Therefore, *b* and *ī* are indivisible phonological units, that is, *phonemes*. That is
all there is to the phonological school's concept of the phoneme.

The definition given above has two important aspects: participation in a
phonological opposition (a sound difference that can distinguish meaning)
and indivisibility into smaller phonological units. And, since the phonological unit itself is defined as a member of a phonological opposition, *the fundamental concept of phonology is not the phoneme but the phonological (or distinctive)
opposition.* Whoever accepts this idea must accept the phoneme (in the sense
given above), for the phonological school's concept of the phoneme is only a
necessary logical consequence of the concept of the phonological opposition.
Since Schmitt seems to accept the existence of phonological oppositions ("for
otherwise the individual speech gestures could not be kept apart"), his rejection of the concept of the phoneme can be due only to misunderstanding.

3

The misunderstandings between Schmitt and the phonological school stem
primarily from differing views on the distinction between language and
speech. Phonemes belong to the domain of language (*langue*), not speech
(*parole*), and rejection of the phoneme usually goes hand in hand with the failure to acknowledge this distinction. Schmitt does acknowledge it in theory,
but his interpretation of it is different from the one offered by phonologists.
For phonologists, language (Bühler's "language construct") is a system of nor-

mative values to which all utterances must refer in order to be understood. The norms of the language construct and the phenomena of the speech event are fundamentally different, incommensurate entities.

It is true, as Schmitt says, that "the levels of speech and of language, which must be strictly distinguished in theory, are intertwined in the individual speaker's consciousness" (1936, 65). But language and speech are nevertheless different objects of study and require different research methods. Speech (Bühler's "speech act," "speech event") can be registered only in concrete situations, in the speaker's linguistic activity; it must be studied with reference to the individual speaker and hearer, regardless of whether the approach is physical, physiological, or psychological. Language (*langue*), on the other hand, is a superindividual, objective, social institution, a system of values, norms, and relations that must be investigated by special methods. For such investigations it is irrelevant to what degree, if at all, the individual speaker or hearer is conscious of linguistic norms, since the research object is language itself as superindividual entity, not the relations of language to the individual's consciousness. Language and speech must be distinguished both in practice and in theory.

The phonological school has always made every effort to observe this distinction. Schmitt, on the other hand, is so taken with the ostensible intertwining of language and speech "in the individual speaker's consciousness" that he tends to blur the line between linguistic norms and the phenomena of speech and to consider the norms as real objects of study only insofar as they "are concretely embodied in individual acts of speaking and hearing" and as "the individual becomes conscious of them" (1936, 65).

This is the source of the disagreement between Schmitt and the phonological school. Schmitt concedes, for example, that an "individual tempo" (in this case, apparently a phoneme) "can receive an independent meaning." But this happens, according to him, only in the rare case that two words distinguished by one phoneme actually occur in close proximity to each other, for example, when misunderstood speakers deliberately repeat themselves: *nicht* bunt *machen, sondern* kund*machen!* 'Don't *color* it, *announce* it!' [cf. Engl. 'Don't *color* it, *cover* it!']. Only in such cases does the "individual tempo"—in this example the *k* of *kundmachen*—constitute "the one part of the whole that is illuminated by conscious attention, . . . while the rest, since it is already known, remains in shadow" (1936, p. 91, sec. 69). For Schmitt, this possibility is no proof of the existence of the phoneme because in the overwhelming majority of situations the speaker's and hearer's attention is not focused on the individual phonemes. The implication seems to be that a linguistic norm can be acknowledged to exist only if it is always consciously (not just unconsciously!) present in the individual's mind. If this thesis were followed to its logical consequence, one would have to deny the existence of grammatical rules, perhaps even all linguistic norms.

The fact that in certain situations individual phonemes are the focus of attention and that each word contains only a fixed number of such "potential foci" (as many as there are phonemes in the word) is indeed an ancillary proof of the reality of the phoneme. But phonology does not need to have recourse to this argument, for what goes on in the individual consciousness of the speaker and hearer during conversation concerns phonology only indirectly. As norms, linguistic values lead an objective, superindividual existence, irrespective of the extent to which individual members of the linguistic community are conscious of them. And, just as the grammatical system of a language must be investigated without regard to how often speakers' and hearers' attention may be focused on a given grammatical form, so must the phonological system of a language be studied independently of the attention paid by speakers and hearers to individual phonemes.

4

The theoretical and practical distinction between language and speech, between linguistic norm and speech phenomenon, necessitates the introduction of the *concept of function* and the *principle of abstract relevance* so masterfully brought out and developed by Bühler. Both concepts are absent from Schmitt's work, which results in additional misunderstandings. In section 19 (1936, 66), Schmitt appears to consider them, although he does not express himself clearly. The statements that he makes in this section do suggest, at any rate, that he acknowledges the division of the sound current into elements endowed with different functions. But it is an oversimplification to distinguish only between the "normal form of the individual speech gesture" (i.e., of the word) and the form conditioned by the context of the "entire gesture" (i.e., of the whole utterance with its "ideational, emotional, and intentional values"). Following Bühler's "organon model," we may distinguish three aspects of every utterance—expression, appeal, and representation [5]—and within the latter at least two more functions.

In any case, it is not clear why in the perception of an utterance a distinction should be made only between features relevant for individual words and those relevant for an entire sentence. If we admit the existence of different functions in one and the same utterance, then certain conclusions will follow. Let us take the two *l* sounds of British English (a situation treated by Schmitt [1936, p. 83, sec. 56]). Before consonants only the "dark" *l* is permitted, but before vowels both "dark" and "light" *l* may occur: "light" *l* if the following vowel belongs to the same word as the *l* (*we learn*), "dark" *l* if it belongs to a different one (*will earn*).[6] In other words, the difference between the two *l* sounds in English is important solely for word division; it is a nonphonemic boundary signal (see Trubetzkoy 1935, p. 30, sec. 38; and Trubetzkoy 1936c). For distinguishing meaning, only those features are relevant that are common to both *l* sounds; the "dark" or "light" coloring serves merely to indicate whether the following vowel belongs to the same word (before consonants the opposition does not exist). The same holds for the two *ch* sounds in German, as Schmitt admits (1936, 79).

This is also true of most so-called combinatory variants. From the general formula, "Only sound β, not sound β', may stand next to sound α within the same word (or morpheme)," it follows that, where β' stands next to α, they are separated by a word (or morpheme) boundary. The features of β and β' thus fall into two groups: those common to both β and β', in opposition to other sounds of the same system, and serving to distinguish words (distinctive features), and those belonging only to either β or β' and serving to mark the presence or absence of a word or morpheme boundary (delimitative features).

There is, however, another kind of combinatory variant. If in Japanese, for example, the phoneme *h* is pronounced as a palatal before *i* and as a bilabial voiceless fricative before *u,* there can be no question of a boundary signal since word and morpheme boundaries in Japanese always fall after a vowel, never after a consonant. Consequently, the palatal or bilabial fricative indicates the presence of a following *i* or *u,* respectively—no small help in Japanese, in which close vowels are often pronounced indistinctly or left out. In a word such as *çito* (or even *çto*) 'person,' the palatal quality of the ç points to a following *i* (which, thanks to this information, does not even need to be pronounced), whereas the voiceless fricative character of the sound and the nonparticipation of the tip of the tongue mark the ç as a realization of the phoneme *h.*

Combinatory variants are thus made possible by the fact that different phonetic features of a sound are employed in different functions. Only some of the "representationally relevant" features are used for the *distinctive* function as such. The others fulfill *nondistinctive* functions: either *delimitative* (by marking a boundary or its absence) or *auxiliary-associative* (by providing supplemental indication of the proximity of another phoneme). Beside these features with representational functions, a sound can also have features with the functions of appeal (various emotional colorings) and expression. All of them are distinguished by the hearer. Schmitt, who seems to recognize the difference between the representational function and those of expression and appeal, has no reason to deny the existence of the various representational functions.

Poetic language proves that different representational functions of sounds are indeed distinguished. In Russian, for example, *sŭd'jöj* 'by a judge' rhymes with *drŭgoj* 'the other,' *tajnŏ* 'secret' (n.) with *slŭcäjnŏ* 'by chance,' *pr'ĭn'ik* 'he cuddled (up to)' with *jĭzuk* 'tongue,' and so on (*u* is a high, back or back-central, nonlabialized tense vowel). Such rhymes are possible because only lip position and height are relevant for the distinctive function of Russian vowels; the choice of front, central, or back tongue position merely helps indicate the palatalization or velarization of the preceding consonant. Since the poetic language disregards nonphonemic distinctions, Russian rhyme observes only (passive or active) lip position and height in vowels, and no Russian notices that the stressed vowels in *sŭd'jöj* and *drŭgoj* are not the same. In Turkic languages with consistent vowel harmony, only height is relevant for vowels of noninitial syllables. All other features (i.e., lip and tongue position) of these vowels are controlled automatically by the vowel harmony; they depend on the quality of the vowel in the first syllable and thus perform a delimitative, not a distinctive, function. In these Turkic languages, such words as *birinji* 'first,' *altunjiu* 'sixth,' *dörtünjü* 'fourth,' and *onunju* 'tenth' all rhyme, but *quz* 'girl' and *yüz* 'hundred' cannot, because in vowels of the first syllable not only height but also lip and tongue position are phonologically relevant (possess distinctive function).

These and many similar facts of the poetic language of various peoples, including those lacking any trace of literacy, teach us that distinctive and non-distinctive representational sound features are clearly distinguished by the so-called naive mind. Different sounds with the same distinctive content (i.e., different realizations of the same phoneme, according to the terminology of the phonological school) in different words are treated as identical.

"It is virtually impossible for us to take ourselves back to the standpoint of illiterate man," says Schmitt (1936, p. 91, sec. 68), quite correctly. For just this reason, attempts to reconstruct the mentality of illiterate man through pure speculation are extremely questionable. Instead of making dogmatic statements based on unproved assumptions, it is better to start with concrete facts and observations such as those provided by the study of poetic language and wordplay. Schmitt's claim that an illiterate would perceive a similarity between the words *Kant* (the name), *Kind* 'child,' and *kund* 'known' and the initial syllables of *Kabel* 'cable,' *Kiefer* 'jaw,' and *Kuchen* 'cake,' but not the existence of the phoneme *k* (p. 91, sec. 68), is completely arbitrary for the very reason that we are unable to return to the perspective of those who cannot read and write. On the other hand, the existence of alliteration in the poetry of peoples without writing is proof that they recognize not just the similarity but the phonological identity of initial consonant phonemes, while the identification of the same phoneme is medial and final position in different words is proved by the existence of rhyme.

Schmitt claims that "illiterate man" would never think of "removing a part of the sound gesture in words like *Haken* 'hook' and *hacken* 'chop' and associating it with the *k* sound in *Kabel, Kiefer,* etc." (1936, p. 91, sec. 68), but this assertion can be disproved by the evidence of popular wordplay. A certain type of Russian folk riddle consists of a sequence of words in which the consonants preceding stressed vowels, taken together in a different order, make up the consonant phonemes of the solution: *č'ornəj kon' prugəĭt v-agon'* (*č . . . k . . . r . . . g*) [*černyi kon' prygaet v ogon'*] 'a black horse jumps into the fire'; solution, *kəč'ĭrga* '(fire or oven) poker.' In another riddle type, the consonant phonemes of the key word are distributed over two words of the question without regard to stress: *s'v'ĭn'ja is-p'it'ĭrə* (*p' . . . r . . .*) *fs'a ĭstuukə̆nə* (*st . . . k . . . n . . .*) [*svin'ia iz Pitera vsia istykana*] 'a pig from St. Petersburg is full of holes'; solution, *năp'orstə̆k* 'thimble.' Both riddle types are traditional, created by and for illiterates.

Even without this kind of evidence, the phonological identity of medial and initial *k* becomes obvious as soon as we approach the issue from the standpoint of oppositions, the only possible standpoint for the investigation of linguistic values. The phoneme is always a member of an opposition. Two phonemes are identical if they stand in the same relations of opposition to other phonemes. Equations such as *Haken : Hasen :: kaum : Saum* or *Laken : lagen :: Keil : geil* ('hook, rabbits, hardly, seam; bedsheet, [we] lay, wedge, lascivious') are no less apparent than *Kinder : Binder :: kaum : Baum* ('children, necktie, hardly, tree'); from them we derive the identity of *k* as a differentiating element that appears in various positions in the word in the same distinctive function and with the same distinctive features (which can just as well be derived by an illiterate consciousness). Since the discussion of "microphonemes" and "macrophonemes" in Twaddell's *On Defining the Phoneme* (1935), the issue may be regarded as closed.

The fact that all sounds with the same distinctive features are identified with each other even when their nondistinctive features are different explains certain phenomena of language contact. It is not surprising that the Japanese, whose language permits (bilabial) *f* only before *u* and prohibits *h* in this position, reproduce the sequence *hu* in foreign words and names as *fu* (e.g., *Fuvaru* for *Hoover*). But, in addition, vice versa, each foreign *f* not followed by *u* is replaced by *h* (*ho:ku < fork*), and before *i* it is pronounced as palatal *ç* (*çirumu < film*). The only explanation can be that the oppositions between *h, f,* and *ç,* which in Japanese perform not a distinctive but rather an auxiliary-associative function, are regarded by the speakers as unimportant. The Japanese consider the three sounds *h, f,* and *ç* as different pronunciations (realizations, combinatory variants) of the same phoneme. Their distribution follows certain rules, and if Japanese speakers encounter them in other languages in unexpected positions, they are treated as insignificant nuances in the pronunciation of a single phoneme.

6

Schmitt makes three arguments against the existence of phonemes. The first is that at any given time the pronunciation of individual words in everyday speech displays considerable instability. Schmitt cites the German word *Morgen* 'morning,' which can assume the most diverse forms, "especially if one includes those used in greetings" (phonetically *mɔrgən, mɔrgŋ, mɔ:gŋ, mɔ:ŋ, mɔŋ:, mɔ̃:ŋ, mɔ̃:, mɔ:jn,* etc.), and he asks "just how many phonemes the word really has." Since the number of phonemes in the different forms "obviously varies," "either some prescribed phonemes are missing in the shorter forms, or some have been added in the longer ones. But this would contradict the position of phonology, which expressly credits the phoneme with independent semantic value" (1936, p. 84, sec. 57).

Schmitt's example is well chosen. The greeting is not *Morgen!* but rather *Guten Morgen!* 'Good morning!' When we simply say *mɔ̃:,* we omit not only several phonemes but also the word *guten,* which both phonology and Schmitt himself credit with "independent semantic value." The situation in which the greeting formula is used is so clear that the phrase does not have to be spoken in its entirety; it can be merely hinted at.[7] If, however, someone has not clearly heard or understood this *mɔ̃:* and asks the speaker for clarification, the speaker will not repeat *mɔ̃:* but rather say something like *Gu:tn mɔ:rgŋ ha:b iç gəza:kt* 'I said "Good morning."'

Each word contains as many phonemes as are necessary to distinguish it from all other words and mark its position in the lexical and grammatical system of the language. *All* these phonemes are always theoretically present, but not all of them must always be realized. Where the social relationship of the two speakers permits (or even requires) careless delivery, and where the situation allows it, certain words are not pronounced in full but only indicated by means of *some* of their phonemes. One can take this principle quite far, as everyone knows. There is always a certain limit, however, that may not be exceeded. As soon as careless pronunciation and the "swallowing" of phonemes leads to misunderstanding (or no understanding at all) and speakers are asked to repeat what they have said, they realize all "prescribed" phonemes of the words in question—regardless of whether they are literate or illiterate.

The fact that Schmitt treats "instability in the realization of one and the same sound unit" as a counterargument to the existence of phonemes is due, once again, to his failure to distinguish language from speech. In addition, however, the problem stems from his disregard of the *sign nature of all linguistic norms.* It is in the nature of a sign that it may serve as the representative of an entire sign complex (more precisely, of a higher-order sign) in the same system. Under certain conditions, a word can represent a sentence of which it is a member, while a phoneme or combination of phonemes can represent a whole word—just as, in writing, a letter can replace a complete written word (*M.P.* = *Maschinenpistole* 'machine gun,' *usw.* = *und so weiter* 'and so on,' *A.G.* = *Aktiengesellschaft* 'public company'). "Instability in the realization of one and the same sound unit" cannot, therefore, be used against the concept of the phoneme; rather, it furnishes indirect proof that phonemes are signs. In swimming, the complete swimming motion can never be replaced by one of its three components, for swimming is neither a sign nor a sign system. Schmitt's comparison of speech with swimming (1936, 81–82) is therefore fundamentally inaccurate.

7

As his second objection to the phoneme, Schmitt mentions the fact that words and forms originally distinct can merge in the course of time: "If we assume, with the phonological school, that phonemes constitute the members of a sign system and guarantee that different sound units are kept apart . . . , then two originally distinct words would never be able to become homonyms: the phonemes would prevent it, since this is supposed to be their main purpose" (1936, p. 85, sec. 59).

Here, the static (synchronic) and the historical (diachronic) perspectives have been confused. For certain generations of speakers and hearers, the phonemes of a given phonological system ensure that words in the corresponding lexical system are distinguished from one another. Even if one word is taken for another in careless, quick speech, the misunderstanding is resolved immediately: a speaker who is asked to repeat a word realizes all its phonemes in such a way that confusion with other phonemes of the system is impossible *for hearers of the same generation.* If, however, a generation arises that *no longer distinguishes* certain phonemes, then, no matter how many times misunderstood speakers of the older generation repeat themselves, younger hearers will not be able to perceive a difference based on a phonological opposition that they do not possess.

Educated Russians have experienced such a phenomenon in recent decades: whereas speakers of an older language form distinguish unstressed *e* and *i* before nonpalatalized consonants, so that for them *l'isá* 'fox' and *l'esá* 'forests' are two different words, this opposition has become irrelevant for the repre-

sentatives of a younger form, who do not hear it (more precisely, do not consider it worthy of attention) and pronounce the words 'fox' and 'forests' in
the same way, that is, regard them as homonyms. The sound change will be
complete when the older generation disappears or capitulates to the younger
one. The next generation will already possess another system of phonemes
and a correspondingly different lexical system: certain word pairs that had
had distinct pronunciations will now be homophones. In the context of this
new lexical system, however, the phonemes of the new phonological system
will once again guarantee the differentiation of nonhomophonous words.

A merger in pronunciation of originally distinct words always begins with
the neutralization of a phonological opposition in a particular generation of
speakers, who thus no longer perceive it (or perceive it only in certain positions) even though it is still observed by older speakers. The rise of a new generation that has lost its sense for a phonological opposition and no longer
hears the sound distinction (or can no longer reproduce it at will) is of course
possible only if the distinction has a low functional yield, to use Mathesius's
term; otherwise, the young generation would learn it in the process of speech
acquisition.

8

A generation that no longer perceives a certain phonological opposition can
replace it with another by making an originally nondistinctive opposition
distinctive; one sound function can take another's place. This brings us to
Schmitt's third objection to the concept of the phoneme: in the course of historical development, as he points out, it frequently occurs that one phoneme
splits into several. Schmitt cites Latin *c*, which yielded seven different phonemes in Old French: *campum* > *champ* 'field,' *pacare* > *paiier* 'pay,' *centum* >
cent 'hundred,' *placet* > *plaist* '(it) pleases,' *lucerna* > *luiserne* 'lamp,' *collum* > *col*
'neck,' and *judico* > *juge* '(I) judge.' "If each phoneme were really a basic semantic element of language, it would not be able to dissolve in such a way over
the course of time" (1936, p. 85, sec. 60).

To understand phonemic split, we must once again examine the concrete
processes from the functional point of view. It will then emerge that phonemic split, that is, the rise of new phonemes from combinatory variants, is
always linked with the abolishment of an old phonological opposition.

Proto-Russian dental and labial consonants were palatalized before front
vowels, but this palatalization had no distinctive value (cf. the palatal pronunciation of gutturals before front vowels in British English): *měl'ĭ* 'sandbank,
shoal' and *mělŭ* 'chalk' were differentiated by the quality of the final vowel;
and, if the *l* was palatalized before *ĭ* and not palatalized before *ŭ*, this was
"natural," that is, phonologically irrelevant, and had no effect on the unity

of the phoneme *l*. A time came, however, in which the vowels *ĭ* and *ŭ* were weakened in certain positions—especially word finally—and eventually disappeared. As soon as the difference between reduced *ĭ* and *ŭ* was no longer perceived, the opposition between palatalized and nonpalatalized consonants assumed the distinctive function: the word for 'sandbank' was now distinguished from the word for 'chalk' only in that the former contained palatalized *l'*, the latter nonpalatalized *l*. The originally undifferentiated phoneme *l* had *split* into two phonemes, *l'* and *l*. Clearly, the split was a compensation for the loss of the difference between *ĭ* and *ŭ*; all the functions of the latter opposition were now assumed by the opposition between palatalized and nonpalatalized consonants.

Often, phonemic split is not a compensation but only the consequence of the partial abolishment of a phonological opposition, that is, the neutralization in a certain position of a distinction between the phoneme in question and another one. In Polish, before nonpalatalized dentals Proto-Slavic **e* is represented by *ⁱo* (*o* with palatalization of the preceding consonant) and Proto-Slavic **ě* (a kind of *æ*) by *ⁱa*, whereas in all other positions both Proto-Slavic phonemes merged into *ⁱe*.

A causal link between phonemic split and the complete or partial elimination of a phonological opposition can be discerned in all so-called regular splits.[8] The dissolution of phonological oppositions is thus one of the most important phenomena of sound change: it paves the way for both the merger of distinct phonemes (if the lost opposition is not compensated for) and the splitting of a single phoneme (as compensation for a lost or partially lost opposition).

The loss of phonological oppositions contains nothing that could logically contradict the idea of the phoneme. It merely signifies the arrival of a generation that does not perceive a certain opposition (in all environments) or is unable to reproduce it in a natural way. From the point of view of the older generation, the new one resembles individuals with hearing defects or speech impediments. But the existence of such individuals is no argument against the distinctive function of phonemes for the nonhandicapped members of a linguistic community.

The failure of a particular generation to keep originally distinct sound units apart is never deliberate, but it always has some inner cause. As pointed out above, an uncompensated failure to distinguish two phonemes is possible only if the opposition between them has a low functional yield. On the other hand, a *compensated* failure to distinguish two phonemes is possible only if the originally distinctive opposition is accompanied by some nondistinctive opposition (e.g., combinatory variants of neighboring phonemes) and thus signaled twice, with the result that no misunderstanding arises if it is ignored.

It often happens that the loss of a distinctive opposition increases rather than reduces the number of phonemes in the system, as in the Russian example given above. This must be taken into the bargain. In political and social history, it is the same way: reforms made to ameliorate some unpleasant condition create an even more problematic situation, which in turn must be remedied by new reform, and so on ad infinitum. If this is possible in political and social life despite the conscious and deliberate action of leading public figures, then how much more so in linguistic evolution, in which only the unconscious collective will participates!

9

Schmitt's objections to phonemic theory are thus unable to shake it. Let us now look at the views he offers in its place. According to Schmitt, language consists solely of units that combine sound and meaning, that is, morphemes (roots, suffixes, prefixes, endings). Schmitt calls these units *acoustic gestures*. Each of them is, in his opinion, an indivisible whole. If we imagine that a morpheme consists of sounds or phonemes, we do this only because we are accustomed to phonetic writing. In reality, he says, acoustic gestures cannot be segmented further from the point of view of either content or sound. Two "gestures" may display similarities in their sound pattern at the beginning, in the middle, or at the end, but these similar parts are only similar, never identical, because they are always merely parts of various unities; they have no independent existence. In the consciousness of the members of a linguistic community, morphemes exist as indivisible wholes, as "gestures" carrying meaning.

Two indivisible "gestures" (as conceived of by Schmitt) can have segments in common, with the restriction that only maximum similarity is possible, not complete identity. They will differ in the remaining parts, but these other parts, in turn, are maximally similar to corresponding segments of certain other "gestures." Each "gesture" thus has segments in common with various other "gestures"; its entire sound pattern is nothing but a series of shared segments of this kind, and there is no segment that does not occur in some other "gesture." Schmitt himself concedes that the total number of such shared segments in each language is relatively small, in any case much smaller than the number of "gestures." From this admission it is only a very small step to the claim that a morpheme *is made up of* certain parts (sound segments, tempi, phonemes, or whatever). But Schmitt is unwilling to take this step. According to him, *words are not made up of phonemes, but rather phonemes are parts of words.* They belong *only to words, not to any phoneme system.* In these two sentences, apparently, Schmitt sees the core of the difference between his view and that of phonology.

I must admit that I do not understand why this difference should be important. Phonologists have never seriously considered phonemes as elements from which words are constructed the way houses are from bricks; nor have they ignored the fact that children learn whole words first, not isolated phonemes, in learning to speak. When phonologists say that words are made up of phonemes, they mean that each word contains a certain number of parts that also occur (more precisely, are recognized) in other words of the same language, that only the selection and the order of these parts vary from word to word, and that all words can be analyzed into these parts and shown to contain nothing else.[9] Certainly, phonologists treat phonemes not only as parts of words but first and foremost as members of phonological oppositions and, consequently, as members of a system. Are these two kinds of structural "membership" irreconcilable? Is a word in a particular grammatical form, for example, not a part of a sentence and also a member of a grammatical paradigm?

Let us compare language with music. A melody is a whole, of which the individual tones are only parts. The "naive" folksinger learns a folk song melody as a whole and performs it correctly without knowing anything about musical theory and notation. If this melody is composed on the major scale, it will not contain any tones that do not belong to this scale. May we not say, in this case, that the melody is made up of the tones of the major scale? There are an infinite number of melodies composed on the major scale, and they are all "made up of" the tones of this scale—only their order varies. But the order is not always completely different: the same tone sequence can occur in different melodies (subjectively, of course, these sequences are not identical, only similar, since they are parts of different wholes). The individual tones and their combinations differentiate the various melodies; they are thus parts of the melodies (conceived of as wholes) and also parts of the major scale. But the latter is a system of relations, of oppositions ("intervals").

There are peoples whose music is based on a single scale, and an improvising singer automatically uses only its tones: any other tone would be rejected as inappropriate ("wrong"). It is not necessary for the singer to be conscious of the existence of the scale. This scale, this system of "intervals" or musical oppositions, is not a natural phenomenon linked with innate anthropological characteristics of the ethnic group but rather a social institution, a law with historical origins and a capacity for change, although at present it regulates the entire musical output of the group.

The phonological system can be described in a similar way: we may compare it to the whole tone–pentatonic scale, which for so many peoples (e.g., the Incas, the Chinese, the Bashkirs, the Welsh, the Irish) is the only scale in use and which thus controls the choice of tones for all folk songs and other melodies. It is an ordered system of members of phonological oppositions, and these members are identical with the elements into which every word in the language may be analyzed.

Which is more important: that the phoneme belongs to a word or that it belongs to the system? Schmitt believes that the evidence of language change permits him to give priority to the word: "The similarity of . . . oppositional pairs [e.g., *kund*: *bunt*: : *Kant*: *Band*: : *Kinder*: *Binder*] is only a factual, not a fundamental, one: the inclusion of the individual tempi in the whole is stronger than their relation with one another, which is why the latter can be lost in the course of linguistic change" (1936, p. 92, sec. 69). We have seen that the historical facts must be interpreted differently. Returning to the synchronic (static) point of view, we may observe that the inclusion of the phoneme in words and its membership in the phoneme system exist side by side; now the one, now the other is in the foreground. The membership of the phoneme in the phoneme system and its position in this system attract our attention whenever the opposition of this phoneme to the others or the repetition of the same phoneme in different words (i.e., in different phonemic contexts) is emphasized, for example, in wordplay, rhyme, alliteration, assonance, or other situations such as those mentioned by Schmitt (see, e.g., p. 91, sec. 69).

10

The simultaneous inclusion in a context and in a system of oppositions is characteristic of many elements of language. As with phonemes, we are not always aware that such elements are both members of oppositions and parts of a given context. As children, we learn to construct the forms of specific words and to use them in specific phrases. It is only with great effort that we can extrapolate the rules governing grammatical forms and their usage, and we notice then, somewhat to our dismay, that these rules are not arbitrary but constitute systems. If Schmitt's approach were taken to its logical consequence, grammatical systems would have to be denied.

According to Schmitt, phonemes have no existence of their own but are organizing concepts foisted on language from without. Of course phonemes are organizing concepts! But all language (*langue*), unlike speech (*parole*), can be reduced to such concepts. Are grammatical rules not organizing concepts? Is the grammatical system not an "organizing net thrown over" speech? Only someone who thinks that there is no reality except speech (*parole*) would speak of the "ordering net" of language (*langue*) as something brought in "supplementally from outside." On the contrary, speech is possible at all only because it is subject to the superindividual system of normative linguistic values, the "organizing concepts" of language.

Grammar does not exist in linguists' minds only because at some point grammatical handbooks were invented (owing to a "demand for scientific knowledge" about language and "practical tools for language instruction" [Schmitt 1936, p. 76, sec. 42]); nor were phonemes created by phonetic writing. In claiming that the phoneme is nothing but the concept of the letter transferred from phonetic writing into linguistics, Schmitt has the situation backward. It is for psychologists to decide whether phonetic writing would ever have been invented if phonemes did not exist. That phonetic writing arose only gradually and that the oldest writing represents not phonemes but larger units, that is, words (the most primitive pictographs represent whole sentences), is hardly proof of Schmitt's theory, for the history of grammar teaches us also that our ancestors discovered the elements of grammatical structure and its system only very slowly and with great effort.

The claim that illiterates have no conception of phonemes is not supported by any concrete observation. As mentioned above, it is not confirmed by the evidence of the poetic language of illiterate peoples. Those who have collected linguistic data from such peoples can testify that the "natives" sometimes have a precise conception of the phonemes of their language. They often provide information on the dialectal characteristics of a neighboring village in the form of regular "sound laws" that could not have been formulated better by a Neogrammarian. During my stay with the Circassians on the Black Sea coast, I heard the following statement by a member of the Š'apsəɣ° tribe on the dialect of the Hak°əc°: "Where we pronounce a strong s, the Hak°əc° pronounce it that way, too; but in words where we pronounce a very weak s, they replace it by č" (examples followed). The sound law was formulated correctly! And the man was "illiterate": at that time (1911) only the Circassian clergy could read and write at all, and then not Circassian but only Arabic and Turkish. Similar examples can be adduced for other illiterate peoples. Every phonologist knows that the investigation of the phonological systems of such peoples is less difficult than the study of written languages, in which a feeling for the phonemes has been obscured by the orthography. This is just the opposite of what one would expect according to Schmitt's theory.

11

Since phonology addresses not so much phonemes as phonological oppositions, it offers a new approach to both the synchronic and the diachronic study of sounds and bridges the older methodological gap between phonetics and grammar. Phonology, which investigates the functions of sound oppositions, and morphology, which investigates the functions of form oppositions, are two branches of one discipline addressing the functions of oppositions of normative linguistic values, and all branches of this discipline employ the same methods. The way the study of sounds is treated by the so-called phonological school implies also a comparable treatment of the other areas of linguistic study, that is, a new *structural linguistics*.

The difference between Schmitt and the phonologists stems from widely diverging conceptions of the nature of linguistics. It is no coincidence that Schmitt closes his article with a quotation from Paul's *Prinzipien der Sprachgeschichte* (1960). Schmitt does indeed speak of a holistic approach, but the highest unity for him is the spoken word and the sentence. The concept of the *system* is foreign to him, as are the concepts *function* and *opposition*. Schmitt still holds to the positivist-naturalistic view of language, a view from which one is afraid to acknowledge order in the static and logic in the diachronic aspect of language.

There was a time when the positivist-naturalistic approach contributed to the development of linguistics. This time is now past.[10] Schmitt's article demonstrates that one-sided positivism can have only a destructive influence on modern linguistics. He has arrived at the denial of any scientific study of sounds; it is easy to show that the consistent application of his principles would also lead to the rejection of morphology, syntax, and semantics. Neither linguistics nor any other social science can develop without the concepts of norm and system. A superindividual system of normative values, which as a nonmaterial but nevertheless objective reality makes the perception and reproduction of elements of a social institution possible, is a fundamental and necessary concept for every social science, especially for linguistics. The denial of the system concept, even for only part of language (e.g., sounds), would lead to its denial elsewhere and thus to the rejection of linguistics as such. I am convinced that Schmitt cannot be happy with such a denial. When the misunderstandings that led this astute scholar to take the false step of rejecting phonology have been resolved, I hope that he will rejoin our ranks to take an active part in the development of a new structural linguistics.

6. Phonology and Linguistic Geography

Phonic differences between dialects fall into three groups: they can concern the *phonological system*, the *phonetic realization* of individual phonemes, or the *etymological distribution* of phonemes in words. Accordingly, I will speak of *phonological, phonetic,* and *etymological* dialect differences.

Phonological differences must be divided further into *differences in inventory* and *differences in function*. A difference in phonological inventory exists when one dialect possesses a phoneme unknown in another, a difference in function when a phoneme occurs in one dialect in a position it never occupies in another. Northern and southern Russian, for example, differ in phonological inventory: northern Russian has four unstressed (reduced) vowel phonemes (ŭ, ŏ, ă, ĭ), while southern Russian has only three (ŭ, ă, ĭ). A difference in phonological function exists, for example, among southern and central Russian dialects: the phoneme ă is permitted in some dialects only after hard (nonpalatalized) consonants but in others after both hard and soft (palatalized) consonants. Within this second group, there is a difference in phonological function between dialects in which unstressed ă may occur after soft consonants only if a hard one follows (the type *v'ădu* 'I lead' – *v'ĭd'oš* 'you [sg.] lead') and those without this restriction (the type *v'ădu* – *v'ăd'oš*).

Phonetic differences are *absolute* when they affect the pronunciation of a phoneme in all positions, *restricted* (*combinatory*) when they occur only in certain positions. There is an absolute phonetic difference, for example, between Polish dialects with ł realized as ļ (a somewhat retracted *l*) and those with ł realized as u̯. A combinatory phonetic difference exists between the southern Polish dialects, in which *l* is palatalized before *i* (*l'is* 'fox' ~ *las* 'forest'), and the northern ones, in which *l* remains unchanged in this position.

Etymological differences are also of two kinds. One is linked with differences in phonological function. When the function of a phoneme in one dialect is more limited than it is in another, some phoneme usually enjoys a wider distribution (it occurs in positions in which the first phoneme does not), compensating, as it were, for the functional restriction of the first. These may be named *compensatory* etymological differences. Where the etymological differences are not linked with a difference in function, however, they may be called *free*. The relation between western and eastern Belorussian dialects is an example of a compensatory etymological difference: whereas unstressed ă occurs in all positions in western Belorussian, in eastern Belorussian it cannot occur before a syllable with stressed *á,* and, where western Belorussian has *ă* in this position, eastern Belorussian usually has *ĭ* (w. Beloruss. *vắda – vắdi̯* 'water' [nom. and g.] ~ e. Beloruss. *vĭ̯da – vắdi̯*). A free etymological difference is evident in the reflexes of Proto-Polish close *é* in the dialects of Lesser Poland: some have *i,* others *e.* If we set historical explanations aside, we can observe only that certain words that have *i* in one group of dialects have *e* in the other; the phenomenon is not bound to any particular phonological position.

2

Up to now, dialectology has always operated with diachronic concepts and interpreted every phonic difference as the result of divergent development. In conscious opposition to the principle that sound laws admit of no exception, modern dialectology, or linguistic geography, claims that each word displaying a sound change has its own area of distribution, which makes it impossible to draw the geographic boundaries of a change exactly. This claim is due to the failure to distinguish the three types of sound differences mentioned above—phonological, phonetic, and etymological.

The idea that dialect boundaries are imprecise, or blurred, is correct as long as by *dialect differences* we mean only *etymological* ones. In this case, the distribution is certainly irregular. An area in which a given sound change has been carried out consistently—that is, where an old phoneme (or combination) has been replaced in all words by a new phoneme—usually borders on areas in which some of the relevant words display a phoneme other than the expected one, without any apparent reason for such exceptions. But not far from these areas there are generally still others in which such exceptions are already the rule. Between areas with maximum etymological difference (i.e., areas in which a given sound difference appears in the maximum number of words), there are always transitional areas in which individual words display sometimes the one, sometimes the other of the two reflexes of the old phoneme, and the areas of distribution of the different forms of the individual words are mutually independent.

With *phonetic* differences, it is another story. If a phoneme is realized in two dialects in two different ways, this must be true of all words in which the phoneme occurs in a certain position. Otherwise, dissimilar phonetic realizations would be used for semantic distinctions and acquire phonological value; the phonetic difference would become a phonological one. It can indeed be difficult to draw a precise border between two geographic areas even with regard to phonetic differences, but this is because areas with maximally opposed phonetic realizations may be separated by areas with a "mediating" realization, so that the transition from the one realization to the other is only gradual, or because they are separated by areas in which both realizations exist side by side as optional variants of the same phoneme. In both cases, however, all words containing the phoneme in question must behave in the same way. The meaning of the term *transitional area* thus depends entirely on whether we are dealing with phonetic or etymological differences.

In the context of *phonological* differences, on the other hand, the term *transitional area* makes no sense at all. A phoneme or phoneme combination can either exist or not exist in a given dialect—*tertium non datur*. Now it is true that a phonological opposition in one dialect can be prepared, so to speak, by a phonetic opposition in a neighboring one or, conversely, that a phonological difference can degenerate into a phonetic one in a neighboring area (both interpretations are equally justified from the point of view of static observation). The opposition between western Belorussian *văda* – *vădi̦* 'water' (nom. and g.) and eastern Belorussian *vi̦da* – *vădi̦* (w. Beloruss. *ă/á* ~ e. Beloruss. *ĭ/á*) was mentioned above. Eastern Belorussian proper is bordered by certain western Belorussian dialects in which *ā̆* is realized as *ə̆* (a vowel of an indefinite timbre) before a syllable with stressed *á*. This *ə̆* is identical with neither *ĭ̦* nor *ă*, but in the speakers' linguistic consciousness it is perceived as a combinatory phonetic variant of *ă*, not as an independent phoneme. The area of the pronunciation *və̆da* – *vădi̦* can be considered a kind of transitional area between eastern Belorussian (*vi̦da* – *vădi̦*) and western Belorussian (*văda* – *vădi̦*), but only from a phonetic standpoint: phonologically it belongs to western Belorussian. The difference between the western Belorussian area proper and the *və̆da* – *vădi̦* area is purely phonetic, while the difference between this area and eastern Belorussian is phonological.

Although the first of these borders may not always be easy to draw (because of the gradual, transitional nuances between *ă* and *ə̆*), the second poses no problems: where the vowel in the first syllable of *vi̦da* is perceived as identical with the vowel of the first syllable of *bi̦ła* 'was' (f.), we have eastern Belorussian phonology; where this is not the case, we have western Belorussian phonology. It is the same in all similar instances. In contrast to the gradualness of phonetic sound transitions, which complicate the mapping of phonetically distinct dialect groups, phonological differences yield clear, sharp boundaries.

From these considerations, we may deduce guidelines for the cartography of dialectal sound differences. *Etymological* differences cannot be expressed by means of uniform isoglosses; they can be expressed only through the word-geographic method. The isoglosses of all words containing a given sound change must be drawn on individual maps and these maps then superimposed. On a synthetic map of this kind, common (shared) isoglosses appear as thick, dark stripes, divergent ones thin and light. Transitional areas are identified by an increased number of these light lines, while areas in which sound changes have been consistently carried out are more or less free of them. *Phonetic* differences can best be drawn on the map with different colors or types of hatching. Areas with transitional pronunciation or the optional coexistence of two pronunciations can be shown by mixed colors or combined hatching, so that the gradual transitions in phonetic realization are expressed symbolically. For *phonological* differences, either their geographic borders can be represented on the map by simple, sharply drawn lines, or the areas can be identified by different colors, or both techniques can be combined. In any case, the cartography of phonological differences is easy, since there are no transitional areas.

3

In order to identify sound differences and their geographic distribution, the dialect pronunciation of the same words in different parts of the language area must be recorded. The questionnaire used for this purpose asks, "How is such and such a word pronounced in such and such a dialect?" Since the investigation of *etymological sound differences* presupposes the existence of a more or less *uniform vocabulary,* such research is possible only within one language, at most within a group of closely related languages.

Phonetic sound differences and their geographic distribution must be identified by investigating local pronunciations (i.e., phonetic realizations) of the same phoneme. It is irrelevant whether the same words are chosen as examples everywhere, as long as the words chosen in a given dialect display the phoneme in question. The investigation of *phonetic sound differences* is thus independent of the lexicon, but it requires the presence of the *same phonological system,* or at least similar systems, in all dialects under study.

For the investigation of phonological sound differences, the phoneme inventory and the functions of the individual phonemes must be established for each dialect. The dialectologist must answer the questions "Does such and such a phoneme occur in such and such a dialect?" and "In which phonological positions is it used?" and it does not matter whether all dialects under study possess the same lexicon or even the same grammatical structure. In contrast to etymological differences, *phonological sound differences* can also be investigated *outside the boundaries of one language* and even outside the boundaries of a *language family.* The remarks made above about the cartography of phonological differences apply equally to the study of more than one language.

That phonological dialectology must sometimes cross language boundaries without regard to genetic relations is beyond any doubt. Certain phonological phenomena are distributed geographically in such a way that they occur in several unrelated but neighboring languages or, conversely, are lacking in large contiguous areas occupied by different languages. Jakobson has demonstrated this for the oppositions of timbre [*Eigenton*] in consonants and pitch [*Verlauf*] in vowels, and the same could be done for other phonological features. Thus, for example, the correlation of recursion (with ~ without glottal stop) is found in all languages of the Caucasus, regardless of their origin (not only in North and South Caucasian but also in the Indo-European and Turkic languages of the region), but it occurs otherwise neither in Europe nor in the neighboring areas of Asia and Eurasia. Distribution areas of this kind can be established for individual phonemes, too. The important thing is that the boundaries of phonological phenomena do not necessarily coincide with language boundaries; since they often cut across language areas, they can be identified only through phonological-dialectological research.

The occurrence of common phonological characteristics in a group of neighboring but unrelated languages or dialects has often been noticed, but scholars have been too hasty in invoking substrate theory or the assumption of a "dominant" language to explain this fact. Such interpretations are worthless as long as they address only individual cases; it would be better to abstain from interpretation until all the relevant material has been collected. What is needed is the exhaustive collection of data, to establish the facts. A comparative phonological-geographic description of the world's languages is our most pressing task, but its prerequisite is the phonological dialectology of individual languages.

7. Quantity as a Phonological Problem

There can be no doubt that, as a physical event, each sound has a certain duration. It is not so obvious, however, to what extent the duration of sounds fulfills a genuine function in the language structure. The distinction between languages with externally determined quantity and those with internally determined quantity was introduced into the study of sounds by our esteemed president, Otto Jespersen, and is now common knowledge. In some languages, the duration of sounds serves no true linguistic function; it is irrelevant for distinctions of meaning or, as we would say today, phonologically nonexistent. But what about the other languages, those with internally determined quantity? Does duration really have the power to differentiate meaning in them? Is it phonologically relevant? This question is not as easy to answer as it might appear.

Phonologically irrelevant is everything that can be taken for granted from the point of view of the sound system. In a language without voiced consonants, for example, the voicelessness of consonants is obvious and therefore phonologically irrelevant. Likewise, it may be taken for granted that each syllable has some duration; the minimal duration of a short vowel as such is thus phonologically irrelevant even in a language with internally determined quantity. It is a point outside time, and its duration is of no consequence. But the duration of long vowels cannot, then, have any phonological relevance either. Since speakers recognize relative, not absolute, duration, the long vowel can be perceived only as exceeding the short one; and, since the duration of the short vowel is from the phonological point of view nonexistent, the long vowel would have to be considered as exceeding a nonexistent quantity, which makes no sense. So it is not any particular duration but rather *the property of having a duration at all* that distinguishes long from short.

From the phonological perspective, the long vowel is related to the short one not as a longer period of time to a shorter one but as a one-dimensional unit to a dimensionless one, that is, as a *line* to a *point*. In languages with internally determined quantity, *short* and *long* are two different *modes of realization,* the punctual and the linear. A long vowel may be extended without affecting meaning or requiring compensatory measures, while a short vowel may not. This definition of *long* as linear and *short* as punctual brings us to another: *long* is extendible, *short* nonextendible. But this definition is not completely satisfactory, for a capability must be grounded in some characteristic feature of the object in question, something that gives it the particular capability. So we are ultimately looking for the cause of the extendibility of long vowels and the nonextendibility of short ones; *this* is the search for the phonological nature of quantity. Although this search fails to yield a single phonological nature of quantity that would hold true for all languages, there are a very small number of types into which languages may be classified. Let us begin with the quantity of syllabics, that is, vowels, diphthongs, and diphthong combinations.

In very many languages, quantitative distinctions in syllabics express distinctions of intensity. Such languages differentiate between two kinds of syllabics, strong and weak. The strong ones are extendible ("long") by virtue of their strength, the weak ones incapable of extension ("short") by virtue of their weakness. Proof that quantity here reflects intensity is furnished by the fact that the languages in question do not employ any other form of intensity (stress) in a phonological way. Either expiratorial stress is absent (as in Tamil and Tungus), or its position in the word is fixed automatically, so that it fulfills no distinctive function and is thus phonologically irrelevant. In most languages of this type (e.g., Gaelic, Icelandic, Czech, Slovak, Hungarian, Ostyak, Mongolian, Kalmuck, Yakut, Chechen, and Lak), expiratorial stress falls on the first syllable and is merely a signal of the beginning of the word. In others, such as Turkmen, expiratorial stress falls on the last syllable and signals the end of the word. In still other languages (e.g., Latin, Prakrit, Arabic, and Ossetic), the position of the stress is determined by the quantity of the outer (first or last) syllables. In all these cases, the position of the stress is determined externally and has no phonological value; the phonological intensity of the syllabics is expressed through quantity instead. This is a *quantitative* realization of intensity, in contrast to the dynamic realization of intensity in languages with free expiratorial stress and without free quantity (e.g., Italian, Modern Greek, Russian, Avar).

In another group of languages, quantitative distinctions signal whether a syllabic consists of two parts or one. This is the situation in Ancient Greek, Lithuanian, Slovenian, the Čakavian dialect of Croatian, the North Kashubian dialects of Polish, Japanese, etc., that is, languages in which two types of stress ("accents") are possible on long bases but only one type on short ones. It is of no consequence whether the two accents are tonal or expiratorial or whether falling is opposed to rising, falling to level, rising to level, and so on. The important thing is that the different treatment of the beginning and the end of a long base distinguishes meaning, while a short base is treated as an indivisible whole without beginning or end and is either emphasized (stressed) or not emphasized (unstressed). In these languages, the long base has two prosodic foci, the short base only one. That the long base can be extended shows that its two prosodic foci are distinct; they can be separated by a segment of any length. That the short base, on the other hand, cannot be extended is a consequence of the fact that its beginning and end coincide. Short bases may sometimes seem to possess distinctions of tonal movement, but these apparent exceptions are illusory. The North Chinese dialect of Mukden, for example, distinguishes two short and two long accents: one short accent is falling, the other rising, while one long accent is rising-falling, the other falling-rising. But the short rising tonal movement is only an expression of emphasis, while the short falling movement reflects nonemphasis. The short bases are either emphasized or not, while in the long bases either the beginning or the end is emphasized—a normal state of affairs for a language of this type.

The distinction between prosodically indivisible and prosodically bipartite syllabics appears also in languages with *stød,* or glottal closure, such as Danish, Latvian, Livonian, and others. The fact that the closure occurs only on long bases—that is, long vowels, diphthongs, and combinations of vowels with sonorants—proves that in these languages the beginning and the end of long syllabics are treated as separate foci and that the length of these syllabics is an expression of their bipartite nature.

This distinction can also be expressed by other means than quantity. In many of the so-called tone languages of Africa, there are syllables whose beginning displays a different tone than the end, and such distinctions of tonal movement are capable of differentiating meaning. According to descriptions of some of these languages, the tonally bipartite syllabics are longer than the tonally indivisible ones (e.g., in Efik). For most such languages, however, no information is given on this point. In some cases, this silence may be due to the observers' negligence, but this cannot be the only explanation; rather, we must assume that in many African tone languages the prosodically complex syllabics are indeed no longer than the simple ones. The bipartite nature of the syllabic is sufficiently indicated by the tonal movement and does not need to be expressed through increased duration.

One type remains, which is represented by a much smaller group of languages, including English, Dutch, and German. Here, length is the expression of a vowel running its course unchecked, whereas short vowels are checked, cut off by the onset of the following consonant. The opposition is not between long and short but between full and curtailed vowels, and the distinction of quantity is only the expression of a distinction of syllable cut. For this reason, quantitative oppositions exist in such languages only before consonants (Ger. *Saat* 'seed' – *satt* 'satiated,' *Miete* 'rent' – *Mitte* 'middle,' *Hüte* 'hats' – *Hütte* 'hut,' etc.), while in open final syllables all vowels are long.

Languages may therefore be grouped into three types with respect to the phonological nature of syllabics. The length, or extendibility, of a syllabic is in the first type the expression of its strength (as opposed to the weakness of short syllabics), in the second type the expression of its complex nature (as opposed to the indivisibility of short syllabics), and in the third type the expression of its running its full, unchecked course (as opposed to the interrupted course of short syllabics).

The first two types may also be observed with respect to consonantal quantity. The opposition between geminated and nongeminated consonants is clearly nothing more than a distinction between bipartite and indivisible phonemes. This type of quantitative relation in consonants is most evident in languages that permit long consonants only between vowels, where the onset of the consonant is assigned to the preceding and its offset to the following syllable, as in Ancient Greek, Prakrit, Italian, Tamil, Japanese, and Chechen. The same holds for languages that permit long consonants only medially or only in those positions in which consonant groups may appear, as in Finnish. In languages that treat them differently from consonant groups, however, long consonants cannot be considered bipartite, for it turns out that they are not only longer but also more energetically articulated than the corresponding short ones and that their longer duration is only a concomitant, nonobligatory feature. In such cases, length in consonants can be considered only as a reflection of their strength, their intensity. This is the situation in most languages of Daghestan, such as Avar, Lak, Kuri, and others.

The two kinds of consonantal quantity may be combined in various ways. In some languages of Daghestan, for example, such as Andi, Tabasaran, and Kubachi, liquids and nasals display the opposition of gemination, obstruents the opposition of intensity. A complicated type is represented by Lapp, in which consonants are either short or geminated. The geminates occur only medially and fall into two groups, stronger (longer) and weaker. Phonetically, the situation in Lapp is further complicated by the fact that the vowels, too, display phonologically relevant distinctions of quantity and that every consonant is pronounced somewhat shorter after a phonologically long vowel than after a short one. The result is six degrees of quantity in the consonants and just as many in the vowels, since the duration of a vowel in Lapp stands in inverse relation to the duration of the following consonant. But this picture is accurate only from the point of view of phonetics. Phonologically, Lapp has only three kinds of consonants: nongeminated, weak geminates, and strong geminates.

The oppositions of gemination and intensity in consonants are combined in another way by the remarkable African language Gweabo (in Liberia), which has been described by Edward Sapir (1931). Gweabo, too, recognizes nongeminated, weakly geminated, and strongly geminated consonants. Reinforcement is expressed primarily through increased articulatory energy, however, rather than quantity, and the strong geminates are divided into two types, according to whether the emphasis is distributed equally over the entire consonant or falls only on its end (it is irrelevant that in the second type the beginning of the following vowel is also affected). There are thus four types of consonants in Gweabo: nongeminated consonants, geminates without emphasis, geminates with even emphasis, and geminates with increasing emphasis. (It must be noted that all four types occur only in voiced consonants.)

To sum up, the opposition between short and long sounds in languages with internally determined quantity is always the expression of some deeper phonological opposition. A quantitative distinction reflects either a distinction of intensity, a distinction between indivisible and bipartite units, or (only in syllabics) a distinction in the structure of the syllable cut. None of these has any intrinsic connection with duration, which is understandable since the language structure (*langue*) is timeless; it is only in speech (*parole*) that temporal relations emerge, as the elements of the language structure are expressed through sounds, measurable physical phenomena. It is the task of phoneticians to measure their duration, and the more precisely they do so, the better. But we must not forget that, with the tools available to them, phoneticians can study only the act of speech, not the language structure. Phonologists, on the other hand, have the task of investigating the language structure, something that cannot be done with the methods of the physical science of phonetics, but only with those of the linguistic science of phonology, that is, mutatis mutandis, with the same methods employed by the grammarian in elucidating the grammatical system of a previously unknown language or in identifying the grammatical meaning of a particular form. Phonetics and phonology are distinct sciences. Each must refer to the other in the study of its minimal units, but each must also be aware of its own limitations.

Responses from Conference Participants

J. Kuryłowicz: The bipartite nature of the syllable in Lithuanian and that of the syllable in Greek seem to be two different things, since in Greek the whole morphological system is based on the proportion long : short :: 2 : 1 (e.g., εὐγεν-ῆ 'well-born' [m./f. nom. sg.] : ἐλπ-ίδα 'hope' [acc. sg.]), which is not the case in Lithuanian.

A. Belić: In which language type should one put Serbo-Croatian, which has two short accents with phonological value (*jàrica* : *jȁrica*)? If we take beginnings with other kinds of accents, we will see that there are four or even five possible beginnings: ̑, ́, ̀, ̏, ˘ (without accent). The various Slavic languages suggest the existence of prosodic systems with two different accents.

Trubetzkoy [Response to Björn Collinder, whose remarks were not transmitted in the conference proceedings:] Certainly, observers who intend to describe a language must proceed phonetically, that is, begin with the sounds. But for their description to be of any use, they must also be able to interpret the material that they have collected.

[Response to Kuryłowicz:] Despite their differences, Lithuanian and Greek have one thing in common, the phonological autonomy of the beginning and the end of long syllabics, and that is what is important.

[Response to Belić:] The falling accents of the Serbo-Croatian literary language occur only on the first syllable of the word and are transferred to proclitics if any appear. So they are not true accents but rather boundary signals, as Roman Jakobson (1931a) has convincingly demonstrated.

8. The Phonological Basis of Quantity in Various Languages

1

As a physical event, each sound has a duration. Since phonetics is a natural science concerned with the physical aspect of speech sounds, it should measure their duration as precisely as possible. The more the investigations and the more accurate the measurements, the deeper our knowledge of sounds as they occur in actual pronunciation. But, from the point of view of phonology, we are entitled to ask whether duration possesses *sign value,* that is, whether it belongs to the linguistic function of the sound. Only those aspects that fulfill a *function in the language structure* pertain to phonology.[1]

Following his British teacher Henry Sweet, the Danish scholar Otto Jespersen distinguished between languages with externally and internally determined quantity in his *Lehrbuch der Phonetik* (1904). Phonology is interested only in languages with internally determined (or, as we would say today, phonologically relevant) quantity, that is, languages in which oppositions of quantity serve the differentiation of meaning.

Only relative, not absolute, quantity is meant, of course. This distinction, like that between externally and internally determined quantity, is not new. But phoneticians have not followed it to its logical conclusion; the analogy of music has led them astray. In music, the relative difference in duration between a half note, a quarter note, and an eighth note remains constant, whatever the variations in tempo (in absolute duration), only because these values, as parts of the measure, are subordinate to higher rhythmic units and governed by the inflexibility of the meter. The same can hold for the recitation of poetry, but never for normal "prose" speech. The terms *speech measure* and *prose rhythm* are only metaphors, after all. A language that recognized eighth, quarter, half, and whole notes phonologically (i.e., for sense differentiation), on the model of music, would have to give up the freedom of speaking tempi, establish one standard tempo for an entire utterance, and thus transform relative duration into absolute duration. But this would be contrary to human nature, since speech tempo is a function of the concrete situation and individual temperament.

Languages with phonologically relevant quantity distinguish only *two degrees of it.* Where observers find more than two, something has been misunderstood, as closer examination from the phonological perspective shows. Baranowski, for example, asserted that his East Lithuanian dialect distinguished long, half-long, and short syllables (Baranauskas and Weber 1882, introduction). But in his transcriptions the quantity values are distributed in the following way: pretonic syllables before a short stressed final syllable are either long or short, never half-long; the other unstressed syllables and all stressed final syllables are either half-long or short, never long; stressed nonfinal syllables are either long or half-long, never short (except those with *a,* which are always short). In each position, only two degrees of quantity are distinguished, a shorter and a longer one, and the half-long syllable turns out to be a phonetic variant of either the longer or the shorter quantity. This case is typical: as a rule, languages for which more than two degrees of quantity are claimed have only externally conditioned variants of long and short phonemes, so in each position only two quantities are possible.

In other cases, the misinformation stems from the confusion of quantity with tone movement. The Serbo-Croatian grammarian Šimo Starčević, for example, believed that his mother tongue possessed not only two short accents but also a "somewhat protracted" and a "fully lengthened" one (Starčević 1812, 113, quoted in Ivšić 1912, 67 n. 3). Yet his examples reveal that by the "somewhat protracted" and the "fully lengthened" accent he meant the falling and the rising tones of long syllables, respectively. The phonologically significant difference between these two accents is not in their duration but in their tonal movement. Comparable mistakes occur in the description of other languages.[2] If we correct them and consider quantitative relations from a purely phonological standpoint—insofar as the language recognizes phonological oppositions of quantity at all—the result is always that only two quantities are distinguished, short and long. (On Lapp, see sec. 7 below.)

The evidence shows further that short vowels are much more stable than long ones. Changes in speaking tempo are brought about primarily by altering the duration of the long vowels, while the duration of the short ones remains relatively constant. Similarly, affective emphasis usually lengthens only long vowels. *A long vowel is characterized by unlimited freedom to exceed the duration of a short one, while a short vowel is characterized by not exceeding this duration, by staying strictly within its limits.* Naturally, a short vowel also has some duration, but this fact is irrelevant for the phonological consciousness; it is always conceived of as a unit devoid of duration, as a point. In language structure, *short* and *long* are not two temporal segments of different length (like eighth notes or quarter notes in music) but rather two modes of realization—*a point versus a line.* A short vowel is punctual, nondimensional, nonextendible; a long vowel is linear, dimensional, indefinitely extendible.

The opposition between the point and the line is used in almost every sign system. We may also note that in many languages it forms the basis of so-called verbal aspect and affects the entire conjugation system. The most important thing about it is that, like many other elements in the system of language (and other sign systems), it can be reduced to a yes-no formula: long is that which may be extended, short is that which may not. If we regard extendibility as a correlation feature, then long is the marked and short the unmarked member of the correlation of phonological quantity (see Trubetzkoy 1931d, 96–99).

Therefore, internally determined, or phonologically relevant, quantity and physical duration are fundamentally different concepts. Duration can always be measured, however short it is. Physical science can compare shorter and longer time segments only with each other, not points with extendible lines. Is the definition of *quantity* as a difference in the extendibility of phonemes sufficient for phonology? We are used to thinking of *capability* as the result of some essential *characteristic:* a bird can fly (has the ability to fly) *because it has wings. What, then, are the characteristics that make one phoneme capable of extension and another incapable of it?* What is the real phonological nature of quantity? Careful investigation of numerous languages has convinced me that there is no uniform answer to this question. Several (at least three) different phonological properties can be expressed by so-called quantity, and the languages of the world can be grouped into several types in this respect. In what follows, quantitative relations are investigated first in syllabics, then in nonsyllabic (consonant) phonemes.

3

The simplest type of quantitative relation occurs in languages with the nonculminative correlation of intensity. In such languages, the syllabics are divided into "heavy" ("strong") and "light" ("weak"). The former are extendible, owing to their weight (strength), while the latter are not. Extendibility is here the consequence of and the expression of intensity, for no other form of phonological intensity (i.e., no sense-discriminating free expiratorial stress) is allowed in the syllabics and the position of stress is regulated mechanically: either by the word boundary (e.g., initial stress in Finnish, Hungarian, Czech, Slovak, Chechen, Lak, Kalmuck, etc., and final stress in Persian, Yakut, etc.) or by the length of the boundary syllables (counted from the end of the word, as in Classical Latin, Arabic, Polabian,[3] Prakrit, etc., or from the beginning, as in Ossetic). The position of stress serves here not to differentiate meaning but to separate words. Wherever we find "free quantity" and "fixed expiratorial stress," we also find this "energetic" interpretation of quantity, that is, extendibility as an expression of intensity.

Languages with free expiratorial stress differ from the type just mentioned only in that the intensity of the syllabic is used to form the word peak, so it is then impossible for intensity to assume any other function. Such languages do not have free quantity; rather, all stressed syllables have long vowels, and unstressed syllables have short ones (e.g., Spanish, Italian, Modern Greek, Bulgarian, Romanian, Ukrainian, Russian, Avar, and Lezghian [Kuri]).[4] Intensity is realized as free quantity in those languages that do not use it to form word peaks; in languages that do use phonological intensity in this way, extendibility is a nonobligatory by-product, and distinctions of intensity are realized mainly as differences in "weight." The phonological nature of the correlation of intensity remains the same in both cases, however: it is the opposition between heavy (strong) and light (weak) syllabics.

4

In another interpretation of quantity, long vowels are treated as phonemes with a distinct beginning and end (hence their extendibility), short ones as phonemes whose beginning and end coincide. The most widespread characteristic of this analytic, or arithmetic, interpretation of quantity is the presence of *differences of tonal movement* capable of distinguishing meaning in long vowels and the absence of such differences in short vowels. Whether the differences in this movement are more tonal or expiratorial, whether a falling intonation is opposed to a rising one, or a falling one to a level one, or a rising one to a level one—all this is relevant only for phonetics. The important thing phonologically is that just *one part* (the beginning or the end) of the long syllabic is emphasized; the vowel is split in two. A short vowel does not permit such a division: the whole syllable must be either emphasized or not emphasized, that is, stressed or unstressed. This system is most clearly evident in Lithuanian, North Kashubian, Slovenian, the Čakavian dialect of Serbo-Croatian, and so on, but the principle remains the same even if the position of the stress is somehow restricted, as long as differences of tonal movement are recognized, as in Japanese, Ancient Greek ("law of three syllables"), certain Kaikavian-Croatian dialects (where stress may fall only on one of the last two syllables), and Latvian (with initial stress).

In Chinese, where the so-called tones occur in compound words only in the syllable with culminative function, there is a distinction in tonal movement in the "long" syllables (first and third tone): in the third tone the last phase is clearly emphasized, while in the first tone sometimes the first phase, sometimes neither of the two phases, is emphasized. In the "short" syllables (second and fourth tone), tonal movement is phonologically irrelevant (non-distinctive): it is important only that the second tone be higher, the fourth lower.[5] There are Chinese dialects in which the fourth ("short low") tone is not only low but also falling, and the second ("short high") not only high but also rising (e.g., the dialect of Mukden). But these rising and falling tone movements are only the expression of emphasis and nonemphasis, respectively: the first tone (with emphasized beginning and nonemphasized end) appears in such dialects as rising-falling, the third tone (with emphasized end) as two peaked and falling-rising (see Polivanov and Popov-Tativa 1928, 90–91; Polivanov 1928, 118–19). Thus, although the rise in the second and the fall in the fourth tone are constant features, they are phonologically irrelevant and must be considered as the expression of emphasis versus nonemphasis.[6]

The same analytic, or arithmetic, interpretation of quantity is the rule in languages that make a phonological distinction between a smooth articulation and one interrupted by glottal closure (Danish stød) in long bases (i.e., long vowels, diphthongs, and sequences of vowel + sonorant). In the phonological consciousness of speakers of these languages, the long bases must consist of a beginning and an end, between which there can be either an unbroken sound stream or an interruption (compare the concepts legato and staccato in music), whereas short bases cannot make this distinction since they consist of only a point.[7] Danish, Latvian, Livonian, and many other languages belong to this group.

An analytic (arithmetic) interpretation of quantity can be assumed also for those languages, mainly African and North American, in which oppositions of pitch (or, rather, of voice register) are used without culminative function. The Gweabo language of Liberia described by Sapir (1931) is especially instructive, as its prosodic principles are followed with unusual consistency. The mora serves as both quantitative and tonal unit here. Each mora has its own tonal characteristic: in addition to four registers, rising and falling morae are distinguished. Long syllables consist of two morae with either the same or different tonal characteristics: the syllable mū means 'door' when its first mora occupies the highest register and its second the lowest, but 'I cause to go' when its first mora occupies the highest register and its second the normal one, and 'you (pl.) cause to go' when the first mora rises to normal register and the second is pronounced in a somewhat lower (middle) register. In polysyllabic words, each syllable has its own tonal characteristic, as does each mora.

The example of Gweabo shows with particular clarity the nature of the analytic, or arithmetic, interpretation of quantity, which is present in languages with the correlation of tone movement or tone interruption in long bases as well as in those with the nonculminative correlation of tone register. Languages with the "energetic" interpretation of quantity have only uniform *syl-lables,* some heavy, some light, whereas the unit in languages with the analytic interpretation of quantity is the *mora.* In the latter, the distinction is not between heavy and light but between bimoric and monomoric syllables. The mora must be conceived of not as a temporal unit but rather as an indivisible component of the syllabic base.[8] Languages with the analytic interpretation of quantity may be called *mora-counting,* as opposed to *syllable-counting,* languages.[9]

5

A third interpretation of quantity may be found in languages such as German, Dutch, and English. The long vowels are here treated as full, unchecked, while the short ones are incomplete, cut off, checked by the beginning of the following consonant. In such languages, therefore, only long (i.e., full) vowels may stand word finally, and the quantitative oppositions appear only before consonants;[10] the free vowels are extendible, the checked ones are not. These languages have a *correlation of syllable cut,* not of quantity.[11] And because syllable cut has nothing to do with culminative intensity, the two can coexist. A combined correlation of this type exists, in fact, in German, Dutch, and English, which have free expiratorial stress.

It seems that the correlation of syllable cut can also go together with the correlation of tone movement. Such a combination seems to exist in Siamese, if I (as a layman) understand the complicated prosodic features of this language correctly. Long and short syllabic bases here are distinguished only before final obstruents;[12] if the syllabic base occurs in final position, it is always long. This situation, reminiscent of English, Dutch, or German (e.g., Ger. *satt* : *Saat* : *sah* 'satisfied, seed, [I] saw'), testifies to a correlation of syllable cut. On the other hand, there is an opposition in Siamese between falling and rising tonal movement in long bases ("returning" and "rising" tone, according to Trittel). This opposition exists only when the voice register is relatively high, that is, when the long (unchecked) base is emphasized; in lower registers, unchecked bases have level tone. Oppositions of tone movement are unknown in short bases, which distinguish only a higher, emphatic level and a lower, softer one (high fading and low fading tone in Trittel's terms). The situation is thus similar to that of Lithuanian, for example, in which long syllabic bases can be falling stressed (abrupt), rising stressed (smooth), or nonemphasized (unstressed), while short ones can be only emphasized (stressed) or nonemphasized (unstressed). But it is a peculiarity of Siamese that the triad of returning, rising, and level tone exists only in long (unchecked) bases in syllable-final position, whereas unchecked bases before syllable-final *k, t,* and *p* (and probably before the glottal stop)[13] possess only two tones (Trittel's falling and "suppressed" tones), whose phonological value is difficult to establish.

If my interpretation of the Siamese evidence is correct, we have evidence that the correlation of syllable cut is possible not only in syllable-counting but also in mora-counting languages, in which unchecked bases count as bimoric. On the other hand, the interpretation of quantity underlying this correlation seems to be incompatible with the energetic interpretation. This explains the paradoxical fact that many Czechs and Hungarians, who possess clear quantity distinctions in their mother tongue, are incapable of keeping apart the short and long vowels of German. Vice versa, it is difficult for many Germans to distinguish the short and long vowels of Czech correctly (especially word finally and in unstressed syllables). The reason that the Czech and Hungarian quantities are not identified with their German counterparts can only be that the former are based on a (nonculminative) correlation of intensity and the latter on a correlation of syllable cut, and that it is difficult for a person used to one interpretation of quantity to learn another one.

6

The interpretation of quantity on which the correlation of syllable cut is based can be applied only to syllabics, while the other two interpretations, the energetic and the analytic, can also be applied to nonsyllabic consonants.

The analytic interpretation of quantity is the basis of the *correlation of consonant gemination.* Geminated consonants differ from simple ones phonetically in many ways, including longer duration and stronger articulation. Phonologically, however, the only relevant fact is that in geminated consonants the onset (beginning) and offset (end) are assigned to different syllables (or morae), whereas in nongeminated consonants onset and offset constitute a whole belonging to one syllable (mora). The correlation of consonant gemination is thus based on the interpretation of quantity identified above as analytic, although the involvement of the syllable boundary establishes a link to the correlation of syllable cut.[14]

As a rule, the correlation of consonant gemination exists only medially. In Gweabo, however, we also find it initially. The beginning (onset) of such a geminate forms a special mora, which, like all morae in Gweabo, displays a particular tonal characteristic: it is always pronounced in the lowest voice register (geminated consonants in Gweabo are either sonorants or voiced obstruents).[15] This unusual language also provides evidence that the consonant gemination is based on the same interpretation of quantity as the opposition between monomoric and bimoric vowels. As discussed above, the analytic interpretation of quantity often manifests itself in the fact that distinctions of tonal movement are recognized in long (bimoric) vowels but unknown in short (monomoric) ones. A similar process can be observed in Gweabo consonants. Besides the normal geminated consonants (designated by Sapir as 'b, 'd, 'm, 'n, 'ñ, 'n̠, 'y, 'w), there are also emphatically geminated ones distinguished by strong, or fortis, articulation. These emphatic, or reinforced, geminates are also of two kinds. The one kind (in Sapir's transcription "B, "D, etc.) has "a slight delay" in its first part and a rise in intensity that reaches its high point at the beginning of the following vowel, with the result that this vowel "begins with unusual strength," although it then "dies out rapidly at the end" in a "steep descrescendo." In the other kind (in Sapir's transcription 'B, 'D, etc.), the articulatory force is distributed more evenly in both the consonant and the following vowel (Sapir 1931, 36–37). This is a clear case of a *difference of tone movement,* which, characteristically, appears only in geminated consonants with expiratorial emphasis (reinforcement): the one type emphasizes the final part of the consonant (the effect on the beginning of the following vowel must have a purely phonetic explanation); the other type does not. The relation "B : 'B : 'b in Gweabo corresponds to the relation between bimoric vowels with emphasis on the final mora, bimoric vowels with equal emphasis on both morae, and bimoric vowels without emphasis on either mora—a triad that recurs in numerous mora-counting languages with the correlation of tone movement.[16]

7

In geminated consonants, the assignment of onset and offset to different syllables (or morae) implies that the beginning and the end are independent. In other long consonants, however, onset and offset cannot be considered as discrete points. This is the case in languages in which long consonants occur initially or finally (although without the prosodic properties of a syllable or mora) as well as medially. Since such consonants tend to have not only longer duration but also a more energetic articulation than the corresponding short ones, we may speak of a *correlation of consonant intensity* based on the same energetic interpretation of quantity as the correlation of intensity in vowels. A difference in duration is not even necessary, for the impression of greater intensity can be created by increased articulatory energy (tensing of the muscles, firmer closure or constriction, stronger expiration, and so on): this is what happens, for example, in most East Caucasian languages, where differences in duration may be considered nonobligatory by-products of the correlation of intensity in consonants (cf. Trubetzkoy 1926, 1931b). Even in languages in which longer duration is an indispensable feature of strong, or heavy, consonants (e.g., in Hungarian), it is accompanied by an increase in articulatory energy, so that here, too, longer duration and increased articulatory energy form an indivisible whole, a complex feature. The designation long ~ short can thus be replaced for consonants (and in certain languages for vowels) by strong ~ weak or heavy ~ light.

The correlations of intensity and of gemination can best be compared by investigating languages that have both. Those languages must be excluded, however, in which long and energetically articulated consonants occur finally or initially with no connection to the syllable boundary, but medially with onset and offset spread over two syllables. For a Hungarian, the long *s* in *hossz* 'length' (pronounced *hɔs·*) is identical with the long *s* in *hosszú* 'long' (pron. *hɔs·/su·*), although onset and offset belong to the same syllable in the first case but are split by the syllable boundary in the second. And since the syllable-final *s* in *hossz* cannot be considered a geminate, the phonological consciousness also treats the distribution of onset and offset over two syllables in *hosszú* as an insignificant, "natural" consequence of the realization of a heavy consonant between two vowels. Only the correlation of intensity is phonologically significant in such cases.

A true coexistence of the correlations of gemination and intensity in consonants is possible only in two forms. First, the two correlations can be distributed among the different consonants: in Lak (Central Daghestan), for example, the nasals participate in the correlation of gemination and the voiceless obstruents in that of intensity. Second, they can form a "bundle" (on this concept, see Trubetzkoy 1931d, 105ff.). This occurs in Lapp, for example, in which distinctions of intensity are made only in geminates, so that, from the phonological standpoint, there are three kinds of consonants: nongeminates, light geminates, and heavy geminates. Phonologically, nongeminated consonants in Lapp differ from geminates only in that, in the latter, onset and offset are assigned to different syllables; that the geminates are also longer than the nongeminates is a "natural," concomitant but phonologically irrelevant phenomenon. The heavy geminates differ from the light ones only in their greater articulatory energy and longer duration. Observers interested in phonetic reality alone have the impression that Lapp distinguishes three degrees of quantity in consonants: short (in the nongeminates), long (in the light geminates), and overlong (in the heavy geminates). This interpretation is unacceptable from the point of view of phonology, because it takes into account only phonetic features (and, of them, only duration) and ignores the fundamental circumstance that the three alleged degrees of quantity differentiate meaning only in medial position.[17]

Gemination combined with intensity in consonants was also identified above for Gweabo. In Gweabo, in contradistinction to Lapp, intensity in the geminates is expressed mainly through articulatory energy, whereas in Lapp duration plays a role, too. Also, as we have seen, the heavy (emphatic) geminates in Gweabo are of two kinds, according to whether the first or the second mora is emphasized—a distinction foreign to Lapp.[18]

8

The present investigation has shown that the opposition between extendible and nonextendible sounds is always the manifestation of a deeper phonological opposition. In some languages, it is an expression of intensity (weight, strength), in others a result of the independence of the beginning and the end of the phoneme (as opposed to phonemes whose beginning and end coincide). In still other languages, the extendibility of a syllabic stems from its running its full course unchecked by the following consonant (as opposed to checked syllabics). None of these phonological properties has anything to do with duration. This is natural, since *the structure of language as such is timeless*. Time (duration) does not become involved until the act of speech. This fundamental difference between speech and language, between the sound and the phoneme, between phonetics and phonology, cannot be emphasized enough: it is just as important as the distinction between the coin and the monetary unit, between numismatics and finance.[19]

There are also practical conclusions to be drawn in connection with terminology. The term *sound duration* should be used only in the branches of science concerned with the investigation and normative description of the phonic aspect of speech (phonetics, speech therapy, orthoepy, and so on). The terms *quantity, long,* and *short* borrowed from classical grammar may be used by disciplines concerned with the structure of language (phonology, grammar) as well, but sparingly and with extreme caution: they should serve as temporary labels, that is, only in cases in which the phonological nature of the phenomenon under study has not been established or cannot be established, owing to a lack of reliable evidence. When the phonological picture is clear, it is advisable to replace them with the corresponding terms used and explained in the present study.

9. How Should the Sound System of an Artificial International Language Be Structured?

Creators of artificial international languages try to keep the grammar as simple as possible, to facilitate the process of acquisition for speakers with the most diverse mother tongues. Phonics is ignored, however, even though a difficult sound system presents just as great an obstacle to language learning as complicated grammar. Communicating with foreigners in languages that they pronounce incorrectly is sometimes close to impossible, as anyone will agree who has ever spoken with a Chinese, Korean, or Japanese with incomplete mastery of German, French, or English. And language teachers in China and Japan know from experience how unbelievably difficult it is to teach the natives of these countries a halfway acceptable pronunciation of European languages. But it is no great problem for a Japanese to learn the correct pronunciation of Chinese or Burmese, so it cannot be the case that Japanese, Koreans, or Chinese have no gift for languages. It is the sound structure of European languages that presents them with almost insurmountable difficulties.

An artificial language intended for truly international use must have a sound system that can be learned by all peoples of the world. It may not be necessary to take the interests of very small, endangered groups into account, such as certain North American Indian tribes. But the requirements of non-European *Kulturvölker* and major colonial peoples must be considered since their need for an international language is especially strong—much stronger than that of the Romance, Germanic, and Slavic peoples, of which every educated member can communicate with other Europeans without serious difficulty. The phonic dimension of a good artificial language must be constructed in such a way that not only a European but also a Chinese, a Malay, or a Sudanese can learn it without excessive effort. The great disadvantage of artificial languages heretofore has been that they did not meet this requirement.

The difficulty of mastering a sound system consists not so much in learning to pronounce foreign sounds correctly as in focusing one's attention on sound distinctions that carry meaning in the new language but are insignificant in the mother tongue. It is easy for a German to sing a vowel on a high, middle, or low note or to let the voice rise or fall during its articulation, but if a German wants to learn Chinese in its southern (Cantonese) pronunciation, the famous "nine tones" of this language form an insurmountable barrier. It is impossible to remember that, whenever the word *fan* 'divide' occurs in a sentence, the *a* must begin on a high pitch, but the *n* on a medium pitch, so that the whole syllable has a falling tone. If the high pitch is sustained until the end of the *n,* the word *fan* means not 'divide' but 'sleep'; and, if the falling pitch movement begins too low, so that the *a* starts on a medium pitch and the *n* ends on a very low pitch, the word means 'burn'; and so on. The problem lies in learning to pay attention to intonation and pitch and in training one's memory, not in learning any particular articulation. An artificial language must avoid anything that could cause problems of this kind and restrict itself to the level of the most basic linguistic awareness. For Germans, learning the tones of South Chinese is difficult, but for South Chinese, it is no problem to learn a language without distinctive tones: they simply remember to pronounce every syllable on a medium pitch, and everyone understands them. It follows that artificial languages should not make use of distinctive tones; in this way, the interests of European speakers are respected and those of East Asians are not compromised. The same principle must be followed in other cases of this type.

An artificial international language must be designed for situations in which speaker and hearer represent different mother tongues and thus different linguistic habits. It is well known that the same phonetic feature can be interpreted differently by speakers of different languages. Russians are used to pronouncing stressed vowels long and unstressed vowels short; to them, stress and quantity are synonymous. Czechs always stress initial syllables; to them, stress is a signal of the beginning of a word, while vowel quantity is independent of stress and often distinguishes meaning: *pīt'i* 'drink' (v.) – *pit'ī* 'drinking' (n.), *lāska* 'love' – *laskā* '(he) caresses,' etc. Russians speaking Czech will either pronounce initial syllables stressed and long and noninitial syllables short, or interpret long vowels in Czech as stressed, pronouncing them stressed and long and failing to stress the initial syllable when it is short. Frequently, a Russian speaker will make both kinds of mistakes and distort the prosodic system of Czech beyond recognition. On the other hand, Czechs speaking Russian cannot master the Russian stress system: they stress the initial syllable as in their mother tongue and interpret Russian stress as vowel length (so that a Russian sentence like *přin'is'ít'i mn'e stakán vadý* 'bring me a glass of water' sounds like *priňisīt'i mňe stakān vadȳ*), or, to avoid this, they shift the stress forward without lengthening any vowel, with the result that all Russian words acquire stress on the last syllable without being lengthened. Since stress distinguishes meaning in Russian, constant misunderstandings are the result.

Even if a sound opposition distinguishes meaning in two languages, misunderstandings can still arise between the speakers of those languages if the opposition is not realized in quite the same way. The French claim that the Germans (especially speakers of the Alemannic dialects) confuse French *b, d, g* with *p, t, k*, which is surprising since the oppositions *b–p, d–t, g–k* differentiate meaning in German, too: *Bein* 'leg' – *Pein* 'torment' (n.), *raube* '(I) rob' – *Raupe* 'caterpillar,' *Drohnen* 'drones' (pl. n.)' – *thronen* 'preside,' *geil* 'lascivious' – *Keil* 'wedge,' *lagen* '(we) lay' (pret.) – *Laken* 'bedsheet.' The explanation seems to be that Alemannic *b, d, g* and *p, t, k* are not identical with the corresponding French sounds. Alemannic *b* and *p* both lie between French *b* and *p*: when speakers of Alemannic pronounce French *bière* 'beer,' the result is something between French *bière* and *pierre* 'stone,' and, noticing the difference from the pronunciation to which they are accustomed, French hearers think they hear *pierre*. Such cases (which are very common in international communication) should suggest to the creators of artificial languages that the so-called correlations should be avoided as far as possible. The distinction between long and short vowels, the distinction between voiced and voiceless (or fortis and lenis, aspirated and nonaspirated) consonants, the position of stress in the word— none of these should be used to differentiate meaning in an artificial international language. This prohibition is all the more important as such distinctions are unknown in the majority of languages.

Sounds that certain peoples find difficult to articulate must be avoided. Again, half-extinct languages may be left out of consideration. The fact that the Aleuts, Tlingit, and Hupa Indians possess no labial stops in their native tongues and have problems with the pronunciation of *p* and *b* in other languages cannot stand in the way of using labial stops in the sound system of an artificial language. But *h,* which is foreign to French, Italian, Modern Greek, Tamil, and other languages, should probably be omitted from such a system.

Following the principles outlined above, let me sketch out an ideal sound system for an artificial international language.

Virtually all peoples will be able to pronounce the five Latin vowels—*u, o, a, e, i*. Languages with poorer inventories do exist, but either their cultural sphere of influence is so small that they may be ignored (e.g., Lak), or they turn out to possess the missing vowels after all under certain conditions. Persian has only three long and three short vowels; but in educated pronunciation the long ones have the values *ū, ā, ī*, the short ones the values *o, ä, e*. Persians are thus able to produce the entire set *u, o, a, e, i;* they would tend to pronounce *o* and *e* shorter than the other three, but this would have no adverse effect on communication since vowel quantity would not be used to distinguish meaning. So the vowels *u, o, a, e, i* are all acceptable for the sound system of an international language. These five will have to suffice, however; neither *ü* or *ö* nor open and close *o* and *e* sounds can be employed as independent elements with distinctive function. The realization of the five vowels must be left up to each people. It could, however, be recommended to the English (and especially the Americans), the Germans, the Arabs, and others—in whose languages short *u* and *i* are quite open, dialectally tending toward *o* and *e*—that they always pronounce *u* and *i* in the international language long. Further, the oppositions *u–o* and *i–e* should not be exploited too heavily; there should be as few pairs of words as possible that are distinguished solely by these oppositions, such as German *Russ* 'soot' – *Ross* 'horse' or *winden* 'wind' (v.) – *wenden* 'turn' or French *doux* 'sweet' – *dos* 'back' or *prix* 'price' – *pré* 'meadow.'

The consonant system of an international language should contain three stops: the labial (*p*), the dental (*t*), and the guttural (*k*). There seem to be no languages in the world without dental stops. Labial stops are lacking only in a few native languages of North America (Aleut, Tlingit, Hupa, and others), guttural stops only in minor dialects of various languages (e.g., the Rosental dialect of Carinthian Slovenian and the Kasimov dialect of Volga Tatar). So *p, t,* and *k* are certainly acceptable. Their realization, like that of the vowels, must be left up to each people. Some will pronounce them with voice, others without; some aspirated, others nonaspirated, and so on. Since distinctions of voice, strength, and aspiration will have no effect on meaning in the international language, differences in the pronunciation of the three stops will not cause misunderstanding. For many peoples, only one pronunciation will be possible. The Greeks, for example, have in their language only voiceless, nonaspirated *p, t, k* but after nasals only voiced *b, d, g:* naturally, they will pronounce the stops of the international language this way, too.

Some languages permit only one kind of stop in certain positions but two stops in others. Estonian, for example, has only voiceless stops word initially but distinguishes voiced and voiceless stops medially. Conversely, some Scots Gaelic dialects possess only nonaspirated voiceless stops medially while recognizing a distinctive opposition between aspirated and nonaspirated stops in initial position. In such cases, it is advisable to recommend that speakers pronounce the stops of the international language in all positions the way they are pronounced in the native language in the position of minimal differentiation (thus, in Estonian as in initial position, in the Scots dialects as in medial position). It is harder to determine how the *p, t, k* of the international language should be pronounced by speakers of languages that recognize two or three kinds of stops with distinctive function in all positions, such as English, French, Chinese, or Siamese. One could only establish rules of the following type: Speakers who distinguish voiced and voiceless stops in their native tongue should pronounce "international *p, t, k*" without voice; those who distinguish aspirated and nonaspirated stops should pronounce "international *p, t, k*" without aspiration; those who distinguish strong (fortes) and weak (lenes) stops should pronounce "international *p, t, k*" strong. Despite such rules, the pronunciation of *p, t, k* will vary with the speaker's nationality; the Arabs, for example, will pronounce international *p* as voiced *b* but international *t, k* as voiceless aspirated *tʰ, kʰ*. In any case, international *p, t, k* will be recognizable, which is the only necessary factor in communication.

Of the nasals, the international language may contain only *m* and *n,* since the others (e.g., the palatal *gn* of French and the guttural *ng* of Germanic) do not occur in all languages and cannot be pronounced by many peoples. Whether *n* is pronounced gutturally before *k* or palatally before *j* by some speakers is then immaterial.

Fricatives are difficult to select. The labial fricative *f* cannot be pronounced by many of the world's peoples; it is lacking in Finnish, Estonian, Latvian, Lithuanian, Armenian, Tamil, Burmese, and Mongolian, for example, and occurs in Japanese and Korean only before *u.* The velar fricative *x* is foreign to Italian, French, English, Norwegian, Swedish, Lithuanian, Latvian, Bengali, and other languages. Therefore, neither *f* nor *x* may assume any role in the sound system of a truly international language. Of all the fricatives, only *s* is acceptable in such a system, for it occurs in every language of the world (except for an isolated few, such as Nuer, in the Egyptian Sudan, or the Australian aboriginal languages, whose cultural significance is so limited that they may be left out of account). The pronunciation of *s* varies widely from people to people, but it can always be recognized, as long as the sound system of the international language contains no other fricative similar to it. The introduction of a second sibilant, say, *š,* would be inadvisable also for the simple reason that many would be unable to pronounce it.

As mentioned above, the sound *h,* which is lacking in French, Italian, Greek, and other languages, must not be included in the system of an international language. The semivowels *j* and *w,* however, may be accepted without hesitation. There are indeed languages without *j,* such as Georgian, but their speakers are able to pronounce it in the form of nonsyllabic *i,* for *i* exists in all languages and the nonsyllabic pronunciation of a close vowel is never problematic. It may be left up to individual peoples whether they wish to pronounce *w* as labiodental *v,* bilabial *w,* or nonsyllabic *u;* the recognition of the single international *w* in these three pronunciations will hardly pose a problem.

The liquids present the most formidable difficulty. There are languages with four, three, or two liquids and some with just one; the latter group includes such important languages as Chinese and Japanese. According to the principle enunciated above, we should follow the poorest sound system and accept only one liquid into the inventory of the international language, but which one should be given the honor? Chinese has (before vowels) only *l,* Japanese only *r.* The single liquid of an international language would be spoken by the Chinese as *l* and by the Japanese as *r;* in a conversation between a Chinese and a Japanese speaker, each would be able to recognize the single international liquid in the partner's *r* or *l*, respectively. But how should the sound be pronounced by those whose languages recognize two, three, or four liquids? Languages and dialects present extremely diverse realizations of *l* and *r*. Even in languages with only one *r* sound (e.g., English, French, Italian, Spanish, and Danish), its pronunciation varies so widely that one people will often fail to recognize another's *r* as such. Arabic speakers will tend to identify the French (Parisian) *r* in *trois* 'three' with their *x* and Danish *r* with their *ayin*. The pronunciation of *l* in different languages varies much less, however. Especially in languages with two *l* sounds, one always approaches a certain median value: in Russian, for example, the "palatalized" *l* is closer to this value, in Serbo-Croatian the "dental" *l*, in Slovenian the "palatal" *lj*, and so on. So the risk of misunderstandings is much less if *l*, rather than *r*, is given the function of unique liquid in the system.

The inventory of the international language may thus contain only the following fourteen sounds: five vowels, *u, o, a, e, i*; three stops, *p, t, k*; two nasals, *m* and *n*; two semivowels, *w* and *j*; one fricative, *s*; and one liquid, *l*.

The inventory of permissible combinations is just as important as the sound inventory itself. Not all combinations in a given language can be pronounced by speakers of other languages, and speakers of one language may pronounce combinations in such a way that their elements are not recognized by speakers of another. Two kinds of vowel combinations must be distinguished, monosyllabic and polysyllabic (disyllabic). Monosyllabic combinations of two vowels, that is, diphthongs, are called *falling* or *rising* according to whether the first component is more open or less open than the second. Falling diphthongs with *i* and *u* as the second component cannot easily be distinguished from those with *e* and *o*; very few languages (dialects) possess such a distinction. For a language with five vowels, therefore, only six falling diphthongs may be considered: *ou, au, eu, oi, ai, ei*. But not all peoples would be able to keep these diphthongs apart easily. The Germans confuse *ou* with *au* (e.g., in pronouncing Czech names), *ei* with *ai* (e.g., in speaking English), and *eu* with *oi*. The English pronunciation of *au* is frequently close to *eu*. Many languages have only *ai* and *au*, and their speakers are unable to distinguish the other diphthongs accurately. It is advisable, then, to select for the international language only the two falling diphthongs *ai* and *au*. Since the monosyllabic pronunciation of rising diphthongs is insurmountably difficult for many speakers whose native language does not contain them, rising diphthongs should probably be excluded from the international language altogether.

Disyllabic vowel combinations are uncommon in the languages of the world, but there does not seem to be any people that cannot pronounce them, so they are acceptable for the international language. It is necessary to ensure that they are kept distinct from certain other combinations, however. Most important, disyllabic combinations with *u* and *i* as the second component must not occur (*o-u, a-u, e-u, i-u, u-i, o-i, a-i, e-i*), as speakers could tend to confuse them with diphthongs. Disyllabic combinations with *u* and *i* as the first component should occur only in environments in which they cannot be confused with combinations with *w* or *j* + vowel. Finally, combinations of two identical vowels must be avoided because speakers of certain languages would contract them to long vowels, which could be interpreted as simple (short) vowels by speakers of other languages. Therefore, of the twenty-five possible disyllabic vowel combinations, thirteen are excluded (*uu, oo, aa, ee, ii, ou, au, eu, iu, ui, oi, ai, ei*), six are admissible under certain conditions, and only six are admissible unconditionally (*oa, oe, ao, ae, eo, ea*).

Some combinations of consonants with vowels must be excluded from the international language if misunderstandings are to be avoided. The combinations *wu* and *ji* cannot be pronounced by many peoples and can easily be confused with simple *u* and *i*. The combinations *tu* and *ti* must be excluded as well since they are unacceptable for the Japanese, who pronounce foreign *tu, ti* as *tsu, či* (the pronunciation of *ti* as *či* is also characteristic of Korean), and speakers of other languages would hardly recognize international *tu* and *ti* in a Japanese speaker's *tsu* and *či*. And, since the Japanese are among those most interested in the creation of an international auxiliary language, their pronunciation must be taken into account. Another such people, the Chinese, has great difficulty with a clear pronunciation of the combination *ki*, which in northern Chinese Mandarin is nonexistent; instead, something between *tçi* and *či* is spoken, which no non-Chinese would identify with *ki*. The combination *ki* will thus have to be deleted from the inventory of the international language. In all, only five of the forty-five possible consonant-vowel combinations must be excluded (*wu, ji, tu, ti, ki*); the remaining forty may be used without restriction.

Of the combinations vowel + consonant, only *ij* and *uw* must be excluded. Before vowels, they would be confused with the disyllabic combinations *i/u* + vowel, before consonants (or word finally) with simple *i* and *u*. All other combinations of vowel + consonant are permissible. The same is true, mutatis mutandis, of the diphthongs *ai* and *au:* the combinations *aij* and *auw* must be forbidden, but *ai* and *au* may occur before all other consonants.

Languages have many kinds of restrictions on combinations of two consonants, and in this respect speakers display especially little adaptability to the requirements of other languages. Extreme examples are furnished by certain languages of East Asia and South Africa. Burmese permits no consonant groups at all (consonant + *j* is spoken as a palatalized consonant, consonant + *w* as a labialized consonant, so neither can be treated as a combination). Japanese permits only the combination of a nasal with a homorganic consonant. The same is true of Chinese, at least of northern and central Chinese (in root compounds), and of Zulu and certain other Bantu languages. This system may be considered the poorest of those eligible for consideration. And, since there does not seem to be any language that prohibits the combination of a homorganic nasal with a following consonant, the international language should model itself on Japanese in this case (languages without such combinations—e.g., Burmese—have nasalized vowels that substitute for the combination vowel + homorganic nasal). Of the seventy-two possible combinations of two different consonants, the international language may permit only seven: *mp, nt, nk, ns, mw, nj, nl.* Any other solution would lead to breakdowns in communication for speakers of East Asian languages. Even after a lengthy stay abroad and careful study of European languages, educated Japanese are unable to pronounce consonant groups. They always insert *u* or *i* between the consonants, pronouncing, for example, *Berulini, Raipitsiçi, Kirisuto, sipitaru, niçito,* and *Nafuto* for German *Berlin, Leipzig, Christ* 'Christian,' *Spital* 'hospital,' *nicht* 'not,' and *Napht* 'naphtha,' with the result that they are scarcely understood. The same happens to the Chinese. If additional consonant groups (beyond the seven named above) were introduced into the international language, the East Asian peoples that need this language the most would speak it in a way unintelligible to others, which would defeat its purpose.

Whether double (geminated) consonants should be permitted is a difficult question. They are found in the most diverse languages (including Japanese), and even speakers of the other languages generally have no difficulty in reproducing them once heard. On the other hand, such speakers often find the acoustic differentiation between simple and double consonants difficult, so the inclusion of consonant geminates in the international language might well lead to misunderstandings. Furthermore, some speakers can produce certain sounds only as geminates. In Tamil, for example, there are either geminated voiceless stops or fricatives between vowels, so Tamil speakers will pronounce international *p, t, k* intervocalically as *pp, tt, kk* and would be unable to distinguish the geminates from the nongeminates. For this reason, consonant gemination ought to be excluded from the international language.

A further problem is presented by the relations of sounds and sound combinations to the beginning, end, and middle of the word. Most languages permit both consonants and vowels in initial position; those permitting only consonants are relatively insignificant and may be left out of consideration. Of the consonants, liquids are frequently avoided initially. This is the case, for example, in the majority of Turkic languages; but, under the influence of Arabic and Persian, the Islamic Turkic peoples (the only significant ones for our purposes) have abandoned this restriction. In Japanese, too, in which the liquid (*r*) originally could not occur word initially, the restriction has dissolved under the influence of the numerous lexical borrowings from Chinese (e.g., the Japanese linear measure *ri*, well known to crossword puzzle solvers). Of the modern languages with a larger sphere of cultural influence, only Korean seems to prohibit liquids in initial position, so there seems to be no reason to extend this prohibition to the international language. The consonant combinations (*mp, nt, nk, ns, mw, nj, nl*) must not occur initially, of course, as most peoples would not be able to produce them. All sounds and groups of sounds in the international language may occur medially. Only the combination of the diphthongs *au* or *ai* with a following consonant group (*mp, nt, nk, ns, mw, nj, nl*) must be excluded as unpronounceable for many.

There seems to be no language in which vowels are not permitted word finally, so there is no reason to exclude any of the vowels of the international language from this position. The number of consonants permitted word finally is severely limited in many languages, however. In Ancient Greek, only *n, s,* and *r* were tolerated in this position; Modern Italian allows only *n, r,* and *l,* Finnish only *n, t,* and *s,* and so on. The most radical stance is assumed, once again, by Japanese and northern and central Chinese, which permit only a nasal word finally. If a foreign word ends in a different consonant, the Chinese leave it off, and the Japanese add a vowel to it: English *pound* = Chinese *pan,* Japanese *pando,* etc. This occurs unconsciously and "with the best of intentions": since Japanese and Chinese speakers are used to speaking and hearing nonnasal consonants only before vowels, they either do not notice a final nonnasal consonant in a foreign word or imagine that they hear a short vowel following it. If such misunderstandings are to be avoided in the international language, no other consonants than *n* should be permitted in final position.

An artificial international language with a phonic inventory drawn up according to these principles can employ only 110 monosyllabic and 10,542 disyllabic elements. These figures are derived as follows:[1]

 1. Monosyllables beginning with a vowel: 5 monovocalic + 2 diphthongal + 5 with final n = 12.

 2. Monosyllables beginning with a consonant: 40 (= 9 × 5 − 5) with simple vowel + 18 (= 9 × 2) with diphthong + 40 with final n = 98.

 3. Disyllables beginning with a vowel:

  a) With no consonant between the two vowels: 6 with simple vowel (*eo, ea, ae, ao, oa, oe*) + 4 with diphthong (*oai, oau, eai, eau*) + 6 with nasal in the second syllable = 16.

  b) With a consonant between the two vowels:

   i) With simple vowel in the first syllable: 120 (= 3 × 40) with open vowel (*e, o, a*) in the first syllable and a vowel word finally + 72 (= 2 × 36) with close vowel (*u, i*) in the first syllable and a vowel word finally + 192 (= 3 × 40 + 2 × 36) with final n + 54

(= 3 × 18) with open vowel in the first syllable and final diphthong + 32 (= 2 × 16) with close vowel in the first syllable and final diphthong = 470.

ii) With vowel + nasal in the first syllable: 200 (= 5 × 40) with a vowel word finally + 200 (= 5 × 40) with final *n* + 90 (= 5 × 18) with final diphthong = 490.

iii) With diphthong in the first syllable: 72 (= 2 × 36) with a vowel word finally + 72 (2 × 36) with final *n* + 32 (= 2 × 16) with final diphthong = 176.

In all, 470 + 590 + 176 = 1,136 disyllables beginning with a vowel.

4. Disyllables beginning with a consonant:

a) Without a consonant between the two vowels: 62 (= 31 × 2) with final diphthong + 39 (= 13 × 3) with close vowel in the first syllable and simple vowel word finally + 54 (= 9 × 6) with open vowel in the first syllable and simple vowel word finally + 93 (= 13 × 3 + 9 × 6) with *n* = 248.

b) With a consonant between the two vowels:

i) With simple vowel in the first syllable: 1,080 (= 27 × 40) with open vowel in the first syllable + 468 (= 13 × 36) with close vowel in the first syllable + 1,548 (= 27 × 40 + 13 × 36) with final nasal + 558 (= 31 × 18) = 3,654.

ii) With nasal before the consonant of the second syllable: 1,600 (= 40 × 40) with simple vowel word finally + 1,600 (= 40 × 40) with final *n* + 720 (= 40 × 18) with final diphthong = 3,920.

iii) With diphthong in the first syllable: 648 (= 18 × 36) with a vowel word finally + 648 (= 18 × 36) with final nasal + 288 (= 18 × 16) with final diphthong = 1,584.

In all, 9,158 (3,654 + 3,920 + 1,584) + 248 = 9,406 disyllables beginning with a consonant.

It has often been claimed that linguistic evolution leads toward monosyllabicity and that an artificial international language should therefore contain no disyllabic words, or at least no disyllabic roots. Phonic considerations make this demand impossible to fulfill. Monosyllabicity would require either a rich inventory of sounds, a great diversity of permissible sound combinations, or distinctive tones. Burmese, which in essence has only monosyllabic roots and permits no consonant groups, distinguishes sixty-one consonants and vowels (including differences of quantity and tone). English, which tends toward monosyllabicity, displays in monosyllabic words various consonant combinations initially and finally and has an inventory of forty-one[2] consonants and vowels (including diphthongs). Such richness of material cannot fall to the lot of an international language. To be truly international, that is, equally pronounceable for all peoples, the language must contain few sounds and allow little freedom in their combination. The smaller the sound inventory and the more limited the possibilities of combination, the smaller the number of possible monosyllabic words will be.

We must resign ourselves to the idea that an international language cannot be monosyllabic; its vocabulary will consist mostly of polysyllables. But this tendency must not be carried too far. A language made up of long words is difficult to learn, especially for speakers whose mother tongue prefers monosyllables. The more easily a long word can be analyzed morphologically, the more easily it can be remembered. So long words should be permitted in the international language only if they can be clearly analyzed into smaller parts. The basic lexical elements, the roots or stems, must be short.

I have already mentioned that more than ten thousand words can be constructed with the phonic inventory and rules proposed here for the international language. Taken as the definitive count of complete words, this number would be very small for a civilized language; but if it represents the number of roots or stems, it is completely adequate, and some of the available possibilities could even remain unused. Stems could be derived from disyllabic roots by means of monosyllabic affixes: the 110 monosyllables are more than sufficient for this purpose. Clear etymological analysis would be ensured if the affixes were always monosyllabic and always attached at the same place, for example, at the end of the root or stem; in a word of more than two syllables, all but the first two would then be affixes. Under this system of word formation, however, monosyllabic roots should not be permitted: otherwise, a stem consisting of a monosyllabic root and an affix could be homonymous with a disyllabic root, which could lead to misunderstandings. Monosyllabic words could be permitted exclusively as nonindependent words with grammatical function.

This rational morphological structure will require clear word boundaries, all the more so as the poverty of the sound system implies considerable phonic monotony. The only suitable means of delimitation is stress on the first syllable of every independent word. Many languages already have such a system (Irish, Icelandic, Finnish, Estonian, Lapp, Latvian, Czech, Slovak, Hungarian, Tamil, Mongolian, and others), so their speakers will have no difficulty with this feature in an artificial language. Nor will it present any problem for speakers of languages with free stress, such as English, Dutch, German, Danish, Norwegian, Swedish, Lithuanian, Russian, Ukrainian, Romanian, Bulgarian, Greek, Albanian, Serbo-Croatian, Italian, Spanish, and others. Difficulties could arise only among speakers of languages in which stress is fixed on the final (French, Armenian, Turkish, Persian) or penultimate (Polish, Swahili, Zulu) syllable or of those with no stress at all (in the sense employed here), such as Japanese and Korean. In most cases, however, these hurdles can be overcome. Speakers used to stressing the final or penultimate syllable of words in their native languages can generally accustom themselves easily to a different fixed place of stress, in this case the initial syllable. Only the French, in whose language stress falls not so much on the final syllable of words as on the final syllable of sense groups, will find it difficult to give up this pattern: for them, the reinforcement of the last syllable of a sense group signals an ensuing pause, and they transfer this signal to every foreign language whenever a pause occurs. Since this habit has no effect on the delimitation of words within the sentence, however, there is no reason why French speakers cannot retain it in the international language, as long as they also stress the first syllable of each word—something they can easily learn with practice. The Japanese and Chinese, in whose speech the nonnative perceives no reinforcement of the individual syllables at all (although close observation does reveal a certain accent, more tonal than expiratorial), should probably be advised to insert short pauses between the words when they speak the international language.

This investigation demonstrates how little the previous experiments in artificial international languages have met the requirements of general phonology. Esperanto, Ido, Occidental, Novial, and so on are relatively easy to learn only for native speakers of Romance and Germanic languages; for many other peoples, their pronunciation is impossible. But it is the non-Romance and non-Germanic peoples who genuinely need an international language. If one takes their needs into account, the logical conclusions are those sketched here. The ideal international language cannot simply use Romance and Germanic vocabulary, for it would differ fundamentally from those languages in both its phonic system (only one kind of stop, no fricative except *s,* only one liquid, no consonant clusters except nasal + consonant, no final consonants except *n*) and its morphological structure (disyllabic roots, monosyllabic affixes and grammatical words).

10. On Morphonology

Besides phonology (the study of the system of phonemes, conceived of as the simplest acoustic-articulatory units differentiating meaning) and morphology (the study of the system of morphemes), grammar must include a chapter on the morphological exploitation of phonological distinctions, which may be called *morphophonology* or, for short, *morphonology*.

Although morphemes do not necessarily display sound alternations, they do so in most branches of Indo-European, including all the Slavic languages. In Slavic, a morpheme varies phonetically according to the morphemes with which it combines to form lexical or syntactic wholes. Thus, in the Russian words *ruka* 'hand' and *ručnoj* 'pertaining to the hand,' the sound strings *ruk* and *ruč* are treated by the linguistic consciousness as two forms of a single morpheme that exists in both, namely, in the form *ruk/č*, where *k/č* represents the idea "the phonemes *k* and *č*, capable of replacing each other according to the morphological structure of the word." Such complexes of *two or more phonemes alternating according to the morphological structure of the word* may be called *morphophonemes* or *morphonemes*. (The term *morphophoneme* and its abbreviation, *morphoneme*, were invented by H. Ułaszyn, although used by him in a different sense.)

It must be emphasized that these are alternating phonemes, not sounds. In the Russian word *ruka* 'hand' (nom.) the sound *k* is velar, in *ruki* (g.) it is palatalized, but the two sounds are merely phonetic realizations of a single phoneme, the choice depending exclusively on the phonetic environment: the phoneme *k* is realized before *a* as a velar voiceless stop, before *i* as a palatalized one, irrespective of morphology. The relation between *k* and *č* in *ruka* : *ručnoi* is different: *k* and *č* are phonemes that can occupy identical positions, with the result that their distinction signals a difference in meaning (*kuma* 'godmother' : *čuma* 'plague,' *kot* 'tomcat' : *čot* 'even number'). Both of them can occur before *a* (*kaša* 'cereal, porridge' : *čaša* 'cup, chalice') or before *n* (*na knut* 'onto the whip' : *načnut* '[they] will begin'). Likewise, the phonemic alternation in *ruka* : *ručnoi* is due not to any phonetic circumstance but to the morphological structure of the word; it is not at all the same as the alternation of the velar stop with the palatalized one in *ruka* : *ruki*.

For different phonetic forms of one phoneme to be perceived as members of an alternation, the morphonemes of the language must be clearly identified. In each Slavic language, there are only a limited number of them. The place that a morphoneme may occupy within a morpheme is just as strictly defined. Thus, for example, in all the modern Slavic languages, the morphonemes *k* : *č* and *x* : *š* are permitted only as the final element of a morpheme. In Russian, in cases of the type *ruka* : *ručnoi* or *uxo* 'ear' : *ušnoi* 'pertaining to the ear,' the alternations *k* : *č* and *x* : *š* do not affect the unity of the morphemes, while, in *kosa* 'scythe' : *česat'* 'comb, scratch; heckle' or *xodit'* 'walk' : *šedšij* 'gone' (past part. imperfective), this unity is disrupted (despite the fact that in analogous cases, such as *voz* 'cartload' : *vezet'* '[he] transports' or *vodit'* 'lead' [v.] : *vedšij* 'led' [past part. imperfect], the alternation *v* : *v'* in no way obscures the identity of the morpheme). The same happens in the other Slavic languages: the alternations *k* : *č* and *x* : *š* are not permitted morpheme initially, and, where they had existed at an earlier stage of the language (as in *kosa* : *česati, xoditi* : *šьdъši*), the link between the phonetic forms has been lost, with the result that the linguistic consciousness perceives two independent morphemes.

Strict rules govern both the place of the morphoneme in the morpheme and the categories of morpheme that may admit a given morphoneme. Some morphonemes occur only in roots or suffixes, not in prefixes, others (e.g., Czech *í/e, ù/o*) only in suffixes, and so on.

Finally, different functions of morphonemes may be identified. Some morphemes preserve a single phonetic form throughout an entire paradigm, displaying phonetic alternation only in roots, while others show alternation in inflected forms as well. Certain morphonemes are permitted only in morphemes of the first of these categories, and so on.

Although the morphonological systems of the various Slavic languages differ, this diversity tends to disappear in linguistic handbooks. In presenting the facts of morphonology, Slavicists generally fall back on historical grammar, erasing the individual features of each contemporary morphonological system. The types of phonetic alternation occurring in a given language are simply listed without any distinction between living and dead types or attention to the conditions governing the occurrence of the alternations. Frequently, morphonological alternations are even confused with externally conditioned alternations in the phonetic realization of a single phoneme (e.g., voicing before voiced consonants and devoicing before voiceless ones). This leads to a falsified picture of morphonology. The very idea of morphonology as a special area of descriptive grammar vanishes, and one is left with a mere enumeration of morphonological facts, the only point of which is that the author can return to them later in the chapter on morphology.

As the intersection of morphology and phonology, morphonology plays an extremely important role in the life of a language. The morphonological system must be borne in mind in diachronic as well as synchronic linguistics, in dialectology as well as single-language study. Morphonology is often a factor either favoring or hindering the spread of phonetic and morphological innovations, many of which are induced by the need for reorganization of a morphonological system. In any case, in the study of historical phonetics and morphology, it is important to establish whether a given change did not cause a shift in the morphonological system. I close with the hope that Slavicists devote serious attention to the precise description of morphonological systems in the sense presented here, taking account of morphonology not only in synchronic but also in diachronic and dialectological research.

11. Thoughts on Morphonology

Morphophonology, or morphonology, the study of the morphological uses of the phonetic material of a language, has been the most neglected branch of grammar in Europe. If we compare the teachings of the ancient Greeks and Romans with those of the Hebrew, Arabic, and especially the ancient Indian grammarians, the lack of interest in morphonological problems in classical and medieval Europe becomes apparent. Even now, the situation is basically the same. Contemporary Semitic philology has taken over the morphonological ideas of the Arabic and Hebrew grammarians without adapting them to the demands of modern scholarship. Indo-Europeanists used Indian morphonological teachings as the basis for a morphonology of the Indo-European protolanguage, which, in an expanded form, became the so-called system of Indo-European ablaut, roots, and suffixes. But the true morphonological perspective is absent from these products of modern Indo-European linguistics: the roots ("bases") and suffixes take on the character of metaphysical entities, and ablaut becomes a kind of magic.

One searches in vain for any connection with a living language. Roots, ablaut systems, and the like appear to have been possible and necessary only in a hypothetical protolanguage; in the historically attested languages, all that supposedly remains is their vestiges, and these are so overlaid with younger developments that one can hardly speak of a system. This view was natural for Schleicher, with his fundamental distinction between prehistoric growth and historical decay, but it is still held unconsciously by most Indo-Europeanists today, even though its theoretical underpinnings have been universally discarded. Ablaut and other types of sound alternation in modern Indo-European languages are presented from the historical point of view and traced back to their sources, regardless of the role they now play. Since this procedure mixes productive and nonproductive morphonological facts indiscriminately in disregard of their function, the systemic aspect of the data necessarily remains hidden. Indo-Europeanists have never been willing to acknowledge that morphonology constitutes a special branch of grammar not only for the protolanguage but also for each individual language. It was considered to be the product of compromise or the interplay of historical phonetics and morphology, with the result that some of the relevant phenomena were treated under sounds, some under forms.

This state of affairs can no longer be tolerated. As the link between phonology and morphology, morphonology must assume the place of honor that it deserves, and not only in grammars of Semitic and Indo-European languages. Only languages without morphology proper can do without morphonology; certain topics normally belonging to morphonology (e.g., the phonological structure of morphemes) would then be relegated to phonology.

A full morphonology consists of three parts: the study of the phonological structure of morphemes, the study of combinatory sound changes undergone by morphemes in contact, and the study of sound alternation series serving a morphological function.

Only the first of these applies to every language. Different morpheme types possess characteristic sound features, which differ from language to language. Root morphemes display particular diversity. In the Semitic languages, as is well known, nominal and verbal root morphemes generally consist of three consonants, while this restriction does not hold for pronominal roots. Structural differentiation of this kind may be established for non-Semitic languages, too: in certain East Caucasian languages, for example, verbal and pronominal root morphemes always consist of one consonant, a rule not followed by nominal morphemes. Even Indo-European languages display similar patterns. In Slavic, root morphemes consisting of a single consonant occur only as pronominal roots; root morphemes consisting of a single vowel without consonants never occur (except for relics such as *u* in Polish *obuć* 'shoe' [v.]); nominal and pronominal root morphemes in Russian must end with a consonant; and so on. Other morpheme types as well (ending, prefix, suffix, etc.) have in each language a limited number of possible sound structures, which it is the task of morphonology to identify.[1]

The study of combinatory sound changes in morphemes in contact, which corresponds to the internal sandhi of Sanskrit grammar, does not have equal significance for all languages. In certain agglutinating languages, it makes up all of morphology (together with the study of the sound structure of morphemes); in others, it plays no role at all.

The same may be said, mutatis mutandis, for the third division of morphonology, sound alternation series fulfilling a morphological function. Particular attention must also be paid here to the strict distinction between productive and nonproductive phenomena and to the specialized functions of the alternation series. Morphonological research has shown that in Russian, for example, the alternation series in nominal forms are not identical with those in verbal forms and that those employed in paradigm inflection differ greatly from those employed in derivational word formation. Many other languages can be expected to present a similar picture.

Sound alternation in morphemes is not unique to the so-called inflecting languages (e.g., Indo-European, Semitic, East Caucasian); one need only point to the morphologically functioning quantitative and qualitative vowel ablaut of Ugric and the consonant alternations of Finnic. On the other hand, there are indeed languages in which the sound structure of morphemes is immutable; this third division of morphonology is not applicable to them.

To sum up, morphonology is an area of grammar that plays an important role in almost all languages but has been investigated in almost none. Morphonological study will deepen our knowledge of languages significantly, especially with regard to linguistic typology. The old classification into isolating, incorporating, agglutinating, and inflecting languages is unsatisfactory in many respects. By virtue of its central position in the system of grammar (as the link between phonology and morphology), morphonology is the ideal tool with which to prepare a comprehensive description of the characteristic features of each language, and a roster of language types according to morphonological criteria could perhaps serve as the basis for a rational typology of the languages of the world.

12. The Relation between the Modifier, the Modified, and the Definite

In a collection of articles dedicated to one of the most eminent representatives of the Geneva school, it is unnecessary to point out that comparative linguistic study independent of the genealogical principle is both possible and legitimate. Whereas the comparative grammar of a group of languages sharing a genetic bond aims to discover the origin of some phenomenon observed in each of them and thus takes a *diachronic* approach, the comparative study of languages lacking such a bond proposes to illuminate the *synchronic* relations in one language by contrasting them with the corresponding relations in another in a different context.

The relation between the element modified and its modifier is one of the most common of all syntagmatic relations, but others also exist. For example, I very much doubt whether the subject and the predicate can be considered as modified and modifier. There are many languages with a special means of marking the relation of modified to modifier, and in most of them this marker is not applied to the subject-predicate relation. In the Turkic and Mongol families, and in many Finno-Ugric languages, the modifier *precedes* the element modified: the adjective, demonstrative pronoun, or numeral precedes the noun; a noun in the genitive case precedes the noun it modifies; the adverb precedes the adjective or verb it modifies; and the direct or indirect complement precedes the verb. But the predicate (verbal or nominal) *follows* its subject; it is evidently not considered the subject's modifier. In Gilyak (a Paleo-Siberian language spoken in the north of Sakhalin Island and at the mouth of the Amur), two adjacent words linked as modifier and modified undergo certain phonetic changes: among other things, the initial consonant of the second term becomes a fricative. These changes occur in the groups adjective + noun, genitive + corresponding noun, complement + verb, etc. But they do not occur in the group subject + predicate (see Kreinović 1934). In Ibo (a Sudanic language spoken in Nigeria), in which three tones are distinguished, the tones of both terms of a group modifier + modified or modified + modifier undergo certain changes: the final syllable of the first term and the initial syllable of the second acquire a high tone if they have a middle or low tone in other positions (details are given in Ward 1936; see also my review, Trubetzkoy 1936d). These changes are observed in the groups adjective + noun, noun (in the genitive) + noun, noun + numeral or demonstrative/relative pronoun, and main clause noun + subordinate clause verb linked with this noun. But the change in tone never occurs in the group subject + predicate.

These examples could be multiplied; they prove that, in languages of the most diverse structure, the relation between subject and predicate is not conceived of as a relation between modified and modifier. Counterexamples are rare and inconclusive. We are justified, therefore, in distinguishing *modifying* phrases (composed of modifier and modified) and *predicative* phrases (composed of subject and predicate).

A third class is represented by *associative* phrases, in which both terms stand in syntagmatic relation to some other member of the utterance: two subjects with the same predicate, two predicates with the same subject, two modifiers modifying the same element, and so on.[1]

Modifying phrases fall into types and subtypes, the number of which partly depends on the grammatical structure of the language in question. Some occur in many languages and have received conventional names: the modifier in a phrase composed of two nouns is usually called *genitive;* where one of the terms is a noun (or pronoun) and the other a verbal form, the latter is designated *participle* if it is the modifier, while if the noun (or pronoun) is the modifier, it is called *complement* and further classified as direct or indirect. This terminology has a certain justification and is practical enough. But it often gives a false idea of the relations between the various grammatical categories of the language.

Every transitive verb in a predicate presupposes at least two nouns (or pronouns), of which the one designates the doer, the other the object to which the action is directed. Of the two phrases formed by the transitive verb and each of the nouns (pronouns), one is predicative, the other modifying. Hence, there are two types of languages: those in which the modifier of the transitive verb names the doer and those in which it names the object. In languages of the first type, the nominative (subject case) is opposed to the *ergative;* in those of the second type, the nominative is opposed to the *accusative.* The first type is represented by Eskimo, Tibetan, the North Caucasian languages, and others, the second by the Sudanic, Semitic, Indo-European, Finno-Ugric, Turkic, Mongol, and other languages. From the point of view of the individual languages, the terminological pairs nominative/ergative and nominative/accusative are convenient, but from the point of view of general grammar, both types of languages display an opposition between the subject case and the "case directly modifying a verb." Although the ergative is indeed the opposite of the accusative, in the syntagmatic systems of their respective languages these two cases play the same role of directly modifying a transitive verb; all other modifying cases of such a verb presuppose the existence of a direct modifier (see Jakobson 1936, 254).

If the accusative or the ergative (according to language type) is the case directly modifying a verb (thus adverbal), the *genitive* can be designated as the adnominal modifying case. This explains the partial or total coincidence of the accusative or ergative (according to language type) with the genitive in many languages. In Classical Arabic, the genitive coincides with the accusative in the dual and (regular) plural of all nouns and in the singular of proper names. In the Slavic languages—with the exception of Bulgarian, which has lost declension—nouns designating masculine living things (as well as pronouns and adjectives referring to such nouns) use the genitive with accusative meaning in the singular. In certain Turkic languages, such as Balkar or Karachay (in the northern Caucasus), the genitive always coincides with the accusative. On the other hand, in certain East Caucasian languages, including Lak (in central Daghestan) and most dialects of Kuri, or Lezghian (in southeastern Daghestan), the form of the genitive coincides with that of the ergative. Clearly, for languages like Balkar and Lak, it is wrong to speak of a genitive case and an accusative or ergative case: they possess a single direct modifying case opposed to various indirect modifying cases and to a nonmodifying (nominative) case. Likewise, the Classical Arabic dual and plural display an opposition not between nominative and genitive-accusative but between a nonmodifying and a modifying case. These examples are enough to bring out the multitude of nuances that the notion of the direct modifier acquires in the grammatical context of different languages. And this is only the simplest type of modifying phrase.

The concept of the definite article has a long tradition in European scholarship. But informed linguists know that the nuance of meaning expressed in Greek, French, German, or English by the addition of the definite article is expressed in other languages in different ways. Any noun that acquires this meaning—whether through the addition of an article or through other morphological devices—can be said to have a definite form.

Definiteness can be expressed in three ways: (1) by a (modifying) phrase composed of a noun and the definite article, a separate word; (2) by a special form of the noun, that is, a combination of its stem and a special affix; (3) by a form of another word (noun, adjective, verb) that refers to the noun, constituting a phrase (modifying or predicative) with it.

It is sometimes difficult to distinguish between procedures 1 and 2. By definition, a sequence of two words will allow another word to stand between its members, whereas an affix cannot be separated from the stem except by other affixes with grammatical meaning. In the modern European languages in which the definite article exists as a separate word (Greek, Italian, French, Spanish, Portuguese, English, German, and Hungarian), it is always preposed. Contrariwise, in the European languages in which definiteness is expressed by affixes (Norwegian, Swedish, Danish, Albanian, Romanian, Bulgarian, and certain Russian dialects), these are postposed. In studying non-Indo-European languages, European linguists have the tendency to interpret all external markers of definiteness as articles if they are preposed and as affixes if they are postposed. This is a mistake that should be guarded against. The "definite article" in Arabic is really a prefix since it always stands directly before the noun and cannot be separated from it by another word, while the so-called definite suffix *r* in Circassian and Kabardian is an article since it can be separated from the noun by adjectives and numerals (e.g., Circ. *unedexešir* 'the [*r*] three [*ši*] beautiful [*dexe*] houses [*une*]').

Procedure 3 is often combined with one of the other two. In Bulgarian, definiteness is expressed by an affix added to the noun if the latter is not modified by an adjective (*čovekăt* 'the man'), otherwise to the modifying adjective (*dobriăt čovek* 'the good man'). In Mordvin, definiteness is indicated by an affix to the noun, but, in addition, transitive verbs have different endings according to whether their direct complement is definite or indefinite: *raman kudo* 'I will buy a house' ~ *ramasa kudont'* 'I will buy the house'; *ramat kudo* 'you will buy a house' ~ *ramasak kudont'* 'you will buy the house.' Compare the "strong" and "weak" forms of the adjective in German and other languages.

As with all grammatical categories, definiteness makes sense only insofar as it is opposed to the contrary notion. In all the languages that possess it, the opposition definite-indefinite is *neutralized,* or *suppressed,* under certain conditions, which differ from one language to the next. In most cases, the neutralization seems to be linked with the system of predicative versus modifying phrases.

Predicative phrases display very simple relations, and the opposition definite-indefinite tends to retain its full force in all their members. But in a number of languages this opposition is suppressed for nouns in predicative function. The converse situation, that is, the suppression of this opposition in subject nouns (and its preservation in predicate nouns), does not seem to occur in any language.

Relations in modifying phrases are more complicated and vary from one language to another. Very often, the opposition definite-indefinite is suppressed in the modified element, for example, when the modifier is a demonstrative or a possessive. Nouns modified by demonstratives stand outside the opposition definite-indefinite in almost all languages.[2] In many other languages, the same is true for nouns modified by possessive pronouns (e.g., in French), by all possessives (e.g., in Old Church Slavonic, Circassian, Abkhaz), and by certain types of possessives (e.g., in English, German, and Danish by possessive pronouns and genitives in -*s* preceding their referents). But in many languages the opposition definite-indefinite exists even in nouns modified by possessive pronouns (e.g., in Greek, Italian, and Arabic).

When the modifier is a qualitative adjective, the modified element preserves the opposition definite-indefinite in all languages known to me. What is more, in certain languages, nouns modified by a qualitative adjective are the only ones to display this opposition. Such is the case in Serbo-Croatian and Old Church Slavonic, where the opposition definite-indefinite is expressed by special forms of the adjective (procedure 3). In French, the same restriction exists with respect to proper names, which do not permit the article except when they are modified by an adjective: *il y avait parmi vos élèves* un petit Jean, *qui ne voulait pas apprendre; et bien,* le petit Jean *paresseux—c'est moi!* 'Among your pupils there was a little John who never wanted to study; well, the little lazy John is me!'

In Kabardian, there are in effect only two cases, the modifying case (genitive, dative, locative, ergative) and the nonmodifying case (for the subject of intransitive verbs, the direct complement of transitive verbs, and the predicate of nominal sentences); the other "cases" are merely combinations with postpositions. In this language, the opposition definite-indefinite exists only in the nonmodifying case and is suppressed in the modifying case.[3]

Finally, in some languages, the situation is just the reverse of that in Kabardian: they display the opposition definite-indefinite only in modifiers. In the Turkic languages, the direct complement of a transitive verb (i.e., the nominal modifier of this verb) can be expressed in two ways, according to whether it is indefinite or definite: in the first instance, it has no case marker; in the second, it receives the accusative ending. For most modern Turkic languages, this is the only syntactic construction in which the notions of definiteness and indefiniteness are distinguished formally. In Modern Russian, and perhaps in certain other Slavic languages, a possessive adjective derived from a personal noun indicates an affiliation to a specific person, while the construction with the genitive of the personal noun does not have this restriction: *mel'nikova doč'* always means 'daughter of *the* miller,' while *doč' mel'nika* can mean either 'daughter of *the* miller' or 'daughter of *a* miller.' This is the only instance where Russian (at least standard Russian) presents a hint of the opposition definite-indefinite, and, curiously enough, it appears in connection with the modifier in a modifying phrase.

The opposition between the definite and the indefinite can thus be suppressed in the modified element (e.g., in French after possessives and demonstratives) or in the modifier (e.g., in Kabardian), but it can also be restricted to the modified element (e.g., in Old Church Slavonic) or to the modifier (e.g., in Turkish). It would be useful to study these possibilities in the context of the grammatical systems of various languages.

13. The Problem of Genetic Relations among the Great Language Families

To prove that two languages or language families are related, one must be able to point to a considerable number of words with regular sound correspondences. Linguists who refuse to observe this principle are unable to prove or disprove a relation in any concrete case, let alone the degree of such a relation. For such linguists, languages are either all related or all unrelated, which amounts to the same thing, whereas, when the methods of comparative linguistics are applied to the problem of the relation between clearly defined language families, the differences often appear to be irreconcilable. One can compare only commensurable quantities; certain structural differences between language families make their linguistic elements incommensurable. The stable, invariant vowel of an Altaic root is fundamentally different from the vowel of an Indo-European root, which is subject to ablaut, or from a Semitic vowel, which can change not only its quality and quantity but also its position within the root. In Semitic and Indo-European, all consonants are on an equal footing and possess the same phonological features, regardless of their position in the root. In languages with "Turanic" structure (i.e., Uralic and Altaic), initial consonants possess fewer phonological features than their root-internal and root-final counterparts, while in the vocalism of these languages it is the other way round: vowel phonemes of the first syllable of a word normally display a richer phonological content than those of other syllables. For a Semitic root, the vowels are unimportant; for roots in the East Caucasian (Chechen-Daghestanian) languages, not only the vowels but also the sonorants are unimportant. Semitic verbal roots almost always consist of three consonants; East Caucasian verbal roots usually consist of a single obstruent.

It is very likely that in many cases the triconsonantal Semitic root developed through the accretion of formants and that the East Caucasian monoconsonantal root owes its shape to the loss of the initial or final consonants of an originally polyconsonantal root. Likewise, it is possible that the invariant root vowel of the Altaic languages is the product of the freezing or generalization of one grade of ablaut or that Indo-European ablaut was caused by the operation of originally mechanical sound laws. None of these possibilities can be excluded. But in no concrete case can it be established with certainty what changes a given structural element (phoneme, root, etc.) underwent before reaching the form reconstructed for it through the application of the comparative method within one language family. And since elements from different language families must be "processed" before they can be compared at all, this kind of language comparison always implies a suspicious amount of arbitrariness and speculation, all the more so as the number of reliable word correspondences in such cases is seldom large.

Therefore, I doubt whether it will ever be possible to demonstrate that Indo-European is related to the Semitic, Uralic, or North Caucasian languages. I take the word *related* here exclusively in its *genealogical* sense. A *typological* relation is something else: everyone will agree that it can exist between languages that have nothing to do with each another genealogically. The typological comparison of languages is a very important and potentially very fruitful area of linguistics, although it requires special research methods that have been only incompletely developed as yet.

Contribution to Discussion

The fact that two languages have individual features in common (shared roots, affixes, or syntactic phenomena) can carry weight only if the type of linguistic structure is also similar. Vice versa, a typological similarity between two languages cannot prove anything about their genetic relation if a sufficient number of shared "material" correspondences are not present. The comparative typological and material study of the largest, best-known language families of the Old World is very fruitful and must be continued (especially typological study, which has been sorely neglected), but we must not delude ourselves into thinking that we will ever be able to prove an original relation between these families with the same degree of certainty with which we speak of, say, the relation between Greek and Sanskrit.

14. Thoughts on the Indo-European Problem

The Indo-Europeans are those people whose language belongs to the Indo-European language family. From this definition, the only scientifically possible one, it follows that *Indo-European* is a purely linguistic concept, like *syntax, genitive, sound change* [or *stress*]. There are Indo-European languages, and there are peoples who speak them. The only thing that these peoples have in common is that their languages belong to the same language family.

Today there are many Indo-European languages and many Indo-European peoples. When we look back, we find that it was the same in the past, too —as far as the eye can see. In addition to the ancestors of the living Indo-European languages, there also existed other Indo-European languages that disappeared without leaving descendants. It is usually supposed that, at one time, there was a single Indo-European language, the so-called Indo-European protolanguage, from which all historically attested Indo-European languages are presumed to descend. This supposition is contradicted by the fact that, no matter how far we peer back into history, we always find a multitude of Indo-European-speaking peoples. The idea of an Indo-European protolanguage is not absurd, but it is not necessary, and we can do very well without it.

The definition of a language family does not require the descent of the members from a single source. A language family is a group of languages that display, in addition to similarity of structure, a series of material points of agreement, that is, regular sound correspondences in a considerable number of lexical and morphological elements. To explain the regularity of the sound correspondences, however, we do not need the hypothesis of common descent, for such regularity arises also in loan traffic between neighboring, unrelated languages (the so-called laws of sound substitution). [For example, in the oldest West Finnic borrowings from (East) Slavic, the Slavic intervocalic voiced plosives *b, d, g* regularly correspond to Finnish short voiceless *p, t, k;* the Slavic voiceless posives *p, t, k* to the Finnish geminates *pp, tt, kk;* Slavic ь to Finnish *i,* and Slavic ъ to Finnish *u* (or *i* when Slavic ъ occurred after voiceless consonants in word-final position).] Nor is agreement in basic elements of vocabulary and morphology proof of common descent, since all elements of human language can be borrowed and since, especially at lower stages of development, the most basic words and morphemes wander from language to language.

Kretschmer (1896) has rightly emphasized that the only difference between borrowing and genetic relation is one of chronology. We recognize as borrowings those words that entered Germanic from Celtic or Italic and entered Slavic from Germanic only after the Germanic sound shift [because they do not conform to certain sound laws. Thus, Slavic *tynъ* 'hedge, fence' is a borrowing from Germanic (*)*tûnas* (Ger. *Zaun* 'fence,' Engl. *town*), for in "genuine" cognates Germanic *t* (Ger. *z*, Engl. *t*) must correspond to Slavic *d* (cf. Ger. *zwei*, Engl. *two*, Slav. *dъvě*, *dъva;* Ger. *zu*, Engl. *to*, Slav. *do;* Ger. *zwingen* 'compel,' Slav. *dvigati* 'move'; Ger. *sitzen*, Engl. *sit*, Slav. *sedeti;* Ger. *Zahl* 'number,' Slav. *dolja* 'part, portion, measure'; Engl. *tear* [v.], Ger. *zerren*, Slav. *dьrati;* Ger. [dial.] *zergen* 'mock, irritate,' Russ. *dergat'* 'pull, tug'; and so forth). We classify *tynъ* as a borrowing only because it was taken over by Slavic after the change *d* > *t* in Germanic: if the borrowing had occurred before this change, the Slavic form would have been **dynъ* rather than *tynъ*, and we would have viewed **dynъ* as a "genuine" cognate of German *Zaun* and English *town*. The Germanic word that was the source of Slavic *tynъ* could itself have been borrowed from Celtic (cf. Gaulish -*dunum* in the names of fortified towns: *Neviodunum*, *Mellodunum*, *Eburodunum*, *Uxellodunum*, etc.). But since it reached Germanic before the shift of *d* to *t*, it does not betray its Celtic origin and should be considered as a "genuine" cognate of Celtic *dûnum*.] Words that had taken the same path before the sound shift, on the other hand, are regarded as belonging to the common stock. Strictly speaking, we ascribe to the protolanguage all elements that occur in several branches of Indo-European and for which the direction of borrowing can no longer be determined. [The same happens in other language families.]

There is, therefore, no compelling reason for the assumption of a homogeneous Indo-European protolanguage from which the individual branches of Indo-European descended. It is equally plausible that the ancestors of the branches of Indo-European were originally dissimilar but that over time, through continuous contact, mutual influence, and loan traffic, they moved significantly closer to each other, without becoming identical.

[In language history, both divergences and convergences occur. Sometimes these two lines of development are hard to distinguish. The Romance languages go back to Vulgar Latin, but before Vulgar Latin was assimilated by the Iberians, Gauls, Ligurians, Etruscans, Venetians, Dacians, and so on, there must have been a period in which their languages adjusted to Latin; they absorbed Latin words and modified their morphology and syntax under Latin influence. At the same time, Latin was also undergoing great upheavals, for it had to adjust to the "barbarian tongues." So when the barbarian tongues disappeared from the Roman Empire and gave way to Latin, this newly acquired Latin had its own peculiarities in every province, and linguistic unity was not achieved. Each provincial variety of Latin began to develop independently of its neighbors. This resulted in the creation of the modern Romance languages, which are so dissimilar at present that sometimes different dialects of the same language, let alone those of different languages, have become mutually unintelligible. On the other hand, the Romance languages, especially their standard varieties, have tended to come closer to one another in matters of detail. This is an example of the interplay of convergence and divergence.

Romance shows how a group of languages can develop from a protolanguage. This example has its drawbacks, for the protolanguage in question was a standard with a written tradition. But alongside the Romance group, there are "semi-Romance" languages: those that gradually substituted elements of Vulgar Latin for their original features but stopped halfway. Such is Albanian, for instance. A good deal of its vocabulary is of Romance origin, and its morphology bears a strong imprint of Romance, but it has not come all the way and retains many elements that cannot be explained from Latin. Since Latin is well known from its textual tradition, and since living Romance languages also exist, linguists are usually able (although not without considerable effort) to unravel the tangle of Romance and non-Romance elements in Albanian. But if scholars had only several semi-Romance languages like Albanian at their disposal and applied to them the comparative method as it is practiced in Indo-European studies, they would be obliged to reconstruct a protolanguage for the semi-Romance group as well. In doing so, they would either have to leave the non-Romance elements unexplained or have to explain them by means of some clever artificial provisions in the reconstruction of the "protolanguage." The picture would become even more complicated if history had preserved the descendants of several groups that had begun converging but then stopped. All of them would share some elements, and comparativists would have to reconstruct another "protolanguage" from the common features of their morphology and vocabulary and from regular sound correspondences. This protolanguage would not be particularly difficult to reconstruct, even though it quite obviously never existed.

Thus, a language family can be the product of divergence, convergence, or a combination of the two (with the emphasis on either). There are virtually no criteria that would indicate unambiguously to which of the two modes of development a family owes its existence. When we are dealing with languages so closely related that almost all the elements of the vocabulary and morphology of each are present in all or most of the other members (allowing for sound correspondences), it is more natural to assume convergence than divergence.

Perhaps some indications can be obtained from the inner segmentation of a language family. Some families are characterized by a *net-like*, or *chain-like*, type of segmentation. Such are, for example, the Slavic languages. Here each language is a kind of link between two others, and neighboring languages are connected by means of transitional dialects, with individual threads extending across borders from group to group. Thus, the South Slavic group displays an unbroken chain from Slovenian (via the Kaikavian area) to Serbo-Croatian and from it (via a series of transitional dialects) to Bulgarian; moreover, of all the South Slavic languages, Slovenian (especially its Carinthian dialects) stands closest to the West Slavic group, while Bulgarian (especially its eastern dialect) stands closest to East Slavic. However, if we compare Slavic to the rest of Indo-European, we will see none of this chain-like segmentation. To be sure, the closest group to Slavic is Baltic (Lithuanian, Latvian, and the extinct Old Prussian), but it cannot be ascertained which Baltic language is closest to Slavic and which Slavic language is closest to Baltic. Instead of a "chain," we find "blocks." Different types of segmentation observed in the groups of "related" languages can well go back to the different ways these groups emerged: possibly, the "chain" develops when divergence predominates, while "blocks" are mainly the product of convergence.

Be that as it may, the Indo-European family does not consist of very closely connected branches. Each branch possesses numerous elements of vocabulary and morphology not matched in the others. In this respect, Indo-European differs greatly from such families as Turkic, Semitic, and Bantu. Therefore, it is equally probable that the Indo-European family arose when some originally nonrelated languages (the ancestors of the later branches) converged and that the Indo-European languages developed from a protolanguage by divergence.]

This possibility must always be kept in sight when the Indo-European problem is addressed[, and every statement about the problem should be formulated so as to be valid for either assumption: divergence or convergence]. Since only the hypothesis of a single protolanguage has been considered until now, the discussion has landed on the wrong track. Its primary, that is, linguistic, nature has been forgotten. Prehistoric archaeology, anthropology, and ethnology have been brought in without any justification. Attempts are made to describe the home, race, and culture of a supposed Indo-European protopeople that may never have existed. The Indo-European problem is formulated [by modern German (and not only German) scholars] in something like the following way: "Which type of prehistoric pottery must be ascribed to the Indo-European people?" But scholarship is unable to answer questions of this kind, so they are moot. Their logic is circular because the assumption of an Indo-European protopeople with definite cultural and racial characteristics is untenable. We are chasing a romantic illusion instead of keeping to the one positive fact at our disposal—that "Indo-Europeans" are a purely *linguistic* concept.

The only scientifically admissible question is, How and where did the Indo-European linguistic structure arise? And this question should and can be answered only by purely linguistic methods. The answer depends on what we mean by *the Indo-European linguistic structure.* How do we recognize an Indo-European language? Certainly, we need a number of "material points of agreement," that is, lexical elements, suffixes, and endings that the language in question has in common (according to regular sound correspondences) with other Indo-European languages. But it is impossible to say how high the number of these elements must be to guarantee the Indo-European character of the language. Nor can it be determined *which* lexical or morphological elements must be represented in each Indo-European language. Hardly any single word occurs in all Indo-European languages, and the most widely distributed words present such phonological irregularities that their protoform can be reconstructed only by doing violence to the facts. [Conversely, words that are quite regular from the phonetic point of view usually occur only in a limited number of Indo-European languages.] Morphological elements, too, seldom agree exactly. The usual sound correspondences often fail one here, and special, sometimes very artificial, ad hoc *Auslautgesetze* must therefore be constructed [for individual words]. Then there is the circumstance that a number of the most widely distributed Indo-European lexical and morphological elements are not restricted to the Indo-European languages [(e.g., the negative elements containing *n* and *m,* the pronominal roots *m* 'my, me,' *t* or *s* 'your, you' [both sg.], and *kwo* 'who')]. In the light of all this, one will not attach too much importance to the material points of agreement in determining whether a language is Indo-European. Such correspondences must be present, and their complete absence may be considered as proof of a language's non-Indo-European character. But their number is irrelevant, and none of them is indispensable to the proof that a given language belongs to the Indo-European family.

In addition to material points of agreement, the following six structural features belong to such a proof.

In the area of phonology we find only two points, more of a negative character:

1. *There is no vowel harmony.* That is, the vocalism of noninitial syllables is not conditioned by the vocalism of the first syllable[, in contrast to the Altaic and many Finno-Ugric languages]. Where the term *vowel harmony* is used in the description of certain Indo-European languages and dialects, [for example, in Sublekhitic, some West Ukrainian dialects, and the Rezija dialect of Slovenian,] this is incorrect, for in such cases we are dealing not with vowel harmony but rather with the influence of the degree of openness of a stressed vowel on the degree of openness of a nonstressed vowel or vowels [(e.g., in the Rezija dialect of Slovenian, *koleno* 'knee' remains intact, but *korito* 'trough'

becomes *kuritu;* in Sublekhitic Ukrainian, the ablative *s soboju* 'with oneself' is unaffected, but the dative *sobi* becomes *subi*, etc.). The results of this process are quite unlike the phenomenon called *vowel harmony* in the Altaic and Finno-Ugric languages.]

2. *The consonantism of the beginning of the word is no poorer than that of the middle and end.* Comparison with Uralo-Altaic and Dravidian languages proves that this is an important feature. I disregard here, of course, the geminated consonants, which by their nature cannot occur word initially. [When in an Indo-European language there is a difference between the consonants permitted in initial and in medial position, the first set is always richer than the second. For instance, in some Scots Gaelic dialects, aspirated and nonaspirated consonants are opposed; in some modern Indian languages, the opposition is threefold: aspirated, nonaspirated, and occlusive; but medially all such distinctions are absent (cf. the eastern dialects of Bengali). Nothing like this would be possible in a Finno-Ugric or Altaic language (but a similar picture can be observed in some North Caucasian languages: e.g., Chechen, in which pure voiceless and occlusive consonants are distinguished only word initially).]

The following points belong to the area of morphonology:

3. *The word does not necessarily begin with the root.* There is no Indo-European language without prefixes. Even in the oldest Indo-European languages we find genuine prefixes, that is, morphemes that are not used as independent words (e.g., *n̥-* 'without,' *su-* 'good,' *dus-* 'bad,' the augment *e-*). In the younger Indo-European languages, the number of such prefixes increases greatly.

4. *Words are formed not only by means of affixes but also by means of vowel alternation within the root morphemes.* In all Indo-European languages, the old ablaut[, about whose origin one can only speculate,] is joined by a new one that has arisen through the operation of special sound laws but that, from a synchronic standpoint, is completely free. There is no Indo-European language without traces of (old or new) vowel ablaut. [Although the later vocalic alternations can be traced to various individual sound laws, these laws have lost their force, and from the point of view of present-day languages the later alternations are no longer regulated by mechanical factors: they are as "free" and "grammatical" as old ablaut. Modern Russian makes no distinction between the alternation *e ~ o* in *melet* '(he) grinds' ~ *molotyj* 'ground' (past part. of *molot'* 'grind'), *pet'* 'to sing' ~ *poj* 'sing!' and *teč* 'to flow' ~ *tok* 'current,' yet in the first case the alternation is specifically Russian, in the second it goes back to a Common Slavic change, and in the third it goes back to Pre-Slavic ("Indo-European") ablaut. In all the Indo-European languages, old and new vocalic alternations overlap and form an intricate web. For instance, in standard German, the root meaning 'break' appears with eight vowels; that is, all the German monophthongs are allowed to alternate in it: *Bruch* 'break' (n.),

gebrochen 'broken,' *brach* '(I) broke,' *bräche* '(I) would break,' *brechen* 'to break,' *brich* 'break!' *brüchig* 'brittle,' and *ab-bröckeln* 'crumble.']

5. *Not only vocalic but also free consonantal alternations play a morphological role.* There is no Indo-European language without grammatical consonant alternation. To be sure, this alternation is always the result of some combinatory sound changes whose formula usually can still be reconstructed. From a synchronic standpoint, however, the consonant alternation in each Indo-European language is free. That this is an important feature of the language structure is proved by comparison with other language types, such as Semitic, in which consonant alternations are impossible [(they are also alien to the North Caucasian languages, except for Archi, Kuri, and now Lezghian)], or Altaic, which has only conditioned consonant alternations.

In the area of morphology, only one feature can be named:

6. *The subject of a transitive verb receives the same treatment as the subject of an intransitive verb.* That is, in Indo-European languages in which the case opposition nominative-accusative is expressed through endings, the verbal subject is in the nominative, regardless of whether the verb is transitive or intransitive (e.g., Lat. *pater venit* 'the father comes,' *pater filium amat* 'the father loves [his] son'); and in those languages in which syntactic relations are expressed through word order, the subject occupies the same sentence position regardless of whether the verb is transitive or intransitive (e.g., Fr. *le père vient, le père aime le fils*).

Each of these structural features turns up in non-Indo-European languages as well, but all six together occur only in Indo-European. A language that does not possess all the structural features mentioned above cannot be considered Indo-European, even if it displays numerous correspondences with Indo-European languages in its vocabulary. Conversely, a language that has borrowed the greater part of its vocabulary and morphological elements from non-Indo-European languages is Indo-European if it possesses the six specific structural features mentioned, even if it displays only a very small number of lexical and morphological correspondences with other Indo-European languages.

Languages can thus cease to be Indo-European, and they can become Indo-European. "Indo-European" was born when all six specific structural features mentioned above first came together in a language whose vocabulary and morphology displayed a series of regular correspondences with the later-attested Indo-European languages. It is not impossible that several languages became Indo-European in this sense at roughly the same time. [If this is true, then originally several Indo-European languages existed in a so-called language union, which later developed into a language family.] We can consider them today in retrospect only as dialects of the Indo-European protolanguage, but it is not logically necessary to trace them all back to one common source. Only geographic contact among these oldest Indo-European dialects may be assumed with a high degree of certainty.

The following considerations are decisive for determining the geographic area in which these dialects received their Indo-European character. The wave theory advanced by Johannes Schmidt holds not only for dialects of a language but also for unrelated but geographically neighboring languages. [Even when they are not related, such neighboring languages "infect one another," as it were, and acquire common phonetic and grammatical features.] Every language has structural features in common with its neighbors, and those common features are the more numerous the longer the geographic contact has lasted. The same is true of language families.

If one looks at the geographic distribution of the language families of the Old World from the point of view of their structural type, one sees that they form an unbroken chain. The Finno-Ugric and Paleo-Siberian languages agree in certain points with the Altaic. The Altaic languages agree, on the one hand, with Korean and, through its mediation, with Japanese, which for its part forms a bridge to the Oceanic languages; on the other hand, Altaic agrees in significant respects with Tibeto-Burmese. [The Altaic languages share some common features with the Paleo-Siberian (Paleoasiatic) languages (Yukaghir, Gilyak, and the Kamchatka group, consisting of Kamchadal, Koryak, and Chukchi), and these languages (especially the latter three) are similar in structure to the Eskimo languages, so a connecting link is formed to other languages of North America.] In Africa, a chain of this type leads from Semitic, Hamitic, Berber, and Cushitic via Negroid languages of the type of Fulani and Wolof to the Sudanic languages, which through the mediation of the Bantuoid languages are linked with genuine Bantu. [The Bantu languages are connected with the Nilo-Saharan (Sudanic) languages via the Bantuoid group. The Sudanic languages are not totally unlike certain isolated West African languages (Wolof and Fulani), which, in turn, bear some resemblance to Berber. The Nilotic group seems to share some features with Cushitic. Finally, Berber, Cushitic, Coptic, and the Semitic languages are close enough to justify the common name *Hamito-Semitic*.] If we consider these facts and the circumstance that each of the six structural features of Indo-European mentioned above also occurs individually in non-Indo-European languages, we may place the genesis of the Indo-European linguistic structure in an area that borders on language families with some of the same features.

Two large groups of language families meet this condition. Uralo-Altaic [, that is, Finno-Ugric, Samoyedic, Turkic, Mongolian, and Tungusic,] has the accusative construction in common with Indo-European (point 6), and its most westerly branch, Finno-Ugric, displays a free consonant alternation (point 5) as well. The Mediterranean group, which is represented today by Caucasian and Semitic languages [(North Caucasian, South Caucasian, Semitic, Basque, and perhaps Berber) and in the past by extinct languages of Asia Minor], touches Indo-European at points 1, 2, 3, and 4. [It differs from it, however, in that it lacks consonant alternations and has the ergative construction; the latter feature is, incidentally, alien to Semitic. (The ergative construction presupposes different forms of the subject depending on whether the verb is intransitive or transitive: cf. Avar *vac vekerula* 'a boy runs' and *vocas til bosula* 'a boy takes a stick.')] It is only these two groups of linguistic structures that Indo-European bridges: Dravidian and Uralo-Altaic, by contrast, display points of mutual agreement foreign to Indo-European, which makes the location of the home of Indo-European in Iran or North India unlikely. [Still less probable are localizations further east, for then Indo-European would have to serve as a link between Uralo-Altaic and Chinese or Sino-Tibetan.]

Thus, the area in which the oldest Indo-European dialects arose must be situated somewhere between the areas of the Finno-Ugric and the Caucasian-Mediterranean languages. [To be sure, this localization is rather vague, the more so as we have no idea how far north the Mediterranean language families spread in the remote past (at present we find their representatives by the Bay of Biscay and in the northern Caucasus).] A more precise location cannot be determined. Above all, we must combat the prejudice that the so-called Indo-European protolanguage occupied a narrowly defined area. Given the non-homogeneous character of this protolanguage (recognizable even through Neogrammarian methods of reconstruction), the assumption of a single point of diffusion is not necessary. It is easy, however, to envision the combined effect of several points of diffusion over quite a large area—say, from the North Sea to the Caspian Sea.

The genesis of the Indo-European languages is not an instantaneous act but a lasting process. Like everything in language, the Indo-European linguistic structure is subject to historical development. In principle, every branch of Indo-European evolves in its own direction, but certain evolutionary tendencies are common to most or all branches. If we compare these tendencies with the situation in non-Indo-European languages, interesting facts emerge. For the most ancient period of Indo-European, no fewer than three manners of stop articulation must be assumed. In the historically attested branches, however, this number is reduced to two, and only Ossetic, Armenian, Kurdish, and the Indian languages, which are surrounded by non-Indo-European neighbors, have preserved stop systems with three or four series up to the present day. As it happens, we find three manners of stop articulation in the Caucasian languages and, if we consider the so-called emphatic consonants as a special manner of articulation, also in Hamito-Semitic. The Finno-Ugric languages, in contrast, display only two manners of stop articulation and agree in this respect with Uralo-Altaic.

In the earliest Indo-European, the labials were the least developed of all stop classes, for *b occurred only rarely; in the historically attested Indo-European languages, this deficiency has been eliminated[, with the result that in this respect the modern Indo-European languages come close to Finno-Ugric, Samoyedic, and Altaic]. The North Caucasian languages display the same weakness of the labial class as Proto-Indo-European [(one of the three labial stops, the so-called occlusive p, occurs extremely seldom, and in Avar and Lak, e.g., it is absent altogether)], and the same may be said of Semitic, which possessed emphatic dentals and gutturals but no emphatic labials [(if one existed in the "protolanguage," its frequency must have been very low)]. In the Finno-Ugric and Altaic languages, in contrast, the labial class is as well developed as all the others.

For the earliest Indo-European, at least two classes of gutturals must be assumed. [The type of opposition between the g-like and the k-like consonants is a matter of debate. Some scholars reconstruct pure and labialized gutturals; others define the opposition as nonpalatalized ~ palatalized.] Almost all the historically attested Indo-European languages, however, display only one guttural class; in those Indo-European languages in which a second guttural class exists (Modern Persian, Ossetic, Latvian), it is an obviously secondary phenomenon. As it happens, the presence of two guttural classes is characteristic of the Caucasian languages, whereas in the Finno-Ugric and Altaic languages there is phonologically only one guttural class and the opposition between velar and palatal is conditioned by the vowel environment.

As Kuryłowicz has demonstrated, laryngeal sounds must have existed in the most ancient Indo-European, in which respect it again approached the Caucasian and Hamito-Semitic languages. Later, however, Indo-European lost its laryngeals, and, where these sounds appear in the historical Indo-European languages [(Ger. h, Ukr. g, etc.)], they are secondary [(only in the recently discovered Hittite may h go back to one of the Indo-European laryngeals)]—just as in the present-day Ugric and Altaic languages, which had no laryngeals in their earlier stages of development. [Whenever h occurs in a Uralo-Altaic language, it is relatively late. Thus, Hungarian h developed from x; in Buryat and North Evenk, the source of h is s. In the Kasimov Tatar dialect, the glottal stop can be traced to k, and one can cite an analogous case from the Rosental dialect of Slovenian (Carinthian), in which Common Slavic k also became a glottal stop. Among the neighbors of Indo-European, a wealth of laryngeal sounds has been attested only in North Caucasian and Hamito-Semitic.]

Partial root reduplication played an important role in the earliest Indo-European and still survives in historical times in the older stages of development of the attested Indo-European languages. [Some grammatical forms depend not only on inflection and ablaut but also on reduplication, that is, on the doubling of the first consonant of the root. Such forms are attested in Sanskrit, Old Persian, Ancient Greek, Latin (*posco* – *pŏposci* 'demand,' *tango* – *tĕtīgi* 'touch,' *tundo* – *tŭtŭdi* 'beat, strike,' 1st p. sg. pres. and perf.), Umbrian, Oscan, and Gothic.] Indo-European agrees in this respect with the Semitic and Caucasian languages [(cf. Avar *tese* 'tear off' [perfective] – *tetese* 'tear off' [imperfective]; Lak *cun* 'to be ill' – *cucar* 'it hurts'; *ššaran* 'boil' – *ššarraššar* '(it) boils'; Archi *xuras* 'to laugh' – *xuraxu* 'laughed')]. This morphological device is completely foreign, however, to the younger stages of development of the Indo-European languages, just as it is to Finno-Ugric and Altaic.

[At a relatively early stage of their development, the Indo-European languages distinguished genders in nouns: first (as is now believed) the animate or active versus the inanimate or passive gender, then the masculine, feminine, and neuter. But they tended to lose this distinction or reduce it to a minimum. Armenian and the modern Iranian languages have forfeited it altogether, English and Dutch have retained just a few traces, and the Romance languages, Latvian, and Lithuanian distinguish only the masculine and feminine. Of the languages bordering on Indo-European, genders are consistently opposed in North Caucasian (Chechen, e.g., has six) and to a lesser degree in Hamito-Samitic. In Uralo-Altaic, genders are absent.]

Finally, Uhlenbeck has shown that in the earliest Indo-European the ergative was opposed to the absolute, not the nominative to the accusative, a feature linking Indo-European with the North Caucasian languages (and with Basque and certain extinct languages of the Near East), whereas the later opposition of nominative to accusative has a parallel in the Uralic and Altaic languages.

In all the points listed above, therefore, the Indo-European languages developed from one type, similar to the present-day East Caucasian languages, to another type reminiscent of Finno-Ugric and Altaic. These facts allow of various interpretations. One can suppose them to be the consequence of particular historical events [in the life of the Indo-European "protonation"] and even try to reconstruct these events. With a certain amount of imagination, such a reconstruction can turn out to be quite clever—although it will always be unconvincing. But one can also interpret the facts listed above as the expression of a natural process of development. The hypertrophy of inflection represented by the modern East Caucasian languages would then have to be regarded as a primitive state and the type represented by the Altaic languages as an ideal of linguistic evolution. To be sure, this interpretation would contradict the common egocentric view according to which the inflecting languages stand at a higher evolutionary level than the agglutinating. But that would be no justification for rejecting it.

[There is only one reason that linguists have always considered the agglutinating languages inferior to the inflectional ones: they themselves have been native speakers of the latter group.[1] When we rid ourselves of the Indo-European bias, we will have to admit that purely agglutinating languages of the Altaic type, with their small inventory of phonemes used with the utmost economy, stable roots thrown into relief by their obligatory word-initial position, and unambiguous suffixes and endings, are a much more perfect tool than inflectional languages of, for instance, the East Caucasian type, whose elusive roots with constantly alternating vowels are hidden among prefixes and suffixes, some of which have a stable sound shape but a capriciously changeable meaning, others an identifiable meaning or function expressed in several heterogeneous, mutually incompatible forms.

In most Indo-European languages, inflection is not hypertrophied to the extent that it is in the Caucasian family, but they still cannot touch the technical perfection of the agglutinating languages. Attempts to create artificial languages show that, contrary to what we hear from Indo-European scholars, agglutination appears to be something of an ideal when compared to moderate, let alone hypertrophied, inflection. Charles Bally is right in saying that, although Esperanto consists of Indo-European lexemes, its structure is agglutinating. So when Indo-Europeans want to "improve on nature," they unwittingly abandon inflection and resort to agglutination. The opposite would be unthinkable. One cannot imagine a Finn, an Estonian, a Hungarian, a Turk, or a Japanese who, in planning a new artificial language, would abolish agglutination and introduce inflection.]

I am inclined, therefore, to think that the Indo-European linguistic structure arose through a process of outgrowing a primitive inflecting type, without, however, reaching the more highly developed agglutinating type.

15. Thoughts on the Latin $\bar{a}$-Subjunctive

1

In Indo-European, each *athematic* indicative had a corresponding optative with the formant *$j\bar{e}/\bar{\imath}$. Reflexes of this optative can be found in every branch of Indo-European, so we may assume that it was common to all of them. *Thematic* indicatives had in most Indo-European languages a corresponding optative with the formant *oi. There are two groups, however, that have not preserved any trace of the oi optative: Italic and Celtic. These two families display a verb form with modal function and the formant *$\bar{a}$, a form that cannot be attested with certainty in any other branch of Indo-European.

It would seem natural to suspect a connection between these two peculiarities of Italic and Celtic (the lack of the oi-optative and the presence of the $\bar{a}$-mood), that is, to assume that the optative of the Indo-European thematic conjugation was formed with *$\bar{a}$ as well as *oi and that *$\bar{a}$ was used by the dialects of the extreme West (Pre-Celtic and Pre-Italic), *oi by all others. This assumption fits all the evidence. The $\bar{a}$-mood indeed appears in Italic and Celtic regularly only in the thematic conjugation and has in both families the same meaning and function as the reflexes of the $j\bar{e}/\bar{\imath}$-optative. The Latin correspondence *est* : *erit* : *siet* = *dicit* : *dicet* : *dicat* (3d p. sg. pres. indic., fut., pres. subj. of 'be' and 'say') shows clearly that the $\bar{a}$-mood can only have been an optative.

2

However obvious this conclusion about the nature and original function of the $\bar{a}$-mood may be, it has never been put forward. Since the beginning of comparative grammar, the Italic-Celtic $\bar{a}$-mood has been considered a variant of the Indo-European *subjunctive*. At the time this explanation was first advanced, it seemed to make sense: as is well known, Schleicher reconstructed only $\bar{a}$ for the protolanguage and treated $\bar{e}$, $\bar{o}$, $\bar{a}$ in the classical languages as later alterations of it. From this point of view, Latin *dicat* and *dicet* had to be interpreted as secondary variants of a single original *$daik\bar{a}ti$.[1] But even after the existence of the triad *$\bar{a}$, *$\bar{e}$, *$\bar{o}$ in the Indo-European protolanguage had been universally acknowledged, the interpretation of *dicat* as subjunctive remained, apparently just by reason of inertia. Latin *ferant* could no longer be connected with Greek φέρωσι (both 3d p. pl. pres. subj. of 'carry'), so three different subjunctives—with the formants $*e/o$ (Lat. *erit*), $*\bar{e}/\bar{o}$ (Lat. *dicet*), and $*\bar{a}$ (Lat. *dicat*)—were posited for Indo-European.

Thurneysen (1884) exploded the belief in the antiquity of the $\bar{a}$-mood. Since then, scholars have tended to assume that it is an Italic-Celtic innovation: according to this idea, on Proto-Italic-Celtic territory, "injunctives" of certain verb stems that happened to end in $*\bar{a}$ took on the meaning of subjunctives, and the $*\bar{a}$, originally part of the tense stem or root, was interpreted as a mood formant and then spread to other forms. This theory, supported also by Brugmann in the second edition of his *Grundriss* (1916, 539–42), seems to be the most common one at present. But it addresses only the *age* and *origin* of the $\bar{a}$-mood; the mood's *meaning* and *syntactic function* appear noncontroversial and are taken for granted. It is considered proved that the $\bar{a}$-mood was a subjunctive (whence the term $\bar{a}$-*subjunctive*), and the whole idea of its injunctive origin rests on this belief in its subjunctive meaning and function; as especially Sanskrit shows, the injunctive competed only with the subjunctive (and the imperative), not with the optative. The theory stands or falls with the assumption of the $\bar{a}$-mood's subjunctive meaning. But this assumption (questioned by no one up to now) is completely unwarranted: the evidence speaks for an originally *optative*, not a subjunctive, meaning.

3

If we consider the other forms of the Italic "subjunctive," we will see that none of them can be traced to an Indo-European subjunctive; ultimately, they all derive from the optative.

The *present subjunctive* forms of verbs with athematic indicative, such as Latin *sim, uelim, edim* (1st p. sg. pres. subj. of 'be,' 'want,' 'eat'), are transparent and are unanimously recognized as old $j\bar{e}/\bar{\imath}$-optatives. The present subjunctive of the first conjugation, however, is ambiguous: on the one hand, *dem, stem, inclinem* (1st p. sg. pres. subj. of 'give,' 'stand,' 'incline') could be considered old optatives ($*d\partial$-$j\bar{e}$-m, $*st\partial$-$j\bar{e}$-m, $*klin\partial$-$j\bar{e}$-m), in which case *plantem* 'plant' (1st p. sg. pres. subj.) would have arisen by analogy with *stem;* on the other hand, we could interpret *plantet* (3d p. sg. pres. subj.) as an old $\bar{e}$-*subjunctive* ($*plant\bar{a}j$-$\bar{e}$-ti) and *det, stet, inclinet* (3d p. sg. pres. subj.) as products of analogy with *plantet.* In the light of the fact that all other $*je/jo$-presents employ the $\bar{e}$-subjunctive only with future meaning (*arguet, capiet, finiet* [3d p. sg. fut. of 'make known,' 'take,' 'finish']) and that this subjunctive seems never to have had the ending -$\bar{e}m$ in the first person singular (cf. Gk. παιδεύῃς : παιδεύω [2d p. sg. pres. subj., 1st p. sg. pres. ind. of 'teach'], Lat. *dices* : *dicam*, Old Lat. *dice* [2d p. sg. fut., 1st p. sg. pres. subj. and fut., 2d p. sg. imper. of 'say']), then the first of the two hypotheses (namely, *stem* = opt. $*st\partial$-$j\bar{e}$-m) is the only acceptable one.

With respect to the *perfect subjunctive,* too, it is certain that Latin forms such as *tutuderim, dixerim, fuerim* (1st p. sg. perf. subj. of 'beat,' 'say,' 'be') derive ultimately from the Indo-European *jē/ī*-optative, even though not every detail of their history is clear. The same may be said of Old Latin forms such as *faxim* 'make' and *capsim* 'take.' Oscan-Umbrian perfect subjunctives (Osc. *fuid, fefacid,* Umbr. *pihafi, kombifiançi* [3d p. sg. of 'be,' 'make,' 'be atoned for' (pass.), 'announce']), whose *i* derives from Indo-European **ē,* have been interpreted as old *ē*-subjunctives, but this is certainly incorrect: the Indo-European *ē*-subjunctive could appear only where the corresponding indicative was thematic, whereas the Italic perfect derives exclusively from Indo-European verb forms that were conjugated athematically in the indicative (Indo-European perfect, *s* aorist, and root aorist of the type of Skt. *abhūt* [3d p. sg. aorist of 'be']). We are justified, therefore, in looking on Oscan *fuid* rather as the direct continuation of an Indo-European **bhū-jē-t,* that is, a *jē/ī*-optative of the root aorist of **bhū* (cf. Skt. *bhūyāt*). Oscan *sakrafír* 'hallow' (fut. imper.) and Umbrian *pihafi* probably contain the enclitic form of this same Proto-Italic **fūē-* (< Indo-European **bhū-jē-*), and all other forms of the Oscan-Umbrian perfect subjunctive must have arisen on the model of **fued : fuíd, amanaffed : amanaffid* (3d p. sg. perf. indic. of 'order').

The origin of the Italic *imperfect* (and *pluperfect*) *subjunctive* is obscure; none of the suggested hypotheses is completely satisfactory. The meaning and syntactic function of the Italic imperfect subjunctive all but rule out its derivation from an Indo-European *ē*-subjunctive, however.

Thus, not a single Italic "subjunctive" form can be traced back to an Indo-European subjunctive. Verb forms that definitely stem from the Indo-European subjunctive have on Italic territory a future, not a subjunctive, meaning (e.g., Lat. *erit, dicet*). And since the *ā*-mood in Italic (except for the first person singular) displays not a subjunctive, but rather a future, meaning, this mood must be regarded as an optative from the point of view of Pre-Italic.

The evidence of the Celtic languages is much less clear, but there is nothing that would contradict the Italic data and support the assumption of a subjunctive function of the *ā*-mood.

There is, therefore, no reason to assume that the Indo-European *ā*-mood ever had subjunctive meaning. In terms of its meaning and syntactic function, it was not a subjunctive but an *optative.*[2] Accordingly, I designate it as the *ā-optative.*

4

In those branches of Indo-European that have the *oi*-optative, it occurs only in the thematic conjugations, and the *jē/ī*-optative occurs only in the athematic. In Italic, too, the *jē/ī*-optative occurs exclusively in the athematic forms of the relevant indicative. This suggests that the *ā*-optative in Pre-Italic and Pre-Celtic was formed only from thematic tense stems.

The facts bear out this hypothesis. Especially interesting is the situation in Old Irish, which can be summarized as follows. For Proto-Celtic *thematic* indicatives, Old Irish displays *ā*-subjunctives formed from the *same* stem (*berid* : *bera* 'bear' [3d p. sg. indic. and subj.], *lécim* : *lécea* 'leave' [1st p. sg. indic. and subj.], *nascid* : *nasca* 'bind' [3d p. sg. indic. and subj.], *ibid* : *eba* 'drink' [3d p. sg. indic. and subj.], etc., where thematic indicatives **bere-*, **leikje-*, **nasce-*, **pibe-* are to be reconstructed). But where the Proto-Celtic indicative stem is *athematic*, Old Irish has *ā*-subjunctives formed from stems *different* from the corresponding present stems (*crenaid* : *cria* 'buy,' *gainithir* : *-genathar* 'be born,' *is* : *ba* 'be' [all 3d p. sg. indic. and subj.], i.e., in Proto-Celtic terms, **krināti* : **krijā-*, **gᵃnītr . . . : **genā-, *esti* : *bwā*). These correspondences show that the Proto-Celtic *ā*-optative could be formed only from thematic stems, not from athematic ones; each Old Irish *ā*-subjunctive presupposes the existence of a corresponding Proto-Celtic (or Pre-Celtic) thematic indicative. Old Irish subjunctives like *cria, genathar* must be *ā*-optatives of lost thematic indicative stems **krije-, **gene-:* these stems were probably strong thematic aorists of the type of Greek ἔπιον (1st p. sg./3d p. pl. of 'drink'), ἐγενόμην (1st p. sg. of 'be born').[3] Weakened sensitivity to aspectual relations resulted in the paradigmatic linking of originally aorist *ā*-optatives like *cria, genathar* with present indicatives like *crenaid, gainithir.* Old Irish *ba* must originally have belonged to a Pre-Celtic thematic indicative stem **bh(u)we-*. It is true that the Indo-European root **bhū* seems to have had only an athematic root aorist (Skt. *abhūt*, Gk. ἔφυ, Lat. *fui*); in the individual daughter languages, however, it had various present stems as well (with the formants **-je-, **-ā-, **-ndhe-*, etc., but also thematically, as in Indo-Iranian). The reconstruction of a thematic present stem **bh(u)we-* (later lost) for Pre-Celtic is thus possible, and Old Irish *ba* makes it probable.

In Italic, as in Old Irish, *ā*-optatives are formed from all thematic present stems: for example, Latin *dicam, capiam, finiam, habeam, moneam, pleam, induam, arguam, noscam, sternam, linquam, bibam, gignam* (1st p. sg. pres. subj. of 'say,' 'take,' 'finish,' 'have,' 'warn,' 'implore,' 'clothe,' 'make known,' 'know,' 'spread,' 'leave,' 'drink,' 'beget'). Old Latin *fuat* '(he) be,' *tulat* 'bear' (*attulat, abstulat*), *uĕnat* 'come' (*ad-, con-, e-, per-uenat*), for which no corresponding thematic indicatives are attested, suggest that here *ā*-optatives were formed from athematic stems. But since such a hypothesis would contradict everything we know about the Italic verb system, these forms must be explained partly as regular *ā*-optatives of old, abandoned indicatives, partly as products of analogy. *Fuat,* which seems to be identical with Old Irish *ba,* must be considered as the regular *ā*-optative of a Pre-Italic **bh(u)weti*,[4] which disappeared early as a simplex but perhaps survives in *amābo, habēbo,* etc. (1st p. sg. fut. of 'love,' 'have'). After the Proto-Italic thematic indicative **fuet(i)* fell into disuse, the optative **fuat* was necessarily associated with the perfect *fuai.* On the model of **fuai : fuat, tulat* was formed for *tuli* (1st p. sg. perf. indic. of 'bear');[5] the same may be said of *uĕnat,* which was formed for the Proto-Italic perfect **gʷĕnai.* The latter form, admittedly, does not agree with Latin *uēnī,* but it must be reconstructed for Proto-Italic because of the Umbrian future perfect *benust* (3d p. sg.).

5

The formation of the optative in Indo-European may thus be summarized in the following way: *The optative of athematic temporal stems was formed with *jē/ī in all Indo-European languages; the optative of thematic temporal stems was formed with *oi in most Indo-European languages but with *ā in Pre-Italic and Pre-Celtic.*

The optative formants **oi* and **ā* are equally old and equally "Indo-European," although neither was common to *all* languages. There is no reason to consider one of the formants as the only original one and explain the other by assuming innovations in individual languages.

It is possible that some Indo-European languages used both optative formants. In Slavic, for example, the third person plural imperative *bǫdǫ* 'be,' attested a number of times in Old Church Slavonic texts, may be derived from **b(h)und(h)ānt* (Vondrák 1906–8, 2:165 [1924–28, 2:137]), whereas the other forms of the Slavic imperative are based on the Indo-European *oi*-optative (*beri* 'take' = **bherois, berěte* = **bheroite,* etc.). Perhaps the enigmatic Old Church Slavonic imperative forms such as *pijate* 'drink,' *plačate* 'weep' (beside *pijite, plačite* = **pijoite, plōkjoite*), too, are to be derived from *ā*-optatives (Meillet 1908–9a, 37).[6]

16. The Pronunciation of Greek χ in the Ninth Century A.D.

The writing systems of the Christian Orient that developed on the basis of the Greek alphabet are a source of some importance for the history of Greek sounds. Until now, historians of the Greek language have paid little attention to the Glagolitic Old Church Slavonic alphabet created by St. Constantine-Cyril in the 860s, even though it contains valuable evidence for the pronunciation of Greek. To be sure, the transmission of Old Church Slavonic leaves much to be desired. The oldest text written in Glagolitic (the *Kiev Fragments*) is at least one hundred years younger than the invention of the Glagolitic alphabet, and the bulk of Old Church Slavonic manuscripts are no older than the eleventh century. When these texts were written, the pronunciation of both Slavic and Greek was no longer the same as at the time of the apostles of the Slavs. Nor had the alphabet remained stable: certain characters had fallen into disuse; new ones had been introduced; still others must have changed their sound value. Fortunately, however, in addition to the Old Church Slavonic texts proper, we possess other sources that tell us something about the original makeup of the Glagolitic alphabet. The most important among them is the acrostic *Alphabet Poem* of the Presbyter (later Bishop) Constantine, a learned Bulgarian cleric who seems to have known St. Methodios (the brother and collaborator of St. Constantine-Cyril) personally and based his poem on the original form of the Glagolitic alphabet. In what follows, I will discuss a case in which the testimony of the Glagolitic alphabet can help identify the pronunciation of a Greek phoneme.

In the Old Church Slavonic texts in Glagolitic, two different letters are used for the guttural spirant *x*. One of them occurs in our texts only twice—once in the *Assemani Gospel* and once in the *Sinai Psalter*—and consists of a ringlet to which four hooks are attached, two on the upper and two on the lower part; in Slavic paleographic literature this letter is usually called the "spider-shaped" *x* (although spiders, as everyone knows, have eight legs, not four!). The letter otherwise used for *x* consists of an almost vertical but somewhat right-slanting ascender, from the lower end of which a short line rises slightly to the right and ends with a loop; in the oldest manuscripts, the bottom of the loop extends down to the level of the bottom of the ascender.

The Presbyter Constantine's alphabet poem proves that both *x* characters existed in the original Glagolitic alphabet, for in this poem two verses (24 and 33) begin with *x*. Another very old Church Slavonic alphabet poem by an unknown author, a copy of which has been preserved in the Old Russian manuscript of the *Jaroslavl' Prayer Book,* agrees in this respect with Constantine's alphabet poem. Finally, both of the oldest Church Slavonic abecedaria (the Munich one, written in the margin of the famous Hrosvitha von Gandersheim manuscript, and the Paris *Abecenarium Bulgaricum*) attest the two *x* characters. It follows that these two letters belonged to the oldest form of the Glagolitic alphabet.[1]

What could have motivated the creator of the Glagolitic alphabet to include two different *x* characters? The answer depends on the interpretation of the evidence contained in the Presbyter Constantine's alphabet poem. Of the two verses beginning with *x,* one begins with the word *xerovĭskǫ* (which corresponds to *xerovimĭskǫjǫ* in the anonymous poem in the *Jaroslavl' Prayer Book*), the other with the word *xvalǫ* (corresponding to *xvalami* in the *Jaroslavl' Prayer Book*). The word *xerovĭskǫ* or *xerovimĭskǫjǫ* is the feminine accusative singular of a possessive adjective derived from the loanword *xerov(im)ŭ* 'cherub,' whereas the word *xvala* (acc. sg. *xvalǫ,* instr. pl. *xvalami*) 'praise' is native Slavic. The Ljubljana Slavic scholar Raiko Nahtigal assumes that the first *x* character rendered only the palatal variant of *x* that occurred in loanwords before front vowels and that the second *x* character denoted normal velar Slavic *x* (as well as Greek χ before back vowels and consontants).

Nahtigal (1923, 174) refers to the fact that the Glagolitic alphabet also possessed a special letter for the voiced palatal spirant that had arisen in Greek words from older γ before front vowels. This parallel is invalid, however, as was shown by the Russian Slavic scholar N. N. Durnovo (1929, 71): the letter rendering Greek γ before front vowels in the extant Glagolitic texts seems to have represented in the original Glagolitic alphabet a native Slavic phoneme that did not occur word initially, which is why the verse corresponding to this letter in the alphabet poem of the Presbyter Constantine begins with another letter (see also Trubetzkoy 1936a). Durnovo observes correctly that the creator of the Glagolitic alphabet had no reason to invent a special character for the palatal variant of Greek χ before front vowels: although in Slavic the gutturals were not tolerated in this position, a Slav who had acquired the correct pronunciation of palatal Greek χ would not need a special letter for it (in Greek, after all, the same χ is written before front vowels as before back vowels and consonants), while those who found the correct pronunciation of the Greek sound sequence χ + front vowel difficult would not be helped by a special letter.

Durnovo considers still another interpretation of the evidence of the alphabet poem, namely, that the second *x* letter (as in *xvalǫ*) designated a labialized velar spirant which is supposed to have developed from Proto-Slavic *xv in the dialect of St. Constantine-Cyril, but he rejects this idea. Indeed, the change *xv > f* in many Bulgarian and Serbian dialects, which could perhaps be cited in support of this interpretation, seems to be relatively late, since the combination *xv* in Church Slavonic, Old Serbian, and Middle Bulgarian texts is always represented by *x* + *v;* the essence of this change appears to have been that *v* became devoiced after *x*, whereas *x*, following the general tendency of Serbian and Bulgarian dialects, lost its articulatory identity and then disappeared (cf. Stevanović 1933–34, 48).

Thus, no satisfactory explanation of the presence of two *x* characters in the original Glagolitic alphabet has yet been advanced. The problem is solved, however, if we consider the position of these letters in the alphabet and the numerical value that this position determines. On the model of Greek, the Glagolitic alphabet was split into nine-character rows: the first nine letters designated the ones, the next nine letters the tens, and so on. As pointed out above, verse 24 of the Presbyter Constantine's alphabet poem begins with *x* (namely, with the word *xerovĭskǫ*). Therefore, the corresponding letter had to occupy the sixth position in the third nine-character row (24 = 9 + 9 + 6) and possess the numerical value 600. This value belongs in Greek to the letter χ. If we compare the order of the Glagolitic and the Greek alphabets, we see that the *relative order* of the letters common to both alphabets is the same but that agreement with Greek with respect to the *absolute numerical value* is found only for those Glagolitic letters that occupy the first position in a nine-character row (*a* = 1, *i* = 10, *r* = 100) or occur only in loanwords (*v* = 400, ϕ = 500).[2]

The fact that the first *x* character possessed the numerical value of Greek χ shows that the creator of the Glagolitic alphabet wanted this character to represent Greek χ, the sound of which he could not identify with any Slavic sound. This is why it is illustrated in both of the oldest alphabet poems by borrowings rather than by Slavic words. The second *x* character, represented in the Presbyter Constantine's alphabet poem by the native Slavic word *xvalǫ*, must, according to the evidence of the poem, have been the thirty-third letter of the Glagolitic alphabet and thus have stood outside the series of letters common to Glagolitic and Greek, namely, in the last nine-character row, which contained only specifically Slavic letters (*č, š, ĭ, ŭ, ě*, etc.). In the light of these circumstances, we can conclude that in St. Constantine-Cyril's time Greek χ could not be identified with Slavic *x*. And the reason can only have been that Greek χ had not yet become a spirant but was rather an aspirate.

This conclusion becomes especially attractive if we compare the testimony of the Glagolitic alphabet with that of its Coptic, Armenian, and Georgian counterparts. Holger Pedersen has pointed out that a prerequisite for the Coptic alphabet, which arose around A.D. 200, was the pronunciation of Greek χ as *kh*, since the Greek letter (only slightly distorted) is used in this alphabet to represent a guttural aspirate, whereas a special character (borrowed from the Demotic alphabet) had to be introduced to represent the guttural spirant. The fifth-century Armenian alphabet displays the same peculiarities. Pedersen believes that the situation reflected in the Armenian alphabet corresponds not to fifth-century Greek pronunciation but rather to Greek pronunciation at the time when "the Armenians first came into contact with the Greeks through the introduction of Christianity," that is, about A.D. 300: "If the Armenians at that time heard and acquired the pronunciation . . . *kh,* it is conceivable that they later preserved it without regard for the changes that Greek pronunciation underwent in other regions" (1923, 68).[3] But this supposition is unlikely: contact between Armenia and Byzantium in the fourth and fifth centuries was so intense that an archaic Greek pronunciation could have been preserved in Armenia only if such a pronunciation was also preserved among educated Byzantines.

Comparison between the Armenian and the Coptic characters for *kh* and *x* reveals their genetic relation. In both alphabets, the *kh* character corresponding to Greek χ is a combination of four hooks linked crosswise, and the *x* character consists of a more or less vertical ascender, from the middle of which an incomplete loop extends to the right and down (the Armenian *x* character displays, in addition, a short horizontal serif at the bottom right of the ascender). The two Glagolitic *x* characters display the same motifs (with the characteristic Glagolitic predilection for ringlets and full loops); the Glagolitic "spider-shaped" *x* corresponds to the Coptic and Armenian *kh* characters, and the "normal" Glagolitic *x* corresponds to Coptic and Armenian *x*:

	Coptic	Armenian	Glagolitic
kh	✕	ⴼ	Ⰶ
x	Ⴆ	ⴓ	ⱈ

This similarity need not surprise us, since other points of contact between the Glagolitic alphabet and the Coptic and Caucasian alphabets exist and have often been noted.[4] The Georgian "religious" alphabet (*xutsuri*), which was developed at about the same time as the Armenian, has a *kh* character with the same features as the Coptic, Armenian, and Glagolitic letters, whereas its *x* character deviates considerably from the Coptic and Glagolitic ones but displays an unmistakable affinity with the Armenian *x*. For our purposes, however, the important thing is not the form but the order of these Georgian letters in the alphabet, together with their numerical value. Like the Glagolitic, the Georgian alphabet contains many more letters than the Greek. The fourth nine-character row, missing in Greek, is used in the Georgian writing system to designate the thousands. This must also have been the case originally in Old Church Slavonic, and we may assume that the Glagolitic alphabet was influenced by the Georgian in the ordering of the letters in the fourth nine-character row. In any case, it seems to be no coincidence that the twenty-eighth letter of the alphabet, which begins the fourth nine-character row and possesses the numerical value 1,000, has the sound value *č* in both the Georgian and the Glagolitic alphabets. As it happens, the word *xvalǫ* stands in the Presbyter Constantine's alphabet poem at the beginning of verse 33, which indicates that the second *x* character of the Glagolitic alphabet occupied the sixth position in the fourth nine-character row ($9 + 9 + 9 + 6 = 33$) and thus evidently had the numerical value 6,000. It is just this position in the alphabet that the Georgian *x* with its value 6,000 occupies, whereas the Georgian *kh* (like the first Glagolitic *x* character) stands in position 24 and possesses the numerical value of Greek χ (namely, 600).

These points of agreement cannot be coincidental. If Greek χ had been a guttural spirant in St. Constantine-Cyril's pronunciation, the creator of the Glagolitic alphabet would have had no reason to represent this sound by a special character and to draw on the oriental alphabets for the Slavic guttural spirant. Although at that time the Slavic gutturals, which occurred only before back vowels and consonants, were probably much more velar than the Greek ones, this difference in place of articulation could not have prevented the identification of the Slavic gutturals with the Greek ones. This is demonstrated, among other things, by the fact that the character for Slavic *g* in the Glagolitic alphabet comes directly before the character for *d* and the character for Slavic *k* directly before the character for *l*—the same relative order that Greek γ and κ display. Clearly, the difference between Slavic *x* and Greek χ was not in the *place of articulation* but in the *manner of articulation*. Slavic *x* was a guttural spirant, while Greek χ, at least in the pronunciation of St. Constantine-Cyril, was an aspirate (*kh*).

Thus, Greek χ must still have been spoken as an aspirate (*kh*) in the ninth century. This pronunciation was probably more or less affected and current only among the educated. Nevertheless, St. Constantine-Cyril found it impossible to represent the χ of Greek words (or of Hebrew words borrowed through Greek) and normal Slavic *x* by the same character. His example does not seem to have been followed faithfully, however, and Greek χ in borrowed words very soon began to be represented in Glagolitic manuscripts by the normal *x* character, which clearly was due to the fact that even those Greeks who pedantically clung to the artificial pronunciation of their literary language articulated Greek χ in the popular way as a spirant. The old difference in numerical value between the spider-shaped and the normal *x* character was also quickly forgotten since the representation of the thousands by the letters of the fourth nine-character row was gradually displaced by the representation normal in Greek (by preposed letters of the first nine-character row).[5] The distinction between the two *x* characters became pointless. The spider-shaped *x* fell into disuse, and in those texts that still used it sporadically it appeared no longer in loanwords but only in the native Slavic word *xlŭmŭ* 'noise, dalliance,' where originally it was not permitted.

17. The Phonetic Evolution of Russian and the Disintegration of the Common Russian Linguistic Unity

1

That there once existed a Common Russian or Common East Slavic proto-language may be considered certain. The opposing view, advanced by Smal-Stockyj and Gartner, was rejected by all leading Slavicists with such rare unanimity that today probably no one would so much as question, let alone attack, the idea of a pan-Russian protolanguage. Unanswered, however, remains the question when and how this pan-Russian linguistic unity disintegrated. To answer it, we must first agree on the concept *disintegration*. If we understand it to mean that the speakers of different dialects of an originally homogeneous language begin to have difficulty understanding one another, it should be borne in mind that such breakdowns in communication usually arise through the divergent development of the lexicon, not of sounds and morphology. Determining the point in time at which such situations arose and describing the processes leading up to them is a task for the history of words or, more precisely, the history of the lexicon, that is, the most neglected area of historical linguistics. East Slavic philology lags especially far behind in this respect; given the almost complete lack of East Slavic word studies, a definitive treatment of the *disintegration* conceived of in this way cannot even be attempted.

But *disintegration* can also mean that the individual dialects of a language lose the ability to participate together in important phonetic and morphological changes. From this perspective, the disintegration of a linguistic community becomes a problem of historical phonetics and morphology. And, since these areas of linguistics are the only ones to have been explored with any degree of thoroughness in both substance and methodology, researchers interested in such matters have no choice but to take *disintegration* in this second sense as the object of their study.

However, even if the disintegration of the Common Russian linguistic unity is considered only in this second sense, plenty of difficulties remain. The Old Russian texts are of little use in tracing the development of the living language: the conservative orthography, the influence of South Slavic source texts, and the artificial, traditional pronunciation of Church Slavonic often make the dating of the most important sound changes on philological grounds alone impossible. Only by chance can philology provide some chronological foundation stones; the gaps can be filled in only by applying the method of comparative reconstruction to dialectology. In describing the history of Russian sounds, this method plays a much greater role than the purely philological one.

In what follows, I try to present the sound changes that led to the disintegration of the Common Russian linguistic unity in their chronological and *logical* context. My point of departure is the conviction that, like every other historical development, the development of sounds possesses its inner logic, which it is the task of the historical linguist to understand. I am thus concerned first and foremost with establishing general principles.

2

For the oldest period (prior to the first written records), the late A. Šaxmatov (1915) assumed the existence of three East Slavic dialects: North, South, and East Russian. One part of the East Russians allegedly mixed with the South Russians, another part with the North Russians. According to this scheme, the Belorussian people arose from the mixture of the East and South Russians, the Great Russian people from the subsequent union of the other part of the East Russians with the North Russians. The part of the South Russians remaining after the emergence of the Belorussian people developed into the Ukrainian people.[1] The modern tripartition (Great Russian, Belorussian, Ukrainian) is thus not a direct continuation of the older one (North, South, and East Russian): it arose from it through partial mixings.

If we examine the reasons that moved Šaxmatov to set up this older tripartition, we will notice that the divisions were grounded neither in the historical facts nor in the Old Russian linguistic data. He offered a working hypothesis necessary for determining the chronology of sound changes that for various reasons do not appear in the old texts. The sound changes that occur in all East Slavic dialects are assigned to the Proto-Russian period (prior to the older tripartition); those that link Belorussian with Ukrainian are considered as belonging to South Old Russian; those that distinguish North Great Russian from South Great Russian are considered as old features of North Old Russian before its union with East Old Russian; all others are assigned to the period after the end of the older tripartition. Šaxmatov devised this system only in order to be able to assign individual sound changes to one of three periods (before, during, and after the older tripartition) and order them chronologically; it is a consequence of his working method. Although he (like his teacher Fortunatov) theoretically rejected Schleicher's family tree theory, he was never able to free himself of its influence: perhaps unwittingly, he always imagined the development of language as the branching of a family tree.

Belorussian is a connecting link between Great Russian and Ukrainian. For advocates of the wave theory, there is nothing strange in this fact: given the geographic position of Belorussian, it is only natural. For proponents, even unconscious ones, of the family tree theory, it is a different matter: they are puzzled by any kind of transitional dialect and know only one solution, the assumption of ethnic or dialect mixing.

Since Schleicher's family tree theory has been rendered obsolete (even Šaxmatov rejected it *theoretically*), Šaxmatov's view of the genesis of the modern tripartition—Great Russian, Belorussian, Ukrainian—must also fall. This view, incidentally, was accepted by no other Slavicists: they were as unanimous in their rejection as they were in emphasizing the insightfulness of the individual observations that make Šaxmatov's *Outline,* despite the weakness of its main thesis, one of his most valuable achievements.

Šaxmatov's theory of the older tripartition was countered by Lehr-Spławiński (1921–22) with the theory of an older bipartition, according to which only two dialects existed in Old Russian before the beginning of writing: the northern, essentially Novgorod's sphere of cultural influence, and the southern, which covered all other parts of the East Slavic language area. For a follower of the family tree theory, this view must appear paradoxical: the differences between Ukrainian and Great Russian are said to have arisen later than those between North and South Great Russian. Nevertheless, it seems to be the only one that fits the historical facts and the state of our philological knowledge. For the preliterary period,[2] therefore, I adopt Lehr-Spławiński's view. I deviate from this scholar only in details.

First, of the features that Lehr-Spławiński assumes to have been characteristic of the two preliterary dialects, I can accept only some as such. In my opinion, only the following four dialectal oppositions are old: (1) the North Old Russian stop g corresponded to the spirant γ in South Old Russian; (2) the sounds $\check{c}$ and c were strictly distinguished in South Old Russian, while in North Old Russian they had merged; (3) Proto-Slavic *tl, dl* became in South Old Russian *l* (without exception) but in North Old Russian *kl, gl;* (4) the combinations $\check{s}\check{c}$, $\check{z}d\check{z}$ remained unchanged in South Old Russian, but in North Old Russian they became $\check{z}\grave{\gamma}$, $\check{s}\grave{\chi}$. The other features mentioned by Lehr-Spławiński arose much later; I will justify this statement below.

Second, it must be emphasized that the southern boundaries of the four characteristics of North Old Russian mentioned above do not have to coincide. In the course of time, individual dialect boundaries must have shifted considerably, so it is impossible to determine the original spread of individual North Old Russian features on the basis of their present-day distribution. There is no reason to assume the existence of a single, sharp dialect boundary at which all North Old Russian features suddenly stopped. Rather, it is likely a priori that each of the four features originally had its own southern boundary, so that, for example, the southern boundary of the plosive g did not co-incide with the southern boundary of the confusion of $č$ and c. As always in such cases, there must at that time have existed transitional and border dialects that combined North Old Russian and South Old Russian features; the general principle of the bipartition was not compromised by this fact. With these (insignificant) modifications, I can accept Lehr-Spławiński's view of the dialectal situation in the oldest, preliterary, period.

3

Before going further, it is necessary to look at the preliterary period from the point of view of Common Slavic. Let us first consider the features that arose through sound changes in South Old Russian. The change from g to $γ$ must be assumed for Proto-Czech, Proto-Slovak, and Proto–Upper Sorbian in addition to South Old Russian. Czech h, which appeared in the textual record about the middle of the thirteenth century and, according to Gebauer (1894–1929, 1:456), in the spoken language somewhat earlier, must have arisen not directly from g but from a fricative $γ$. The chronology of the Czech change of g to $γ$ cannot be determined precisely since the letter g in the Bohemica of the twelfth century designates both g and $γ$ (cf. the spelling g for fricative $γ$ in Old and Middle High German manuscripts). The change is undoubtedly old, however, for the new g that arose from *k before voiced stops after the loss of $ъ$ remained unaffected by it: for example, Czech kde, kdy (pronounced gde, gdy) from $kъd$- as opposed to $tehdy$ from ($tъ$-)$γъd$-. Therefore, the change $g > γ$ in Czech must be older than the loss of the semivowels, that is, much older than the oldest preserved Bohemian texts; so the hypothesis of a direct connection between the Czech–Slovak–Upper Sorbian change $g > γ$ and the South Old Russian one seems to be very probable. Likewise, the assumption of a direct connection between the South Old Russian change tl, $dl > l$ and the same change in the South Slavic languages is not only very probable but unavoidable.[3]

Thus, both of the sound changes that South Old Russian underwent separately from North Old Russian are tied to corresponding sound changes in certain neighboring Slavic languages and may be considered dialectal phenomena of the late Proto-Slavic period.

The sound changes characteristic of North Old Russian in the preliterary period look different. The change tl, $dl > kl$, gl (especially typical of the old dialect of Pskov) is reminiscent of the same phenomenon in Lithuanian and Latvian, as Karinskij (1909) already pointed out. The merger of $č$ and c (in contrast to the strict distinction of the corresponding fricatives $š$, $ž$ – $ś$, $ź$) is reminiscent of the West Finnic languages, in which Proto-Finno-Ugric $č$ and $ć$ have merged while š and ś are treated differently. And the change šč, ždž > šх́, žγ́ is another form of the same tendency toward eliminating the affricates č, dž from the sound system.

Consequently, the difference between the two Old Russian dialects of the preliterary period is linked to geographic and cultural factors. From the start, communication between the Russian-speaking world and the rest of the Slavic-speaking world had been restricted to the West and South, while the speakers of Russian in the North stood in contact with the non-Slavic peoples of the Baltic coast. Certain sound changes in neighboring Slavic dialects penetrated to the East Slavs from the South and West, but they did not always have the energy to spread over the entire East Slavic area and did not affect its northern part, which remained more independent of the Slavic world and was exposed instead to the influence of the languages of the Baltic. The difference between the northern part of the East Slavic area, gravitating toward the Baltic, and the Slavic-oriented South can have begun very early: only later did it crystallize in the formation of two cultural centers, Novgorod in the East and Kiev in the South. It was characteristic of this period that the East and Southeast of the Russian language area lay fully within the sphere of southern cultural influence.

4

The dialectal situation described above for the oldest, preliterary, period continued for a long time, probably into the 1160s: with respect to the sound system, at least, the interrelations of the Old Russian dialects hardly changed significantly. The spellings и or e for ѣ, which occur sporadically in texts of this period, hardly reflect a real sound change but rather, at most, the nondifferentiation between ě and i or e.[4]

A new period in the dialectal differentiation of Old Russian begins in the second half of the twelfth century. One of its most important phonetic phenomena was the loss of the weak semivowels ŭ, ĭ, ĭ and the parallel change of the strong semivowels ъ, ь to o, e.[5] This was a Common Russian phenomenon that eventually affected the entire Russian language area, even though it spread gradually and relatively slowly. It came to an end in the South in the 1160s and in the North not until the last quarter of the thirteenth century (Šaxmatov 1915, 203ff.): the Galician-Volhynian *Dobrilo Gospel* of 1164 may serve as a chronological landmark for the South, the Novgorod *Kormčaia* (statutes) of 1282 for the North.[6]

The texts give us no information about the semivowels in the West and East of the Russian language area in this period. The oldest East Russian texts that could be of use here are of much more recent date, while the oldest West Russian text (a Smolensk deed from the year 1229) displays all signs of the transformation of the semivowels and thus cannot be considered a terminus a quo. It is only for general, theoretical reasons, which I hope to make clear below, that I assume a parallel treatment of the semivowels in the West and the South, on the one hand, and in the East and the North, on the other.

There was, therefore, a fairly long period (more than a century) in which the semivowels were present in the North and East but had disappeared in the South and West. The Russian linguistic unity could not be undermined by the circumstance that in the Northeast overshort and very weakly pronounced vowels were spoken in positions in which no vowels were heard in the Southwest or that in the Northeast the vowels ъ, ь (roughly, open *u, i* tending toward *o, e*) corresponded to *o, e* in the Southwest, especially since between these extremes there must have existed transitional dialects whose boundaries were gradually shifting northward and eastward. But this minor difference was nevertheless able to prevent certain sound changes that appeared in various parts of the Russian language area in this period from spreading over its entire territory. A whole series of sound features separating Great Russian from Ukrainian and Belorussian can be explained in this way. I proceed now to the listing and discussion of such features.

5

1. Great Russian *svin'ja* 'pig,' *sud'ja* 'judge,' etc. ~ Ukrainian *svyn'n'a, sud'd'a,* Belorussian *svin'n'a, sudz'dz'a,* etc. The assimilation *n'j, d'j,* etc. to *n'n', d'd',* etc. could not occur until the weak semivowel *ĭ* between the palatalized consonant and *j* had been lost. This loss of *ĭ* took place, as we know, earlier in the South and West than in the North and East. The fact that the assimilation *n'j >* *n'n* etc. did not penetrate Great Russian indicates that it occurred at a time when the North still had *sud'ĭja* (trisyllabic) but the Southwest already *sud'ja* (disyllabic), that is, in the period 1164–1282.

2. (*a*) Great Russian *igrat'* (or *iɣrat'*) 'play' (v.) ~ Ukrainian *hraty,* Belorussian *hrac'*; (*b*) Great Russian *błoxa* 'flea' ~ Ukrainian *błyxa,* Belorussian *błyxa.* In open, unstressed syllables after *j,* Proto-Slavic *i* was "weak." After the Proto-Russian loss of word-initial *j* before front vowels, this weak *ĭ* often assumed word-initial position. Like all weak vowels, it had to disappear. In Ukrainian and Belorussian, this is indeed the case: Ukrainian *hraty, hra, s'katy, mu,* etc. < Old Russian *ĭɣrati* 'play,' *ĭɣra* 'game,' *ĭskati* 'seek,' *ĭmu* 'him' (dat.), etc. (Proto-Slavic *jĭgrati* etc.). On the other hand, Great Russian has only forms with preserved *i: igrat', igra, igołka* 'needle,' *iskat', imět'* 'have,' etc. Since weak *i* is otherwise lost in Great Russian (cf. *jajca < jajĭca* 'eggs'), it must have become strong specifically in word-initial position before the beginning of the Northeast Rus-

sian loss of semivowels, and, since this strengthening of weak word-initial *i* did not spread to the other parts of the Russian language area, it must have taken place at a time when in the South and West of the Russian language area the loss of all weak vowels (including word-initial *ĭ*) was already complete.

The relation between Great Russian *głotat'* 'swallow' (v.) and Ukrainian *hłytaty*, Belorussian *hłytac'*, etc. must be interpreted in the same way. Where Old Russian weak *ъ, ь* followed a word-initial group consonant + liquid, Ukrainian dialects mostly have consonant + liquid + *y* (*hłytaty, słyzy* 'tears' [n.], *pobryde* '[he] will wander,' *dryžaty* 'tremble, shiver') as well as other sound combinations (Lemkish *sylza* 'tear' [n.], *hyrmity* 'thunder' [v.], Galician dial. *kervavyj* 'bloody,' *tervoha* 'alarm,' etc.). In such cases, weak *ъ* and *ь* seem to have been lost according to the general rule, and the awkward sound combinations consonant + liquid + consonant later developed epenthetic vowels. Belorussian forms of the type *hłytac', słyzy, n'a kłyn'i* 'to one's knees, in one's lap,' *hrym'ec', dryžac'* cannot be separated from the Ukrainian ones and must have arisen in the same way. Great Russian, on the other hand, has forms with *o, e* after the liquid (*głotat', sleza, gremĕt', drožat'*), and, since *o, e* otherwise represent only strong *ъ, ь*, we must assume that the weak semivowels were strengthened in this position, that is, after the word-initial groups consonant + liquid. This strengthening can have occurred only before the Northeast Russian loss of semivowels; the weak semivowels in Southwest Russian must already have been lost, however, since otherwise the strengthening would have spread to the South and West.

Lehr-Spławński assigns the strengthening of weak *ъ, ь* after word-initial groups consonant + liquid to the oldest period and regards it as a feature of the North Old Russian dialect that can be grouped together with other North Old Russian features (such as the plosive *g* and the merger of *č* with *c*). I cannot share this view. The isogloss *błyxa ~ błoxa* coincides essentially with the isoglosses *svin'n'a ~ svin'ja* and *myju ~ moju* 'I wash' and does not touch the isoglosses of specifically North Great Russian features. There are indeed certain South Great Russian dialects that possess the forms *błyxa, dryžat'*, etc., but these are border dialects that display other Belorussian features as well (esp. *s'v'in'n'a, myju*, often also *jost'* for *jest'* 'is') (see Durnovo 1918, vol. 1, pt. 1, pp. 18ff., pt. 2, pp. 29ff.).

3. Great Russian *mòju* 'I wash,' *slĕpòj* 'blind,' *šèja* 'neck,' *kostèj* 'bones' (g. pl.) ~ Ukrainian *mỳju, slïpỳj, šỳja, kostỳj*, Belorussian *mỳju, sl'apỳj, šỳja, kas'c'ij*. Before *j*, Great Russian *y* and *i* became strong *ъ, ь*, which then became *o, e*. The texts give us no information about the chronology of this change: новгородьскъѥ in the *Kormčaja* (Nomocanon) of 1282 proves only that the change *yj > ъj* was complete before the change *ъ > o*, which is clear even without this example; and, when older and later North Russian texts systematically write

ы, и before *j*, such spellings can be explained simply by orthographic tradition. The reasons why Šaxmatov (1915, secs. 309–402, 405–6, 419, 525) postulated two separate sound changes, *ij* > *ej* (directly) and *ị̈* > *ь̣i* > *ẹ̈*, are not clear to me. Wherever Great Russian has *oj*, *ej* for older *yj*, *ij*, I assume the single change *yj*, *ij* > *ьj*, *ьj*, irrespective of the position of the accent and the nature of the vowel following the *j* (thus, *slěpòj*, *mòju*, *Lukoján* [proper name], *kostèj*, *šèja*, *ručejòk* 'rivulet'): this change must have preceded the Northeast Russian change ъ, ь > *o*, *e*.[7]

The change *yj*, *ij* > *ьj*, *ьj* did not spread to the southern and western parts of the Russian language area: apparently, some factor inhibited its operation. This factor can only have been the absence of ъ and ь from the sound system of the southern and western dialects of Russian at that time. The change *yj*, *ij* > *ьj*, *ьj* in the Northeast must have taken place at a time when ъ, ь no longer existed in the sound system of the Southwest: in weak position they had disappeared; in strong position they had changed to *o*, *e*.[8]

4. Great Russian *bok* 'side,' *p'eč* 'stove, oven' ~ Ukrainian *bik* (dial. *buok*, *buek*, *buik*, *buk*, *bük*, etc.), *pič* (dial. *pieč*), South Belorussian *buok*, *pieč*. The so-called loss of semivowels (apocope) is to be distinguished from the quantitative reduction of semivowels in weak position. The reduction was much older than the loss, for it took place in the Proto-Slavic period, whereas the loss did not begin on Russian territory until the twelfth and thirteenth centuries. The reduction caused compensatory lengthening of short vowels in the preceding syllable. In the eastern Proto-Slavic dialects (i.e., in those dialects of Proto-Slavic from which Russian later developed), the lengthening must have been older than the development of full vowels (*o*, *e*) in the second syllable of forms with pleophony, so the new *o* and *e* were unaffected by it. The chronological sequence was (1) *bokъ* > *bōkъ*, (2) *gorrdъ̌* 'town' > *gorodъ̌*. Before the loss of weak ъ̌, ь̌, therefore, the vowels *o* and *e* were long in *bōkъ̌*, *p'ēčъ̌*, but short in *gorodъ̌*, *p'er'edъ̌* 'in front of.'

The Ukrainian (and South Belorussian) diphthongization (or breaking) *bōk^ь* > *buok* (> *bik*) must not—in contrast to Czech, for example—be regarded as a spontaneous development of *o*, *e*. Where long *ō did not precede a syllable with a weak semivowel, it remained a monophthong: for example, Ukrainian *koža* 'skin' (Czech *kůže*), *može* '(he) can' (Czech *může*), etc. On the other hand, the Ukrainian diphthongization must not be regarded as a consequence of apocope alone since apocope did not occur in *moroz* 'frost,' *horod* 'town,' *pered* 'in front of,' etc., although here, too, a semivowel was lost. The Ukrainian diphthongization was brought forth by the simultaneous operation of two factors: the length of *ō*, *ē* and the loss of the semivowel in the next syllable. In physiological terms, we can picture it as follows. A semivowel in the process of disappearing always displays a tendency to become much closer or narrower, and this narrowing can be anticipated already at the beginning of the preceding syllable, but only if the vowel of the preceding syllable is not too close and not too open (thus, in *o*, *e* but not in *u*, *y*, *i*, *a*) and if for the linguistic consciousness the beginning and the end of the vowel articulation do not coincide, that is, if the vowel (*o*, *e*) is long.[9]

It follows that the Ukrainian and Southwest Russian diphthongization (breaking) took place simultaneously with the loss of semivowels, a chronology confirmed by the textual record. Since the breaking affected only long *ō*, *ē* while short *o*, *e* remained unchanged, the loss of semivowels in South Russian must have occurred at a time when the old quantitative distinctions still existed.

In Great Russian, we find a different state of affairs: *otca* 'of the father' and *bok* have the same *o* as *gorod*. Since we know from Ukrainian that *o* followed by an apocopated syllable remained unchanged only if it was short before apocope, we must assume that the loss of semivowels in North and East Russian did not take place until after the loss of the old quantitative distinctions. Therefore, the Common Russian loss of the old quantitative distinctions occurred in the period 1164–1282.

Thus, a whole series of phonetic features that separate Great Russian from the other two East Slavic languages is explained by the fact that the chronological difference between the Northeast Russian and Southwest Russian treatment of the semivowels prevented the spread of certain sound changes over the entire Old Russian language area. The period 1164–1282 was of great importance for the development of the East Slavic sound system. In this period fall (1) the Southwest Russian assimilation *n'j*, *t'j*, etc. > *n'n'*, *t't'*, etc.; (2) the Northeast Russian strengthening of weak vowels in the first syllable, namely, in word-initial position and after the group consonant + liquid; (3) the Northeast Russian change *yj*, *ij* > *ъj*, *ьj*; and (4) the Common Russian loss of quantitative distinctions. The following oppositions between Great Russian and the other East Slavic languages go back to these sound changes: (1) Great Russian *svin'ja* ~ Ukrainian *svyn'n'a*, Belorussian *svin'n'a*; (2a) Great Russian *igra* ~ Ukrainian and Belorussian *hra*; (2b) Great Russian *błoxa* ~ Ukrainian and Belorussian *błyxa*; (3) Great Russian *mòju*, *xudòj* 'bad,' *šèja*, *čej* 'whose' ~ Ukrainian and Belorussian *myju*, *xudyj*, *šyja*, *čyj*; and (4) Great Russian *bok*, *p'eč* ~ Ukrainian *bik*, *pič*, South Belorussian *buok*, *pieč*.

6

There is one other Great Russian feature whose origin must be dated to the same period: this is, Great Russian *ω*, which has recently been the subject of considerable discussion. The Great Russian dialects (northern as well as southern) that distinguish systematically between old *ě* and *e* also make the same distinction between two kinds of *o*, of which the one (*ω*) corresponds to Proto-Slavic acute *o*, the other (*o*) to Proto-Slavic short, or circumflected, *o* or to Old Great Russian *ъ*.[10] Since the distinction between *ě* and *e* existed at one time in all Great Russian dialects, the distinction between *ω* and *o* must have existed in them, too, and was only later abandoned in most of them, together with the distinction *ě* : *e*. For older Great Russian, we must set up forms such as *kωža* 'skin,' *pωpъ* 'priest,' *prωs'išь* '(you) ask' (sg.), *tωn'ešь* '(you) drown' (sg.), *zabωta* 'care' (n.).

How we imagine the origin of Great Russian *ω* depends on our idea of the Proto-Slavic system of accents; my view of this subject can be found in two articles [chaps. 19 and 20 in this volume]. I picture the origin of Great Russian *ω* in the following way. Proto-Slavic acute *o* was always long. In the Slavic languages under consideration, (*a*) the vowel *o* in Proto-Slavic *kőža* 'skin' is identical in quantity and accent with the vowel *i* in *lĩpa* 'linden tree' (Serbo-Croatian *kȍža-lĩpa*, Slovenian *kóža-lípa*, Czech *kůže-lípa*); (*b*) the same relation holds between the *o* of genitive singular *nārŏda* 'of the people' and the *a* of *lopáta* 'spade, shovel' (Serbo-Croatian *nárŏda-lòpăta*, Sloven. *naróda-lopáta*, Czech *nárŏda-lopăta*); (*c*) in Serbo-Croatian and Slovenian, the *o* in the first syllable of Proto-Slavic trisyllabic words like *mőžešь* 'you can' (sg.) and *xŏdišь* 'you walk' (sg.) has the same quantity and accent as the *a* of *jăgoda* 'berry' (Serbo-Croatian *mòžeš, hȍdiš–jàgoda*, Sloven. *móžeš, hódiš–jágoda*); and (*d*) the same relation holds in these languages also between the *o* of *bőbъ* 'bean' and the *a* of *răkъ* 'crayfish' (Serbo-Croatian *bȍb-ràk*, Sloven. *bòb-ràk*).[11] Besides acute long *o*, Proto-Slavic also had long *o* with circumflex: for example, *bōgъ* 'God,' *gōdъ* 'year,' *grōmъ* 'thunder,' *bōkъ* 'side,' etc. (Serbo-Croatian *Bôg, gôd, grôm, bôk,* etc.). I believe that in North and East Old Russian every long *o* acquired a diphthongal pronunciation, such that broken *o* sounded *o̧o* rather than *uo* (where *o̧* stands for close *o* and *o* for open *o*). This must have been the first step in the development of *ω*. According to my interpretation, Proto-Slavic "acute" and "circumflex" were both rising-falling accents, the only difference being that in the acute the first (rising) part was longer than the second (falling) one while in the circumflex it was shorter. I also believe that the boundaries of the two components of Old Great Russian broken *o̧o* coincided with the boundaries of the musical parts of the rising-falling accent: acute *ō* was *o̧ŏ*, circumflex *ō* was *ŏo* (*bo̧ŏbъ-bŏokъ*). The second step in the development of *ω* must have consisted in the qualitative assimilation of the shorter part of the diphthong *o̧o* to the longer part: acute *o̧ŏ* produced close *ǭ*, while circumflex *ŏo* produced open *o*. In this way, a qualitative opposition between acute and circumflex *o* arose, which later survived the abandonment of accentual and quantitative distinctions and resulted in the opposition *ω* : *o*.

The opposition between *ω* and *o* is foreign to Ukrainian, in which *koža* 'skin,' *prosyš* 'you ask,' *toneš* 'you drown,' and *zabota* 'care' have the same *o* as *vodu* 'water' (acc. sg.) and *mox* 'moss', and *pip* (dial. *pup, puop,* etc.) 'priest' has the same *i* as *bik* (dial. *buk, buok,* etc.) 'side.' This lack of a distinction between *ω* and *o* in Ukrainian (where, on the other hand, the distinction between *ě* and *e* is strictly observed) can be explained only by the assumption that the old accentual distinctions were lost in South Russian earlier than in North and East Russian and that, at the time when *o* was diphthongized to *o̦o* (*o̦ŏ, o̦o*) in Northeast Russian, quantitative distinctions had already been abandoned in South Russian. As we know, the loss of quantity did not take place in South Russian until after the transformation of the semivowels.

On the other hand, the two steps postulated above in the development of Great Russian *ω* ([1] *ō > o̦o;* [2] *o̦ŏ > ō, o̦ŏ > o̦*) presuppose quantitative and accentual distinctions in North and East Old Russian. We know that the quantitative distinctions were lost in Northeast Russian before the completion of the changes in the semivowels. Direct information on the time of the loss of accentual distinctions is lacking. But if we consider the general principle that languages with musical stress but without quantitative distinctions and languages with both free quantity and free expiratorial stress occur nowhere in the world, as far as I know,[12] we may safely assume that the loss of quantity occurred simultaneously with the replacement of musical stress by expiratorial stress.

It follows that (*a*) the development of Great Russian *ω* must be dated to the time between the completion of the South Russian and the Northeast Russian transformation of the semivowels (thus to the period 1164–1282) and (*b*) the replacement of the old musical accent by a purely expiratorial accent, which occurred simultaneously with the loss of quantitative distinctions, was completed earlier in the South of the East Slavic language area than in the North and East.

A special case is the history of *ω* in Belorussian. Scholars disagree on the origin of the diphthong *uo* occurring in certain Belorussian dialects: some (such as Karskij) would like to identify it with North Ukrainian *uo,* others (such as Lehr-Spławiński) with Great Russian *ω.* Perhaps both views are correct: this would fit well with the geographic position of Belorussian and its role as intermediary between Great Russian and Ukrainian. In my opinion, the oppositions Great Russian *bok* ~ North Ukrainian *buok* and Great Russian *kωža* ~ Ukrainian *koža* rest on chronological differences in the emergence of certain Common Russian sound changes: in Ukrainian the loss of accents and quantity occurred earlier than in Great Russian but after the changes in the semivowels, while in Great Russian this loss occurred later than in Ukrainian but before the changes in the semivowels. Both phenomena (the transformation of the semivowels and the loss of accents and quantity) spread from the Southwest to the Northeast, but not at the same speed: the loss of quantity and intonation spread faster than the changes in the semivowels. From the Northeast came the change *ŏ > ω. It took place at a time when neither the changes in the semivowels nor the loss of intonation and quantity had reached the Northeast, and it did not penetrate the extreme Southwest (the Old Ukrainian area) because both processes were already complete there. We do not know the situation in the transitional areas between North and South, that is, in the Old Belorussian area. It is possible that in some parts of this area at this time the transformation of the semivowels had been completed while the loss of accents and quantity had not yet begun: in such areas both *buok* and *kuoža* would have been possible.

7

In the two preceding sections, I have shown that all the important sound features separating Great Russian from the other East Slavic languages arose in the period 1164–1282.

The sound features that separate Ukrainian from the other East Slavic languages are the result of a single sound change, namely, the hardening (depalatalization) of soft consonants before syllabic front vowels. This sound change caused the merger of *y* and *i* (more precisely, the change of *i* to *y*); it also prevented the penetration of the change *e > o* into Ukrainian territory (as Šaxmatov assumed) and made the merger of *ě* with *e* in Ukrainian impossible (as Lehr-Spławiński correctly saw). As far as the nature of this Ukrainian hardening is concerned, I see no reason to accept the complicated interpretation suggested by Šaxmatov and endorsed by Lehr-Spławiński and Vondrák. The phenomenon in question is a timbre dissimilation, something that one can often observe with palatalized and labialized consonants in various languages: for palatalized consonants compare, for instance, Bulgarian, where in most eastern dialects soft consonants are weakly palatalized or even hard before *i* and *e*, whereas they remain soft before back vowels (and before *a* from *ě*); for labialized consonants we may compare the essentially identical loss of labialization in the labiovelars before and after labialized vowels (especially *u*) in most Indo-European *centum* languages.

Since Old Russian orthography possesses no means of indicating soft and hard consonants before front vowels, it is impossible to establish the date of the Ukrainian depalatalization on the basis of the textual record. Yet we can reconstruct the chronology of this exceptionally important change, which determines the whole character of Ukrainian phonetics. Soft consonants in Ukrainian preserve their softness before lost ь but become hard before ь that has become *e:* compare, for example, Ukrainian *den'* 'day' with hard *d* and soft *n'* from **d'ьn'ь*, etc. It follows that the hardening took place after the completion of the South Russian transformation of the semivowels. On the other hand, the consonants have remained soft before *e* in Ukrainian *žyt't'e* 'life,' *bil'l'e* 'past time,' *znan'n'e* 'knowledge,' *pol'is's'e* 'lowlands,' so the hardening preceded the South Russian assimilation of *t'j, l'j, n'j, s'j* to *t't', l'l', n'n', s's',* which, as we know, antedates the Northeast Russian transformation of the semivowels. Consequently, the Ukrainian hardening must have occurred in the first half of the period 1164–1282. This seems to have been the only sound change of this period that for no apparent reason failed to spread past the borders of South Russian (Old Ukrainian).

Thus, toward the end of the period 1164–1282, the Russian language area was already divided into the same major dialects as today. Great Russian distinguished itself from the other East Slavic languages by forms like *s'v'in'ja, im'ět', móju, čej, bok, p'eč, kωža,* while within Great Russian the distinction between the North with plosive *g* and the South with spirant *γ* still remained. Ukrainian had hard consonants before *e.* Belorussian shared with Ukrainian forms like *znan'n'e, hra, błyxa, myju* (dial. also *buok, pieč,* perhaps also *koža*) and with Great Russian soft consonants before *e* and dialectally perhaps also forms like *kωža.* Since most of these features were the product of chronological differences in the emergence of Common Russian sound changes in different parts of the Russian language area, the geographic boundaries of the individual features must have been indeterminate and fluid even then. In the course of time, these boundaries shifted again and again, so that the modern situation is no reliable guide for details of the older period. In principle, however, transitional dialects must have existed in border areas from the beginning, just as they do today.

8

If we consider the sound changes of the period 1164–1282 from the point of view of the comparative phonetics of all Slavic languages, the following observations can be made.

We have seen that the character of the Great Russian sound system and its deviation from the other East Slavic languages were caused by the fact that two Common Russian sound changes of the period 1164–1282, namely, the loss of quantity and accents and the transformation of the semivowels, spread over the East Slavic area relatively slowly. Also, the change *ky (gy, γy, xy) > k'i* (*g'i* etc.) was complete in the South by about the middle of the twelfth century but did not reach the North until the second half of the thirteenth century.[13] The period 1164–1282 is thus characterized by three Common Russian sound changes that gradually spread from the Southwest over the entire Russian language area. Let us examine them more closely.

The loss of the weak semivowels, together with the change of strong ъ, ь (which were originally *high-wide* in English phonetic terminology) to normal vowels of middle height (*midback* and *midfront* in English terminology), is a phenomenon common to all the Slavic languages. It took place first among the South Slavs (among the Slovenians perhaps already in the tenth century) and then spread northward over the entire Slavic area; the North and East Russians seem to have resisted it the longest.

The replacement of the old accents by expiratorial stress is also common to all the Slavic languages except Serbo-Croatian and Slovenian. Where the expiratorial stress is fixed, the quantitative distinctions remain (Czech, Slovak, Old Polish); where it assumes the position the musical stress had held, the old quantitative distinctions are lost (Russian, Bulgarian). Incidentally, the tendency to eliminate quantitative distinctions is found even in languages with fixed expiratorial stress (Modern Polish, Sorbian, certain Czech, Slovak, and Macedonian dialects). Thus, the loss of accents and quantity may also be regarded as a sound change linking Russian with other Slavic languages.

Finally, the change $ky > k'i$ is known also in other Slavic languages: we find it in the Lekhitic languages and in Sorbian.

Consequently, all three of the Common Russian sound changes that spread from the Southwest to the Northeast in the period 1164–1282 are attested in the neighboring Slavic languages. The circumstance that all of them appear in the Southwest and spread from there is explained by the fact that the Russian language area touches the areas of other Slavic languages only in the Southwest and West.

The sound changes that arise at the same time in the Northeast of the Russian language area and whose spread is hindered by the aforementioned sound changes (moving in the opposite direction) are of a completely different nature. The strengthening of weak semivowels after the word-initial combination consonant + liquid occurs only in certain Kashubian dialects. Nor is the change $yj, ij > ьj, ьj$ known in the other Slavic languages. And the qualitative differentiation of $ō > o$ and $ő > ω$ hardly has analogues outside Russia.

Unlike the more or less pan-Slavic sound changes spreading from the Southwest, those originating in the Northeast have a decidedly individual character. The external, geographic opposition finds its counterpart in an inner opposition of evolutionary tendencies. The history of sounds in this period is dominated by the struggle between the conservative Southwest, steeped in the Slavic spirit and clinging to Slavic forms of development, and the Northeast, hostile to pan-Slavic traditions and passionately seeking its own identity.[14] It was this struggle that caused the collapse and disintegration of the Common Russian linguistic unity.

Externally, the development of sounds in the period treated here is distinguished from that in the preliterary period by the rise of different geographic oppositions: earlier, only the northern part of the Russian language area (gravitating to Novgorod and the Baltic) was opposed to all the rest; now the East, too, goes hand in hand with the North. However, the division of roles remains the same as before: the area bordering on other Slavic languages is still a bearer of Slavic evolutionary tendencies, an intermediary between the Russians and the rest of the Slavic world, whereas the part of the Russian linguistic community isolated from other Slavic areas strives to take its own independent path—and, indeed, there is no longer any trace of the influence of non-Slavic languages that we observed in the preceding period. This, of course, has to do with the fact that the area dominated by evolutionary tendencies that we may call *separatist* from the Slavic viewpoint has expanded in this new period and is no longer bound to the Baltic.

9

We have seen that Common Russian, formerly more or less homogeneous, fell into three great dialect groups, Ukrainian, Belorussian, and Great Russian, of which the last split further into North and South Great Russian,[15] in the period 1164–1282.

This process also signified a disintegration of the finer dialect distinctions within East Slavic. None of the isoglosses of later sound changes coincides exactly with the boundaries of the four dialect groups mentioned above (Ukrainian, Belorussian, and North and South Great Russian): either the sound change extends beyond the borders of the language area in question, or parts of the area remain unaffected by it. In principle, each sound change has its own isogloss.

The thirteenth-century hardening (depalatalization) of *š, ž* covers Great Russian, Belorussian, and most of Ukrainian, but certain Ukrainian dialects are not subject to it. The hardening of *č* that took place about the same time covers Belorussian and a large part, although not the whole, of Ukrainian. The hardening of *c,* probably simultaneous with the others, covers South Great Russian, Belorussian, and certain Ukrainian dialects but leaves most of the Ukrainian area unaffected. So the process covers the entire Belorussian area, but on Ukrainian and Great Russian territory the isoglosses of the hardening of each individual sound (*š, ž, č, c*) are different.

"Broken" *e* and *o* (*ě, ω, ie, uo*), regardless of origin, are contracted to monophthongal *e, o* in most Belorussian, North and South Great Russian dialects, but the contraction takes place earlier in some dialects than in others and does not reach all Belorussian, North and South Great Russian dialects. (This contraction began in certain dialects already in the thirteenth century, but in most others much later.) Nor are $\widehat{ie}$ and $\widehat{uo}$ treated in a uniform way in Ukrainian dialects.

The hardening of r' covers Belorussian and parts of South Great Russian and Ukrainian; the assibilation of t', d' to c', dz' crosses the southern border of the Belorussian area proper; the change of syllable-final ł to ų covers Belorussian and Ukrainian and certain South Great Russian dialects (the same phenomenon arose independently in certain North Great Russian dialects).

The so-called *akan'e,* or, better, the reduction of the number of vowels in unstressed syllables, is certainly no older than the end of the thirteenth century.[16] This phenomenon consists of a series of individual changes, of which the most important are the following: (1) the monophthongization of unstressed $\widehat{ie}$, $\widehat{uo}$ to e, o (thus, the merger of ě with e and South Belorussian uo with o in unstressed syllables); (2) the delabialization of unstressed o and its merger with unstressed a, resulting in ɒ (midback-wide-unround); (3) the change of unstressed a (or ɒ) to e after soft consonants; (4) the raising of the unstressed vowels e, ɒ, o to ẹ (or ɛ), ɒ̣ (or α), ọ; and (5) the lowering of unstressed ɛ, α (or ẹ, ɒ̣) to a in positions varying from dialect to dialect. These changes cover the entire South Great Russian and Belorussian area and certain North Ukrainian dialects, but only their southern boundaries more or less coincide (with the exception, perhaps, of the southern boundary of the raising of unstressed vowels, which extends somewhat further into Ukrainian territory). Their northern boundaries are independent of one another: changes 1, 3, and 4 occur also in some purely North Great Russian dialects, and the so-called Central Great Russian dialects combine all five changes with the unambiguously North Great Russian plosive g. In details, even the individual South Great Russian and Belorussian dialects vary significantly, and therefore the *akan'e* constitutes neither conceptually nor geographically a uniform whole.

From our survey of the sound changes that took place in the East Slavic languages (Ukrainian, Belorussian, North and South Great Russian) after the disintegration of the Common Russian language in the period 1164–1282, it is evident that, with respect to its further phonetic development, none of these languages can be considered as a closed, self-sufficient entity. Each of the languages that arose through the disintegration of the Common Russian linguistic unity represents a group of dialects sharing certain common features but also participating in sound changes together with dialects of other groups.

Theoretically, therefore, it would not have been impossible for a sound change to spread over the entire East Slavic language area even after 1282. With the hardening of š, ž this came close to happening. There is a further sound change that left no Slavic dialect untouched, even though its spread for the most part falls in the period after 1282: this is the development of prothetic v before initial broken o (uo, ω).

The conditions of this change may be seen most clearly in Ukrainian. Here, prothetic *v* develops before every initial **uo* (> *i*): *vid* (= Gr. Russ. *ot*") 'from,' *vit'ca* (= Gr. Russ. *ot'ca*) 'of the father' (g. sg.), *vin* (= Gr. Russ. *on*") 'he,' *viv'ca* (= Gr. Russ. *ov'ca*) 'sheep,' *vis'* (= Gr. Russ. *os'*) 'axis,' *vil'xa* (= Gr. Russ. *ol'xa*) 'alder,' etc. Where this *v* stands before *o*, this is easily explained by the influence of related forms with **uo*: for example, *vona* 'she,' *vono* 'it' (nt.) under the influence of *vin*.

In Great Russian, the individual dialects vary considerably with respect to prothetic *v*. However, if we compare all dialectal and standard forms with prothetic *v* before *o*, we will notice that this *v* always stands before old initial *ω*, which is still preserved dialectally: standard and colloquial *vòsem'* (dial. *vωs'em*), Proto-Slavic *ŏsmь* (g. *osmì*) 'eight' must have had acute *ŏ* according to the same rule as *bŏbъ* (g. *bobà*) 'bean'; standard *vòbla* (a kind of fish), *vòtčina* 'patrimony,' dialectal *vòspa* 'smallpox' (in almost all dialects; in the eighteenth century also in the standard language), *vòl'xa* 'alder,' *vòbža* 'measure of land, shaft of a plow' must have had *ω* since *a*-stems with root stress always had the acute in root syllables; dialectal (almost universal) *vòstryi* 'sharp' (attested also as *vωstroi*) must have had *ω* according to the same rule as *gωlyi* 'naked' (**gołŏ* : **gŏłyjь* :: **ostrŏ* : **ŏstryjь* 'sharp'); standard and colloquial *votъ* 'here!' from *otъ̀* < *otò* with stress shifted to the first syllable, which had to produce **ŏtъ*, etc. On the other hand, we never find prothetic *v* in words with Proto-Slavic (or Proto-Russian) initial short or circumflected *o* (Old Great Russian *o*, not *ω*): *os'* 'axis' (**ŏs'ъ*, g. *ŏs'i*), *on*" 'he' (**ōnъ*, nt. *ŏno* 'it'; cf. *vo vrèmia ŏno* 'long ago, in days of yore'; the form *onò* has been influenced by the f. *onà* 'she'), *ŏlovo* 'tin,' *ŏzero* 'lake,' *ŏsen'* 'autumn,' *otèc"* 'father,' *osìna* 'aspen,' *odìn"* 'one' (m.), *odnà* 'one' (f.), etc. have been attested in Great Russian dialects only without *v-*.

It may be considered certain that the Great Russian *v* prothesis regularly occurred only before initial *ω*.[17] The cases in which *v* stands before unstressed *o* are explained by the influence of related forms with *ω*: thus, for instance, standard and colloquial *vos'mòi* 'eighth,' *vos'mì* 'eight' (g.) under the influence of *vòsem'* 'eight' (nom.),[18] likewise dialectal *vostrò* 'sharply,' *vostrit'* (in the language of educated people only in the facetious idiom *navostrìt' lyži*, lit. 'sharpen one's skis,' i.e., 'prepare to flee')[19] under the influence of *vòstryi* 'sharp.' It is more difficult to explain the lack of *v* before initial *ω* in some cases. Standard and colloquial *òstryi* 'sharp' (in addition to dial. *vωstroi*) can be attributed to the influence of *ostrò* 'sharply'; *òtčina*, dialectal *ωtčina* 'patrimony' (in addition to *vòtčina*, the form in the standard language) can have arisen under the influence of *otèc"* 'father,' *otčìzna* 'native land,' *òtče* 'father' (voc.); the varying stress in the word for 'alder' explains the fact that in addition to *ol'xà* and dialectal *vol'xà* a compromise dialectal form *òl'xa* has been attested. But for *òspa* (in addition to *vòspa*) 'smallpox' and *òbža* (in addition to *vòbža*) 'measure of land, shaft of a plow' such an explanation is impossible because no related forms with unstressed *o* exist. The explanation is provided by a passage in the *Second Sofia Chronicle:* under the year 6986 we read in one and the same sentence *7 sotъ obežь . . . 20 (dvadesjatь) obežь* '700 measures . . . twenty measures' and immediately thereafter *pol" 300 sta vobež' i tri vobži* '150 measures and three measures'; thus, we have *vω-* after words ending in a vowel (*trista* '300,' *tri* 'three') and *ω-* after words ending in a consonant (*sot, dvadesjatь*).[20]

Originally, the insertion of *v* must have been due to external sandhi. The words beginning with *ω* appeared in two forms (with and without *v*), according to whether the preceding word ended in a vowel or a consonant; in time, the rule was neglected and forgotten, and the *vω-* and *ω-*forms were used interchangeably until finally the one or the other was generalized, which occurred for each word and each dialect independently. The important thing about the *v* prothesis is that it developed regularly only before *ω* (i.e., *u͡o*) in Great Russian as well.

For Belorussian, we lack exhaustive collections of material. Prothetic *v* sometimes appears in various Belorussian dialects where we would expect *ω* in Great Russian (e.g., *vòstryj* 'sharp,' *vòspa* 'smallpox,' *vòkna* 'windows'), sometimes where we may reconstruct *uo* in Old Ukrainian (e.g., in the word for 'louse': *vos', vòu̯cy, vojcú*), which is understandable in the light of what was said above about the two possible origins of Old Belorussian **u͡o*. Unfortunately, given the present state of research, it is impossible to determine the frequency and geographic distribution of these forms on Belorussian territory. In any case, the Belorussian material does not contradict the principle that the *v-* prothesis appeared in all East Slavic languages systematically before old broken *o* (*uo, ω*).[21]

The oldest Ukrainian attestations of the *v-* prothesis (*jęko vovьcę* 'as a sheep,' *Galician Gospel Book* of 1266) go back to the second half of the thirteenth century, the oldest Great Russian attestations only to the fourteenth. We are thus dealing, as before, with a sound change that spread from the Southwest over the entire East Slavic language area. This seems, however, to have been the last Common Russian sound change: it arose in the period 1164–1282, but its spread took place only much later.

If we compare this last pan-Russian sound change—the only one that spread across the whole East Slavic language area after 1282—with the pan-Russian sound changes of the period 1164–1282, we immediately notice the difference in the consequences for the rest of the system. The loss of accents and quantity altered the system fundamentally; the change *ky > k'i* introduced new sounds into it (*k', g', γ', x'*)[22] and the transformation of the semivowels eliminated old ъ and ь. But the *v*-prothesis created nothing essentially new, for *v* already existed in the sound system of Russian.

After the loss of accents and quantity, every word—and, after the changes in the semivowels, most words—acquired a different pronunciation, or at least they were perceived differently; the change *ky, gy, xy* > *k'i, g'i, x'i* also affected numerous words.[23] In contrast, the prothetic *v* was a marginal phenomenon: as noted above, it occurred originally only after words ending in a vowel. If we also take into consideration that the most important changes of the period after 1282 (e.g., individual instances of the reduction of vowels in unstressed syllables, the elimination of *ě* and *ω*, and the hardening of *r', c, č, š, ž*) affected not all East Slavic but only limited areas, we will realize that the comparatively small structural significance of the only Common Russian sound change of this period (the *v*-prothesis) is the norm rather than an exception. After the conclusion of the Common Russian sound changes of the period 1164–1282, fundamental changes no longer had the strength to spread over the entire East Slavic language area. And this inability of the dialects of a language to undergo significant sound changes collectively indicates that their unity has dissolved.

10

We have now traced the development of Russian sounds from the emergence of the oldest dialectal distinctions to the conclusion of the last Common Russian sound change. The southwestern and western parts of the East Slavic language area, which border on other Slavic languages, early on adopted various sound changes from their neighbors; these changes spread from the Southwest and West over the remainder of the language area, meeting strong resistance from more isolated regions along the way. In the oldest period (the beginning of which probably extends back into Late Proto-Slavic times), the part of East Slavic that resisted the southwestern sound changes was geographically very limited, but it gradually increased, and the changes proceeded at a slow pace. This is how new dialectal distinctions arose, and, since all the sound changes spread in roughly the same directions, the dialectal distinctions acquired roughly the same geographic distribution.

Even when a sound change succeeded in overcoming the resistance of all parts of the language area, the dialectal distinctions created by the slow pace of the spread remained. As the number of distinctions grew, the linguistic unity became differentiated to such an extent that finally no significant sound change had the strength to spread over the entire language area. This situation was quite different from the old one: before, each sound change strove to cover as much territory as possible, stopping only when it reached a dialect that either had not yet acquired or had already eliminated the phonetic conditions it needed; now, the individual changes stalled without inner motivation, simply from the lack of strength to expand. From now on, dialect distinctions were created not only by the slow pace of the spread but also by the fact that each sound change was circumscribed in its geographic range and faded out in different parts of the language area for no apparent reason. The collective evolution of the sounds of the linguistic whole came to an end; the sole subject of linguistic development was now the individual dialect. This was the disintegration of the linguistic unity.

The picture of the development of Russian sounds sketched above leads also to conclusions of a general, methodological nature. A slow-moving change that eventually covers an entire language area can produce greater dialect differences than a local change that spreads to only limited areas. Therefore, it is important to consider the speed and direction of spread even of gradual changes.

Further, I have shown that the Russian linguistic unity did not split first into three or four daughter groups but dissolved directly into an indeterminate mass of dialects. No homogeneous "Proto-Great-Russian" ever existed because the characteristics that distinguish North from South Great Russian are much older than the so-called Common Great Russian features. The distinctive character of the Ukrainian sound system arose in the first half of the period 1164–1282, that is, before the Common Russian linguistic unity ceased to exist: Proto-Ukrainian is older than the disintegration. Moreover, the disintegration of the Russian linguistic unity coincides with the end of the transformation of the semivowels, the last sound change common to all Slavic languages, so we may say that Russian participated in Common Slavic sound changes as long as the individual East Slavic dialects were able to undergo Common Slavic sound changes collectively. It follows that the end of a daughter language community is not necessarily younger than the end of a mother language community.

18. On the Chronology of Some Common Slavic Sound Changes

Common Slavic is not a language that was spoken during a narrowly defined historical epoch; it represents a long period of development that began when a certain group of Indo-European speakers, whom we designate as Proto-Slavic, found itself separated from neighboring groups (Proto-Iranian, Proto-Baltic, Proto-Germanic, etc.) by the first isoglosses. It is impossible to date this event precisely. However, Proto-Slavic shares certain sound changes with Indo-Iranian (such as the change of *s* to *š* after *i, u, k, r*), while lacking others that are older (such as *ə* > *i, l* > *r*), so it is clear that by the time Indo-Iranian emerged as an independent language—around 1500 B.C. at the latest, to judge by the inscriptions of the kings of Mitanni—Proto-Slavic must already have had an inventory of features distinct from that of any other Indo-European dialect.

The Common Slavic period ended when the Slavic languages stopped participating in changes as a group. The last common change seems to have been the loss of the weak *jer's*, which occurred in all the Slavic languages under almost identical conditions between the tenth and the twelfth centuries A.D.; this is the terminus ad quem of Common Slavic. So the development of Common Slavic stretches across at least two millennia and a half—a period no shorter than that separating Modern Greek from the language of Homer or present-day French from the oldest Latin inscriptions. Since in the course of this development the phonetic and morphological systems of Common Slavic must have been reorganized from top to bottom several times, reconstructing Common Slavic is a matter not of identifying one single phonetic or morphological system but of discovering the chronology according to which different systems were superimposed one on the other: a dynamic scheme, not a static tableau.

The development may be divided into three periods: First is the *Proto-Slavic* period, during which Common Slavic was an Indo-European dialect still maintaining close relations with the other neighboring dialects. Most of the changes of this period are shared by Proto-Slavic with certain other Indo-European dialects; only the catalog of changes as a whole sets Common Slavic apart.[1] Second is the period of *independent unity,* during which Common Slavic was independent of all other Indo-European languages but did not yet comprise distinct dialects. Third is the period of *dialectal differentiation,* during which dialect groups formed within Common Slavic. Some changes of this period affected all of Slavic; others failed to extend beyond the borders of individual dialects. The period could be subdivided into two parts: in the first, dialectal changes were less numerous than common ones, while, in the second, the reverse was true.

Almost all the changes of the Proto-Slavic period are shared by other Indo-European dialects, and they will not be examined here as the discussion would necessarily involve questions of general Indo-European linguistics. In what follows, I will try to establish the chronological order of certain sound changes of the "period of independent unity."[2]

1

One of the oldest phenomena of the period of independent unity was the change of *a* to *o*. Kretschmer's (1905) view that this change is later than the first contacts between the Slavs and the Greeks has been disproved by Vasmer (1907, 157ff.). Greek *o* was a tense vowel, quite different from the nontense, open *o* of Common Slavic. What struck the Greeks about the Slavic phonetic system was the degree of openness of its vowels, and they exaggerated this impression by rendering Slavic *o* by their own *a*. Endzelins's (1911, 107) objections can be refuted by the fact that Lithuanian renders Slavic *o* by *a* even in loanwords of very recent date (Lith. *mada* < Pol. *moda* 'mode, fashion'). The same exaggeration of the wideness of Slavic *o* may also explain the *a* of West Finnic *pappu* 'broad bean' (= Slav. **bobŭ*), *akkuna* 'window' (= Slav. **okŭno*), *palttina* 'linen cloth' (= Slav. **poltĭno*), etc.[3] In any case, it is notable that the oldest loanwords contain Finnish *u* for final Slavic **-u*, at least after voiced consonants:[4] Finnish *papu* (= *bobъ* 'broad bean'), *laatu* (= *ladъ* '[good] order'), *turku* (= *tъrgъ* 'market'). This **-ŭ* from **-on* (and **-os?*) is definitely more recent than the change of **a* to **o*: the Slavic prototype of Finnish *papu* can only have been **bobŭ*, not **babas*. So there is no reason to believe that the change of *a* to *o* followed the first contacts of the Slavs with the Greeks and the Finns. On the contrary, it must have predated the appearance of the Slavs on the stage of history and occurred at the beginning of the period of independent unity.

The only difference between Proto-Slavic *a* and *ā* was length. Since the change from *a* to *o* was a purely qualitative one, it must have affected *ā* as well as *a*. In the historical period, the reflex of Indo-European **ā* in Slavic is *ā* (OCS *mati* = Lat. *māter* 'mother'), but this same Slavic *ā* also represents old **ō*: not only Indo-European **ō* (OCS *darъ* = Greek δῶρον 'gift') but also the **ō* in the combinations **tōrt, *tōlt* from **tort, *tolt* in certain Common Slavic dialects (OCS *strana, glava*; cf. Pol. *strona* 'country, land,' *głowa* 'head'). So there is no reason not to assume that **ā* changed to **ō* at the beginning of the period of independent unity, after which every *ō changed to *ā in the period of dialectal differentiation. General considerations support this conclusion, too. Numerous languages change ā to ō without changing ă to ŏ (Common Germanic, Albanian, Lithuanian, certain Iranian and Polish dialects, to cite only Indo-European languages); others change every a to o in certain positions without regard to distinctions of length (e.g., certain High German dialects). But one would be hard put to name a language that changed ă to ŏ without changing ā to ō.

The early parallel changes of *ă to *ŏ and *ā to *ō reshaped the Slavic vowel system in a remarkable way. Two vowel series were created: the palatal series, comprising nonlabialized palatal vowels (e, ē, ĭ, ī), and the labiovelar series, comprising *only labialized* velar vowels (o, ō, ŭ, ū). This structure was the point of departure for the entire phonetic development of the period of independent unity, and some sound changes can be understood only with reference to it.

2

The vowels o and ŭ became e and ĭ when they were preceded by j or a palatalized consonant. Meillet (1896, 137ff.) has shown most convincingly that *ō also changed to *ē under the same conditions: only later did this *ē become ā, as did all ē's preceded by j or a palatalized consonant. Further, *ū became ī, again under the same conditions (OCS šiti < *sjūtei 'sew').

One is tempted to suggest the following rule: All labiovelar vowels lost their labialization and became palatal when preceded by j or a palatalized consonant. But it would have numerous exceptions if formulated in this way. For one thing, Common Slavic *ǫ, which was a labialized velar vowel, seems to have preserved its labialization and its velar articulation even after j and palatalized consonants. This exception is sometimes dealt with by supposing that *on[t] became *ǫ[t] before the aforementioned change set in. Yet such an "explanation" explains nothing. If one considers the movement of the tongue from the palatal to the velar position as being opposed to the movement of the lips from a retracted to a protruding, rounded position, then the change in question would have had the function of eliminating the evidently inconvenient simultaneous combination of two opposite movements. How could the lowering of the velum in the denasalization of *on[t] to *ǫ[t] make this combination more convenient? Moreover, the change was circumvented not only by *ǫ but also by u from ou, for example, in the dative singular Old Church Slavonic konju 'horse, stallion', etc.

To explain these two exceptions, we must first define more precisely the value of ǫ and u in forms such as veljǫ '(I) command' and konju. The Glagolitic alphabet possessed special characters for *ju* and *jǫ* that cannot be traced back to ligatures for *j* + *u* and *j* + *ǫ*. Certain Old Church Slavonic and Old Russian texts systematically use the character *ju* after *č, š, ž,* and *c,* even though their palatalization did not have to be indicated by any special sign since they were always palatalized. This circumstance led Fortunatov and Šaxmatov to the conclusion that *ju* and *jǫ* differed from simplex *u* and *ǫ* not only in their "iotation" but also in their timbre, which would have been something like *iü* and *iǫ̈* (Šaxmatov 1915, 9, 10, 12).

It follows that *u* and *ǫ* did not completely withstand the influence of palatalized consonants: they remained labialized but acquired palatalization. In this respect, the sound law formulated above must be emended: after *j* or a palatalized consonant, all velar vowels became palatal, but, in becoming palatal, some of them lost their labialization, while others did not.

It would seem natural to suppose that labialization was preserved or lost depending on how strong it had been in the vowels in question. And, in fact, *o, ō,* and *ŭ,* which all lose their labial character in becoming palatalized (**xvōljŭši* [f. nom. sg. active past part.] > *xvaljьši* 'praised,' **konjō* [nom. dual] > **konje* > *konja* 'stallions, horses,' **poljo* > *polje* 'field'), were lax vowels with weak labialization, as is proved for **ō* by its change to *ā,* for *ŭ* by its change to *e, ъ,* and *a* in certain Slavic languages, and for *o* by the fact that the Greeks took it for *a*. As the first element in the diphthong **ou,* on the other hand, *o* must have been more tense and thus more strongly labialized than in any other position: the change of *o* to *ǫ* before *u* has numerous parallels (e.g., Russ. *pǫ́ uxu* 'on the ear' in contrast to *pó mъstu* 'along the bridge'). The same tense and strongly labialized articulation may be assumed for *o* in the group **on* since this nasal diphthong eventually changed to *u* in one part of Slavic territory and to nasalized *ъ* (< *ŭ*) in the rest. The narrowing of open vowels (*e, o* > *ę, ǫ, i, u*) before a nasal is known from many languages (Celtic, Common Germanic, Cypriot, Romanian, Armenian, to cite only Indo-European examples). We have seen that **ou* and **on* preserved their labialization when they were palatalized: for example, **koljǫntĭ* (3d p. pl.) > **koljöntĭ* (> Russ. *koljut'*) 'cut, chop,' **poljou* (dat. sg.) > **poljöü* > **poljü* (Russ. *polju*) 'field.'

Only **ū* poses problems, for it must have been tense and strongly labialized since the beginning of Common Slavic and nevertheless lost its labialization in becoming palatalized: for example, **sjūtei* (inf.) > Old Church Slavonic *šiti*. But this is only an apparent exception. In all other positions, **ū* became *ȳ* in Common Slavic. This change can be grouped together with the change of **ō* to *ā* under a common heading: *delabialization of long vowels.* If we assume that at a certain period the long labialized vowels lost their labialization, then at a still earlier period **ū* can have become **ǖ* when preceded by *j* or a palatalized consonant; later, this **ǖ* became *ī,* sharing the fate of all long labialized vowels.

It remains to examine the development of the group *-*jons* in word-final position. Although *-*ons* became $\bar{y}$ in all the Slavic languages (e.g., the accusative plurals *nosy* 'noses,' *ženy* 'wives'), when preceded by *j* or a palatalized consonant, it became *-*ę* in South Slavic and *-*ě* in the other languages (e.g., the accusative plurals OCS *konję*, Slovak *duše* 'souls,' *kl'úče* 'keys,' ORuss. *koně*, Ukr. *konji*). Very early on, *n* before final *s* must have undergone a quantitative and articulatory reduction that triggered the lengthening of the preceding vowel: *-*ons* became *-*ō^{n}s*. (Nasals tend to be reduced before *s*, and especially final *s*, in many languages: suffice it to mention Greek and Latin.) If it is true that *ŏ* was tense (close) before a nasal not followed by a vowel (see above), it is also true for its long counterpart *ō* in the group *-*ō^{n}s*. In accordance with my formula, every long tense *$\underset{.}{ō}$ had to become *$\underset{.}{\bar{ō}}$ after palatalized consonants. Later, in the period of delabialization of long vowels, *$\underset{.}{\bar{o}}{}^n$ became *$\bar{e}^n$, which yielded *ę* in South Slavic and—with loss of the final nasal—*ě* in the other Slavic languages. Since this *ě* is retained after palatalized consonants (ORuss. g. sg. *dušě* = OCS *dušę* 'soul'), the delabialization of long vowels must have occurred after the change of *jē* to *jā*.[5]

In the group *-*ō^{n}s* not preceded by *j* or a palatalized consonant, *$\underset{.}{ō}$ should have become *$\underset{.}{v}$ after delabialization, yet we find *-$\bar{y}$ instead. The delabialization of *-$\bar{u}$ also yields *-$\bar{y}$ instead of *α. Evidently, the nonlabialized, nontense velar vowels (v, α) were relatively unstable and tended to merge as they approached the central ("mixed") series.

Thus, the development of Slavic vowels during the period of independent unity comprises three steps: (1) the change of *a, ā* to *o, ō*, resulting in a system of two vocalic series (labiovelar: *ō, o, ū, ŭ;* palatal: *ē, e, ī, ĭ*); (2) the change of *o, ō* to *$\underset{.}{o}$, $\underset{.}{ō}$ before tautosyllabic *u* or *n*; (3) the law of palatalization: All velar vowels become palatal after *j* or a palatalized consonant, the tense vowels retaining their labialization ($\bar{u} > \ddot{\bar{u}}$, $\underset{.}{ō} > \underset{.}{\bar{o}}$, $\underset{.}{o} > \ddot{o}$) and the nontense ones losing it ($\ddot{u} > \ddot{\i}$, $o >$ *e, ō > ē*). In this way, the earlier system of two vocalic series was supplemented by a new series of palatal labialized vowels ($\ddot{\bar{u}}$, $\underset{.}{\bar{o}}$, $\ddot{o}$), always tense and always preceded by phonemes with *i*-timbre.

The other changes mentioned above belong to the period of dialectal differentiation: (1) the loss of the reduced final nasal, which occurred in Proto-Russian and Proto–West Slavic after all long vowels ($\bar{\i}$, $\bar{y}$, $\bar{e}$) and in Proto–South Slavic only after the close vowels ($\bar{\i}$, $\bar{y}$): accusative plural *pǫti* 'roads, paths,' *syny* 'sons,' *raby* 'slaves'; (2) the change of *ē* to *ā* after *j* or a palatalized consonant; (3) the delabialization of long vowels: *ō > ā;* $\underset{.}{ō}$, $\bar{u} > \bar{y}$; $\underset{.}{\bar{o}} > \bar{e}$; $\ddot{\bar{u}} > \bar{\i}$. The latter two changes led to the appearance of nonlabialized velar vowels ($\bar{a}$, $\bar{y}$), which dealt the final blow to the vowel system that had been established at the beginning of the period of independent unity. The contraction of diphthongs ($\underset{.}{o}u > \bar{u}$, $\ddot{o}\ddot{u} > \ddot{\bar{u}}$, *ei > ī*) and the emergence of nasalized vowels ($\underset{.}{o}$, $\ddot{o}$, $\underset{.}{e}$) belong to a still more recent period.

Baudouin de Courtenay (1893, 1894) thought that the Slavic gutturals *k, g, x* were palatalized after *ĭ, ī, n̦ⁱ, r̦ⁱ, l̦ⁱ* whenever they preceded a stressed vowel. This theory is supported by such forms as *licé* versus *likъ* 'face' (g. *líka*) and *po-dvidzáti* versus *dvígati* 'move.' But there are also counterexamples, such as *zájęcь* 'hare' and *kъnędzь* 'prince,' on the one hand, and *kъnęgýnji* 'princess,' on the other, and this may be the reason why Baudouin de Courtenay's conclusion did not meet with general acceptance. He seems to have been led astray by the striking oppositions of the type *dvidzáti – dvígati* and failed to pay sufficient attention to evidence that contradicted his generalization. A review of the problem is thus in order.

First of all, the cases in which Slavic has the palatalized gutturals *c', dz', s'* before unstressed vowels cannot all be explained by stress shifts or analogy, as Baudouin de Courtenay proposes. Explanations of this type would be plausible in two cases in which the stressed vowel immediately precedes the palatalized guttural: *kъnędzь* and *vodíca* 'water.' Common Slavic *kъnędzь* is a Germanic word (**kuniŋgs*) and thus had initial stress (**kŭnĭŋgŭ*); it was only because of the general rule prohibiting stress on the weak *jer* that the stress was shifted to the second syllable. Feminine words in *-íca* owe their *c* to analogy: *vodíca* (vs. *vodá*) was created on the model of *rýbica* 'fish' : *rýba;* cf. also *bolьníca* 'hospital' : *bolьná* 'sick' (f.) = *žítьnica* 'granary' : **žítьna, učeníca* 'female pupil' : *učeníkъ* 'male pupil' = *mǫ̑čenica* 'female martyr' : *mǫ̑čenikъ* 'male martyr.' The plant names in *-íka* (Russ. *golubíka* 'large blueberry,' *eževíka* 'blackberry,' *gvozdíka* 'carnation,' *černíka* 'blueberry,' *zemljaníka* 'wild strawberry,' *brusníka* 'red bilberry,' *povilíka* 'convolvolus,' etc.) form a more or less closed semantic group; they preserved the guttural unchanged for the most part because they offered no basis for the operation of analogy. Where the stressed vowel is separated from the palatalized guttural by one or two syllables, however, this kind of explanation is not possible. The initial stress in *kládędzь* 'well' (n.), *pěnędzь* 'small coin,' *vítędzь* 'warrior' must be old since these words are of Germanic origin. Nor is there any reason to suspect a stress shift in *mèsęcь* 'month,' *zájęcь* 'hare,' *rýbica* 'fish,' *žítьnica* 'granary,' *mǫ̑čenica* 'female martyr' *žlědica* 'plant name,' *pólьdza* 'profit,' and other similar words. It follows that the position of the guttural before a stressed vowel was not necessary for palatalization: *licé* and *dvidzáti* are just special cases. The main thing is that *the guttural had to be preceded immediately by an unstressed syllable* in order to become palatal. This is the first modification that Baudouin de Courtenay's formula requires.

The second concerns the definition of the phonemes that precede the gutturals and bring about their palatalization. Baudouin de Courtenay names *l̦ⁱ* and *r̦ⁱ* among them. I am not aware of any cases of palatalization after *l̦ⁱ* (= *ĭl*).

For ṛⁱ, only dubious examples can be cited: iteratives such as (sъ-)zьrcáti 'con-template,' mьrcáti 'shimmer,' etc. Meillet justly remarks that, "given the type narekǫ : naricati, iteratives with nonetymological gutturals were formed even in environments other than those in which the type originally arose" (1902–5, 48). Since the *c* in an iterative like mьrcati (< mьrknǫti) does not have to be any more organic than the *c* in vycati 'get accustomed to' (< vyknǫti), and since no examples other than iteratives can be cited for palatalization by preceding ĭr, this phoneme should be struck from the list of those causing palataliza-tion. The same holds for the diphthong *ei*. Wherever Slavic has *c', dz', s'* after *i*, this *i* derives from Indo-European *ī, not *ei. Baudouin de Courtenay assumes that the change of *ei* to *ī* antedates the palatalization of gutturals after *ī*, but this assumption is not supported by any argument, and, as we shall see in note 6 below, it is erroneous. Finally, Baudouin de Courtenay cites n̦ⁱ among the phonemes causing palatalization; it is not clear what he means by this n̦ⁱ. The Slavic phoneme generally designated by *ę* has a twofold origin: it derives partly from *en, partly from *ĭn, which in turn reflects Indo-European *n̦ in certain cases. The *ę* that causes the palatalization of following gutturals can be traced back only to *ĭn: thus kъnędzь, vitędzь, kladędzь, pěnędzь, stьrlędzь 'sterlet,' usьrędzь 'earring' with *ę* for Germanic *iŋ. The *ę* of měsęcь, zájęcь re-flects Indo-European *n̦ because these substantives have old themes in -en/-n̦ extended by the suffix -ko and, "in secondary formations, the element that directly precedes the secondary suffix generally has the zero grade" (Meillet 1922b, 237ff.). In iteratives of the type sъ-tędzati 'argue, quarrel' and bręcati 'rattle,' *ę* must also go back to *ĭn because Slavic iteratives have *i* in the root syllable wherever possible (Meillet 1902–5, 49). No examples of palatalization after an *ę* deriving from *en* seem to exist. So the palatalization of the gutturals took place after ĭ, ī, and *ĭŋ. And, since *ŋ* is a *guttural* (velar) nasal, the rule may be formulated as follows: *The gutturals* k, g, x, *together with the clusters* ŋk, ŋg, *became prepalatal following unstressed* ī *or* ĭ.

This formula explains all instances of the palatalization of gutturals not caused by a following palatal vowel. But there are exceptions in which gut-turals remain unchanged despite their position following unstressed ĭ or ī: for example, Russian starikъ 'old man' (g. stariká), ženixъ 'bridegroom' (g. ženixá), ol'xá 'alder,' Old Church Slavonic žьgǫ '(I) burn,' lękǫ '(I) bend' (< *lĭŋkôn), etc. I begin with two more or less isolated cases.

1. kъnęgýnji (vs. kъnędzĭ). This is the only word in which the guttural (*ŋg), preceded by unstressed ĭ, is followed by ȳ derived from *ū throughout the paradigm, which was probably the cause of its preservation. We have seen that *ū was a tense vowel and that at a certain period all tense velar vowels were strongly labialized. This strong labialization could well have been trans-ferred to the preceding guttural, preventing its palatalization. Consequently,

gutturals preceded by unstressed *ī* or *ĭ* were not palatalized when they were followed by tense velar vowels.

2. *vьsĕmь, vьsĕxъ, vьsĕmъ, vьsĕmi* (various forms of the word for 'all'). In these forms, old **oi* (= *ě*) did not become **ei* (= *i*), which proves that their **x* was palatalized to *s'* under the influence of the following *ě*, not the preceding *ĭ*. All other forms of this pronoun (*vьsego, vьsemu, vъs'a*, etc.), in contrast, display palatalization caused by the preceding *ĭ*. At a certain period, therefore, its locative singular must have been **vĭx'omĭ* (with prepalatal *x'*) and the instrumental **vĭxoimĭ* (with guttural *x*).

As pointed out above, the strong labialization of tense vowels prevented the palatalization of preceding gutturals. There is no reason to believe that *o* would have been more tense (close) in the diphthong *oi* than in other positions, but, while remaining lax, it could have had a higher degree of labialization in this position than elsewhere, the whole perhaps sounding something like *ᵘoi*. After the change of *eu* to *jou, oi* was the only Common Slavic diphthong consisting of heterogeneous elements, the first being labiovelar (*o*) and the second palatal (*i*). A "contrasting" reinforcement of the labialization of this *o* was only natural.

Thus, gutturals preceded by unstressed *ī, ĭ* must have remained unchanged when followed by strongly labialized vowels (*ū, ọ̄, ọ, ᵘoi*). This hypothesis makes the exceptions to the law of progressive palatalization of gutturals understandable.

Let us sketch the paradigm of nouns with the theme *o* ending in the group unstressed *ī* or *ĭ* + guttural + *o*. According to my hypothesis, the guttural became palatalized in six forms of the paradigm (nom. sg. -*ŭ[s]*, g. sg. -*ō*, acc. sg. -*ŭ[n]*, instr. sg. -*omĭ*, g. pl. -*ŭ[n]*, dat. pl. -*omŭ[s]*) and remained unchanged in six others (dat. sg. -*ọu*, loc. sg. -*ᵘoi*, nom. pl. -*ᵘoi*, acc. pl. -*ọ̄ᵘ[s]*, instr. pl. -*ō[s]* or *ū[s]*, loc. pl. -*ᵘoixŭ*). Feminine nouns with the theme *ō* (= **ā*) displayed the same numerical proportion between palatalized and unchanged forms (nom. sg. -*ō*, instr. sg. *ojọn*, g. pl. -*ŭ[n]*, dat. pl. -*ōmŭ[s]*, loc. pl. -*ōxŭ*, instr. pl. -*ōmī[s]* vs. g. sg., nom. and acc. pl. -*ọ̄ⁿ[s]*, dat. and loc. sg. -*ᵘoi*, acc. sg. -*ọn*). It is thus not surprising to find fluctuation between palatalized and nonpalatalized gutturals in this morphological category. Masculine nouns with the themes -*ĭko* (*otьcь* 'father,' *starьcь* 'old man'), -*ĭŋko* (*měsęcь*), and -*ĭŋgo* (*kladędzь* 'storehouse') and feminine nouns with the themes -*īkō* (*rybica*) and -*ĭkō* (*avьca* 'sheep') generalized the palatal form, while masculine nouns with the themes -*īko* (*starikъ, sъtьnikъ* 'centurion') and -*īxo* (*ženixъ*, Russ. *vývixъ* 'dislocation' [of a bone], etc.) generalized the unchanged guttural; feminine nouns with the theme -*ĭgō*, a much smaller group, vacillated between the two possible treatments: cf. Russ. *pól'ga* in addition to *pól'za* 'profit,' *stegá* in addition to *stezjá* 'path,' etc.

Verbal roots ending in ĭ + k, g, ŋk, ŋg and forming a thematic present palatalized their gutturals in the first-person dual (-ovē) and plural (-omŭ) indicative and in the present passive participle (-omo-) while preserving their gutturals intact in the first-person singular (-ǫn) and third-person plural (-ǫntĭ) present indicative, the present active participle (-ǫntjo-), and all persons of the imperative (-ᵘoi-). Unchanged gutturals appeared further in the strong aorist and the past active participle with the formants -ŭš-jo-, since these forms carried initial stress, and in the past active participle in -lo-. In the verbs in question, therefore, the number of forms with unchanged gutturals exceeded the number of forms with prepalatal consonants to such an extent that the generalization of the unchanged forms was virtually inevitable. The picture was different for verbal roots with the infinitive theme a (= *-ō-): here the prepalatals appeared in all forms derived from this theme, which ensured that they prevailed over the unchanged gutturals. Indeed, the verbal roots in ĭ + k, g, ŋk, ŋg that do not have the "infinitive theme a" display unchanged gutturals (Czech řku '[I] say' < *rĭkǫ, OCS žьgǫ, lękǫ, etc.), while the only one of these roots with an infinitive in -ati displays a palatalized guttural (sьcǫ, sьcati 'urinate'). All exceptions, therefore, admit of a clear explanation. It remains only to provide the definitive formulation of the general rule.

The progressive palatalization of gutturals took place at a time when all velar vowels in Common Slavic were labialized, but they displayed two degrees of labialization: tense vowels (ū, ō, ǫ) and the o of the diphthong *oi were strongly labialized, while in nontense vowels (ŭ, ō, o) the labialization was weak. Since gutturals had already become č, ž, š before palatal vowels, gutturals were to be found only before labiovelar vowels and were consequently labialized: strongly before ū, ō, ǫ, oi and weakly before ŭ, ō, o. The rule may be formulated in this way: *Weakly labialized gutturals* (k, g, x, ŋk, ŋg) *lost their labialization and became prepalatal when preceded by unstressed ĭ or ī, while strongly labialized gutturals in this position remained intact.*

4

Two arguments prove that this rule is earlier than the palatalization of velar vowels preceded by j and palatalized consonants. First, the palatalization of velar vowels took place not only after j but also after gutturals palatalized according to the rule under discussion: the paradigms of otьcь (except the vocative), lice, and rybica are completely identical with those of konjь, morje 'sea,' and volja 'will.' So by the time velar vowels were fronted after palatalized consonants, weakly labialized gutturals preceded by unstressed ĭ and ī must have been transformed into prepalatals. On the other hand, gutturals always remained unchanged when the preceding unstressed ĭ went back to ŭ following a palatalized consonant: for example, the Russian diminutives *konëk* 'horse,' *duš(ь)ka* 'soul' < **konjŭkŭ, *dǫušjŭkō* (formed from **konjŭ, *dǫušjō* on the model of **zǫmbŭ* 'tooth,' **ženō* 'wife' : **zǫmbŭkŭ, *ženŭkō*); Russian *rožok* 'horn,' *ruc(ь)ka* 'hand' < **rog'ŭkos, *rǫŋk'ŭkō* (instead of **rogŭkos, *rǫŋkŭkō* by dissimilation, at a period when the prepalatals had not yet become *č, ž, š*). Thus, when weakly labialized gutturals were palatalized after unstressed $\bar{\iota}$, $\breve{\iota}$, velar vowels preceded by *j* or a palatalized consonant had not yet been transformed into palatals.[6]

But, although the two progressive palatalizations (gutturals preceded by unstressed $\breve{\iota}$, $\bar{\iota}$ and velar vowels preceded by palatalized consonants or *j*) did not occur at exactly the same time, they cannot be represented as *consecutive* processes; they were rather successive phases of a single change. At a certain period, Common Slavic possessed phonemes belonging to two opposite articulatory bases: palatals, characterized by retracted lips and the raising of the front of the tongue, and labiovelars, characterized by protruding, rounded lips and the raising of the back of the tongue. The phonemes of each type did not all possess these typical traits to the same degree. The vowels *e, ē* displayed the articulatory properties of palatals to a lesser extent than the vowels $\breve{\iota}$, $\bar{\iota}$, and the vowels *o, ō, ŭ* displayed the labiovelar characteristics with less intensity than *ǫ, ǭ, ų̄*. The two-stage process of progressive palatalization can be described in the following way. When a phoneme with the palatal basis directly preceded one with the labiovelar basis, the latter tended to change its basis and become palatalized. At first, it was only the most palatalized phonemes ($\breve{\iota}$, $\bar{\iota}$) that exerted this effect on the least labialized phonemes (k^o, g^o, x^o, η^o), while those with strong labialization remained intact (k^u, g^u, x^u, η^u). This first phase of progressive palatalization affected only velar consonants, that is, the phonemes characterized by maximum raising of the back of the tongue. The second phase affected velar vowels, this time extending even to those with strong labialization. These retained their labialization, however, and the shift in their articulatory basis was therefore less complete than that of their weakly labialized counterparts.

These two laws of progressive palatalization mark the end of the period of independent unity of Common Slavic. Afterward, the tendency governing them apparently ceased to operate. In the dialects that later gave birth to the West Slavic languages and Russian, liquids followed by consonants and preceded by palatal vowels were indeed palatalized: for example, Polish *wilk* 'wolf' (= *vil'k*), *wierzba* 'willow,' Russian *p'er'vvi, cer'kvf'* (*pervyj* 'first,' *cerkov'* 'church'), and Russian *b'er'eg* (*bereg* 'shore, bank'), implying **ber'ṛ'gŭ < *ber'gŭ*. But this phenomenon is not directly comparable to the two progressive palatalizations discussed here, for liquids (especially *r*) seem never to have been labialized before consonants. In other cases in Slavic, when a palatal phoneme is immediately followed by a labiovelar (or at least nonpalatal) phoneme, it is usually the first that succumbs to the influence of the second. The two laws of progressive palatalization (*otĭkŭ > *otĭk'ŭ and *otĭk'ŭ > *otĭk'ĭ) are thus exceptional in Slavic. They were induced by a phonetic system in which the opposition between phonemes with a palatal basis and those with a labiovelar basis played a uniquely prominent role.

Postscript (Added Seven Months Later)

After writing this article, I read Belić's (1921) instructive discussion of the progressive palatalization of the gutturals. It is my pleasure to observe that my ideas are close to those of the eminent Serbian Slavicist and that, without realizing it, I had propounded a theory that combined elements of his and Baudouin de Courtenay's theories. But Belić and I differ in our attitude toward Baudouin de Courtenay's views: while Belić rejects them out of hand, I am content with certain modifications. Despite Belić's persuasive argumentation, I cannot accept his theory as a whole. We disagree on the following points.

1. According to Belić, *ŭ* was one of the phonemes that prevented the palatalization of preceding gutturals. Old Church Slavonic *nicь* 'down' (adv.) (< *nikŭ*), which is an isolated word and thus not susceptible to analogy, shows that gutturals could also be palatalized before *ŭ*.

2. I cannot bring myself to follow Belić in denying the influence of stress on palatalization. I have shown that all the examples of progressive palatalization after a stressed vowel are dubious. Also, there are cases in which gutturals remain unchanged after stressed *i* or *ĭ*, such as *lĭgŭkŭ* 'light' (adj.) and *mękŭkŭ* 'soft' (< *mĭŋkŭkŭ*), in which the following *ŭ* cannot have been the cause of the preservation of the gutturals; the same explanation applies to the intact *x* in *tixŭ* 'quiet,' *lixŭ* 'devoid of, alien, bad, reckless,' *lixva* 'bank interest,' etc.

3. Belić agrees with Baudouin de Courtenay that the progressive palatalization occurred later than the palatalization of gutturals before *ě* from *oi*. The reasons for my taking the opposite view were outlined above: the monophthongization of *oi* certainly occurred later than the palatalization of velar vowels preceded by *j* or a palatalized consonant (the change of *jo* to *je*);[7] and the progressive palatalization of gutturals occurred earlier than the change of *jo* to *je*, while the palatalization of gutturals before *ě* from *oi* must have occurred later than the monophthongization of *oi*.

4. According to Belić, only the *x* palatalized by a preceding *i, ь,* or *ę* yielded *š* in the West Slavic languages (Czech *vše* 'all' < *vĭxó* < *vĭxó*), whereas *x* palatalized by *ě* from *oi* was represented by *s'* in all the Slavic languages. Belić's arguments do not seem convincing here. It is difficult to explain Czech *mouše* (dat.-loc. sg. of *moucha* 'fly') by the influence of *duše* (voc. sg. of *duch* 'spirit').

But it would be most natural for the relation guttural in nominative singular : sibilant in nominative plural (Czech *pták* 'bird' : *ptáci, vrah* 'enemy' : *vrazi*) to have stimulated the creation of a plural *mnisi* beside the singular *mnich* 'monk' in Polish or Slovak. Isolated words such as Polish *szary,* Czech *šerý, šedý* (= Russ. *seryj* 'gray,' *sedoj* 'gray haired'), which cannot be explained by analogy, prove irrefutably that x became $š$ in West Slavic before $ě$ from $*oi$.

19. On the Original Value of the Common Slavic Accents

1

In discussions of the tonal nature of the two long syllable accents in Common Slavic, the "abrupt" accent is usually described as rising and the "smooth" one as falling.[1] These definitions have been obtained from the accentuation in Russian words, such as *voróna* 'crow' and *vóron* 'raven,' but they fail to explain the evidence of the other Slavic languages. Why is the "falling" accent shifted in Slovenian (Sloven. *bregâ* = Russ. *bérega* 'bank, shore, coast' [g. sg.]) while the "rising" accent retains its old position (Sloven. *vrána* = Russ. *voróna*)? Why does the "rising" accent in Serbian cause shortening of the stressed vowel (Serb. *vrȁna*) and the "falling" accent retain its length (Serb. *grâd* 'town'), whereas in Czech the opposite took place (Czech *vrána, hrad*)? No connection can be established between these facts and the supposed nature of Common Slavic accent.

In one of his last works, Šaxmatov (1915; cf. Kul'bakin 1921, 150) proposed another definition. According to him, the difference between the acute and the circumflex was that acute syllables were half long and bore an accent more dynamic than tonal, whereas the circumflected syllables were long and displayed a strong tonal (falling) modulation without substantial dynamic reinforcement. This definition was suggested solely by the Serbian data and does not seem in any way preferable to the older one. The evidence of Czech presents insurmountable difficulties for Šaxmatov's theory: one would have to assume that in Czech long vowels were shortened while half-long ones were lengthened, which is quite unlikely. To solve the problem, we must consider the old accents in the entire Slavic family in comparison with the Baltic evidence, rather than the facts of just one Slavic language.

2

The tonal nature of Lithuanian stress has not yet been elucidated by experimental phonetics. From the acoustic point of view, the Lithuanian acute is composed of a long, tonally neutral first part and a short second part with falling tone. The circumflex also contains a neutral first part and falling second part, but their quantitative relation is the inverse: the first is short, the second long. In some Lithuanian speakers, the falling part of the circumflex ends with a sudden rise; the accent thus receives two peaks and can give the impression of rising.

As is known, Serbian has a short vowel under the "abrupt" accent where Lithuanian has the acute, and a long vowel under the "smooth" accent where Lithuanian has the circumflex: Lithuanian *várna* = Serbian *vrȁna* 'crow'; Lithuanian *vaĩnas* = Serbian *vrân* 'raven.' The accented syllable in Serbian is short when the second part of the Lithuanian accent is short, and long when the second part of the Lithuanian accent is long; the length of the Serbian accented syllable is therefore identical with that of the *second* part (always falling) of the Lithuanian accent.

Czech presents a completely different picture: Lithuanian *várna* = Czech *vrána;* Lithuanian *vaĩnas* = Czech *vrǎn.* The accented syllable in Czech replicates the quantity of the *first* part of the Lithuanian accent.

The stressed short open vowels (**e, *o*) correspond to short vowels in both Serbian and Czech: Serbian *ȍko,* Czech *oko* 'eye.'

Given such evidence, in the comparable cases in Lithuanian one might expect to find an accent composed of two equally short parts, of which the first is tonally neutral and the second falling. Indeed, stressed *a* and *e* in East Lithuanian are half-long. Baranowski states that half-long vowels in East Lithuanian display more than half the duration of normal long ones: the proportion is about two to three (Baranauskas and Weber 1882, xv–xxxi). Be that as it may, according to Baranowski, the accent on half-long vowels consists of two parts, of which the first is identical (in length as well as in tone) with the first part of the circumflex and the second with the second part of the acute. The West Lithuanian counterparts of the stressed half-long vowels of East Lithuanian are long and circumflected. Stressed short close vowels (*i, u*) are half long in East Lithuanian but short in West Lithuanian, so in Common Lithuanian they must have been shorter than normal short vowels. Since in Common Slavic, too, the corresponding **ь* and **ъ* were shorter than **e* and **o,* the agreement with Lithuanian seems to have been complete.

It follows that, like Lithuanian accents, Common Slavic accents consisted of two tonally distinct parts: the first was short in the smooth accent and long in the abrupt one; the second was long in the smooth accent and short in the abrupt one; the accent on the vowels **e* and **o* was composed of two equally short parts. Serbian has preserved the second parts of the old accents, Czech the first ones. It now remains to determine the tonal quality of the two parts of the Slavic accents.

Serbian, which has preserved the second part of the old accents, has the same length and the same (falling) tonal quality in this part as does Lithuanian. It thus appears that the second part of the Common Slavic accents was falling. Serbian furnishes no clue to the tonal quality of their first part, as it has lost it. Czech is equally uninstructive since the apparent tonal differentiation of Czech vowels depends on initial expiratorial stress, the number of syllables in the word, and other factors irrelevant to the old accent system. More helpful is Slovenian: for Lithuanian *várna* Slovenian has *vránă,* and for Lithuanian *var̃no* (g. sg. of *var̃nas*) it has *vrănâ.* The quantitative relation between the *two parts* of the monosyllabic accent in Lithuanian (- ˘ for the acute, and ˘ - for the circumflex) corresponds exactly to the quantitative relation between the *two syllables* of the old paroxytones in Slovenian. And since in the Slovenian word *vrănâ* the long syllable preserves the tonal quality of the long part of the old accent (cf. Serb. *vrăna*), we must assume the same correspondence for Slovenian *vránă.* At least in the abrupt accent, then, the first part had a rising tone, and by analogy the same must hold for the first part of the other Common Slavic accents.

Schematically, the tonal nature of the Common Slavic accents can be presented in the following manner:

Abrupt accent 

Smooth accent 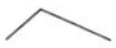

Accent of **e* and **o* 

3

Let us now try to sketch out the development of accentuation in the various Slavic languages according to the definitions given for Common Slavic.

In *Serbian,* three sets of facts are of importance: (1) long bases under the smooth accent are preserved; (2) long bases under the abrupt accent are shortened; and (3) the syllable preceding the old stressed syllable retains its original quantity and receives a rising tone. These facts acquire inner coherence only in the light of the theory put forward above. The definition of Common Slavic accents proposed here yields the following unifying formula: The first part of old accents is shifted in Serbian to the preceding syllable, retaining its rising tone but modifying its quantity in accordance with that of its new locus; the old stressed syllable thus preserves only the second (falling) part of the old accents and has the original quantity of this part.

The regressive displacement of the old accent started as a phenomenon of sentence phonetics: a word with a stressed initial syllable transferred the first part of the old accent to the final syllable of the preceding word. At the time of this change, a syllable with a fall in a Serbian sentence was preceded by one with a rise. Later, each dialect went its own way. Dialects employing the interrogative *što* 'what' preserved only the contour closest to the beginning of the word: **sèlȍ* 'village' became *sèlo* and **cȓná vrȁna* 'black crow' became *cȓna vrȁna.* Dialects with the interrogative *ča* dropped the rise: thus, **cȓná vrȁna* became **cȓnā vrȁna,* just as in Štokavian, but **sèlȍ* became *selȍ.*

The development in *Slovenian* cannot be summarized in a single formula and appears to comprise no fewer than five steps:[2]

1. All stressed syllables become equally long; the accent on *e* and *o* in final syllables becomes abrupt,[3] in other syllables smooth (*selô* > *selő*, *ôko* > *ōko*).

2. The second part of the tonal accent is shifted to the following syllable of the same word; the first part stays in place; both preserve their original quantity and tonal quality (*mēso* > *mèsô* 'meat', *ōko* > *òkô*, *vrâna* > *vránà*).

3. Final syllable accents that could not be displaced earlier—since they did not precede any other syllable in the same word—undergo a regressive displacement as in Serbian, except that the first (rising) part of the accent preserves its original contour and quantity (*vodá* > *vódà* 'water', *roká* > *rókà* 'hand', *selő* > *sélò*, *mlẹkő* > *mlẹ́ko* 'milk').

4. The progressive displacement (2) fails to occur when the part of the accent subject to displacement is short and the following syllable long (e.g., instr. sg. *lîpō* < *lipoi̯ǫ* 'linden tree') or when the following syllable contains a "weak" *jer* incapable of bearing any accent (e.g., *mîška* < *mýšĭka* 'armpit'). In these two cases the accent remains in place and is transformed into a falling long one (Sloven. *lîpo* = Czech *lipou*, Sloven. *mîška* = Serbian *mȉška*).

5. All short syllables lose their contour, and long syllables deprived of their tonal component become short (*mèsô* > *mesô*, *òkô* > *okô*, *vránà* > *vrána*, *sélò* > *sélo*, *lîpō* > *lîpo*).

Bulgarian seems to have participated in certain stages of the Slovenian development, notably stages 1, 2, and 5, with the result that long syllables were shortened and the tonal accent was replaced by expiratorial stress (as in Russian). This explains the agreement between Bulgarian and Slovenian with respect to the position of the stress: for example, Bulgarian *okó*, *mesó*, but *vrána*, *kráva* 'cow' (Sloven. *okô*, *mesô*, *vrána*, *kráva*). The regressive displacement does not appear to have reached Bulgarian, despite the conformity of Bulgarian *mlěko* (*mleáko*), *sélo* (in addition to *seló*) with Slovenian *mléko*, *sélo* (Serb. *mlijèko*, *sèlo*), which could be coincidental. In many cases Bulgarian and Slovenian diverge. It is impossible to reconstruct all the details of the extremely complicated Bulgarian development because tonal differences in the vowels no longer exist in this language. Macedonian dialects have fixed expiratorial stress on the initial syllable, the penult, or the antepenult, according to the dialect. Its emergence is due to the weakening and loss of the old tonal distinctions.

Czech preserves the length of the first part of the accent of old stressed syllables (see above). At some point, the second part must have been shifted to the following syllable, as in Slovenian. Czech and Slovenian developed differently because Czech possessed both tonal accent and initial expiratorial stress. The progressive displacement of the second part of the old accent must have caused quantitative changes like those in Slovenian. But later, unstressed long vowels were shortened; this is why Czech *vrána* 'crow' agrees with Slovenian *vrána* with respect to the length of both syllables, whereas Czech *vrana* (g. sg. of *vran* 'raven') differs from Slovenian *vranâ* in its short noninitial *a*. Words that once bore the tonal accent on the second syllable preserved length in the first syllable because it was protected by initial stress—for example, Czech *mouka* = Russian *muká* 'flour', etc. Long vowels in noninitial syllables in Modern Czech are for the most part the product of contractions (instr. sg. *vodou* < **vodoi̯ǫ* 'water,' *dobrá* 'good!' [interj.] < **dobrai̯a*, etc.) or of compensatory lengthening after the loss of *jer* (*zeměnin* 'country squire' < **zeměninŭ* etc.). With the displacement of the old accents and the shortening of long vowels in noninitial syllables, tonal distinctions on vowels must have become less conspicuous than the difference in intensity between the heavily stressed initial syllable and unstressed syllables. They faded and finally disappeared.

Polish and *Sorbian* have fixed expiratorial stress; it falls on the penult in Polish and on the initial syllable in Sorbian. The traces of quantitative distinctions (partly old and partly new) preserved by these languages do not go back to ancient accents. There is no reason to believe that the old tonal accents in Polish and Sorbian were ever displaced as in Serbian and Slovenian. Rather, it seems that they simply weakened and became so insignificant that they gave way to a new, expiratorial stress, whose position was independent of theirs.

Russian has expiratorial stress in place of old tonal accents. The tonal movement in Proto-Russian seems to have been accompanied by parallel expiratorial reinforcement, such that the tonal peak of the stressed syllable eventually merged with its dynamic peak. When this happened, monosyllabic groups of the type *tert, tort, tolt* became disyllabic. The melody, originally confined to a single syllable, now spanned two. The tonal and dynamic peak of an old syllable with an abrupt accent was closer to the end of the contour, since the first (rising) part of the abrupt accent was longer than the second. On the other hand, the peak of the smooth accent was closer to the beginning of the contour, since its first part was shorter than the second. It is thus only natural that the type **tőrt* yielded *torót* and the type **tòřt* yielded *tórot* (Russ. *voróna* 'crow' = Lith. *várna*, Russ. *vóron* 'raven' = Lith. *var̃nas*). This process can be represented by the following diagram:

Abrupt accent

Smooth accent

The proposed theory of the tonal nature of the Common Slavic accents fits perfectly with the evidence of all the Slavic languages. From the point of view of any other theory, the development in the various dialects appears complicated and devoid of logic, but given the new definitions, it can be reduced to the interplay of two tendencies. The one, operating in the Southwest, consists in distributing the tonal contour—made up of a rising part and a falling part and originally limited to a single syllable—over two adjacent syllables, each syllable becoming the locus of one tonal movement (rising or falling). This tendency manifests itself in two ways: progressive and regressive displacement.[4] The other tendency, operating primarily in the Northeast, consists in eliminating tonal distinctions and replacing them with expiratorial stress. It also displays two variations, according to whether the stress falls on the syllable that had borne the tonal accent or is fixed on some particular syllable (initial, penultimate, etc.) irrespective of the position of the old accent. Serbian and Slovenian represent the tendency of the Southwest; Russian, Polish, and Sorbian that of the Northeast. Czech and Bulgarian are subject to both tendencies. These two languages show that the progressive displacement— a manifestation of the southwestern tendency—is older than the manifestations of the northeastern tendency, and it follows from the Slovenian data that this displacement occurred earlier than the regressive displacement.

The simplicity of the picture drawn here for all the Slavic languages proves that the starting point was reconstructed correctly.

4

Let us now consider the Baltic languages. As pointed out above, *Lithuanian* accents differ from those reconstructed for Common Slavic in the quality of their first part, which must have been rising in Common Slavic while in Lithuanian it is tonally neutral. This state of affairs seems to be quite old, as the shortening of the second (falling) part of Lithuanian final vowels indicates. Where the second part was originally long, it became short; thus, in East Lithuanian, old smooth long vowels in the final syllable received the same accent as the vowels *a* and *e* word internally. Where the second part of the vowel was short, it disappeared; thus, final *a* and *e* acquired the same duration as *u* and *i* in the middle of a word. Old final abrupt vowels had to become half long, having lost their short second part. But as these half-long vowels were tonally neutral, they were reduced again, this time to the length of word-internal *u* and *i*. Yet at one time they must have been longer than the *a, e* of final syllables, for short vowels that go back to old final abrupt long ones have been preserved while *a* and *e* (as well as *i* and possibly *u*) in final syllables tend to disappear.

Latvian possesses expiratorial stress. Stressed syllables in this language are not entirely neutral from the tonal point of view, but the tonal distinctions that do exist are weak; they vary according to the dialect and are less audible than the dynamic distinctions. Long syllables in Latvian can have three types of accent: (1) the "continuous" accent, which displays no significant change in the force of the breath flow for the entire duration of the stressed syllable (ˉ); (2) the "falling" accent, which is composed of a strong first and a closely adherent weak second part (ˆ); and (3) the "interrupted" accent, split into two parts (the first strong, the second very weak, almost whispered) by more or less complete closure of the glottis (ˋ).

These three types of accent, defined by Endzelin (1899), Schmidt (1899), and Schmidt-Wartenberg (1899, esp. 144), are distributed in the following way: The continuous accent occurs on abrupt syllables (Latv. *māte* = Lith. *mótė* 'mother'; Latv. *brālis* = Lith. *brólis* 'brother'; Latv. *vārna* = Lith. *várna* 'crow'; etc.). The falling accent occurs on smooth syllables (Latv. *wil̃ks* = Lith. *vil̃kas* 'wolf'; Latv. *ʃȇma,* cf. Lith. *žȇmą* 'low'; Latv. *rûka,* cf. Lith. *rañką* 'hand'; etc.). The interrupted accent occurs on originally abrupt pretonic syllables (Latv. *gàlva* = Lith. *galvà* 'head,' cf. *gálvą;* Latv. *vèna* = Lith. *vēnà* 'vein,' cf. *vēnas*).

This distribution can be understood if we assume that Proto-Latvian originally had accents identical with those of Proto-Lithuanian but that the dynamic peak of the word was located early in the stressed syllable. The elements furthest from the peak—the beginning of the pretonic syllable and the end of the stressed one—were eliminated. As a result, abrupt accents in stressed syllables lost their short, falling second part and preserved only the long, tonally neutral first part. Where the element furthest from the dynamic peak was the *long* part of the old accent, it remained but forfeited some of its duration: the "breaking" of the voice, that is, the nonhomogeneous character of the syllabic melody, was preserved and—after the replacement of tonal distinctions by dynamic ones—came to be expressed by a change in intensity between the beginning and the end of the syllable. This is what happened to the smooth accent in stressed syllables and the abrupt accent in pretonic syllables. The falling part of the smooth accent was longer than that of the abrupt one, however, so the passage from a relatively high to a low level was slower in the first case than in the second; and, as the end of the smooth accent in stressed syllables experienced the destructive effect of the syllable-final dynamic peak, the falling movement of the second part of the smooth accent in the *stressed* syllable was both slower and less complete than its counterpart in the abrupt accent in the *pretonic* syllable. This distinction was also expressed dynamically: the smooth accent is represented by length with a fall, the abrupt accent by interrupted length. Consequently, the dynamic differences that can be observed at the beginning and end of stressed syllables in Modern Latvian correspond exactly to the differences in tone height in Proto-Latvian.

Smooth accents in pretonic syllables must have lost their neutral, short first part; only the falling, long second part would have been able to remain. Since the tone of the second part was homogeneous, one could expect to find a continuous accent in its place in Modern Latvian, at most a falling one—in any case one without abrupt dynamic leaps. In Modern Latvian, regular reflexes of smooth accents in pretonic syllables are hard to discover because the original state of affairs has been obscured by analogy. We do not know whether the falling accent of Latvian *weĩku, wiĩku* (cf. Lith. *velkù, vilkaũ*) directly represents the smooth accent of a pretonic syllable or whether it is due to the influence of the infinitive *wiĩkt* 'pull' (Lith. *viĩkti*) and other forms with stressed root syllable; the same holds for Latvian *ſẽma, rŭka, baȓda* 'beard', etc. (cf. Lith. *žëmà* [acc. *žë̃mą*], *rankà* [*rañką*], *barzdà* [acc. *baȓzdą*], etc.).

If Proto-Latvian seems to have had accents more or less identical with those of Proto-Lithuanian, the same cannot be said for *Proto-Prussian*. In his fine article on Baltic quantity and accent, Fortunatov (1895) showed that in the Prussian catechism of 1561 old abrupt diphthongs bore the length sign on the second element and old smooth diphthongs on the first (OPr. *ēit* = Lith. *eīti* 'you [sg.] go'; OPr. *lāiku* = Lith. *laĩko* 'hold, support [3d p. sg.]'; OPr. *āusins* = Lith. *aũsys* 'ears'; OPr. *erdērkts* 'poisoned' = Lith. *apdeȓktas* 'soiled, defiled'; OPr. *āntran* = Lith. *añtrą* 'other [m. sg.]'; OPr. *per-traūki* = Lith. *tráukia* 'pull'; OPr. *boūt* = Lith. *búti* 'be' [inf.]; OPr. *soūnan* = Lith. *súnu* 'son'; OPr. *geywas* [= *geĩwas*] = Lith. *gývas* 'life'; etc.). This system is the opposite of what we observe in Lithuanian, and Fortunatov had every reason to conclude that Proto-Prussian accents were different from those of Proto-Lithuanian (and, we may add, Proto-Latvian).

Nevertheless, this difference must not be exaggerated, for it is possible to reconcile the Old Prussian evidence with that of the other Baltic languages. There are two ways to understand this evidence. In *ēit, pertraūki,* etc., the letters *ā, ē, ī (y), ū* could have marked the most salient element of the diphthong (with respect to tone height or force) rather than length; the place of these letters in the digraphs *ān, ēr, eī, aū* and so on would then have indicated the position of the tonal or dynamic peak in the corresponding phonemes of the spoken language. But it is also possible that, at a certain period, the element that bore the tonal peak was lengthened at the expense of the other element; in this case, the letters *ā, ē, ī, ū* in the digraphs could indeed represent long vowels. Be that as it may, the orthographic evidence indicates that at one time Old Prussian accents contained a peak of the tonal curve or of dynamic strength. The second part of Old Prussian accents was therefore falling. But the first part cannot have been neutral, as in Lithuanian or Proto-Latvian; most probably, it was rising, as in Common Slavic. Correspondences such as Old Prussian *ēit* = Lithuanian *eīti* and Old Prussian *pertraūki* = Lithuanian *tráukia* prove that the Old Prussian tonal peak was closer to the beginning of the syllabic melody in the smooth accent, closer to the end in the abrupt: it thus occupied the same place in Proto-Prussian as in Proto-Russian (Russ. *voróna* = Lith. *várna*, Russ. *vóron* = Lith. *vaȓnas*).

Since the tonal structure of Proto-Prussian and Common Slavic accents seems to have been identical, the accents that I have attributed to Common Slavic can also be reconstructed for Common Baltic. The divergent character of Lithuanian and Proto-Latvian accents is then an innovation. The rising movement of the first part of the old accents was replaced with a neutral movement owing to an anticipation of the tonal peak: instead of rising gradually toward the relatively high tone of this peak, the voice reached it at once and maintained its level until the descent began.

5

The accents proposed for Common Slavic have turned out to be those of Common Baltic as well. It remains to determine their relation to Common Indo-European.

The tonal structure of Indo-European accents is known imperfectly, but it must have been different from the one sketched out above for Common Slavic and Baltic. The accentual contour in abrupt long bases in Indo-European seems to have been homogeneous; it contained only one movement of the voice, which, to judge from Ancient Greek, was rising. According to the evidence of Ancient Greek and Sanskrit, the accent on normal short bases was distinguished from that on abrupt long bases only by shorter duration and perhaps by greater rapidity in its ascent. The accent on smooth long bases seems to have contained two tonally distinct parts, the first of which displayed a tonal movement identical with that of the abrupt accent (i.e., rising) and the second a falling movement. The composite nature of the smooth accent may explain why, in the Vedas as well as in the metrical parts of the Avesta, a smooth long base is sometimes treated as two short ones. Nowhere, neither in Vedic Sanskrit nor in Ancient Greek, is there any indication that one part of the smooth accent was longer than the other: the two parts seem to have had equal duration but different—even opposite—tonal characteristics.

If we compare this system with the one reconstructed for Common Slavic and Baltic, we will notice that the Slavic and Baltic accents always differ from their Indo-European prototypes by the addition of a falling appendage that prolongs the falling movement of old smooth bases and transforms the homogeneous contour of the old abrupt long and short bases into composite melodies. Schematically:

	IE	Balto-Slavic	Latvian-Lithuanian
Smooth	◁	◁	◁
Abrupt	◁	◁	◁
Short (a, e, o)	◁	◁	◁

The difference between the systems of Balto-Slavic and Common Indo-European is thus the result of an innovation in Baltic and Slavic that consisted in extending all the Indo-European accents by a short, tonally falling element. Only the maximally close short vowels *i and *u were not affected by this process, by virtue of their closeness (see Meillet 1908–9b).

The Balto-Slavic innovation caused a drastic change in the Indo-European accent system. Since each syllable (with the exception of those with *i and *u) now contained two opposite tonal movements, the melody of words and sentences became richer, more varied, and the tonal character of the language more distinct. It is perhaps for this reason that, of all Indo-European languages, Baltic and Slavic retained the principle of chromatic accent the longest. But the saltatory nature of the Baltic and Slavic accents was also the cause of many changes. The Fortunatov–de Saussure law, the lengthening of short vowels before a short or smooth syllable (Czech *půchod* 'origin, cause,' Serb. *prórok* 'prophet'), the shortening of long vowels before syllables with abrupt accent (Serb. *rùkama* 'hands' [dat. pl.], *knègiňa* 'princess,' *kràvica* 'small cow,' *mlàdica* 'offshoot,' etc.; Czech *kravice* 'small cow,' *mladice* 'young woman,' *hvězdice* 'star, rosette,' *slanina* 'bacon,' *sudidlo* 'criterion,' *sudište* 'court of law,'[5] *starucha* 'old woman,' etc.), the change of noninitial short and smooth long syllables to abrupt long syllables (Russ. *ogoród* 'kitchen garden' in addition to *górod* 'town,' *pozolóta* 'gilt' in addition to *zóloto* 'gold,' dial. *naruòd* 'people, nation' in addition to *rod* 'kin,' etc.) — these facts, and a number of others, find their natural explanation in the light of the theory of Common Slavic accents presented here. And they are all the result of the fundamental Balto-Slavic innovation that we have observed.

Not only did this innovation affect word and sentence intonation, but it also brought forth a profound upheaval in the rhythm of the language. Indo-European had opposed bimoric long bases to monomoric short bases. In Balto-Slavic, this simple and transparent system collapsed. The duration of the short open vowels (Indo-European *e, *o, *a) approached that of the long vowels; the quantitative distinction between *ā and *a became weaker than in Common Indo-European. On the other hand, the short close vowels (Indo-European *i, *u) differed from all others in their duration: the distinction between *ī and *i became much greater than before, and *i ceased to be metrically identical with *e.

This rhythmic upheaval had far-reaching consequences for vowel quantity. In Slavic, short open vowels tend to side with old long ones, and none of the Slavic languages has retained intact the old quantitative distinction between *e, o* and *ě, a, u, ī, y.* Contrariwise, the short close vowels tend to dwindle: they forfeit their timbre and disappear in certain positions, especially where juxtaposition with a vowel of normal length (short open or long) emphasizes by contrast their own minimal duration. The Baltic languages were more conservative; nevertheless, Upper Lithuanian eliminated the quantitative distinction between short open and long vowels, at least in stressed syllables, and East Lithuanian (like Latvian) gave up the quantitative distinction between short open and short closed vowels.

The transformation of the rhythmic structure of the language could not remain without consequences for Baltic and Slavic metrics. The simple one mora–two morae opposition in Indo-European had made quantitative meter possible (see Meillet 1913a, 151ff.). But the more complicated distinction of three degrees of length resulting from the Balto-Slavic innovation destroyed the older metrical system, which was replaced by a syllabic one. We find this syllabic character in the meter of the folk poetry of most Slavic peoples, and Korš was mistaken in deriving it from a tonic meter based on Russian folk poetry. The latter cannot have received its tonal structure until after the replacement of the old accents by expiratorial stress. Before this change, the Russians must have possessed a syllabic metrics comparable to that of the Serbs and Bulgarians. This Proto-Russian syllabic system may have been the model for the metrics of Mordvin folk poetry, the principal meters of which (4 + 3, 4 + 4, 5 + 3, 5 + 5, and their variants produced by the insertion of feet from three to five syllables between the two halves of the line, e.g., 5 + 3 + 3, 5 + 4 + 3, 4 + 3 + 4) are attested in Serbian and Bulgarian folk poetry but have no exact parallels elsewhere—neither among the other Finnic peoples nor the neighboring Turkic peoples (Tatars, Chuvash, Bashkirs). Paasonen's (1910) hypothesis attributing this characteristic of Mordvin poetry to Ukrainian influence is highly improbable from the historical and geographic points of view; we can conclude only that it was the Russians who supplied the Mordvins with the model for their syllabic metrics, at a time when expiratorial stress had not yet altered the rhythm of the Russian language and its principles of versification.[6]

20. On the Proto-Slavic Accents

In an article in *Revue des études slaves* (Trubetzkoy 1921 [chap. 19 in this volume]), I suggested that, with regard to their musical characteristics, all the original accents of Proto-Slavic—acute, circumflex, and grave[1]—had been rising-falling. In the acute, the first (rising) part was longer; in the circumflex, the second (falling) part was longer; in the grave, both parts were equally short. The short vowels (*e, o*) were normally somewhat more than half as long as a long vowel, the "semivowels" (*ĭ, ŭ*) less than half as long. I attempted to show that my theory offered a simpler explanation of the development of accent in the individual Slavic languages than the old view, according to which the acute was rising, the circumflex long and falling, and the grave short and falling. The Proto-Serbo-Croatian development, for example, can be shown to express a single principle: only the second (falling) part of the original accent remained in place, while the first (rising) part was transferred to the preceding syllable without changing this syllable's quantity. The different accentuation of pleophonic combinations in Russian (acute *$\overline{or}$* > *orò*, circumflected *$\overline{or}$* > *òro*) can be explained as follows: the acute, whose first (rising) part was longer than the second, reached its tonal peak in the second half of the syllable, whereas the circumflex, whose first (rising) part was shorter, reached its peak in the first half.

The more I work on Slavic accents, the more I am convinced that my theory is correct. But, in applying it to the history of the individual languages, I made some statements in the earlier essay that no longer satisfy me. In particular, my description of the development in the West Slavic languages (1921, 177–78 [see chap. 19, pp. 144–45 above]) seems to have been mistaken, and I should like to correct it here.

For Proto-Czech, Proto-Slovak, Proto-Polish, and Proto-Kashubian-Slovincian, we can assume a progressive accent shift. Only the first (rising) part of the old accent remained in place; the second (falling) was transferred to the following syllable or—if already in final position—dropped. Let us designate the length of a normal long vowel by 3, a length greater than half this by 2, and a length less than half this by 1. If we use the symbol ˝ for the Proto-Slavic acute and ˜ for the Proto-Slavic circumflex and, otherwise, Vuk Karadžić's intonation symbols, we can represent the West Slavic progressive accent shift as follows: $vo_1dã_3$ > $vo_1dá_2$ 'water'; $ko_1pý_3to_1$ > $ko_1pý_2tò_1$ 'hoof'; $tra_3vã_3$ > $tra_3vá_2$ 'grass'; $sã_3dlo_1$ > $sá_2dlò_1$ 'saddle'; $mę̃_3so_1$ > $mè_1sò_1$ (or $mè_1sò_2$?) 'meat'; $kô_2lo_1$ >

kò₁lò₁ 'wheel.' The result of the accent shift was thus a system of three length grades: short (1), mid (2), and long (3).

This system was replaced in West Slavic by a two-grade system of short and long vowels. In Proto-Polish and Proto-Kashubian-Slovincian, all mid-length vowels were shortened: *vo₁dá₂ > vŏdă; ko₁pý₂tò₁ > kŏpȳtŏ; sta₁ri₃ká₂ > stărīkă* 'old man (g.)'; *sá₂dlò₁ > sădlŏ*. In Czech, mid-length vowels were lengthened in the first syllable of a word (*sa₂dlo₁ > sādlŏ*), shortened in the others (*vo₁da₂ > vŏdă; ko₁py₂to₁ > kŏpȳtŏ; tra₃va₂ > trāvă*). The difference between Proto-Czech and Proto-Polish is due to the fact that in the former each word-initial syllable had strong expiratorial stress regardless of its accent. Polish, too, seems to have had initial stress at one time, but it must have been weaker than that in Proto-Czech, as it was abandoned in all words of more than two syllables, while in Czech initial stress survived. The weak expiratorial stress of Proto-Polish was unable to increase the duration of mid-length vowels in initial syllables.

Proto-Slovak appears to have been halfway between Proto-Czech and Proto-Polish with respect to initial stress. In principle, all mid-length vowels are shortened in all positions in Slovak (*līpă* 'linden tree,' *sădlŏ*), but old initial stress is preserved in most dialects even in polysyllabic words,[2] and there are also dialectal forms with a lengthened mid-length vowel in the initial syllable. Sorbian apparently possessed the same stress and quantity as Proto-Czech. In Kashubian-Slovincian, initial stress seems to have prevailed only in the southern dialects. In the northern Proto-Kashubian-Slovincian area, the progressive accent shift appears to have left expiratorial stress in its old place. A word like **kopȳto* sounded **ko₁**pý₂**tò₁* after the accent shift (boldface designates reinforcement of the syllable *pý₂*); but the shortening of the mid-length syllable was linked to the reinforcement of the preceding one: *ko₁**pý₂**tò₁ > **kŏ**pȳtŏ; sta₁ri₃**ká₂** > stă**rī**kă.*

I believe that this explanation fits the facts of the individual West Slavic languages better than the one offered in my earlier essay.[3]

The 1921 essay treated only the original accents of Proto-Slavic: the normal acute, circumflex, and grave accents. But Proto-Slavic also possessed later accents, products of metatony. A considerable amount has been written on the causes of and requisite conditions for metatony, but no one has tried to define the tonal nature of the new accents. It has merely been observed that the new circumflex in syllables with original acute was similar to, although not identical with, the old circumflex and that the same relation holds between the old and the new acute in syllables with original circumflex. Just what the similarities and differences were has remained unclear; I will try to fill in the gap.

The new circumflex appears in Slovenian as a long falling tone that—in contrast to the old circumflex—retains its original position and is never transferred to the following syllable. Since the Slovenian progressive accent shift was a result of the rising-falling character of the old accents (1921, 175–76 [see chap. 19, pp. 144 above]), I conclude from the Slovenian treatment of the new circumflex that this accent was not rising-falling and that its most important element was a tonal descent. In Russian words with Proto-Slavic new circumflex, we find stress on the second syllable of the pleophony: for example, the genitive plurals *koróvъ* 'cows,' *berëzъ* 'birches,' *vorónъ* 'crows.' This proves that the tonal peak came in the second half of the syllabic melody. The combined evidence of Slovenian and Russian indicates that the new circumflex was falling-rising, that is, two-peaked; its first (falling) part was longer than the second (rising) part, and the second peak—at least in Proto-Russian—was higher than the first.

Unlike the normal acute, which produces a short vowel in Proto-Polish, the new acute in Polish preserves its length. Since the Proto-Polish shortening of the old acute was a result of the progressive accent shift (see above), it follows that this shift did not affect the new acute. And, since the shift otherwise operated on all rising-falling accents, the new acute cannot have been rising-falling. In Slovenian and Čakavian, and in the dialects of Posavina, the new acute is represented by a long rising tone: a tonal ascent must therefore have been one of its essential elements. Štokavian, however, has a long falling tone in place of the new acute, so the latter cannot have been only rising; a tonal descent must also have been present. These facts can be reconciled only if we agree that the new acute was a falling-rising intonation whose second (rising) part was longer than the first.

Consequently, the difference between the old accents and the new ones produced by metatony was that the new accents were falling-rising, the old ones rising-falling. The new circumflex resembled the old one in that both possessed a long falling and a short rising part, but the respective position of these parts was different. The same is true, mutatis mutandis, of the relation between the new and the normal acute.

More important from a historical point of view is the relation between the new acute and the old circumflex, since the new acute falls on originally circumflected long vowels: in both accents, the first part is shorter than the second. On the other hand, the new circumflex, which falls on syllables with the old acute, and the normal acute have in common that the first part is longer than the second. Proto-Slavic long stressed vowels consisted of two tonally distinct parts: in old long syllables with the acute, the first part was longer than the second, while in circumflected ones the second part was longer than the first. The tonal movement was rising-falling; in metatony, it was falling-rising. I will call this kind of metatony *accent inversion*. Accordingly, I would also suggest replacing the names *new circumflex* and *new acute* with *inverse acute* and *inverse circumflex,* respectively.[4] My view can be diagrammed as follows.

	Normal accent	Inverse accent
Acute	⌃	⌄／
Circumflex	⌃	⌄／

What follows is a brief sketch of the development of the new (inverse) accents in the individual Slavic languages.

Serbo-Croatian dialects treat the inverse circumflex differently. Štokavian, which had a tendency to give the first of two opposite tonal movements expiratorial reinforcement and to neutralize the second tonally (e.g., Proto-Serbo-Croatian *rúkà* 'hand,' *vòdà* 'water' > Štok. **rûka, vòda**), did just this with the inverse circumflex, and the result was a long falling tone: **krȁálj* > **krȁālj* > **krâlj* 'king.' Čakavian, which displayed the opposite tendency (e.g., Proto-Serbo-Croatian *rúkà, vòdà* > Čak. *rūkȁ,* vo**dȁ**), reinforced the second part of the inverse circumflex and neutralized the first (**krȁálj* > *kraálj*). Belić's (1909, 204) description, however, indicates that, at least in some areas, the Čakavian rising tone has retained its original complex tonal nature.

The inverse acute yields a long falling tone in both Štokavian and Čakavian, so the short rising part must have been assimilated to the long falling one already in the Proto-Serbo-Croatian period (*lîpъ* > *lîpъ* 'linden tree' [g. pl.]). In many cases, the inverse acute was transformed in Proto-Štokavian into the normal acute, whose regular product was a short falling tone. In nonfinal and nonpenultimate syllables, this change seems to have been carried out systematically: **gỳnešъ* > Štokavian *gȉneš* 'perish, languish' (2d p. sg. pres.), **màžešъ* > Štokavian *màžeš* 'smear' (2d p. sg. pres.) (cf. Čak. *gȋneš, mâžeš*).[5] The reason is obscure.

In *Russian,* pleophonic combinations have the accent on the second syllable in both inverse accents: **kòrvъ* > *koròvъ* 'cow' (g. pl.), **gólvъ* > *golòvъ* 'head' (g. pl.), **móltišъ* > *molòtišь* 'grind' (2d p. sg. pres.), etc. Apparently, the second peak of both falling-rising accents in Proto-Russian had been higher than the first, and therefore, when the syllabic melody was distributed over two syllables, the second was emphasized. This can be displayed schematically in the following way:

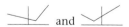 and ‿⌄／‿

In *Slovenian,* the inverse acute yields a long falling tone, the inverse circumflex a long rising one; neither is shifted. The shorter parts of both falling-rising accents were assimilated to the longer parts, and there was no reason to shift the tonally homogeneous accents that resulted.

For the *West Slavic languages,* the same assimilation must be assumed as for Slovenian. After this process, however, the falling accent derived from the inverse acute was the only one to begin with a descent. It was therefore replaced in all West Slavic dialects by the normal circumflex, the accent most similar to it. Consequently, unlike all other Proto-Slavic dialects, the West Slavic dialects permitted a normal circumflex not only in the first syllable of disyllabic words but also in other positions: *mǎžešь* (for *mǎžešь*), *kobȳlъ* 'mare' (g. pl.) (for *kobýlъ*), etc. In the progressive accent shift, the circumflex derived from the inverse acute was treated like the old circumflex; that is, it produced a short vowel. But the rising tone that had developed from the inverse circumflex was not affected by the accent shift since it had no second part that could have been transferred to the following syllable. Nor did it undergo shortening, which affected only mid-length syllables, not long ones. In northern Proto-Kashubian, shortening of a mid-length syllable caused expiratorial reinforcement of the syllable preceding it; but under the rising tone derived from the inverse circumflex this accent transfer could not occur, for here no shortening took place. Nor could the accent transfer apply to the circumflex derived from the inverse acute, for this circumflex had produced a short syllable under the accent shift and was not subject to any further shortening. This explains the fact that, as Lehr-Spławiński showed (1917, 41ff.), the northern Kashubian and Slovincian metatonic accents retain their old positions.

21. On the Development of the Gutturals in the Slavic Languages

1

In his essay "De moderne phonologie en de omlijning van taalkategorieën" (1932), Van Wijk criticizes modern phonology. In contrast to the so-called phonological school, which emphasizes the teleological (goal-oriented) nature of sound changes and sees their purpose in the creation of regular and efficient phonological systems, Van Wijk believes that sound change is essentially devoid of inner meaning. Alongside changes that apparently strive to eliminate irregularities in the organization of the sound system, there are some that, according to Van Wijk, destroy an existing state of harmony without replacing it with a new one. He cites the change $g > \gamma > h$ in certain Slavic languages as an example. The change $g > \gamma$ provided a voiced counterpart for old x but deprived old k of such a counterpart, with the result that the newly created system was in no way superior to the old one. Moreover, when γ from g became h (in Ukrainian, Slovak, Czech, and Upper Sorbian), both k and x were isolated, and all symmetry was lost. "It is true," Van Wijk adds, "that the correlation $x : h$ is still felt to exist in paradigms such as Czech $b\bar{u}\chi$ (written *bůh*) : *boha* ['God,' nom. and g.], but the system has nevertheless lost something of its structural regularity, which is all the more surprising as the various Slavic languages underwent the change $g > \gamma > h$ independently of one another" (p. 74).

As a representative of the "phonological school," I would like to show here that the development of the gutturals in the Slavic languages is not at all purposeless and that its explanation lies in a striving for regularity and efficiency in the structure of the sound system.

2

First, certain statements made by Van Wijk must be corrected. From the *phonetic* standpoint, voiced h cannot be regarded as a "voiced counterpart" of x since these two sounds belong to different places of articulation. From the *phonological* point of view (i.e., from the standpoint of the linguistic *function* of the sounds in question), it is a different matter. The speakers of the Slavic languages that underwent the change $\gamma > h$ *perceive h* as the voiced counterpart of x, and therefore in their minds the equation $h : x = z : s = \check{z} : \check{s}$ is perfectly valid.[1] This is why even the modern languages still have γ as a phonetic variant of h

(and, to some extent, of *x*), without phonetically untrained Czechs, Slovaks, and Ukrainians being aware of this fact.[2] Dialectally, this γ can replace *h,* as appears to be the case, for example, in the Ugro-Russian dialects of Ukrainian (Broch 1895, 337; Broch 1900, 17). Occasional alternation between γ and *h* can also be observed in South Russian dialects bordering on Ukrainian-speaking territory: the same speaker will pronounce the same word sometimes with γ, sometimes with *h.* The transition from pure South Russian γ to pure Ukrainian or Belorussian *h* is so gradual and displays such extensive individual deviation that no exact isogloss can be drawn for it, the reason being that we are dealing with a phonetic, not a phonological, distinction (see Trubetzkoy 1931c, 230–31 [see chap. 6, pp. 40–41, in this volume]).

In the Slavic languages, voiced laryngeal *h* and velar γ are nothing more than two phonetic realizations of one phoneme, namely, the voiced counterpart (correlate) of *x.* Slavic *x* displays a fairly open articulation and hence relatively weak velar friction (Broch 1911, 40).[3] In the acoustic perception of *x* and (voiced) *h* by the Ukrainian, Czech, and Slovak ear, only the difference in voice is relevant, while the presence of weak velar friction in *x* and its absence in *h* is merely an irrelevant, "natural" by-product of the opposition of voice. Therefore, the change $\gamma > h$ had no effect on the phonological systems of the Slavic languages in question, and Novák (1930, 20) is correct in saying that it was a purely phonetic change.[4]

3

Van Wijk's claim that the individual Slavic languages introduced the change $g > \gamma > h$ independently of one another cannot be accepted, at least not as far as the phase $g > \gamma$ is concerned. In his objective and convincing review of the debate over the age of this change in Czech, Liewehr concluded: "Trávníček's assumption that old Slavic *g* began to yield γ from the beginning of the twelfth century . . . is no better supported than the hypothesis that the γ pronunciation dates back to Proto-Czech times" (1929, 25–26). The same is true of Slovak and Upper Sorbian.[5] The external evidence is worthless: the orthography of the old texts proves nothing, for the letter *g* can also represent a fricative γ (as in Old and Middle High German manuscripts); nor are loanwords of any value since languages with γ but without *g* reproduce the latter with γ (cf., e.g., South Russ. *cÿγarkă* = Russ. *cygarka* 'cigarette,' *t'ĭl'ĭγraf* = Russ. *telegraf* 'telegraph,' *γăz'etă* = Russ. *gazeta* 'newspaper')[6] and, vice versa, a language lacking γ can represent it only by means of *g* (cf., e.g., the representation of Turkish and Modern Greek γ by *g* in Bulgarian and Serbo-Croatian).[7]

Internal evidence permits only *termini ante quos* for the change $g > \gamma$ in the individual languages, no *termini post quos,*[8] and Šaxmatov's (1915, sec. 62, sec. 71n) view that the change was a dialectal phenomenon of the Proto-Slavic period has not been refuted. In the light of the fact that this change occurred not at geographically disparate places in the Slavic world but rather in a group of languages (dialects) that either share common borders today or did so at one time (as Upper Sorbian and Czech), Šaxmatov's assumption is much more probable than the idea that by chance South Russian, Belorussian, Ukrainian, Slovak, Czech, and Upper Sorbian all carried out the same change $g > \gamma$ independently of one another. Therefore, we should accept Šaxmatov's reconstruction and treat the change as a late Proto-Slavic dialectal phenomenon.

The change $\gamma > h$ belongs to a much later period. Since only a change in the phonetic realization of a phoneme is involved, the process must have begun with the appearance of voiced h as an unusual "stylistic" (optional) variant alongside γ. The two variants (γ and h) must have coexisted for a time; that is, the same speaker could pronounce the same word sometimes with γ and sometimes with h without creating the impression of a speech error. Perhaps h was originally preferred only in certain positions, but with time its use increased until it finally became the principal variant.[9] The process may have taken a long time; reliable points of reference for its chronology are lacking.[10]

Since medieval scribes associated the letter h with German voiceless h or with x (= "ch"), it probably would not have been employed to designate the voiced guttural fricative γ if this γ had not had voiced h as an optional variant (a different but generally accepted pronunciation of the same phoneme).[11] The first h-spellings of Slavic names in Latin documents thus show that, at that time (for Czech, the second half of the twelfth century [Bergmann 1921, 237; cf. Schwab 1925]), voiced h already existed as a phonetic realization of the voiced counterpart of x. But the texts tell us nothing about when this voiced h became the principal variant of the phoneme in question or when it first appeared as an optional variant alongside γ. It is likely that the definitive victory of the variant h occurred relatively late.[12] The first signs of the change $\gamma > h$, however, the weakening of the velar friction of γ and perhaps the first sporadic appearance of the optional variant h (if only to a very limited extent, such as between open vowels and in hurried or careless speech), may be very old, perhaps dating back to the late Proto-Slavic period.

4

Let us now turn to the main point, the phonological explanation of the development of the gutturals in Slavic. The most remarkable event in this development is the change $g > \gamma$.

This change took place in all Slavic dialects in which dz (< g') *had become* z, *except for (a) those in which Proto-Slavic* c *and* č *had merged and (b) those in which Proto-*

Slavic x had become a laryngeal aspirate [Hauchlaut] and displayed the tendency to disappear completely.

For the correct interpretation of these facts, the phonological concepts *correlation* and *disjunction* are necessary. In every language, two or more phoneme pairs display the same relation, such as, in Latin, the pairs $d : n = b : m$ or $p : t = b : d$. If a relation of this kind is perceived as the opposition between the presence and the absence of a certain feature, it is a *correlation*. All other relations between two phonemes are *disjunctions*. The relation $d : n$ in Latin is thus a correlation because, first, it is equivalent to the relation $b : m$ and, second, it is perceived as the absence versus the presence of nasalization. The relation $p : t$ in Latin is a disjunction because it cannot be perceived as the opposition between the presence and the absence of any feature, and the relation $s : l$ in Latin is a disjunction because it is not equivalent to any other relation between Latin phonemes. For a feature to be perceived as correlative, it must appear in more than one pair of phonemes in the same sound system. Thus, a given phoneme pair can be perceived in one language as a correlation, in another as a disjunction, depending on whether other equivalent phoneme pairs exist in the same language. Correlations can be combined in *bundles;* in Ancient Greek the relation media : tenuis : aspirata ($\delta : \tau : \theta = \beta : \pi : \phi = \gamma : \kappa : \chi$) is an example of a correlation bundle with three terms. Correlations give the phonological system a regular structure, and most languages tend to keep the number of isolated phonemes—those not participating in any correlation— to a minimum (see Trubetzkoy 1931d and the literature cited therein).

The Proto-Slavic obstruent system possessed only two correlations, that of voice and that of constriction or closure. By *correlation of voice* is meant the opposition between voiced and voiceless obstruents; the *correlation of constriction* is the opposition between obstruents with complete closure and those with incomplete closure. In this second correlation, it is irrelevant whether the obstruent with complete closure is a plosive or an affricate; the important thing is that in the one member of the correlation the closure at a certain place in the mouth is complete, whereas in the other member there is only incomplete closure, a constriction.

The correlation of constriction originally involved only two phoneme pairs, $k : x$ and $č : š$. No clear link to the correlation of voice existed, the only rule being that, as members of the correlation pair, both had to be voiceless. This meant that only one of the two members of each correlation pair could have a voiced counterpart: in the pair $k : x$, it was the stop ($k : g$); in the pair $č : š$, it was the fricative ($š : ž$).[13]

The situation changed when the palatals k' and g' (products of the second and third palatalization of the gutturals) became c and dz. Two new phoneme pairs, $c : s$ and $dz : z$, joined the old ones, $k : x$ and $č : š$.[14] Of these four pairs, the only one with voiced members was *dz* : *z*. Most Proto-Slavic dialects treated this as a disruption of the system and abandoned the distinction between *dz* and *z*. It remained only in the extreme Northwest (in the Pre-Lekhitic dialects) and the extreme South (in a part of the Pre-Bulgarian dialect area); in all other dialects, *z* and *dz* merged, the rarer *dz* becoming *z*.

The elimination of *dz* from the phonological systems of most Slavic dialects created a new state of affairs. In the obstruent systems of all these dialects, two groups of phonemes now existed. One comprised the pure stop pairs *t* : *d* and *p* : *b* (and *t'* : *d'* in dialects in which the palatalized stops derived from **tj, *dj* had not yet undergone further modification),[15] displaying the opposition of voice. The other was made up of the phoneme triads combining the opposition of voice with that of constriction. Two of these bundles displayed a clear structure: a voiceless fricative was opposed to a voiceless stop (affricate) and a voiced fricative (*c* : *s* : *z*, *č* : *š* : *ž*). The third—guttural—phoneme bundle did not fit into this pattern. Although the relation *k* : *g* was the same as *t* : *d, p* : *b,* the gutturals were unable to join the pure stop pairs because alongside *k* there was also *x* and the difference between *k* and *x* was clearly one of degree of constriction. On the other hand, the gutturals were also prevented from aligning with the other three-member bundles (*c* : *s* : *z*, *č* : *š* : *ž*) because of their dissimilar structure. For all Proto-Slavic dialects that had lost *dz,* the failure of the gutturals to fit into the phonological system was a problem that urgently needed solving.[16]

The simplest solution was the transformation of *g* into the fricative *γ*. Voiceless *x* acquired a voiced counterpart, while *k* retained only the role of stop counterpart of the fricative *x*. The gutturals were now organized like the sibilants, and the complete obstruent system acquired a regular structure: two (or three) pure stop pairs (*t* : *d, p* : *b,* and dialectally *t'* : *d'*) and three three-member phoneme bundles (*c* : *s* : *z*, *č* : *š* : *ž*, *k* : *x* : *γ*). Understandably, this was the path chosen by most of the Proto-Slavic dialects in question: Pre-South Russian, Pre-Slovak, Pre-Czech, and Pre–Upper Sorbian.[17]

Two phonological conditions were necessary for the change *g* > *γ*: the presence of the phoneme groups *c* : *s* : *z* and *č* : *š* : *ž* as models and the perception of an affinity between *x* and *k*. The change could not occur in dialects lacking these prerequisites. This explains why it was able to penetrate neither the Pre–North Russian nor the Pre–Lower Sorbian dialects of Proto-Slavic. In Pre–North Russian, Proto-Slavic *c* and *č* (from *č* and **tj*) had merged in an intermediate sound that I designate for convenience as *ĉ*. This is indicated by the confusion of Ч and Ц already noticeable in the oldest Novgorod texts (see also the merger of Proto-Slavic *sc* and *sč,* as in North Russ. *ščepka* < **scěpъka* 'splinter,' *ščerit'* < **scěriti* 'show one's teeth' [cf. Durnovo 1926 and Jakobson 1929, 46]). The intermediate sound was unable to function as correlative stop counterpart of either *s* or *š;* the correlation of constriction was abandoned. All that remained was the correlation of voice, comprising five phoneme pairs (*t* : *d, p* : *b, k* : *g, s* : *z, š* : *ž*), together with two isolated, "nonpaired" obstruent phonemes, *ĉ* and *x.*

The same development must be reconstructed for Pre–Lower Sorbian. In modern Lower Sorbian, Proto-Slavic **c* and **č* are both represented by *c* when not bound by another consonant, but they are represented by *č* in certain consonant groups (*čk, čm, šč,* etc.). Mucke (1891, 167) concluded from the German form of Lower Lausitz place-names such as *Bretschen, Tschecheln,* and *Tscheren* that Proto-Slavic **č* was "still prevalent" in Lower Sorbian in the twelfth and thirteenth centuries, but numerous place-names in Lower Lausitz have German *z* (*ts*) for Proto-Slavic **č* (e.g., *Zernitz*). Moreover, Mucke himself cites the name *Tschirkau,* which has German *tsch* for Proto-Slavic **c* (Proto-Slavic **cьrkъvь* 'church,' modern Lower Sorb. *cyrkej,* Upper Sorb. *cerkej*). It follows, in my opinion, that in Lower Sorbian, just as in North Russian, Proto-Slavic **c* and **č* had merged in an intermediate sound, **ĉ,* that was reproduced by German speakers sometimes as *z, tz,* sometimes as *tsch, zsch,* and that later became *c* when not bound by another consonant and *č* in certain consonant groups. The merger of **c* and **č* can have taken place already in the Pre–Lower Sorbian dialects of Proto-Slavic.

The abandonment of the correlation of constriction brought about by the merger of *c* and *č* provided a satisfactory solution to the "guttural problem."[18] This was the reason why the change *g* > *γ* could not spread to either Pre–North Russian or Pre–Lower Sorbian. And today, in fact, the isoglosses of the plosive *g* and the change *č* > *c* on Sorbian territory coincide. On Russian territory, we find between the area of *cokan'e* (merger of *č* and *c*) and the South Russian dialects proper (with *g* > *γ* and the opposition *č* : *c*) a relatively wide zone consisting of dialects with preserved *g* and the opposition *č* : *c*.[19] They are of relatively recent origin and seem to have arisen through dialect mixing. Earlier, they must have displayed *cokan'e,* as is shown, for example, by the treatment of *č* and *c* in Russian loanwords in Mordvin (Ravila 1932a, 256–57, 261–62). Originally, therefore, the geographic distribution of plosive *g* and of the merger of *č* and *c* on East Slavic territory, too, must have been identical.[20]

A third possible solution to the problem of the gutturals was the laryngealization of *x,* that is, its transformation into a voiceless, laryngeal aspirate [*Hauchlaut*] (which I designate as *ḥ* in order to distinguish it from voiced *h*). In this way, the phoneme ceased to be a member of the guttural group, and the constriction correlation *x* : *k* was eliminated. Velar *x* does still occur in dialects that underwent this change, but merely as an optional (or combinatory-optional) variant of *ḥ,* and it is pronounced so far back in the throat and with such weak friction that it cannot possibly be perceived as a fricative counterpart of *k*. The further development of this *ḫ* in the dialects is characterized by its becoming voiced in certain positions and by the tendency for it to disappear completely (it is often replaced by voiced sounds: *g, v, j*).[21] Today, *ḫ* or its reflexes can be found in Bulgarian and Serbo-Croatian dialects, but the original geographic distribution of the change *x > ḫ* is beyond reconstruction.[22] In any case, the change is to be regarded as a solution to the guttural problem. In the Proto-Slavic dialects that introduced it, a system arose in which all obstruent phonemes except *ḫ* found partners: *t : d, p : b, (t' : d',) k : g, c : s : z, č : š : ž, ḫ.*

The tendency to weaken the velar friction of the guttural fricatives is characteristic of Slavic generally. Even in North and Central Russian and Polish, *x* displays very weak friction, with the result that many observers perceive it as an intermediate sound between *x* and *h* (*ḫ*).[23] But neither Polish nor North Russian went as far as the South Slavic dialects in this respect. The reason for this difference is not far to seek. In North Russian, the weakening of the velar friction of *x* was merely a consequence of the isolation of this phoneme in the phonological system after the abandonment of the correlation of constriction.[24] In Polish, as well, the weakening of the velar friction of *x* is a consequence of its isolation; in the phonological system of modern Polish, it is the only obstruent phoneme without a voiced counterpart.[25] In both languages, the weakening affected only the phonetic realization of the phoneme *x;* the status of this phoneme in the system remained unchanged. In the South Slavic dialects, however, the laryngealization of *x* was not a by-product but rather the direct cause (better, the means) of its isolation in the sound system. The change was phonological, not merely phonetic. This is why it was much more radical than the change in the pronunciation of *x* in Polish and North Russian.[26]

In languages with the change *g > γ*, no significant weakening of the velar friction of *x* was possible since this could have obscured the relation *x : k* (and hence the equation *x : k = s : c = š : č*). On the other hand, nothing prevented these languages from "develarizing" the voiced guttural fricative, since it stood in no direct relation to *k* and its relation to *x* depended mainly on the correlation of voice. In most of the languages in question, the velar friction of *γ* was weakened even to the point of transforming the sound into voiced *h;* but the corresponding phoneme retained its function of the voiced correlate of *x*.

Certain Čakavian and Slovenian dialects treated the gutturals differently. In some of them, *g* became *γ*, just as in the Central Proto-Slavic dialects mentioned above. The Slovenian dialects also display other unusual features: in some of them, *g* and *γ* alternate as optional variants of the same phoneme; in others, *g* is preserved as a stop except word finally, where it has become *x;* in still others, *g* and *x* have merged into *h;* elsewhere, *k* has even become the "rough vowel onset," a kind of glottal stop; and so on. Space does not permit a discussion of these unusual situations here; I intend to treat them in more detail, and also in connection with other topics, in the future. Suffice it to say here that I regard the peculiar development of the gutturals in Slovenian as the result of a struggle between two solutions to the guttural problem: the change $g > \gamma$ and the laryngealization of x.

My points may be summarized as follows. The Proto-Slavic system of obstruent phonemes was governed by the correlations of voice and constriction. In Proto-Slavic dialects that had eliminated dz ($< g'$), a structural rule existed according to which voiced stops could not participate in both correlations at the same time. In order to reconcile this rule with the presence of the three gutturals, the dialects made various changes: (*a*) some of them eliminated the correlation of constriction (by merging c and $č$ into an intermediate sound); (*b*) others retained the correlation of constriction but dissolved the correlative pair $k : x$ (by transforming x into a laryngeal sound); (*c*) still others made the gutturals conform to the rule (by the change $g > \gamma$). All Slavic languages display the tendency to weaken the velar friction of the guttural fricatives. But since velar friction signals the incomplete closure formed at a certain point in the mouth, it can be weakened only in guttural fricatives that do not participate in the correlation of constriction in the language in question. We may indeed conclude that the development of the Slavic gutturals fulfills a purpose and does so quite efficiently.

22. Remarks on Some Iranian Words Borrowed by the North Caucasian Languages

The northwestern, or "Scythian," Iranian dialects have been studied very little. Modern Ossetic, which seems to be the only living remnant of this formerly extensive dialect group, proves by its phonetics, grammar, and vocabulary that North Iranian differed fundamentally from South Iranian: in phonetics, the reflex *ar for old *$\mathring{r}$ could be mentioned (as in Armenian, in contrast to Persian and the other Iranian languages); in vocabulary, the word *bindzä* 'bee,' based on the root *bhei- (which is characteristic of the northwestern Indo-European languages but unknown in Indo-Iranian). Data on the other Iranian dialects of the Scythian group, therefore, would be of prime importance for the comparative grammar of Indo-European. Unfortunately, although Ossetic is the descendant of one dialect of this group, we possess for all the others only insignificant, fragmentary information, such as proper names, and even these facts are sparse. Under these circumstances, any new source of information is welcome. The purpose of the present note is to identify one such source.

The dialect from which Ossetic is descended does not seem to have been the only Iranian language spoken in the steppes and mountains of the northern Caucasus. There must have been others, now extinct, for they have left traces in the native North Caucasian languages. These languages display a great number of words that are clearly of Iranian origin but not to be found in Ossetic and that in part presuppose a linguistic evolution distinct from that of Ossetic. Thus, Chechen has the word *ḥaša* 'host,' Kabardian *-ḥaç'e,* Circassian *hač'ə;* these words reflect the Iranian root *haxay 'friend' (Avestan nom. sg. *haxā,* dat. *hašye*), which does not exist in Ossetic and which contradicts the phonetic laws of that language since in Ossetic initial *h is dropped and all *s*-sibilants become pure (hissing) sibilants. In particular, the Caucasian languages of the western group (Abkhaz, Ubykh, and Adyghe with its two dialects, Kabardian and Circassian) present a large number of words borrowed at a very ancient date from some vanished Iranian dialects.

The Iranian word *fšu-* 'small livestock,' occurring in Avestan primarily in compounds, is unknown in Ossetic, which has only the form *fus,* from *pasu.* But it is attested in the Caucasian languages of the west: Adyghe *p'çi* 'prince' corresponds to Abkhaz *p'ç"ym* 'rich man,' which recalls Avestan *fšumō* 'rich in livestock.' The goddess considered as patroness of sheep and goats in Circassian mythology bore the name *P'çyçan,* which evidently corresponds to an Iranian *fšušanī* 'she who procures (verbal root *san-*) small livestock.' Circassian also displays other mythological terms borrowed from Iranian. The ancient storm god was called Çibλə, and this is the name still given to thunder, lightning, and storm in Kabardian (çyble). Since the palatalized ç of Adyghe generally corresponds to çᵘ in Abkhaz and Ubykh, the original form of the storm god's name must have been *šu̯ible, which could be compared with Avestan xšvīwra 'prompt, rapid.' The Adyghe word for 'tempest' is u̯ái̯e, which recalls the wind god Vāyu- of the Vedas. In Circassian, the word for 'sorceress' is 'udə, which may go back to Iranian *yātu- with epenthesis of u.

Other Iranian words in the West Caucasian languages have no connection to religion. Circassian uostaγa and Kabardian ozdyγa 'candle, light' doubtless reflect an Iranian *us-daγa, composed of the preposition us (Skt. ud) and a derivative of the root daγ 'burn' (Skt. dah, dagh). Circassian nyč'epə 'tonight, last night' is opaque from the point of view of Circassian, and it is tempting to trace it to an Iranian *nū-xšapar 'tonight.' To be sure, Circassian č' for the supposed Iranian *xš is without parallel; but the combination xš is foreign to Adyghe, which has it only in the word axše 'money,' borrowed from Noghay (a Turkic language), and in the word maxše 'camel,' which is surely also a borrowing, although its origin is unclear. The idea of 'speaking' is expressed in Circassian by the verb guš'a'yn, which is evidently Iranian *gaušayati, causative of the root guš- (Skt. ghuš-) 'hear, make noise' (cf. Skt. ghōšoyati 'proclaim, announce'). Circassian fedə, Kabardian xodé 'similar' (Common Adyghe *xu̯ede) goes back to an Iranian *xᵘatah (Skt. svatas); compare Ossetic xädäg 'the same.'

Not having all the necessary materials at my disposal, I am not able to continue the list of Iranian borrowings in the West Caucasian languages here, but I hope I have proved that these words exist. Most of the words cited above are not attested in Ossetic. It goes without saying that the West Caucasian languages also possess words that could have been borrowed directly from Ossetic: Adyghe badze 'fly' – Ossetic bindzä 'bee'; Adyghe ben 'grave' – Ossetic bun 'place' (Avest. buna- 'bottom'); Circassian beurə 'much, for a long time' – Ossetic bëurä (Avest. baēvarə); and so on. But facts of this type only make it all the more obvious that Ossetic (or Proto-Ossetic, "Alan") was not the only source of North Caucasian borrowings from Iranian. There are cases in which Ossetic itself borrowed words of Iranian origin from a Caucasian language. One of these cases is very instructive and worthy of mention here.

The peoples of the northern Caucasus possess a common epic tradition, a store of legends celebrating the great deeds of heroes and demigods. These legends vary from one people to another, but their essential subjects remain the same throughout the region. The proper names of the heroes, too, are to a large extent shared by all the North Caucasian tribes, the Adyghe, the Balkars (Karachays, Urusbiys, etc.), the Ossetes, and the Ingush. Closer examination shows that those names that can be derived from Iranian according to the phonetic laws of Ossetic are restricted to the domain of Ossetic folklore: the brother heroes *Äxsnart'* (= *Xšnāθra-* and *Äxsärtäg* (= *Xšaθraka-*) are known and celebrated only by the Ossetes, as is the malevolent *Syrdon,* whose name appears to be Ossetic, although it admits of no certain etymology. In contrast, names of Adyghe origin are known not only among the Circassians and Kabardians but also among the Ossetes: we find in Ossetic folklore a hero *Sauai,* whose name appears in Adyghe folklore in the form *Çau-aiə,* which in Circassian means 'ugly boy,' and the patronymic of another Ossetic hero, *Kuc'yǵifyrt',* recurs in a Kabardian legend in the form *Qujc'yk"o-qo,* literally '(son of the) little bald one.'[1]

Another legendary Ossetic hero, however, bears the name *Bat'raz,* which cannot be indigenous since the cluster *-t'r-* is impossible in native Ossetic words. This hero is known by the Circassians as *P'ät'αräz,* by the Kabardians as *Betyrez,* and by the Ingush as *P'αt'riž.* The Adyghe forms explain the cluster *-t'r-* in the Ossetic name, since Circassian *α,* corresponding to Kabardian *y,* is a very short close vowel that can easily disappear. It is obvious that the Ossetes borrowed this hero's name from Kabardian: in Common Adyghe, it was **Pet'αrez,* not **Bet'αrez,*[2] and Ingush, with its *P'αt'riž,* confirms that the initial sound was voiceless. But the reconstructed Common Adyghe **Pet'αrez* cannot be analyzed into elements proper to Adyghe: the ancestors of the Circassians and Kabardians must have borrowed the name from yet another language.

The legends attached to the name describe its bearer as a cruel and vindictive figure whose principal exploit is vengeance for the murder of his father. The circumstances under which the father was killed cannot be reconstructed in detail since the attested versions differ significantly, but all those known to me (except the Ingush version, which makes no mention of the event and cannot justify the hero's cruelty) agree in linking the murder of the father with the miraculous birth of the son. The Ossetic versions, which are the most detailed, report that the mother of *Bat'raz* was a supernatural being. Pregnant with *Bat'raz,* and determined to leave her husband *Xamyc,* she spits on his back, transmitting to him by this act the embryo of her son, and disappears. *Xamyc* becomes a hunchback. His hump grows visibly, and after nine months he consults a sorceress, who cuts off the hump, delivering him of the infant *Bat'raz.* Among the Circassians of the Tuapse region, I noted a legend of the birth of *P'ät'αräz* that agreed with the Ossetic version in the essential fact that *P'ät'αräz* was given birth to by his father *Xamyš'* in a supernatural manner.[3]

The agreement between the Adyghe and the Ossetic versions of the legend makes it highly probable that the protagonist's name was Iranian, namely, **Pitari-za,* which means 'given birth to by the father.' Compounds of this type with the root *zan-* 'give birth' in the *za*-grade as second term are unknown in Old Persian (including Avestan), but Sanskrit makes widespread use of corresponding forms of the root *an(-ja): dvīja, devaja,* etc.; compare especially *manasija-* and Vedic *pravāteja-* with the first term in the locative case. The reconstructed **Pitariza* is a syntactic compound: its first term is in the locative. A more regular type, such as **Pitarza* (< **pitr̥za*), would not have conveyed the desired shade of meaning. The root *zan-* (Indo-European **ĝen-*) is employed in Indo-Iranian with the locative of the mother and the ablative of the father (i.e., for normal births). The only way of expressing the fact that in the birth of the hero in question the father assumed the mother's role, that is, that he *gave birth to* a son, was the anomalous compound **Pitariza.* Since this etymology accords perfectly with the content of the legend, its degree of probability becomes very high.

*Pitariza's name tells us that, at the time when North Caucasian heroic legend was in the process of forming, the Iranian tribes participating in this formative process still possessed the old nominal inflection, at least the distinction between locative and ablative. More important, the fact that the Ossetic form *Bat'raz* was borrowed from Kabardian proves that the Iranians who supplied Proto-Adyghe with this name were not the direct ancestors of the Ossetes.

These points lead to an additional hypothesis. The heroes of North Caucasian epic legend are designated by the term *nart'* (in Adyghe, Balkar, Ossetic, and Ingush); among the mountain folk of Daghestan, the same word means 'giant.' The word cannot be explained by any of the modern languages of the northern Caucasus. But since we have seen that Iranian **fšuma* yielded Adyghe *p'çy,* we may derive Adyghe *nart'* (or *nart'y, nart'α,* according to the requirements of external sandhi) from Iranian **nartama;* compare Sanskrit *nr̥tama* 'the most heroic,' epithet of Indra in the *Rig-Veda.* This etymology, supported by the etymology of Common Adyghe **Pet'arez,* suggests that the epic tradition was brought to the northern Caucasus by Iranians who were not the ancestors of the Ossetes: Iranian **nartama-* would have yielded **närdäm* in Ossetic (or perhaps **näldäm,* since the Ossetic reflex of Iranian **nar-* 'man' is *nal*).

It has been my goal to draw the attention of linguists, primarily scholars of Iranian, to a new and important source of information for the study of the extinct North Iranian languages. Careful investigation of the indigenous languages of the northwestern Caucasus will perhaps furnish data just as valuable, even if not as voluminous, as those already supplied by Armenian for the study of Middle Persian (Pahlavi). The East Caucasian languages, with the possible exception of Chechen, are less interesting from this point of view: aside from a few words borrowed from Ossetic (such as Kazikumyk *barzuntiu* 'promontory' = Ossetic *bärzond* 'high'), the Iranian elements of the Lezghian languages of Daghestan seem all to be of Persian origin, borrowed by way of Tatar-Azeri. There are no indications that the mountain folk of Daghestan ever maintained cultural relations, however casual, with the North Iranians.

23. On the Prehistory of the East Caucasian Languages

1

The name of the Laks in central Daghestan—singular *lakku-čū*, plural *lak*—was identified with the *Λῆγες* of the Greek geographers already by Uslar (1890, 1-2). This identification is confirmed by historical phonetics. Lak *a* derives partly from older **a* but partly from an older front vowel (**ä*), as comparison with the Samurian languages shows: for example, Lak *maz*, Kuri *medz*, Agul *mez*, etc. 'tongue'; Lak *mašši* 'dairy farm,' Agul *mex* 'winter quarters'; Lak *nak̲*, Kuri *nek*, Agul *nekk*, etc. 'milk'; Lak *maq̇*, Agul *ney°*, Tabasaran *newγ*, etc. 'teardrop'; Lak *marχχa*, Agul *mer'ä* (?) 'root.' Strong *kk* in Lak (which becomes *k* before consonants and word finally) arose from Pre-Lak **g*: compare Lak *kkarčči*, Andi *guži*, Agul *g°ardž* 'tooth'; Lak *kkačči* 'dog,' Avar *guaži*, Archi *g°ačči*, Dargwa *gwadža* 'female dog'; Lak *kkacca*, Archi *g°acci*, Dargwa *gwaza* 'mare'; Lak *kkunuk*, Archi *genuk* 'egg'; Lak *kkuṭ* 'hole, opening,' Avar *goend* 'pit, well'; Lak *kkurtta*, Archi *gertti* (Dargwa *dirga* < *girda*) 'bow, crossbow'; Lak *kkurkki*, Andi *gurguma*, Tabasaran *gurgum*, Agul *girgen*, Ingush *görgə*, Chechen *gωrgan* 'round'; Lak *kkakkan* (perf. *kka-kra*), Chechen *gar*, Dargwa *gwis*, Agul *ag°as* 'see'; Lak *-ukkin*, Andi *-agudu* (pres. *-aguar*) 'count.' The native name of the Laks can thus be traced back to a base form **läg*.

The original meaning of the word **läg* was probably 'person.' Khinalug *ləgə-d* 'man' is undoubtedly related, although the present state of research on the Khinalug language does not permit us to specify the nature of the relation. Ossetic *läg* 'person' is clearly an old borrowing from an East Caucasian language. In the East Caucasian languages bordering on Ossetic (i.e., the Chechen group), **läg* has acquired the meaning 'slave': Bats *lag*, Chechen *laj*, Ingush *ləj*. East Caucasian *g* remains unchanged in Bats, but in the other Chechen languages after vowels it has become *j* or disappeared, according to the environment: the correspondence Bats *lag*, genitive *laga(n)* ~ Chechen *laj*, genitive *lēn* may be compared with Bats *sag*, genitive *saga(n)* ~ Chechen *saj*, genitive *sēn* 'stag'; compare further Bats *gagao* ~ Chechen *gē* 'belly,' Bats *žagn* ~ Chechen *žajna* 'book,' Bats *jeg* ~ Chechen *jī* 'beer,' Bats *c̣ejg*, Chechen *c̣ī* 'blood,' etc. Apparently, the closure of old **g* (and of the other old voiced plosives **b*, **d*) was weakened in postvocalic position, and this lenition led to vocalization.[1]

2

The area between the Lak and the Chechen language groups is occupied today by the Avar-Ando group, in which the form *läg 'person' has no cognates. There is, however, an Avar word laγ 'slave' that is obviously connected with Chechen laj 'slave' in some way, although it cannot be a regular derivation from *läg since old *g is preserved in Avar in all positions. It can only be a borrowing from a language of the Chechen type, in which voiced stops have undergone lenition after vowels: a *g sound of this kind, formed with weak or perhaps even incomplete closure, could have been rendered by the ancestors of the Avars as a postvelar fricative γ. From Avar, laγ 'slave' spread to the other Avar-Ando languages and to Darginian and Lak. Archi must have borrowed the word through the mediation of Lak, as the Archi plural form laγart with its Lak ending shows.

Žirkov pointed out in his Avar grammar that the word laγ 'slave' is treated in Avar as an ethnic name: the ergative plural laγzàdericca displays a structure otherwise typical only of names of peoples or tribes (e.g., χχùndericca from χχùnzaqew 'Khunsak,' baŋqàdericca from bòniqew 'Botlikh,' ʿandàdericca from ʿandissew 'Andi'). The ethnic group from which the Avars borrowed the word laγ 'slave' had used it to designate itself. This people must have had the same native name as the Laks, the same lenition of postvocalic voiced stops as the Chechens, and a homeland somewhere between the area of the Laks and that of the Chechens, that is, probably in western Daghestan.

3

It follows that the Avar-Ando peoples, which today occupy western Daghestan, are not its original inhabitants. This is confirmed by the fact that Lak and the Chechen languages share a number of features that are foreign to the Avar-Ando languages. The emphatic palatalization correlation in Lak and Chechen consonants, completely lacking in the Avar-Ando languages, is not one of them, however (see Trubetzkoy 1931b, 10–11, 34, 47–48); it appears to have existed originally in all East Caucasian languages, so its presence in Lak and Chechen is not the result of a common innovation.

What is significant is, rather, the lack of the correlation of labialization in Lak and Chechen consonants, for the opposition between labialized and nonlabialized consonants was at one time common to all East Caucasian languages, including Lak and Chechen. This is proved for Lak by the different treatment of old labialized and nonlabialized prevelars before a and i. In this position, the originally nonlabialized prevelars have become š-sibilants (Lak irža, g. irglul, Avar erga 'sequence'; Lak ttarḳ, g. tturčal, Agul irkk, pl. irkkar 'bone'; Lak čan, Agul kken 'lower part'; Lak i-čan, perf. i-ḳura, Agul ḳes 'die';

Lak *išin*, perf. *i-xura*, Agul *ixes* 'lay'; Lak *ššar*, Agul *xir* 'woman'; etc.), while the originally round prevelars have not (Lak *kkarčči*, Agul *gᵒardž* 'tooth,' see above; further Lak *kija*, Avar *koeʿa* 'dishonest'; Lak *ukān*, Avar *kuine*, Dargwa *irkwis* 'eat'; Lak *ḳi*, Dargwa *ḳwi* 'two'; Lak *riḳ*, g. *riḳiral*, Kuri, Agul *jaḳᵒ*, pl. *jaḳᵒar* 'axe'; etc.). In the Chechen languages, the originally labialized dorsal fricatives seem to have become *pχ* (e.g., Chechen *pχa*, Lak *xxa* 'vein'; Chechen *pχī*, Agul *ifâ* < **jixᵒâ* 'five'; Ingush *pχar* 'with young,' Kuri *χᵒar* 'mare'), while the nonlabialized ones are represented by *χ* or *tχ*.[2]

Since the opposition between labialized and nonlabialized consonants must have existed in Lak and the Chechen group, its loss may be considered a common innovation of these languages. The Avar-Ando languages did not participate in this innovation. It is true that the correlation of labialization is somewhat limited in Avar-Ando (and in the Darginian group), and the correlation itself was rephonologized, as the labial offset of old labialized consonants merged with the following vowels to form diphthongs, but this is not the same thing as eliminating the distinction labialized-nonlabialized.

Also significant is the agreement between Lak and the Chechen group in the treatment of old lateral affricates. Whereas both lateral affricates remained lateral in Archi and the Avar-Ando languages and became dorsal in the rest of East Causasian, in Lak and the Chechen languages the old voiced affricate is represented by a lateral sound and the voiceless one by a dorsal (which has merged with old **ḳ;* see Trubetzkoy 1922).

The most important Chechen-Lak innovation in the area of phonetics is the merger of the two sibilant affricates that may be reconstructed for the oldest period of East Caucasian as **ç* and **cc* (or **çç?*). The reflex of **ç* is in all East Caucasian languages *ç* (which yields *z* medially in Chechen and Ingush, according to the general rule): Avar *anç*, Archi *wiça*, Dargwa *wiç*, Tabasaran *jiçu*, Lak *aç* 'ten'; Avar *çija*, Archi *maça*, Kuri *çeji*, Chechen *çenin*, Lak *çu* 'new, young'; Avar *çeze*, Archi *aças*, Dargwa *-içis*, Kuri *açun*, Chechen *-uzar* (Bats *-uçar*), Lak *-uçin* 'fill'; Avar, Dargwa, Agul, etc. *ça*, Archi *oç*, Kuri *çaj*, Chechen *çe*, Lak *çu* 'fire'; Avar *baç*, Dargwa *biç*, Chechen *bωrz* (Bats *borç*), Lak *barç* 'wolf'; Dargwa *ʿçirç*, Kuri *çiç*, Chechen *çωz* (Bats *çoç*) 'locust'; Archi *darçan*, Kuri *riçam*, Lak *ittaçani*, Bats *çamçam* 'eyebrow'; etc.

East Caucasian **cc*, on the other hand, becomes in Archi and the Avar-Ando languages *çç;* in Dargwa *r'* (more rarely *dz*); in Tabasaran *cc;* in Kuri *t* finally, otherwise *ţ;* in Rutul and Tsakhur *t* finally, otherwise *d* (in Tsakhur also *ţ*). Only in Lak and the Chechen languages does this sound merge with **ç:* for example, Avar *naçç*, Dargwa *nir'*, Tabasaran *necc*, Agul *nett*, Kuri *net* (pl. *neṭer*), Lak *naç*, Chechen *mezi* (Bats *maç*) 'louse'; Avar *ççar*, Archi *ççor*, Kuri *ṭar*, Agul *ttur*, Rutul *dur*, Chechen *çe* (g. *çerin*), Lak *ça* (pl. *çardu*) 'name'; Avar *ççoa*, Dargwa *ur'i*, Lak *çu-ku* 'star'; Avar *ççino*, Archi *ççan*, Tsakhur *dan*, Chechen *can*, Lak *çumu-kkuţ* 'navel' (Lak *kkuṭ* 'hole, opening, depression'); Archi *marçç*, Tabasaran *marcci*, Agul *martte*, Lak *març* 'clean'; Avar *hoçço*, Archi *imçç*, Dargwa *war'a*, Kuri *wirt* (g. *wirṭedin*), Rutul *it*, Tsakhur *ut*, Agul *üt* (g. *üttan*), Chechen *mωz* (Bats *moç*), Lak *niç* 'honey'; Andi *miçça*, Dargwa *mur'i*, Chechen *merzin* (Bats *maçri*), Lak *naçu* 'sweet' (cf. Agul *itte*, Tsakhur *-uṭu*, Archi *-izdu* < **içç-də* 'sweet'); Archi *açci*, Dargwa *idzala*, Kuri *ṭal* < *jiṭal*, Agul *ittal*, Rutul *jadal* 'pain, illness,' Tabasaran *iccu* 'ill,' Chechen *lazar* (Bats *laçar*), Lak *çun* 'hurt' (intr.).

In the field of morphology, two features may be noted. First, the Chechen languages and Lak have a dative ending in *n* that occurs nowhere else in East Caucasian. Second, these languages have given up every trace of the "nasal conjugation" found in the languages surrounding Lak: in Avar, the verbs with infinitive in *-ine*, present *-una* (as opposed to those in *-ize*, *-ula*); in Archi, the verbs with present in *-an*, *-in*, preterite *-ni* (as opposed to those in *-ar*, *-ir*, *-di*); in Kuri, the verbs with gerund in *-anz*, present *-anda* (as opposed to those in *-az*, *-ada*); in Darginian, the verbs of Uslar's third conjugation.[3]

The common features of Chechen and Lak must have arisen at a time when the region between Lak and Chechen was occupied not by the Avar-Ando group but by some other languages that participated in these innovations.

4

Most of the Chechen-Lak innovations are also found in Udi. This language has abandoned consonant labialization and displays the emphatic correlation of palatalization. The affricates **ç* and **cc* have merged here to *ç*: for example, Udi *wiç* 'ten,' *çi* 'name,' *neç* 'louse,' etc. Udi does not have an *n* dative, but on the other hand it has failed to retain the nasal conjugation, which unites it with Lak and the Chechen languages. So it is very probable that Udi was originally separated from Lak not by the Samurian languages but by languages that participated in the Chechen-Lak-Udi innovations.

Some traces of the lost language of the original inhabitants of the Samur valley may perhaps be found in the modern Samurian languages. The word for 'goat'—Lak *çuku*, Avar *ççe* (pl. *ççani*), Archi *ççej* (pl. *ççahur*)—must have contained **cc*. The Samurian languages, however, display in this word *ç* (Kuri, Agul *çeh*, Tabasaran, Rutul *çih*, Tsakhur *ce'e*), which can be explained only by the influence of a language of the Chechen-Lak-Udi type. Old **b*, **d*, **g* preserve their voice in the Samurian languages. But the cognates of Avar *gorde* (Karata *gurdi*, Khvarshi *gid*, Dido *ged*) 'shirt' are Kuri *ḳurt* 'short pelt,' Tabasaran *kkurtt*, Tsakhur *gurt* 'shirt,' which must be derived from a Common Samurian base form **kkurt* or **kkurtt*.[4] This base form can only be a loan from a language in which the old voiced stops were systematically represented by strong voiceless stops, as in modern Lak (cf. Lak *kkurttu* 'beshmet, short outer garment').

The present-day Laks are thus the last remnant of a group of East Caucasian tribes whose homeland originally extended much farther to the west and the south and who shared borders with both the Chechen tribes and the Udi. The other members of the group were later absorbed in the west by the Avar-Ando and in the south by the Samurian tribes, most likely through a process of immigration and conquest.

The ancient inhabitants of the region occupied today by the Avar-Ando and Samurian tribes apparently bore the name *läg, which was identical with the Λήγες of the Greek sources. But what was the name of the immigrants and conquerors who brought the Avar-Ando and Samurian languages into these areas? Among the designations used by neighboring peoples for the Avars, Karata *halbi* 'Avar' is of special interest,[5] for it is reminiscent of the Caucasian "Albanians" of the Greek sources. The question arises whether the present distribution of the East Caucasian tribes should not be considered the result of an immigration of the "Albanians" into southern and western Daghestan.

24. The Universal Adoption of the Roman Alphabet: Peoples of the Caucasus

As you know, the League of Nations supports the Institut de Coopération Intellectuelle, and one of the institute's committees encourages all languages that do not use the roman alphabet to go over to it. This committee, so typical of the League of Nations, asked me for some data on the romanization of the alphabets among the peoples of the Caucasus. Since my information is very incomplete and partly outdated, I am afraid of making mistakes. In Brno you showed me an article by Jakovlev [1928a, 1928b] on the writing systems of all the peoples of the USSR. Can't you send me this article or write out from it everything concerning the peoples of the Caucasus (not only the autochthonous peoples but also the Indo-European and Turkic ones)? Please hurry!—N. S. Trubetzkoy to Roman Jakobson, 28 May 1932

Of the peoples of the Caucasus, the Georgians and the Armenians possess an ancient literary tradition and national writing systems. As these systems are practical and well adapted to the two languages in question, no need has been felt to replace them with the roman alphabet. The tentative efforts made in this direction have never led to any practical result. The Mingrelians and the Svans, whose languages are closely related to Georgian and who have consistently been dominated by Georgian culture, have virtually no national literature: they read and write in Georgian (all the more so as this is the official language of the Georgian Soviet Republic, to which the Mingrelians and Svans belong), and, when they do make the effort to write in their own language, they use the *Georgian alphabet.*

Before the revolution, the other Caucasian peoples, most of them Muslims, used the *Arabic alphabet* (with some additional characters), insofar as they wrote in their native languages at all. The Arabic writing system, which was inconvenient and poorly adapted to the phonological systems of these languages, was able to survive only under the pressure of Islamic tradition. The efforts of the prerevolutionary Russian government to introduce a writing system based on the Russian alphabet among certain peoples (notably the mountain folk of Daghestan) were foiled by the opposition of the Islamic clergy, who saw these initiatives as attempts at Russification and Christian propaganda. Otherwise, with the exception of the Azeri, who could boast of a periodical press and a mature literature (in the Arabic alphabet) long before the World War, the other Caucasian Moslems possessed only the seeds of national literatures.

The Bolshevik Revolution changed this situation drastically: Communist propaganda required periodicals and popular literature in national languages.

The new government cared nothing for the opinions of the Muslim clergy and, having resolved to destroy the influence of all religion, declared war on the Arabic alphabet, which for every Muslim is closely linked to Islam. In order not to raise suspicions of Russification, it was decided to replace Arabic writing not by Russian characters but by the roman alphabet, with the addition of supplementary characters. This reform was not easy and could not be carried out in one step. For many peoples, it was necessary to revise the writing system several times before satisfactory results were obtained. According to official Soviet information, the roman alphabet is now being used by the following peoples who had previously employed Arabic writing (or none at all): the Avars, the Adyghe (Circassians), the Azeri, the Dargwas, the Ingush, the Kumyks, the Kurds, the Laks (Kazi-Kumyks), the Lazi, the Lezghians (Kuri), the Noghays, the Kabardians, the Karachays (Balkars), the Chechens, and the Talyshes. The roman alphabet has also been accepted by the mountain Jews, who had previously employed the Hebrew alphabet, by the Ossetians, who had possessed an alphabet based on Russian characters, and by the Abkhazians, who had not had any universally accepted writing system.

About thirty Caucasian peoples remain without a writing system at present. These are primarily West Caucasian languages spoken by very small linguistic communities and in very limited areas (Archi, e.g., is spoken by a single village with a population of seven hundred). Since almost all members of these small communities are bilingual (except for children and some women), their mother tongues are tending to disappear and will soon be replaced by more prestigious neighboring languages: by Avar (this is the case for the languages of West Daghestan: Andi, Botlikh, Godoberi, Karata, Akhvakh, Bagulal, Tindi, Chamalal, Khvarshi, Dido, Kapucha, Bezhita, Hunzal, Archi), by Azeri (for certain languages of South Daghestan and neighboring regions: Agul, Tabasaran, Rutul, Tsakhur, Budukh, Jek, Kryz, Khinalug, Tat, Haputli), by Georgian (for Batsbi, or Tushian), or by Armenian (for Udi).

It is difficult to judge the success of the roman alphabet on the basis of Soviet information. Periodicals and booklets in roman letters appear, but do people read them? This question is impossible to answer without on-the-spot research. Nor can one rule out the existence of a literature in Arabic writing parallel to the official Communist literature in the roman alphabet, hand copied, unofficial, and hence unregistered. The adaptation of the roman alphabet to the Caucasian languages is fraught with serious difficulties mainly because their phonological systems are extremely rich in consonants (Abkhaz, for example, has fifty-four), while the roman alphabet is meager in this respect. The introduction of diacritical marks to compensate for this lack is psychologically impossible, for one of the strongest arguments leveled against the Arabic alphabet is precisely the overabundance of diacritical marks, inconvenient for both printers and readers. Digraphs comparable to English *sh,* French *ch,* German *sch* are possible only in the few Caucasian languages that do not possess complicated consonant clusters (such as Chechen and Ingush, in which the graphs *th, kh, qh, ph, gh* designate special phonemes). For most of the languages, recourse has had to be made to additional characters. Thus, for example, in the "romanized" alphabet of Adyghe we find, beside the normal roman letters, characters such as

$$ƀ, ҏ, ҟ, ӿ, ʃ, ʒ, ʕ, ɦ, ɧ.$$

These modified characters are often so numerous that a text written in such an alphabet looks "exotic" indeed; one of the principal arguments cited in favor of adopting the roman alphabet worldwide is thus robbed of almost all its force.

To sum up, if the "romanization" of the alphabets of the Caucasian languages has had a certain degree of success, this has been because (1) these new alphabets are more convenient and better adapted to the phonological systems than the Arabic alphabet and (2) these alphabets do not resemble the Russian alphabet and their introduction cannot therefore be regarded by the peoples of the Caucasus as an attempt at Russification.

25. The Phonological System of Mordvin Compared with That of Russian

The question whether there is an inner connection between the phonological system and the grammatical structure of a language can be answered only after a detailed investigation, primarily involving the comparison of languages with identical or similar phonological systems but fundamentally different grammatical structure. The comparison of Russian with Mordvin is an instructive example.[1] From a grammatical point of view, these languages are completely different, as Russian belongs to the Indo-European family and Mordvin to Finno-Ugric. Yet they possess nearly the same inventory of sounds (Bubrix 1932), even though certain sound oppositions common to both do not have the same phonological value.[2] Their phonological systems are so similar that the Mordvins experience no difficulty in using the Russian alphabet without the slightest alterations.

The similarity ends at the phoneme inventory (the same archiphonemes, the same correlations);[3] in their functional and combinatory phonology, the languages diverge. The difference may be formulated in this way: *The loss (or neutralization) of any phonological feature occurs in Russian under the influence of the following phoneme but in Mordvin under the influence of the preceding one (or the zero phoneme).* This principle applies to the correlations of voice[4] and of palatalization[5] and in Mordvin also to the constriction correlation.[6] We may say, then, that sound laws in Mordvin are generally *regressive,* in Russian generally *progressive.*[7]

This regressive orientation of Mordvin phonology is linked with the *special status of the initial word syllable* in that language. The five vowels *u, o, a, e, i* are treated as independent phonemes only in the first syllable. In other syllables, the occurrence of *o, e, u* is conditioned externally, that is, by rules of regressive assimilation; *o* and *e* may be considered here combinatory variants of one phoneme.[8] Thus, the vocalism of the first syllable is fundamentally distinct from that of the others, and, since initial consonants, too, receive different treatment,[9] the first syllable may be said in general to have a special status.

Finally, we notice that in Mordvin *correlative oppositions have a smaller functional load* than in Russian. The oppositions of intensity in vowels (stressed-unstressed), which play such an important role in Russian, are foreign to Mordvin. The correlation of palatalization, which in Russian extends to dentals and labials, is in Mordvin restricted to the dentals. In Russian speech, 37 percent of obstruents are voiced (i.e., marked), 39 percent voiceless (i.e., unmarked), and only 24 percent phonologically neutral with respect to voice (word final, etc.), whereas, in Mordvin, 18 percent are voiced, 38.7 percent voiceless, and 43.3 percent phonologically neutral.[10]

All these characteristics of the phonology of Mordvin are intimately linked with its grammatical structure. As a typical Turanic language, it has no prefixes. The initial syllable is always a *root syllable,* which justifies its special status from the point of view of grammar as well. The sound shape of the Mordvin root is not changed to serve morphological ends; new forms are produced only by means of agglutination, the addition of formative elements to the unchanged root. Regressive assimilation guarantees the maximum stability of the root and bonds the formative elements tightly to it. But agglutination continues to operate, linking one element to the next, and the rules of regressive assimilation extend its influence over the whole word. The grammatical structure of Mordvin is rational and regular. It permits no exceptions, no unjustified complication of the paradigms. Everything is strictly prescribed; the exercise of free choice is reduced to a minimum. There are a limited number of sharply defined grammatical patterns into which each thought must be forced; the patterns are relatively simple and leave little room for finer nuances. This kind of schematized thought corresponds to Mordvin phonology, which makes little use of correlative oppositions and operates primarily with archiphonemes. The phonological uniformity of Mordvin corresponds to the uniformity of its grammatical structure. Its phonological structure and grammatical structure are completely parallel.

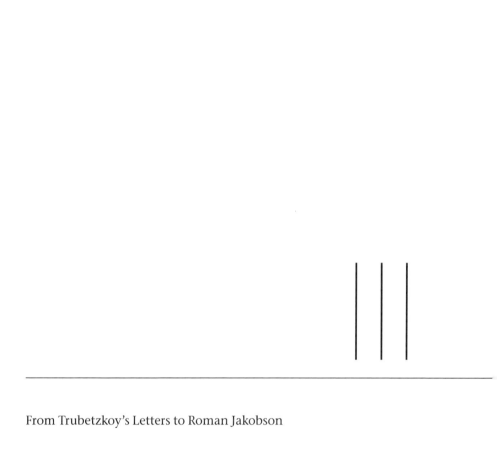

From Trubetzkoy's Letters to Roman Jakobson

Some Considerations on the History of Language

A Systemic View of Language History. The General Laws
of the Evolution of Culture

22 December 1926

In language history, many things seem to be fortuitous, but historians cannot trust this impression. Logic will show that the general lines of language history are never due to chance; consequently, the details are not fortuitous either. The linguist's task is to detect their inner meaning. The meaningful character of language evolution follows from the fact that "language is a system." In my lectures, I always try to point out the logic of evolution. This is possible not only in phonetics but also in morphology (and probably in vocabulary). Some examples are especially instructive, such as the evolution of the numerals in Slavic (this evolution depends on whether the dual has survived as a living category in the language), the evolution of Russian conjugation, etc.

If de Saussure did not dare draw a logical conclusion from his own thesis that "language is a system," the cause must be sought in the fact that such a conclusion would have been at cross-purposes with the universally recognized notion of language history and of history in general. For the only meaning admitted in history is the notorious "progress," an illusory, inwardly contradictory concept that of necessity reduces "meaning" to "meaninglessness." From the point of view of general historians, one may set up only such laws as "the progress of civilization destroys the dual" (Meillet 1922a, 150), laws that are dubious[1] to begin with and not purely linguistic. Yet a close study of the history of languages, with special emphasis on the inner logic of their evolution, shows that such logic exists and that it is possible to formulate many purely linguistic laws independent of the extralinguistic factors of "civilization" and the like.

To be sure, these laws will tell us nothing about "progress" or "regress," and therefore from the point of view of general historians (and all kinds of evolutionists—ethnologists, zoologists, etc.) they will lack the "corpus" of evolutionary laws. This is the reason such an approach to linguistic evolution meets with resistance. Other aspects of culture and folklife also evolve with their own inner logic and according to their own laws that again have nothing to do with "progress." And that is why ethnography (and anthropology) do not want to study them. . . . The Formalists, in their historical studies, have finally turned to inner literary laws: this allows them to discern meaning and inner logic in literary development. From a methodological point of view, the evolutionary sciences have been neglected to such a degree that our "pressing task" consists in rectifying the method in each of them.

There can be no doubt that some parallelism exists in the evolution of the various aspects of culture and that there also exists some law governing this parallelism. Thus, for instance, the entire evolution of Russian poetry, from Deržavin [1743-1816] to Majakovskij [1893-1930], has an inner logic and meaning, and no moment of this evolution should be "derived" from nonliterary facts; but at the same time it is, of course, not fortuitous that Symbolism flourished in the prerevolutionary period and Futurism at the beginning of Bolshevism. It is wrong to "explain" literature by politics (or the other way around), but the connection should be established: we need a special science that will stand outside literature, politics, etc. and study, in a synthesizing way, the parallelism of the evolution of life's various aspects. All this holds for language as well. From a subjective, intuitive point of view, I am, for instance, absolutely certain that there is some inner tie between the general acoustic impression of Czech speech and the Czech psychic (even psychophysical) profile ("national character"). It is an irrational impression, but who knows whether there is no rational law behind it? Thus, when all is said and done, we are quite justified not only in asking why this or that language has chosen a certain path and developed just as it did but also in asking why this language belonging to this people has chosen this particular path of evolution (e.g., Czech has retained length, and Polish has retained palatalization). Only this is not a question for linguistics, but some other science, say, "ethnosophy." [pp. 96–97][2]

*Languages in Contact; the Higher and
the Lower Echelons in Language and Culture*

14 March 1935
In bringing to a close my course in Czech historical phonology . . . I came to the conclusion that the Modern Czech Standard follows the same phonological rules as the Old Czech Standard did. The Old Czech Standard was the language of the aristocrats ("landowners") and strove to preserve phonological distinctions, in disregard of convergences that had occurred in popular speech. [Jan] Huss [ca. 1370-1415] distinguished between ł and l, y and i, r̄ and r̥ at a time when they no longer existed in the pronunciation of the Prague burghers. But similar anachronisms turn up in monuments written between the fourteenth and the seventeenth centuries, and it can often be shown that

the cause is an archaicizing pronunciation rather than conservative orthography.

The difference between Modern Czech phonological purism and the purism of the Old Czech epoch consists only in that a century and a half before the battle of White Mountain [1620] the *oral* tradition of an artificial archaic phonology died out. Huss could distinguish *ł* and *l* because he learned this distinction from some representatives of the higher intelligentsia. At that time, the language of the intelligentsia and the language of common people had different phonological systems.

But when the Modern Czech Standard was being created, the system once used by that intelligentsia no longer existed. One could draw only on the requisite phonological material of popular speech and distinguish what had been distinguished in the Old Standard (although not distinguished in contemporary popular speech)—to the extent that it was possible. The process did not go beyond the etymological redistribution of the phonological elements of *hovorová čeština* [colloquial Czech]: *ej* was retained in *véjce* ['egg'], *dej* ['action, story'], etc. but was replaced by old *í* in *býk* ['bull, ram'], *mlýn* ['mill']; *vo* was retained in *voda* ['water'] but replaced by old *o* in *oko* ['eye']— only because these distinctions had existed in Old Czech and corresponding phonemes were at the reformers' disposal.

The one real innovation and act of violence was the introduction of *é* [the long correlate of *ě*]. This violence was easy to perform, for since *e* existed and the quantitative correlation also existed, it did not require much effort to "build" the phoneme *é*. But to introduce *ł, y*, long syllabic liquids, *ě* and *iu* after all kinds of sibilants—such violence would have been intolerable. So the principle that the phonology of the standard language differs from that of the popular language was valid in both Old and Modern Czech. In Huss's time, the difference between the two phonological inventories was even greater than now: then the Standard had six phonemes alien to the popular language (*ł, y, ȳ, r̄, l̄, ē*), and now there is only one such (*ē*).

I believe that in the history of Czech the influence of German has been decisive since at least the thirteenth century but that it spread mainly to the "vulgar," plebeian language. Were we to visualize a German artisan speaking Old Czech with a Czech landowner, it would appear that the artisan's speech possessed several features of Modern Czech: depalatalization of palatalized consonants, the changes *ł > l, y > i, ü > i*, long and short syllabic liquids, nondistinction of syllabic and nonsyllabic liquids between consonants, monophthongal pronunciation of *o* after consonants (while native speakers of Czech pronounced *ᵘo*), and perhaps the substitution of *wo* for *ᵘo* in word-initial position. It follows from written records that speakers of the Old Czech Standard stubbornly resisted these features of German pronunciation, which spread like a wave to the burghers (and probably to suburban peasants). Huss says unambiguously that at his time the changes of *ł* to *l* and of *y* to *i* were looked on as the result of German influence.

Curiously enough, up to a point this process was two-sided: the language of Czech burghers "deteriorated" under the influence of German, but German, too, deteriorated under the influence of Czech. Schwarz's [1934] article does not give a clear idea of the state of affairs, but in Vienna Bohemian and Moravian Germans are recognized at once by their "Czech" accent. Apparently, the influence of Czech manifests itself in phonetics, while phonology remains unaffected. In any case, the German school and the German theater in Bohemia have always fought this phenomenon, exactly like Huss, who fought the confusion of *ły* and *li!*

Neighboring peoples naturally adapt to one another, and "the guardians of national traditions," "the bearers of the national banner," fight this adaptation, and thereby development in general, for in such areas language development (to give just one example) consists in nothing more than mutual adaptation. [pp. 329–30]

Indo-European among Other Language Families

24 June 1929

From a structural point of view, the Indo-European languages occupy, I would say, a middle position between the Finnic and the Caucasian languages. In an overall classification, the languages [of the former Soviet Union] should be arranged in the following way: (1) isolating (Dungan Chinese in Turkestan), (2) Arctic (Yenissei Ostyak, Gilyak, the settled Chukchi, the nomadic Chukchi, Koryak, Western Kamchadal, Yukaghir), (3) Ural-Altaic (Tungus, Mongolian, Turkic, Samoyed, Finno-Ugric), (4) Indo-European, (5) Northern Caucasian (Eastern Caucasian, Western Caucasian), (6) Southern Caucasian, (7) Semitic (Aisorian or New Aramaic). [p. 134]

General Phonology

Nonbinary Oppositions in Synchrony and Diachrony

24 October 1927

You consider only the simplest case, namely, oppositions of *two* correlative distinctions. But the situation becomes more complicated when there are three or more such distinctions. In all the Caucasian languages (including Armenian and Ossetic), not voiced and voiceless consonants are opposed but voiced ~ voiceless ~ occlusive guttural; in the West Caucasian languages, this opposition covers stops, affricates, and fricatives. Some languages display an even more diverse system of correlative distinctions. In Kuri, four [*sic*] types of stops are opposed (voiced ~ weak voiceless, aspirated ~ strong voiceless, nonaspirated ~ occlusive guttural), and these oppositions are perfectly regular and are an important factor of the static system and of the phonetic evolution of Kuri.

Sometimes the direction of language evolution is determined by the struggle of two correlations with three or four. This happens when some group of phonemes is based on two correlations and another on three or more. At one time, Polabian consonants could be nonpalatalized ~ palatalized in most positions, but before *e* (from old **e, **ь,* and **o*) the distinction was between nonpalatalized, palatalized, and half palatalized. This discrepancy resulted in various changes, and the system of two correlations prevailed. Perhaps the dialectal *mazurenie* in Polish was caused by the fact that, owing to the lisping pronunciation of the sibilants and the depalatalization of *š, ž,* the language acquired three correlative series (*c* – *ć* – *č* etc.), which had to be reduced to two, for the other consonants distinguished only two series. But this tendency to reduce "polycorrelative" systems to two correlations is by no means universal. Many languages tolerate polycorrelative systems in phonology. [p. 110]

A General Theory of Vocalic Systems and Its Role in
Language History and Reconstruction

19 September 1928

Among other things, I undertook a project that greatly interests me: I drew up the phonological vowel systems of the languages I remember by heart (thirty-four) and tried to compare them. Here, in Vienna, I continued this work, and now I have forty-six. I will go on until I get a hundred. The results are most curious. For example, I have never yet run across a language without a symmetrical vowel system. All systems conform to a small number of types and can always be represented by symmetrical schemes (triangles, parallel rows, etc.). Some general laws underlying the formation of such systems become immediately obvious. For example, if a system has labialized front vowels, their number cannot exceed the number of their nonlabialized counterparts. Strong (i.e., long or stressed) vowels are also related to weak (i.e., short or unstressed) vowels in an interesting way and conform to few types, and there is no difference of principle between languages with quantitative and those with expiratorial distinctions. Thus, the same relation

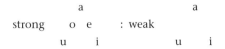

is realized as quantity in Sanskrit and as stress in Russian (and this is not the only example).

I believe that empirical laws obtained in this way may be of great importance, particularly for language history and reconstruction. As a matter of principle, I deal with living languages and turn only to those dead languages that have been investigated especially well, but the laws deduced from this material must have universal validity and also hold for reconstructed proto-languages and the various stages in the development of attested languages. In connection [with the discovery that vocalic systems are always symmetrical], I am now reappraising some of my and your constructions, and not all of them have passed muster. For instance, we seem to be in trouble with the oldest stages of Czech. Three *e*'s (< **e, *ě,* and **ъ*) cannot be arranged into a decent-looking symmetrical system. Something is wrong here, but what? [pp. 117–18]

16 April 1929

You have set up two vowel systems in Old Church Slavonic: soft [after palatalized consonants] and hard [after nonpalatalized consonants]. But, given your solution, both systems appear to be asymmetrical:

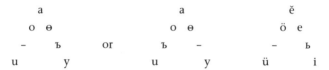

This scheme violates the first main rule, according to which the number of the middle degrees of opening in the "outermost" (maximally low and maximally high) classes should be the same. I have given the vowels of Old Church Slavonic much thought and failed to improve my scheme, which still seems the best to me.

I can perhaps agree with your treatment of the Turkic languages. At least in those of them in which consonants are palatalized in "front vocalic" words and velarized in "back vocalic" words, as in the Kazan dialect, it is indeed permissible to set up a four-vowel system, which has the form

o a
u y

when surrounded by velarized consonants and

ö ä
ü i

in other positions. Unfortunately, we do not know which Turkic languages belong to this group. Instrumental investigations of palatalized and nonpalatalized consonants exist only for Azeri [Šaraf 1927]. But your scheme cannot be applied to the Karagos and Koibal languages, for they have *n', t'* alongside *n, t* in "back vocalic" and "front vocalic" words. [pp. 123–24]

1 May 1929

. . . If this is true [i.e., if *y* = ы existed in the dialect of the First Teachers], we obtain an ugly, skewed system for their dialect:

a		ě	
o		ö	e
ъ			ь
u	y	ü	i

This is impossible. There is only one way out: we must admit that the phoneme *y* (ы) did not exist. And here two possibilities open up. Either *y* in this dialect had become *i,* which is quite improbable, for, if *y* had changed into *i,* the distinction between ъ and ь would hardly have been preserved. Or *y* had the status of a diphthong, whose first part was identified in the linguistic consciousness with ъ and the second with *i.* Objectively (phonetically), this complex was perhaps not ъ*i,* but in any case its beginning and end had different quality. The second hypothesis seems the most probable to me, for then the digraphs in our monuments . . . can be said to have given an exact picture of phonological reality. [p. 128]

The Inner Coherence of Phonological Systems;
Universal and "Ethnically Restricted"
Linguistic Laws; Phonology and Grammar

25 February 1930

According to this table [of numerical relations between vowels and consonants], from the percentages of syllabic and nonsyllabic phonemes one can deduce the types of phonological correlates. It appears that, if, for example, in Slovak there were several consonants fewer, it would inevitably develop musical stress or that if Russian had one or two more consonants, it would forfeit free stress, etc. But all such generalizations are valid only for Slavic. In French, the relation between syllabic and nonsyllabic phonemes is approximately the same as in Slovak (57 percent nonsyllabic, 43 percent syllabic), but the phonological correlates are quite different.

You agreed that the law of the incompatibility of musical stress with timbre differences in consonants is valid only for Slavic. Similar "laws with an ethnically limited sphere of application" can also be formulated for the East Caucasian languages (e.g., the incompatibility between free stress and the opposition of emphatic ~ nonemphatic consonants; this opposition corresponds functionally to the Slavic correlate nonpalatalized ~ palatalized, and in Slavic it coexists beautifully with free stress).

I believe that, alongside the really universal structural laws of phonology, there are laws limited by the morphological (perhaps also lexical) language types. Since language is a system, its grammatical and phonological structure must be interconnected. Any given grammatical structure permits a limited number of phonological systems. This circumstance restricts the free play of evolution and thereby the applicability of comparative phonology. [p. 153]

Acoustic and Physiological Terms in Phonemic Description;
Lack of Analogy between Vowels and Consonants

17 August 1930

Your idea of distinguishing two timbre correlations (and, consequently, four timbres) is clever and useful. But there are terminological difficulties. Your terminology is suitable only for Russian and other Slavic languages; outside Slavic, *soft* and *hard,* with regard to vowels, sound odd and will never be accepted. In describing two types of Latin *i,* Romans used the terms *exilis* 'small, thin, feeble' and *pinguis* 'plump.' But I do not think that, when translated into modern languages, these labels have a better chance of taking root than yours. The only way out is to give up acoustic terminology and to use physiological terms. Unfortunately, acoustic terminology is so poor that one cannot draw on it alone. In the phonological classification of consonants, I do not use it at all (except for the notion of timbre) and work only with physiological terms, although I naturally point out their weakness and one-sidedness.

At one time, analogies between the presentations of vowels and the presentations of consonants seemed tempting to me, too. But later I realized that these analogies are illusory and that no classification can rest on them. For instance, if we compare stressed ~ unstressed in vowels and voiced ~ voiceless in consonants, what shall we do with languages in which both voiced and voiceless consonants can be short and long (such are Italian and Hungarian)? Or with languages in which voiceless consonants are divided into strong and weak? Note that both classes can be opposed to voiced consonants (such is the situation in all the languages of Daghestan except Rutul and among the West Caucasian languages in some Circassian dialects). We would then get several types of intensity. The analogy between the degrees of sonority in consonants and vowels does not fare better. So I have chosen another way. I believe that consonantal oppositions can be classified according to (1) the place of articulation, (2) the type of articulation, (3) intensity (dynamic or quantitative), and (4) timbre. [pp. 166–67]

Correlative Features; the Principal and Subsidiary
Features of the Phoneme; Markedness

31 July 1930

While thinking about phonology, I have come to the conclusion that our theory of correlative phonemes has serious drawbacks. To begin with, the terms *the principal variant* and *the subsidiary ("accessoire") variant* are unfortunate in and of themselves and also because they serve both phonemes and phonetic variants. Under such conditions, one can imagine, for instance, "the principal variant of the subsidiary variant" of the archiphoneme. In general, the analogy between the relation of the archiphoneme to individual correlative phonemes and the relation of the phoneme to its phonetic variants is superficial. There is a fundamental difference here, and it should find its expression in terminology.

The difference between the principal and the "subsidiary" members of a phonological correlation is of great importance, and it emerges with especial clarity when one of these members is determined by nongrammatical factors in some position. Thus, in Russian, in which the palatalization of all consonants except *l* before palatalized dentals and labials is determined by nongrammatical factors, palatalization is far from obvious in this position: an unschooled informant will be hard put to decide whether *s* is palatalized in *svet* ['light' (n.)] and *sled* ['trace' (n.)], and an illiterate person may doubt whether to supply *s* with the palatalization sign [i.e., with *mjagkij znak*]. But, before nonpalatalized dentals, a position in which the absence of palatalization, rather than its presence (also in all consonants except *l*), is determined by nongrammatical factors, the pronunciation will leave no one in doubt, and even an absolutely illiterate native speaker of Russian will not write *snop* ['sheaf'] with the palatalization sign [*mjagkij znak*] after *s*.

This explains the difference in the treatment of vowel letters after *š/ž* and velars in Old Church Slavonic written monuments. In the correlative pairs *a/ě*, *оɣ/ю*, *ѫ/ѩ*, *ъ/ь*, the principal members were *a, оɣ, ѫ, ъ*. After *š/ž*, the "subsidiary" members, that is, the palatal front vowels, were determined by nongrammatical factors, and that is why their palatal character was not perceived clearly—hence the scribes' vacillation between *a* and *ě, оɣ* and *ю, ѫ* and *ѩ, ъ* and *ь*. But after velars, where nongrammatical factors determined the lack of frontness, it was perceived with absolute clarity, and all scribes wrote *a, оɣ, ѫ, ъ* without the slightest doubt. (By the way, it would be interesting to analyze from this point of view the designation of nongrammatically determined voiceless and voiced consonants in Old Czech, i.e., cases like *tbal* [= Modern Czech *dbal* 'took care of'].

The situation with the palatal and nonpalatal vowels in Old Church Slavonic also shows that your definition of the principal [variant] (*variante fon-*

damentale) in *Remarques* [Jakobson 1929, 11] is not quite correct. In Old Church Slavonic, word-initially and after vowels, *a, ot, ѧ* and *ě, ot, ѭ* were permitted, while *ъ* and *ь* were not. In this sense, palatal and nonpalatal vowels were equal and had to be perceived as *variantes équipollentes* [equipollent variants], with neither taking precedence. But the aforementioned facts testify unambiguously that the members of the correlation palatal vowel ~ nonpalatal vowel where not on equal footing.

You must have been led astray by the false analogy with phonetic variants. Among the variants, the one occurring more frequently (or in the position of maximal differentiation) can indeed be looked on as the principal. But in dealing with correlative phonemes, we face a different situation, and statistics has nothing to do with it; what matters is, so to speak, "the ideological content" of the correlation. Probably every (or not every?) phonological correlation appears, in the linguistic consciousness, in the form of the opposition: the presence of a feature versus its absence (or the maximum of a feature versus its minimum).

It follows that one member of the correlation is positive or active while the other is negative or passive. At least this is the case if the opposition is binary. For instance, in objective terms, the correlative distinctions of timbre between consonants can be reduced to the opposition maximally high timbre ~ maximally low timbre, but from a subjective viewpoint it is invariably transformed into raised timbre ~ nonraised timbre (= maximally high ~ maximally low) or nonlowered timbre ~ lowered timbre (= minimally low ~ maximally low); the first type is realized in the correlation palatalized ~ nonpalatalized, the second in the consonantal correlation nonlabial ~ labial in the North Caucasian languages (and probably in the correlation nonemphatic consonant ~ emphatic consonant in the Semitic languages), to give just a few examples.

In both cases, only one member of the correlation is perceived as actively modified, as carrying a positive feature, while the other emerges merely as lacking this feature, as passively immutable. The two members are perceived as equally active, equally deviating from the norm in the opposite directions only when there is a third, absolutely passive or neutral member, that is, only when the correlation is ternary rather than binary. . . . So I believe that we should speak not about the principal and subsidiary variants of the archiphoneme but about the active and passive or positive and negative features of the correlation. In any case, we must reform our terminology in this point. [pp. 161–64] n.d. (ca. 20 December 1931)

The other day I was called in as an expert. A student born in Burgenland has written a phonological description of the dialect of his native village. His main guide was the phonological section of my *Polabische Studien* [Trubetzkoy 1929a]. This is where the hitch is. In his dialect, common German preconsonantal *l* became *ü̦*, which stands in free alternation with *i̦* (at least after back vowels); preconsonantal *r* became *v̦* (close nonsyllabic *a*). These changes are typical of all Austrian Bavarian dialects. But in addition to it, in this dialect Old High German *uo* (from **ō*) went over to *ui*, which stands in alternation with *uv̦* (hence, *Bruder* ['brother'] = *brui̦dv ~ bruv̦dv*).

The result is that the dialect has *ui̦* < **ul ~ uü̦* (e.g., *gui̦n ~ guü̦n* 'Gulden' ['guilder']) and *ui̦* < **uo ~ uv̦* (cf. *brui̦dv ~ bruv̦dv* 'Bruder'). Likewise, alongside *uv̦* that stands in free alternation with *ui̦* (as in *bruv̦dv ~ brui̦dv*), there exists *uv̦* < **ur* (e.g., *k'uv̦ds* 'kurz' ['short']), which cannot be replaced by *ui̦*. Note that *ü̦/i̦* and *v̦* (the one that does not alternate with *i̦*) are separate phonemes because they occur in combinations with other vowels, whereas the diphthong *ui̦* is monophonemic, for no other similar groups ending in *i̦* (which would not alternate with *ü̦*) exist.

The resulting picture is complicated: we have the phonemic groups *uü̦* (~ *ui̦*) and *uv̦* and the phoneme *ui̦* [= *ui̦*] ~ *uv̦* whose variants overlap with different phonemic groups. According to the student, these three phonological units are clearly distinguished in the [linguistic] consciousness: the peasants do not hear the difference between *brui̦dv* and *bruv̦dv* but correct the observer pronouncing *k'uv̦ds* instead of *k'ui̦ds*. This is a curious phenomenon. I believe that something like this can be found only in a transitional dialect. This village is situated almost at the border of Burgenland and Low Austria, where preconsonantal *l* after back vowels has yielded *i̦*, while *uo* is realized as *uv̦*. *Gui̦n* and *bruv̦dv* are Low Austrian, prestigious variants (this is how people speak in Vienna), and *guü̦n*, *brui̦dv* are provincial variants, characteristic of Burgenland. In the remoter localities of Burgenland, *guü̦n*, *brui̦dv* are the only variants, so the problem disappears. This phenomenon (whatever the solution) is of interest because it shows how many corrections and modifications will have to be introduced into phonological theory after a detailed examination of dialectal material. [pp. 230–31]

26 October 1937

Yesterday I saw Pfalz. . . . He denies the phonological status of *ü, ö* in Austrian dialects: they are always more or less diphthongized (*iü, eö*), and their alternation with *ül, öl* is so much alive that they should be considered as realizations of these groups before consonants. He refers to the pronunciation of such borrowings as *Krokodil* ['crocodile'], *Kuratel* ['guardianship'] = *krokodǖ, kurathȫ*. These new *ǖ, ȫ* < *il, el* reach neither the Hungarian border nor the High Alemannic dialects. [p. 407]

The Reality of Correlations and Distinctive Features

n.d. (May 1934)

... We seem to have exaggerated the difference between correlation and disjunction. There are many intermediate states between them. Only those correlations are perceived clearly that occur in a limited number of positions (for in the other positions archiphonemes emerge, and this is when the presence/absence of a feature visibly comes to the foreground). Other correlations are perceived badly, if at all (cf. Russian $o : e = u : i, d : n = b : m$). Differences in the vocalic timbre are perceived as correlations only in quadrangular systems.

By the way it is wrong that in languages having palatalized/nonpalatalized consonants, vowels are always dark or light. Two types should be distinguished: languages like Russian in which this correlation is in principle permitted before all vowels and languages like Bulgarian, Polabian, Lithuanian, and Japanese in which it is absent before *i* and *e*. In the languages of the second type, *i* and *e* are opposed to the rest of the vowels precisely because palatalized and nonpalatalized consonants fail to alternate before them. In this case, labialization is subservient to the opposition of front to back vowels. For example, in Lithuanian, short vowels make up the quadrangle

a   e
u   i

with a clear distinction front/back, regardless of labialization. This is also the reason Japanese *u* is pronounced with weakly protruded lips, as noted by Polivanov. (304)

Prosody

Metrics and the Prosodic System of a Language

20 December 1922

Many thanks for your book [Jakobson 1923], which I have read with great interest. A wealth of fruitful and brilliant ideas! Sometimes even too many of them, and one loses the perspective of the forest for the digressions of the trees. But this is your style — it can't be helped. In any case, each individual "tree" is sufficiently interesting and valuable as not to arouse anyone's chagrin on account of the blocked forest. The general outline is rather clear, and the main conclusions are most persuasive. The only noticeable drawback is the absence of any mention of Czech folk poetry. To tell the truth, I have only a very vague notion of this poetry. Perhaps you had every right to disregard it, but it is a fact that you speak about Chinese, Persian, etc. metrics, while the metrics of Czech folk poetry is given no attention.

I have no serious objections. Perhaps your statement that metrics is independent of the properties of any given language needs modification. Any metrics is of course violence, but the patience of every language has its limits, and for the most part the toleration threshold is not great. Thus, caesural metrics was an act of violence that eighteenth-century Russian could not tolerate. Russian can permit only such a metrics that in some way depends on stress, and the types of stress-based metrics are not many: Pushkin, Majakovskij, and perhaps something in between, and that's all. In Polish and French, metrics must depend on word boundaries, etc. Czech (like Latin, Arabic, Persian, and other languages) is special in that its metrics is allowed free play on a scale unthinkable for most languages. You do not make enough of this circumstance. But this is clearly not an objection. [pp. 36–37]

Free Quantity and Free Stress; Phonological and Morphological Intensity;
the Phonological Nature of Vowel Harmony

16 April 1929

Languages combining free stress with free quantity interest me very much. Your theory breaks down in German since German has long vowels in unstressed syllables, for instance, in the suffixes -*tum* (*tūm*, pl. *tümər*) and -*heit*. It would be useful to examine dialects from this point of view. Preservation of free stress and free quantity may turn out to be an artificial phenomenon. In Plattdeutsch (Low German), two types of stress are distinguished; so this is "musical" stress.

You seem to have misunderstood my idea of morphological intensity. I am saying only that a certain syllable (in this case, the first one) has the same morphological function in all words; namely, it conveys the main material meaning. This phenomenon is, in turn, connected with the absence of prefixes and has as its consequence some other regularities in morphology, syntax (word order), and phonology (e.g., the difference between consonants permitted at the beginning and those permitted in the middle of the word). Morphological intensity cannot be brought under the general rubric of emphasizing a syllable. Such emphasis (be it by expiratorial or musical stress) is always free in that it does not depend on the position of the syllable in relation to word boundaries, while morphological intensity is connected with them. It could rather be compared to fixed stress, which, incidentally, falls on the morphologically intense syllable in at least half the relevant languages.

Languages in which free quantity is independent of morphological differentiation exist. One of them is Finnish. It distinguishes long and short vowels in initial as well as noninitial syllables, yet the vowel system in the first syllable is not identical with that permitted in other syllables. Such, I believe, are also the languages of the Siberian Ugrians (Ostyaks and Voguls). In the Lapp dialects, the distinction between long and short vowels in noninitial syllables plays a role, too, but the vocalism of noninitial syllables is complicated in these dialects, so I preferred not to touch on them. Morphologically weak syllables have fewer *Eigentonklassen* [distinct timbres], whereas phonological intensity rather presupposes differences in *Schallfüllegrade* [sonority] between maximally and minimally intense syllables.

By the way, since finishing my article [Trubetzkoy 1929c], I have familiarized myself with the vowel system of Estonian. Distinctions of quantity occur only in the first syllable:

    a ō ä
    o ö e
    u ü i

(ō is "very open ö"); long mid vowels are realized as diphthongs (*uo, üö, ie,* although in spelling they are designated by *oo, öö, ee!*); all the other vowels are monophthongs. In noninitial syllables, only four vowels occur:

    a e
    u i.

There is no vowel harmony. In general, on closer scrutiny, the notorious vowel harmony appears to be nothing other than the phonetic realization of a morphologically weak syllable that has fewer timbres than a morphologically strong one. If we take into account the main peculiarity of morphologically weak vocalism, it becomes clear why just the so-called Turanian languages so often have systems with mid (one or two) timbres: they need these timbres to differentiate more sharply the morphologically strong syllable from the morphologically weak ones. . . .

I would add that, to the best of my knowledge, no languages combine the differentiation of morphologically strong and morphologically weak syllables with musical stress.

I am not certain whether free quantity can coexist with stress fixed on the penultimate syllable, for I know too few languages with such stress: it is dangerous to set up general rules on the basis of Standard Polish, Polish-Czech and Polish-Slovak dialects, and a few Macedonian dialects. The languages combining free quantity and fixed expiratorial stress (to the extent that I know them) have stress either on the first syllable (Czech, Slovak, Hungarian, Finnish, Lapp, Chechen) or on the last (New Persian, Kalmuck, Yakut, Old Hungarian) or display a dependency on the length of the last syllables (Latin, Prakrit, Arabic, Polabian). [pp. 124–26]

Phonological Relatedness of Tone and Intensity
(Expiratorial Stress and Length);
Classification of Vocalic Features

3 October 1930

While thinking about your new theory of the tonal correlation, I have come to the following conclusion. If musical stress consists in emphasizing one mora while length and stress emphasize a whole syllable, then no difference of principle exists between intensity and the tonal correlation: intensity and intonation should be assigned to the same *group*. This conclusion is borne out by the fact that both phenomena are projected by the linguistic consciousness to one plane. . . . On the other hand, degrees of sonority (*Schallfüllegrade*) and vocalic timbres are also projected by our consciousness to one plane, but a different plane than the one reserved for stress, length, and intonation. Thus, the correlations significant for vowels fall into two groups: qualitative distinctions (*Qualitätsunterschiede*) and distinctions in energy (*Energieunterschiede*) (I propose the term *Energieunterschiede* in connection with the phonetic term *Energiefaktoren* embracing strength, length, and intensity). Qualitative distinctions fall into those of sonority (*Schallfülleunterschiede*) and timbre (*Eigentonunterschiede*). The latter subsume the correlations front ~ back, labial ~ nonlabial, nasalized ~ nonnasalized, whereas distinctions in energy fall into the correlation of intensity (dynamic and quantitative) and tonal. Only what to do with the correlation of tenseness (*Spannungskorrelation*) remains unclear. Perhaps it is a special (third) type of qualitative distinctions. This new phonological classification of vowels follows inevitably from the combination of your understanding of musical distinctions and my understanding of the groups of phonological features. Please write what you think of this matter. [p. 173]

12 October 1930

The term *prosodic distinctions* is better than *distinctions in energy,* and I accept it. Furthermore, I am inclined to think that the correlation *nasalized : nonnasalized vowel* cannot be assigned to the same group as the other qualitative correlations, for it belongs to a different plane. I believe that it should be classified with a special group of so-called distinctions in resonance, which will also include the opposition of "constricted" vowels (*Presstimmvokale*) to pure ones, as it is known in the Caucasian languages, and perhaps a few other similar oppositions. [p. 178]

The Correlation of Quantity and Monophonemic/Biphonemic
Diphthongs; Syllabic and Nonsyllabic Phonemes

Jakobson to Trubetzkoy, 10 February 1931

An interesting idea was expressed by Vachek, the student who recorded the discussion [at the Prague phonological conference]. He asked whether it was possible to consider diphthongs as independent phonemes in languages with the correlation of quantity. Isn't Czech *ou* a group of two short phonemes, the sum short + short being naturally equal to long? Given similar morphological conditions, there is no opposition monosyllabic group versus disyllabic group. This treatment of diphthongs would explain the history of *ě* in Proto-Slavic; *ě* would emerge as a biphonemic group rather than a nonintegrated "orphan," such that, when long vowels were shortened and short *ě* appeared alongside bimoric *ě*, it became necessary to accommodate this waif somehow. [pp. 196–97]

21 February 1931

Vachek's idea about diphthongs in languages with a correlation of quantity, in the general form in which you conveyed it, seems untenable to me. Consider the differences between Czech and Serbo-Croatian. Serbo-Croatian really lacks diphthongs and has either combinations of vowels with *j* (a consonant phoneme) or biphonemic groups of two vowel phonemes, which occur in various morphonological contexts. In Czech, alongside groups like *uj* and *ao* (at the morphological juncture: cf. *naopak* ['on the contrary']), a real diphthong exists, namely, *ou*. In languages with a correlation of quantity, there is an especially easy way to tell a diphthong from a bivocalic group: in the (phonologically) nondiphthongal group, vowels retain their quantitative features, whereas, in diphthongs, they are devoid of them.

This is a rather difficult problem. It is connected with the question whether the correlation syllabicity ~ nonsyllabicity exists and whether a nonsyllabic phoneme can be united with a syllabic one into an archiphoneme. In Sanskrit, *y* and *i, r* and *r̥* are in complementary distribution. So it seems as though *y* is a phonetic variant of *i* and *r* of *r̥* (*v* and *u* are related differently, for *r* and *i* can be preceded word initially by both *v* and *u:* e.g., *vrajati* ['(he) goes'] ~ *uru* ['wide' (f.)], *vyathati* ['(he) trembles'] ~ *uye* ['(I) am woven']). With regard to *i : j, r : r̥*, and *l : l̥*, the situation appears to be the same in Czech, if I am not mistaken (at least in Modern Czech; in Old Czech, *r* and *r̥* could occur in the same position). Yet I would not subscribe to such a conclusion. I believe that in any given language syllabic and nonsyllabic phonemes make up two different, albeit interrelated, systems. A syllabic and a nonsyllabic are fundamentally different phonemes, the difference between them being in their *function*. It is like the dative and the prepositional cases in Russian morphology: they remain different even in words that do not distinguish them formally (e.g., in feminine nouns). To my mind, even in languages with decomposable diphthongs nonsyllabic $i̯$ and $u̯$ are perceived as separate phonemes not identical with syllabic *i* and *u*. [pp. 196–97]

10 May 1933

Vachek's [1933] book is brilliant in form and poses interesting questions; perhaps it even contributes to the solution of some of them. In phonological descriptions, it cannot be ignored. Yet I am not satisfied with his conclusions or, rather, with his starting point. All of it looks like phonetic opportunism. An English scholar has a hard time doing phonology, for English phonetics is known exceptionally well; one cannot help falling under its influence. Nor has Vachek avoided this danger. He has failed so signally in his dealing with English prosody because he approached it as a phonetician, not as a phonologist.

His theory of diphthongs rests on two false premises: that a syllabic feature cannot be phonologically distinctive (but compare Old Czech monosyllabic *krvi* ['blood'] with disyllabic *prvý* ['first'] or Serbian *gròce* ['(bottle)neck'] with *grob* ['grave, tomb']) and that there cannot be phonemes occurring in only one environment (I can cite such phonemes by the dozen). He disregards neutralized phonemes. But, in Czech, in which length in the phonemes *a, e, i, u* is free, *u*, neutralized with regard to length in the diphthong *ou*, is a unit essentially different from *ŭ* and *ū* and should be treated as a separate phoneme ($u̯$) (such was my interpretation of Polabian diphthongs) or as part of the phoneme *ou* (= phonologically *ō*). In choosing phonetic realization as the criterion of biphonemicity in diphthongs, Vachek "capitulates before phonetics" and destroys the only foundation on which this question can be solved in every concrete case. The phonetic concepts *Stellungsdiphthong* ['diphthong ending in -ə'] and *Bewegungsdiphthong* ['diphthong ending in -i, -u'] are too vague and fluid. I have written Vachek a nineteen-page-long letter. If you are interested, ask him to show it to you. . . .

As far as *j* in East Slavic is concerned, it should be noted that, in many dialects with *okan'e* [= pretonal *o* distinct from *a*] in which *ě* became *i*, the groups *ij, ji* occur not only at the morphemic juncture but also within a morpheme (*jis't'* = *ěstъ* ['to eat'], *pos'ij* = *posěj* ['sow!']). I cannot tell you offhand how frequent forms like *vyjti, vyjtit', vyidu* ['to go out,' 'to go out,' '(I) will go out'] are in dialects with *akan'e* [= with pretonic *o* and *a* merged]. In any case, the interpretation of *ĭj* as *ĭí* (for, if *j* is a combinatory variant of the featureless *i*, it is consequently a variety of *í*) seems extremely artificial to me; it would appear that in words with *ĭj* there are two stressed vowels (*íníĭ* [= *inej* 'hoarfrost']). Equally untenable is the interpretation of *jí* as *íí*. It seems that under Vachek's influence you are also forgetting about phonemes neutralized with regard to some feature and ignoring syllabicity as a phonological property. *J* can be treated neither as a combinatory variant of *í* nor as a variant of *ĭ*: the concepts *stressed/unstressed* (or, rather, *full/reduced*) are inapplicable to it, for it is neutral with respect to intensity. But the phonemes of Russian neutral with respect to intensity are called *consonants*. It follows that *j* is a consonant. If you insist on linking *j* and *i*, I can offer such a formula (for dialects with *akan'e*): The archiphoneme *i* before and after vowels is neutralized with regard to intensity, and we designate it by *j*. [pp. 272, 274]

Ancient West Indo-European Culture
and Prosody; Latin Prosody

1 September 1922
As far as I can judge, the poetry of the Roman aesthetes is a highly artificial phenomenon "divorced from native soil." These aesthetes were completely hypnotized by Greek culture, looked on all things Greek as beautiful, and could not conceive of beauty outside Greek forms. Yet they were given a really wonderful, euphonious language, Latin, that surpassed Greek in mellifluousness and phonetic richness. Against their will, they were "tempted" to create works of art from this remarkable material. But since they treated all non-Greek forms as barbaric, they naturally had to squeeze Latin into the prosodic forms worked out for Greek verse, even though these forms were at variance with the "spirit" of Latin. The mistakes that Virgil and Lucretius constantly make in the hexameter show how difficult this process must have been.

The original, so-called Saturnian, Latin verse rests on entirely different principles. Only this verse can be studied on its own terms, disregarding non-Latin prosody. The prosody of the Roman classical poets requires a broader framework for its study, for their Latin was affected, pronounced *à la grecque*. As far as the Saturnian verse is concerned, one should bear in mind the following. The Proto-Italic dialect of Indo-European, along with Proto-Celtic and Proto-Germanic, was part of the so-called West Indo-European group. This group did not display such inner unity as did Balto-Slavic and Indo-Iranian, but the remarkable similarity of its members' vocabularies and numerous common features in their phonetics make them into some sort of whole. It is clear that their ancient linguistic unity went together with the unity of their culture, and, most probably, this unity also extended to their poetry. The best proof of such an assumption is the development of initial expiratorial stress in all the western dialects, a change of crucial importance for the subsequent phonetic development of these dialects and their descendants and of no mean consequence for prosody. So I believe that the Saturnian verse should be studied in the light of ancient Germanic and Celtic metrics. This is merely a supposition on my part, for I have never studied Latin prosody and do not have the faintest notion of Celtic metrics. [pp. 33–34]

Stress and Scansion in Latin; Stress in Finno-Ugric;
Alliteration and Initial Stress

12 August 1922

. . . The question of Latin scansion is difficult because it is connected with the broader one of the nature of Latin stress, which remains unsolved. There are two schools: French (headed by Vendryès [1902]), which looks on Latin stress before the fourth century as musical, and German, which teaches that Latin stress was expiratorial throughout the historical period, that is, from the beginning (prehistoric initial stress is treated as expiratorial by both schools). Immisch [1912, 31] made an attempt at a compromise. In his opinion, stress in the Latin of the lower orders was always expiratorial, but the higher, educated classes replaced it with musical stress under Greek influence (as they replaced Latin nonaspirated consonants with aspirated ones, also under Greek influence). You will find the literature in Walde [1916, 150–62].

With regard to versification, all this is even more complicated. Here, Immisch's suggestion sounds quite plausible, for together with Greek metrics the Romans naturally also borrowed Greek scansion and turned their stress (which could have been expiratorial in ordinary speech) into musical and began to put expiratorial stress on the *temps fort* [strong measure] independent of where it fell in conversation. Plautus and Terence, neither of whom deviated too much from the popular norm, tried to place "metrical stress" (*temps fort*) according to the rules of everyday speech, and this is the main argument of the German school.

In principle, quantitative metrics ignoring "normal" stress is possible only when stress is not expiratorial at all or very weak, while quantitative distinctions are strong. As far as we can judge by the extant Greek scores, the Greeks indeed put metrical stress on the *temps fort,* while in everyday speech stress consisted in a metrically neutral modulation, stylized as a melody. Gruška's scansion is undoubtedly artificial. Horace, for example, must have *sung* his verses.[3]

In the Finnic languages, stress is in general not strong. In Mordvin, it is usually so weak that it is hard to perceive, and many people do not hear it. True, vowels are often lost in noninitial syllables, which seems to indicate that at one time initial syllables had strong stress. But vowels in initial syllables have not always been preserved either, so this fact proves nothing. In Finnish, initial stress can be perceived, but it is, of course, weaker than in Russian and Czech; secondary stress on the odd syllables (counting from the beginning) is also rather apparent, but on the whole, the even syllables (the ones without any stress) are also rather strong, so the difference between stressed and unstressed syllables is not great, and this produces the impression of "babbling." Hungarian strikes one as even more babbling. At first sight, stress (on the first syllable) seems to be very weak; I have had no chance to check my earlier observations.

Alliteration as the principle of versification is consistent only in the West Finnic languages. In Mordvin and Ob-Ugrian, it exists as a tendency; the other languages (to the best of my knowledge) lack it (the Perm languages—Komi and Votyak—have fixed stress on the *final* syllable). To my mind, alliteration is in no way connected with initial stress, although such stress can be one of the factors contributing to its rise. Thus, alliteration exists in Circassian folk poetry, but stress in Circassian is very weak, hardly perceptible at all (perhaps it falls on the penultimate syllable). In the poetry of the Mongols, Buryats, and Kalmucks, alliteration coexists with word-*final* stress. I believe that, like all types of qualitative rhythms and qualitative rhythmic embellishments (rhyme, assonance, repetition), alliteration is historically tied to internal rhythm and stylistic devices. Rudimentary rhyme is the result of parallelism. The same is, by and large, true of alliteration. That is why it occurs so often in the poetic systems relying on pedantic parallelism, as is the case in all the Ural-Altaic peoples. Of importance are also some stylistic turns of speech; compare Mordvin *čudi ved čudi* 'flowing water flows' or *paly tol paly* 'burning fire burns' with counterparts elsewhere in Finno-Ugric poetry: Ostyak *anžet êding anžiŋ ûr* 'birdcherry tree forest made up of birdcherry trees' (I am not sure that it is indeed *birdcherry tree,* but no matter), and so forth.

The properties of the phonetic system are also important for the rise of alliteration. In the Ural and Altaic languages, alliteration is supported by the poverty of consonants in initial position. In most Finnic and all Samoyed languages, only voiceless obstruents are permitted word initially, while voiced ones are excluded (except for *v* and *j*, probably from $u̯, i̯;$ and in the majority of the Samoyed languages *b* occurs in this position, probably also from $u̯$). Some Turkic languages follow the same pattern, others deviate from it, but an indiscriminate use of voiced and voiceless consonants exists only in Osman and Azeri. Contrariwise, in the Mongolian languages, of all obstruents only voiced plosives are permitted word initially. To sum up, in the Ural-Altaic languages, there are severe restrictions on the type of consonant occurring in word-initial position. It is no wonder that alliteration frequently springs up by chance, and later this "chance" is generalized, stylized, and elevated to a rule of versification. As you see, initial stress is not at all necessary in any of such cases. [pp. 28–30]

Stress and Quantity in Finno-Ugric;
the Origin of Stufenwechsel

1 September 1922

I cannot say anything definite about lengthening of initial consonants under initial stress in the Finnic languages, for I have never tried to observe it myself and am not sufficiently versed in the literature. But I have certain vague ideas that I am offering here for what they are worth; to develop them, I lack the necessary books.

In West Finnic and Lapp, consonants at the beginning of the second syllable behave differently, according to whether this syllable is open or closed: for example, the essive (locative) of Finnic *kota* 'house' is *kotana,* whereas the inessive (locative-internal) is *kodossa;* likewise, the inessive of *kukka* is *kukassa.* Setälä [1912] suggested that originally stress fell on the initial syllable only when it was open; when the second syllable was closed (and, consequently, *positione longus*) it attracted stress to itself. According to his hypothesis, consonants within a word were treated differently, depending on the vowel that preceded them. Setälä calls the position after a stressed vowel a strong grade and the position after an unstressed vowel a weak grade.

The law of the alternating grades [*Stufenwechsel*] comes down to the following. (1) A long consonant in the strong grade corresponds to a short consonant in the weak grade; (2) a voiceless consonant in the strong grade corresponds to a voiced consonant in the weak grade. Setälä reconstructed this state in the Common Finno-Ugric period, for sporadically such alternations (but independent of the type of syllable!) occur in Hungarian and (once!) in Komi. He ascribes the absence of the *Stufenwechsel* in languages other than West Finnic and Lapp to the later analogical generalization of the weak grade (why just weak?). I have always thought that in this respect Setälä's reconstruction is wrong, and I can represent the picture as follows. Originally, stress in Finno-Ugric fell only on the initial syllable. Later, in Proto–West Finnic and Proto-Lapp, stress was shifted to the next syllable if it was long (i.e., closed), for these dialects developed a system of accentuation in principle analogous to the one we find in Latin, Prakrit, Old Iranian, etc. Only after this shift did a law emerge, according to which posttonal short voiceless consonants (as well as liquids and nasals) became long and voiced obstruents became

voiceless; still later, voiced stops—insofar as they were preserved intervocalically—turned into fricatives. This is how Finnic *kota* developed from *koda,*
kodassa (pronounced *kóðassa*) from *kodásna, kukka* from *kúka,* and *kukassa*
from *kukásna,* etc.

Two circumstances bear repetition. (1) In Common Finnic, stress was also
initial; (2) from the Finnish point of view, the change of a voiced consonant
to a voiceless one is equivalent to consonant lengthening (*kóda* > *kota* ‖ *kúka* >
kukka). Note that of all obstruents in Common Finnic only voiceless ones were
permitted word initially (for *v* and *j* go back to *u* and *i;* they were not originally obstruents), and you will get an approximation to the answer you need:
as far back as in Common Finnic, there existed the reinforcement (devoicing)
of initial consonants; this is not lengthening but a phenomenon of the same
order. Incidentally, in Mordvin, the presence of voice in initial obstruents is
not distinctive: in connected speech, initial voiceless obstruents constantly
acquire voice (this substitution is especially frequent in folk poetry, in nouns
preceded by fixed epithets, for example, *od zëra* 'young fellow' [*ë* = Russian *ë*],
ine guĭ 'big snake,' although *zëra* and *guĭ* are understood as *sëra* 'fellow' and
kuĭ 'snake'). [pp. 34–35]

30 November 1932
Paavo Ravila, a Mordvin scholar from Finland, sent me a letter showing that
he does not understand anything in phonology. He also sent me his dissertation [Ravila 1932b] on the quantitative system in a Lapp dialect. The work is
hopelessly atomistic and purely phonetic, but the material is interesting.

Most consonants within a word display *three* degrees of length, and it seems
that all three are phonologically distinct. Before extralong consonants, all
vowels are short, but before long consonants, both long and short vowels are
permitted (the same is true of the position before short consonants). Phonetic
distinctions in the *Silbenschnittkorrelation* [the correlation of syllable cut] exist,
but they are determined by the length of the vowel in the next syllable rather
than by the length of the postvocalic consonant. A strange system emerges.
Two consonantal correlations seem to interact here: geminated ~ nongeminated consonants and long ~ short geminated consonants. Probably the short
nongeminated consonants are unmarked. Incidentally, nongeminated stops
do not exist at all, and *d'* appears only as a short geminate. [p. 263]

Stress in Sanskrit

28 May 1932
I have certain ideas about the Sanskrit (Vedic) system of accents. Not every-
thing is clear there, as you remember. Stress consists in the raising of the voice.
The pretonic syllables are rising, the posttonic syllables are low (the first post-

tonic syllable is probably falling), but nothing testifies to the existence of two distinct accents in the stressed syllable. Both stress and quantity are free. So this is what I think. In Vedic texts, three categories of words never have stress: enclitics (conjunctions and the short forms of the oblique cases of personal pronouns), nouns in the vocative, and the finite forms of the verb in main clauses. Enclitics could have been fully unstressed, but in the other two categories, some of which contained rather long words (*dhārayiṣyāmahē* [first person plural future causative (or iterative) of the root *dhr-* 'support']), there must have been stress of some sort, that is, the reinforcement of one mora.

In the accented texts in which the accent of "stressless" syllables is designated, all such syllables are marked as having the low tone. I think that we are dealing with an analogue of the Štokavian system: insofar as stress consisted in the rising tone, it could fall on any syllable in a word, or on none, in which case the first syllable acquired expiratorial reinforcement under the falling tone. The trouble is with grammar [= morphology] and syntax: the vocative, that is, a form of address, indeed remains outside the intonation of the sentence (it is *incise* [parenthesis], as Karcevskij calls it), but the verbal forms are a puzzle, for in subordinate clauses they have etymological stress (*dhā̂rayiṣyāmahē* in the main clause, *dhārayiṣyā̂mahē* in the subordinate); it appears that the opposition between the stressed and the unstressed forms did not affect meaning. [p. 244]

Germanic Prosody (Mainly German)

8 January 1931

While thinking about German (and Dutch) prosody, I have come to the conclusion that in these languages the place of the syllable peak, rather than length, is distinctive: the peak either coincides with the implosion of the postvocalic consonant (the marked series) or not. The shorter duration that can be observed in the first case is a concomitant phenomenon. I called this correlation *Silbenschnittkorrelation* ['the correlation of syllable cut'] or *Gipfelstellungskorrelation* ['the correlation of the peak placement']. . . .

My conclusion does not contradict your theory of musical stress. Under musical stress, a long vowel is perceived as two moments, with stress falling on either one. Given the German type of prosody, it is not the place of stress but the place of the syllable peak (whether stressed or unstressed) that is distinctive, and this peak hits either the vowel or the juncture between the vowel and the consonant. The *Tonverlaufkorrelation* ['the correlation of tone movement'] presupposes a vowel consisting of two morae (or rather of two moments), that is, a quantitative correlation. The *Silbenschnittkorrelation* presupposes a dynamic correlation (a correlation of strength), not a quantitative one.

Even if the *Silbenschnittkorrelation* and the *Tonverlaufkorrelation* are not identical, they are related. Therefore, it is worthy of note that from the geographic perspective the European languages with the *Silbenschnittkorrelation* border on the Baltic polytonic union (and at the other end German borders on Slovenian). At the same time, German appears to be a connecting link between Baltic polytony and the purely quantitative systems of the Hungarian-Czech type. However, the immediate neighbors of the Hungarian-Czech type are German dialects with somewhat different prosody. German dialects display rather great prosodic variety. It would be good to find a Germanic scholar who could explain all these things. [pp. 187–88]

28 January 1931

The *Silbenschnittkorrelation* is valid only for Standard German, probably for Low German dialects, and for Dutch. But in High German the situation is different. In the dialects of the Marchfeld type, as it has been described by Pfalz [1912], only the correlation of strength exists, and quantity is a nondistinctive factor depending on the intensity of the following consonant. In Swiss and some other High German dialects, the prosodic relations are more complicated, and I do not understand them yet. In Swiss dialects, vowel length does not depend on the next consonant, and the *Silbenschnittkorrelation* is absent; so far, I am quite in the dark here. In some Carinthian dialects, the first syllable of old disyllables is long, but the first syllable of old tri- and polysyllabic words is short, although at present all of them are disyllabic: compare *Leder* ['leather'] (< Old High German *ledar*) = *lēdə* with *Feder* ['feather'] (< Old High German *fedara*) = *fĕdə*. A hard nut to crack. So the question is not settled yet. And I have not yet formed an opinion about English. [pp. 190–91]

28 July 1933

There are many more German dialects with the correlation of tone than you thought, and they are situated not only on the shores of the Baltic Sea. It is characteristic of the deplorable state of European dialectology that no one has defined the borders of this phenomenon or put all these facts together (for musical distinctions are of different origin in different dialects and dialectology is oriented toward origins). So far, I have found out that such dialects exist on the Rhine and, what is especially interesting, in Switzerland.[4] It is not improbable that the Baltic and the South Slavic polytonic unions are connected by a string of archaic polytonic dialects. [pp. 282–83]

20 September 1937

On the whole, the prosody of the Germanic languages (at least as far as the standard varieties are concerned) is almost clear, and soon we can move on to the synthesis. I believe that in the Germanic prosodic system two aspects are important: several (at least two) tiers of stress and the opposition of two types of contact of the prosodic element (the mora in Danish, the vowel elsewhere). Icelandic seems to be entirely different. We must by all means find someone to study Icelandic phonology. [pp. 400–401]

Historical Phonology

Long/Short and Close/Open in the History of Vowels

11 November 1924

Narrowing of long vowels is connected with the circumstance that, the closer a vowel, the smaller its duration [*Eigendauer*]. In making long vowels close and short vowels open, language strives to diminish the difference in their duration. When this process is weakly developed ($\bar{e} > \underset{\circ}{e}$ or $\bar{\imath} > \underset{\circ}{\imath}$), the overall picture remains the same, and the quantitative principle is preserved, as happened, for instance, in Latin and German. But when this process goes far enough ($\bar{e} > \bar{\imath}$ or $\bar{\imath} > \breve{e}$), it usually results in the elimination of quantity (cf. Polish, Armenian, and the Romance languages). Languages in which long vowels become close, bypassing the stage of diphthongization, are moving toward the loss of quantitative distinctions, and where narrowing has been complete, the elimination of quantity is usually also complete. Czech does not belong to this type. It lacks any tendency in the direction of eliminating quantity. Therefore, the idea that it underwent "total" narrowing (i.e., bypassing the diphthongal stage) is a priori rather improbable. The opposite is true: diphthongization, that is, the differentiation of the vowel's beginning and end, reinforces quantitative distinctions and would fit Czech. [pp. 71–72]

Syntactic Phonetics and Speech Tempo as Factors of Sound Change

12 January 1927

Your explanation of $o < e$ in Russian, in word-initial position, does not satisfy me. . . . Nor do I subscribe to the hypothesis about the connection of *j* with the place of the word in the sentence. It is at best possible to prove that *prothetic* j *did not arise* at the beginning of a sentence or sense group. It is ill advised to operate with such concepts as *place in the sentence* and *speech tempo;* these are euphemisms disguising our inability to give a proper explanation. (103)

The Teleological and the Genetic Motivation of Sound Change

12 January 1927

"Teleological" explanations of sound change can and will help us discover many new and important things. But I do not think that it will wholly supersede and abolish "genetic" explanations. Both factors influence the life of language: an unconscious striving for "an ideal transformation" of the system and inexpedient changes that introduce disorder into the system and have "mechanistic causes." [p. 104]

Markedness and Sound Change

14 April 1931

I am not sure that when a correlation is abolished, only the marked series is changed. Two examples occur to me. In the so-called Belok dialect of Kashubian (described by Bronisch [1896–98, 4]), *ł* went over to European *l* and merged with *l'*, which corresponds to European *l* everywhere in Kashubian; the same seems to have happened in Czech. So the correlation was abolished owing to the change of the nonpalatalized, that is, unmarked consonant. Also in Russian, when musical-quantitative prosody gave way to expiratorial prosody, all stressed short vowels were lengthened and unstressed vowels shortened. Here, the quantitative correlation was abolished owing to the change of both the marked and the unmarked member.

You cite examples of a correlation becoming a disjunction, the change affecting only the marked member of the correlation. This creates the impression that such is always the case. But the same result can be achieved by changing the unmarked series. In Carinthian Slovenian dialects, *k* became the glottal stop, while *g* remained unchanged. In Lak, the front variety of nonlabialized palatals became *š, ž*, but their labialized counterparts did not change (the correlation of labialization stopped existing). In some Circassian dialects, the same process took place, but the correlation of labialization— represented by other phonemes—survived. In the Khakuch dialect of Circassian, "strong" (long and energetically articulated) *šš* did not undergo any modification, whereas regular (lenis) *š* went over to *č*. In Vulgar Latin, when the quantitative correlation collapsed, *ī* and *ū* continued into the new system, but *ĭ* and *ŭ* became *e* and *o*. [pp. 201–2]

Sound Change Caused by the Content of a Phonemic Series

n.d. (ca. 20 December 1931)

. . . There seems to be a law valid for some languages that a phoneme cannot contain more than one *Artikulationsartmerkmal* [feature of the type of articulation]; in such languages, the unmarked member of the *Annäherungskorrelation* [correlation of occlusion] is the fricative. This could have caused the change of *dž, dz, g* to *ž, z, γ* in some dialects of Old Church Slavonic. Such a possibility is not the only one. Originally, in Common Slavic, the correspond-

ing phonemes had two features each. What do you think of my explanation?
[p. 233]

Phonology and Statistics; Laws of Biological
and of Linguistic Evolution

4 August 1932

Van Ginneken's [1932] biology is unbelievable nonsense. But there are some facts worthy of consideration. First of all, attention must be paid to the statistical aspect of phonology. It is probably also governed by some laws. And, second, we must familiarize ourselves with biology. Van Ginneken's causal explanation is unconvincing and unverifiable. But it is quite possible that some analogy does exist between the laws of biological evolution and the evolutionary laws of language systems. [p. 250]

The History of Palatalized Consonants and Affricates in
Serbo-Croatian: Systemic Factors and Relative Chronology

10 May 1933

I have succeeded in connecting several facts of Serbo-Croatian dialectology: (1) Čakavian *d > j ~ Štokavian *d > d ($ʒ$), (2) Čakavian *t > t' ~ Štokavian $ć$, (3) Čakavian $šč$ > $šć$ (= $št'$) ~ Štokavian $šč$ > $št$, (4) Čakavian $če$, $že$ > $ča$, $ža$ ~ Štokavian $če$, $že$.[5] All these differences find their explanation in the circumstance that $č$, $š$, $ž$ were depalatalized earlier in Štokavian than in Čakavian. Once the depalatalization had been completed, it became possible to pronounce the palatalized plosives like affricates, without the risk of dephonologizing the difference between *t (> $ć$) and $č$. But Čakavian did not allow t > $ć$, for it still had $č$ (palatalized), and its merger with t would have caused upheavals in the system. On the other hand, the weakening of the voiced occlusion in Čakavian resulted in the change *d > j, but this change could not spread to Štokavian, which had lost *d. Even before Čakavian d > j and Štokavian t, d > $ć$, d, but after the depalatalization of $č$, $š$, $ž$ in Štokavian, $č$ and $dž$ shed their fricative part after $š$ in all Serbo-Croatian dialects. But since the groups $šč$, $ždž$ were palatalized in Čakavian and nonpalatalized in Štokavian, the results were $št'$, $žd'$ (> $žj$) in Čakavian and $št$, $žd$ in Štokavian.

At the same time (after the Štokavian but before the Čakavian depalatalization of $č$, $š$, $ž$), e (e^n?) became a after palatalized consonants. This change could not affect Štokavian, in which palatalized fricatives and affricates had lost palatalization, and e did not occur after palatalized plosives in the same morpheme. Since Štokavian e failed to go over to a even after j, I conclude that at that period Štokavian j was no longer treated as a palatalized consonant and had the status of the nonsyllabic variant of the archiphoneme *I*. The decisive factor in the reinterpretation of *j* was, to my mind, the loss of word-initial *j* before *i* in Štokavian. (In Čakavian dialects, *ji-* and *i* seem always to be differentiated.) [p. 273]

The Rise of "Artificial" Phonemic Systems;
the Case of English

1 January 1935
Your ideas about the historical absurdity of English (and French) phonology and about the Russian-Norwegian and Russian-Chinese jargons appear fully convincing. I have spoken a good deal with [Daniel] Jones's pupil [A. C.] Lawrenson and come to the conclusion that English has more than one system, partly differing according to region. Standard English is an artificial compromise regulated by orthoepic authorities (not the same in America as in Europe). Given such circumstances, the phonological aspect of language of necessity loses its significance. [pp. 317–18]

Languages in Contact: Russian and Finnish

5 May 1935
I have very little knowledge of the historical phonology of the West Finnic languages. Their vowels have been barely investigated. In my lectures, I explained the rendering in Finnish of Russian *o, e, ъ, ь* by *a, ä, u, i* exactly as you did it in your letter: *u* and *i* are the two intrinsically shortest sounds of the Finnish system. As far as the rendering of Proto-Slavic *ū, ī* by West Finnish *uo, ie* (= *ō, *ē) is concerned, I now think that Proto-Slavic *ū, ī* developed from *ou, ei* via the stage *ọ̄, ẹ̄* and that this is the pronunciation that western Finns heard when they first came into contact with eastern Slavs. German place-names in Austria show that the Slavs who inhabited this territory also had *ọ̄, ẹ̄* at approximately the same time. [p. 335]

Phonemic Split

12 August 1936
. . . It is doubtful that the second component of the group *šč* [in Russian] should have stopped being a combinatory variant of *ĉ* [palatalized] after the rise of *cokan'e* [*č* > *c*]: *č* and *ĉ* retained their articulatory and acoustic similarity and were in complementary distribution (*č* occurred after *š*, *ĉ* in all other positions). One could perhaps offer a simpler explanation. In the period between the emergence of *cokan'e* and the change *ky* > *k'i*, North Old Russian *ĉ* was a

combinatory variant of *k* before front vowels. A third variant of the same phoneme, only after *š*, was *č*. But the voiced partner of this phoneme (*k–ĉ–č*) was *g–dž*, and it was natural to render *dž* by the letter *g*.

One could object that, if this understanding of the North Old Russian phonological system was correct, *k'* (palatal) should have been regularly replaced by *ĉ*. But in church names (*Kyprijanъ, Kyrilъ, Kyrikъ, Marъkelъ*) and technical terms (*kel'ia* ['monastery cell'], *sakellarij* ['sacrist'], and so forth) the old pronunciation could have been preserved artificially (cf. the popular variants *Čurilo, Čuprijan*). Finnish (Karelian, Veps) place-names like *Kemozero* could have been borrowed later. According to your interpretation of *ky ~ k'i*, after *ky* changed to *k'i*, that is, after the fall of weak vowels, *k* and *ĉ* were no longer combinatory variants of the same phoneme.

But this theory may turn out to be wrong. It occurred to me only today, while I was reading your article [Jakobson 1937], and on closer scrutiny my whole construction may prove to be sheer nonsense. [p. 366]

An Overview of the History of the Slavic Languages

12 December 1920

In Kislovodsk, I began to write a dissertation entitled "An Attempt at the Protohistory of Common Slavic." This is the continuation of my paper "The Method of Reconstructing Common Slavic in A. A. Šaxmatov's *Outline* [1915]," which I gave at a meeting of the Dialectological Committee. I attempted to reconstruct the history of the emergence and disintegration of Common Slavic with the help of the method that I defended in that paper against Šaxmatov. I rather decisively parted company with the Moscow school (if you remember, I was ready to break with its dogma even in the paper), so Porzeziński would have been very angry with me. Many other dogmas had to be given up as well. Suffice it to say that I date the end of Common Slavic to the tenth century and that I deny the existence of nasal vowels in Common Slavic.

If my work ever appears, it will probably enrage not only the Moscow school. Yet I hope that some of my thoughts will find universal approval. I had a hard time writing, for most of my books stayed behind, and in my area the library of Rostov University presented nearly a Torricellian vacuum. However, I more or less finished the chapters on phonetics and was ready to go on to morphology. But then we had to evacuate from Rostov, and all my manuscripts and books remained there; I managed to take only a few notebooks. Now I am busy doing the work all over again. The library here [in Sofia] is not bad, so I am making progress, but there are irritating gaps. For example, Šaxmatov's *Outline* (1915), my main source, is absent, and, without it, especially in the section on stress (my greatest pride!), I am as good as lost. Although I keep working, sometimes

I feel desperate. The book is going to be voluminous, and publishing it at my own expense is out of the question. Institutional support means that the work will come out in Bulgarian, and I am not enthusiastic about this idea. Perhaps I will bring out some parts as articles, but journals seem to be on their last legs. [pp. 2–3]

1 February 1921

I start with an assumption that Common Slavic is not a moment but an epoch or, rather, a series of epochs. The beginning is marked by the first dialectal features that appeared in the so-called Proto-Slavic dialects. I mean the Indo-European dialects that with time developed into Common Slavic. The marker of the end is the latest set of phenomena that spread to all the Slavic languages, namely, the fall of ъ and ь, which, mutatis mutandis, had the same history in all the Slavic languages. Consequently, the "epoch" of Common Slavic lasted at the most conservative estimation two millennia and a half.

Given such conditions, it is absurd to define the phenomena of Common Slavic without dating them to a concrete period and determining their relative chronology; it is like tracing Napoléon's and Alexander the Great's conquests on the same map. Therefore, I attempt to reconstruct the relative chronology of various Common Slavic changes. It is an established fact that the first palatalization of velars preceded the second; similar sequences can be worked out for other changes.

As a result, I obtain the time line, a synchronistic table that includes nearly all the Common Slavic and most Common Russian, Common Polish, etc. changes, for many peculiarities of the individual dialects of Common Slavic arose at a period in which some features belonging to all dialects were still arising. This line of phonetic change can also be made to embrace some morphological innovations, which are, in turn, ordered chronologically. Thus, we witness the gradual emergence of the phonetic and morphological makeup of the dialects that lie at the foundation of the individual Slavic languages. My most important conclusion is that no sharp line separates the so-called protoepoch from the epoch of the individual languages; the emergence of Proto-Slavic is also its disintegration.

I divide the "protohistory of the Slavic languages" into four periods. The first period is the disintegration of Indo-European and the emergence of some "Proto-Slavic" dialects. At that time, Proto-Slavic changes spread actively to a few other Indo-European, notably Proto-Baltic, dialects. These two groups are especially close to each other. The second period is characterized by the complete unity of Common Slavic, which had differentiated itself from the other descendants of Indo-European. Common Slavic does not share any changes with its neighbors but has not yet split into dialects. The third period is the rise of dialects. Beside the changes spreading to the whole of Common Slavic, changes arise that are peculiar to individual dialect groups, even though they are relatively few, and the dialect groups have not been isolated once and for all (e.g., the West Slavic group does not yet exist: we see only the Proto-Sorbian-Lekhitic group going east and the Proto-Czech-Slovak one going south). In the fourth period, the emergence of dialects comes to an end. Individual changes now predominate over those common to all dialects, and dialect groups become more differentiated and stable.

The book falls into two parts: phonetics and morphology. That on phonetics contains a section on vowels and a section on consonants; if I succeed in reconstructing stress, I will add one more section. Each section falls into chapters, according to periods. Here is a tentative table of contents of part 1.

Section 1: Vowels. Chapter 1: The First Period: (1) *e > o* in open syllables before *u̧;* (2) *eu > iou;* (3) the merger of *a* and *o;* (4) the change of schwa [*irratsional'nyi glasnyi* 'irrational vowel'] to full front vowels; (5) opening of short high front vowels; (6) *ę̄ > ę̄;* (7) *e > i* in open syllables before *i̧*. Chapter 2: The Second Period: (1) *ă̄ > ŏ̄;* (2) palatalization of back vowels after *i̧* and palatalized consonants; (3) changes in word-final position; (4) the change of vowels in closed syllables before nasals. Chapter 3: The Third Period: (1) the evolution of the diphthongal groups vowel + nasal; (2) the evolution of the diphthongal groups vowel + liquid; (3) the evolution of the diphthong *oi.* Chapter 4: The Fourth Period: (1) the so-called depalatalization in Russian, Polish, and Sorbian; (2) the evolution of the open variants of the front high vowels ъ and ь.

Section 2: Consonants. Chapter 1: The First Period: (1) *s > š > x;* (2) the evolution of Indo-European affricates and cerebrals; (3) the evolution of aspirates; (4) the first palatalization of velars; (5) some consonantal groups (*sr, u̧r, ps*). Chapter 2: The Second Period: (1) progressive palatalization of velars (Baudouin de Courtenay's law); (2) groups of two plosives (two nasals; two fricatives). Chapter 3: The Third and the Fourth Periods: (1) dentals and labials before *j;* (2) the second palatalization of velars; (3) dentals + *l,* dentals + *n, m,* labials + *n.* Conclusion.

Prehistory of Slavic Phonetics: An Overview

1 February 1921

. . . I have a backlog of essays on Indo-European, rather than Slavic, linguistics in which I put forward dissenting views on many problems. Since in my work, especially in the opening chapters of each section, I argue constantly from Indo-European, I must insert these essays as excursus into my text, so the book—already voluminous—keeps expanding, and my argumentation also suffers because the overall picture becomes blurred. Therefore, I would now much rather publish my excursus in journals, to be able to refer to them later as articles. [pp. 6–8]

24 February 1925 (D)

The methods that I apply in my article [Trubetzkoy 1924] to the historical phonetics of Russian I now also apply widely to the historical phonetics of other Slavic languages and to Slavic comparative phonetics, and the results look very interesting. I have obtained an original picture of the disintegration of Common Slavic, and the relations between individual languages often appear in a new light. Most important, the evolution itself acquires an inner logic that, for the most part, comes as a complete surprise to the investigator. [p. 427]

20 October 1925 (D)

In your defense of Šaxmatov, you say that he based his linguistic reconstruction on history. And this is exactly what is wrong with him. Historians know very little about the most ancient period of the Russian tribe and turn to us, linguists, for information. They now constantly refer to Šaxmatov and supply their references with notes like "as has been proved by modern linguists." Yet what has allegedly been "proved" does not come from Šaxmatov the linguist but rather from Šaxmatov the historian, who could not have had the same weight in the eyes of professional historians as Šaxmatov the linguist.

All this is a sheer misunderstanding. I believe that, in order to avoid such misunderstandings, linguists should first offer their conclusions without regard to history, using only the evidence of linguistics. Later, their linguistic constructions should be subjected to historical analysis. In this case, they will be much more valuable to historians than constructions like Šaxmatov's, which are no more than linguistic interpretations of a preconceived theory of old historians. [pp. 435–36]

An Overview of the Phonetic History of Russian

18 July 1923

In the history of Russian, as in the rest of Slavic studies, I mainly try to see the forest for the trees, which, I think, has become a practicable task, even though few people are working in this direction. A bird's-eye view of the development and disintegration of Common Russian, its history observed *à vol d'oiseau,* as it were, provides a picture of amazing inner coherence and logic. The whole of it can be reduced to an extremely simple fact: Russian territory borders on the territory of other Slavic languages only in the west and southwest. Hence the consequences: all the phenomena common to all or several contiguous Slavic languages arise in the western and southwestern dialects and spread northeast.

Special cases are of two types: (1) Some such phenomena failed to spread to the Russian dialects that do not border on other Slavic territories. This situation occurred twice in the most ancient epoch, and both times several northern dialects remained unaffected. I mean the change *tl* > *l, dl* > *l* that originated in the Slavic south and passed by some northern Russian dialects and the change *g* > *γ* that originated in the west (cf. Czech, Slovak, and Sorbian) and did not reach most northern dialects. (2) Some phenomena common to the contiguous Slavic languages finally spread to the entire Russian territory, but in the southwest and west they arose much earlier than in the north and east; naturally, the changes that took place between these moments had dissimilar consequences in the north and east, on the one hand, and in the south and west, on the other. Such are (*a*) the Common Slavic loss of weak vowels (in the Russian southwest, it took place soon after the middle of the twelfth century, and in the southeast, in the second half of the thirteenth century), (*b*) the Common Slavic (except for Serbian and Slovenian) loss of musical [= tonal] distinctions, and (*c*) the Polish, Sorbian, and "coastal Polabian" change *ky, gy* (*γy*) > *k'i, g'i* (*γ'i*) (approximately the same chronology as in *a* above).

Between the end of the southwestern and the beginning of the northeastern abolition of musical distinctions, diphthongization of *o* under the acute took place; apparently, this diphthongization could not spread to the southwestern and western dialects that no longer possessed such distinctions. Between the end of the southwestern and the beginning of the northwestern fall of weak vowels (and the subsequent acquisition of full timbre by them), the following phenomena occurred: (*a*) shortening of long vowels, with the result that Russian *kon'* ['stallion'] and *moroz* ['frost'] now have the same [stressed] vowel (cf. northern Ukranian *kuon'* vs. *moroz*); (*b*) assimilation in the group palatalized dental + *j*, with the result that this assimilation did not happen in the northeast, where the dental and *j* were still separated by a weak vowel; (*c*) reinforcement of word-initial *i*, which could not affect the dialects of the southwest in which the weak vowels had been lost (cf. Ukrainian *z khati* 'from the house,' *grati* 'sing or play a musical instrument'); (*d*) reinforcement of weak ъ, ь after the word-initial group consonant + liquid, which could not seriously affect the southwest, where ъ, ь had been lost and interconsonantal liquids were turning into new combinations with vowels; (*e*) the change ы, *i* into ъ, ь before *j*, which could not spread to the dialects of the southwest, for they no longer possessed ъ, ь.

Thus, all the phenomena that spread before the fourteenth century from the southwest to the northeast were common to Russian and its neighbors.

Most remarkably, the phenomena that arose in the southwest but remained alien to the neighboring Slavs for some reason did not spread northeast. Such is the Ukrainian depalatalization of palatalized dentals and labials before syllabic front vowels (it took place after the southwestern fall of weak vowels but before the assimilation *t'j* > *t't'*), which—as though only because it was unknown to the neighboring Slavs—never spread beyond the Ukrainian area. This phenomenon had several consequences for Ukrainian, namely, the merger of *ы* and *i*, the nonmerger of *e* and *ě*, and the absence of *ë* in forms like *mëdu* ['honey,' dat. or partitive].

In contradistinction to the phenomena that spread from the southwest to the northeast, the phenomena that arose in the north or in the east always remained local and either had no counterparts in Slavic (Russ. *móju* ['I wash'], *šéja* ['neck'], *drožat'* ['tremble, shiver,' inf.], *sleza* ['tear, lacrima'], the second pleophony) or (less frequently) smack of borrowing: Sobolevskij [1909] compares *kl, gl* < *tl, dl* in Pskov and the change *tl, dl* > *kl, gl* in Lithuanian (more precisely, in Lithuanian-Latvian), while *cokan'e* [= *č* > *c*] can be brought into connection with the West Finnic merger of old *č* and *ć*.

As you see, before the fourteenth century, the development of Russian phonetics was governed by a single principle that can be understood as the logical consequence of the geographic situation of Russian territory in relation to the territory of other Slavic languages. The result of this development is the disintegration in the fourteenth century of the Russian language into four main groups of dialects: Ukrainian, Belorussian-Russian, northeastern Russian, and southeastern Russian (naturally, with transitional vernaculars).

At the beginning of the fourteenth (perhaps even at the close of the thirteenth) century, the development loses its coherence and is no longer governed by uniform principles: the unity is lost, and individual dialects enjoy considerable autonomy. One can see it in the changes of the early fourteenth (if not of the late thirteenth) century: the depalatalization of *š, ž, c* and qualitative modifications of unstressed vowels fall into this epoch. It is difficult to unravel the confusion that ensued.

Thus, it seems that depalatalization of *š, ž, c*, attested in all the Slavic languages bordering on Russian, should have spread from the southwest to the northeast. Yet many Ukrainian dialects were unaffected (including the western ones!), and in Ukrainian written monuments it was recorded even later than in those stemming from Moscow. One more phenomenon is worthy of note. In southern Russian dialects with the dissimilative *jakan'e* of the Obojan'-Don and Sudža type, unstressed *o* (< *ö*) and *a* after *š, ž* and after old nonpalatalized consonants are treated similarly and do not merge with *e*: compare *žana* ['wife'], *šagat'* ['march' (v., infinitive)] ~ *šistnadcat'* 'sixteen'; *šatër* 'marquee' ~ *žirëbaja* 'with foal.'

Conversely, in both the Russian dialects with *ekan'e, ikan'e,* and moderate *jakan'e* and the Russian and Belorussian dialects with the *jakan'e* of the Žizdra type, unstressed *a, o* after *š, ž* merge with *e,* as they do after palatalized consonants. Thus, in all such dialects, *š* and *ž* must have been depalatalized after the change of *v* (from unstressed *a, o*) to *e* preceded by a palatalized consonant, while, in the dialects of the Obojan'-Don and Sudža type, depalatalization occurred before the change *v > e;* to put it differently, in these dialects, which, on the whole, are situated southeast of Belorussian territory, *š* and *ž* were palatalized earlier than in Belorussian. I cannot make head or tail of it. In general, the areas with these types of dissimilative *jakan'e* were colonized relatively late, but the types as such are archaic. Even the assumption of resettlements does not clarify the picture.

To trace the history of the qualitative changes of unstressed vowels, it is necessary to regroup an enormous mass of currently used material. In this question, the methodological fallacy of Šaxmatov's school is especially obvious: Šaxmatov determined the borders of dialects rather than of phenomena and worked with fully established dialects, which are said to "mix" later. This is the sequence of the main phenomena: (1) the change of unstressed *ě* to *e* in the Belorussian area (it took place concurrently with $\widehat{uo} > o$); (2) the merger of unstressed *o* and *a* in *v* (back, mid, nonlabialized); (3) the change of unstressed *v* (and *a*) to *e* after a palatalized consonant; (4) the change of unstressed *v* and *e* to *a* in the immediately pretonic syllable. Each of these changes has its own territory: 1 and 3 reach partly the northern Russian area, whereas 2 and 4 stay away from it. The borders of 2 and 4 overlap, but it is not clear whether the same is true of 1 and 3. The traditional division of the northern Russian dialects as one finds it on the Moscow dialect map gives no answer to this question. One needs additional fieldwork, which cannot be done abroad.

Between 3 and 4, one more change must be placed, namely, the narrowing of unstressed open *e* to closed *e* and of *v* to *ъ*. Both processes took place in the limited area of dialects with dissimilative *akan'e,* only in the immediately pretonic syllable and only under certain conditions (before *a* in the next syllable, etc.). Other dialects either display no traces of narrowing or had it only in unstressed syllables that did not immediately precede a stressed one. In addition to the narrowing of open *e* to closed *e* and of *v* to *ъ*, one should consider the narrowing of *e* before palatalized consonants, a change that is hard to separate from the change of stressed open *e* to closed *e* before palatalized consonants. Naturally, only that unstressed *e* was affected that had not undergone narrowing earlier. In the dialects of the Obojan'-Don and Žizdra type, the change *e > a* (*jakan'e*) takes place even before palatalized consonants. It follows that here *akan'e* is later than dissimilative narrowing but older than the narrowing of *e* before palatalized consonants.

In the dialects with moderate *jakan'e,* dissimilative narrowing did not occur, and the narrowing of *e* before palatalized consonants occurred prior to the change of *e* in the immediately pretonic syllable to *a.* Thus, in the areas with Obojan'-Don and Žizdra *jakan'e,* the change *e > a* began earlier and narrowing of *e* before soft consonants later than in the regions with moderate *jakan'e.* But between these two areas there is an intermediate one of Sudža *jakan'e* in which both the dissimilative narrowing and the narrowing before palatalized consonants predated the change *e > a* (Durnovo seems to be only partly right [Durnovo, Sokolov, and Ušakov 1915; Durnovo 1918]; to account for the Sudža type, it is necessary to recognize a purely phonetic factor, that is, narrowing before palatalized consonants). If we look at the picture from this point of view, we must map not the various types of *akan'e* and *jakan'e* but the types of narrowing (and combinations of them), individually for each type; otherwise, the borders will cross.

However, these are all details, "trees." For the whole, it is important that even such main phenomena as depalatalization of *š, ž* and qualitative changes of unstressed vowels that occurred at the close of the thirteenth and the beginning of the fourteenth centuries appear to be the sum of smaller processes, each of which covers certain groups of dialects and spreads from group to group in a chaotic chronological sequence.

As regards later phenomena, they seem to have set in without rhyme or reason. Strictly speaking, there is not a single common Great Russian, Ukrainian, or Belorussian, let alone common Russian, change after the middle of the fourteenth century (perhaps only the change *-l > -u̯* in Belorussian and Ukrainian and the rise of prothetic *v* before *ω* in Great Russian, if my conception of these changes is correct), for *dzekan'e* [*dz < d'*] and depalatalization of *r* cannot be called a common Belorussian phenomenon and the change *ě > e* did not affect all southern Great Russian dialects. The fourteenth century witnesses the disintegration of Common Russian. The period before the fourteenth century is interesting precisely because the disintegration can be observed, and it runs its course according to rules one is able to identify and comprehend. [pp. 51–55]

Slavic (and Baltic) Accentuation and Metrics

Stress and Quantity in the History of Czech

20 December 1922

I would like to dwell on the origin of quantity in Czech (re n. 33 [in Jakobson 1923]). The last paragraph of this note does not convince me at all: no obligatory connection exists between the strength of expiratorial stress and the number of unstressed vowels. I am convinced only by your first objection. My scheme [Trubetzkoy 1921] indeed fails to explain the difference between *beran* ['ram, wether'] (or *lopata* ['shovel']) and *rukáv* ['sleeve']. Everything depends on whether Trávníček [1921] is right, that is, whether pretonic long vowels are indeed preserved only in the penultimate syllable and whether they are always preserved in this position. Exceptions to Trávníček's law (i.e., cases like *jazyk* ['tongue'], *táhnouti* ['pull, drag']) are so many that at first I rejected it. But recently I have changed my opinion and modified my scheme of the evolution of Czech, although not as you suggest it.

You returned to the old formula: shortening of long vowels under the grave and their preservation under the acute. This formula ignores the principle of parallelism in phonetic evolution and denies the causal link between phonetic evolution and the inherent properties of changing sounds, and my article is directed first and foremost against such views. My present reconstruction of the evolution of Czech is as follows: (1) Long and half-long vowels were preserved only in final and penultimate syllables (so, if we designate length by 3, half-length by 2, and what is less than half-length by 1, we will get mu_3kva_3 ['flour'], $ru_1ka_3va_3$ ['sleeve' (g. sg. or nom./acc. pl.)], vo_2da_3 ['water'], $do_1bro_2ta_3$ ['kindness'], etc.). (2) Posttonic syllables did not serve as the locus of quantitative distinctions ($ja_1h\breve{o}d\ddot{a}$ ['berry'], $lo_1pa_3t\ddot{a}$ ['shovel'], $zla_3t\breve{o}$ ['gold'], $vra_3n\ddot{a}$ ['raven' (g.)]). (3) The difference between the acute ($vr\tilde{a}_3na$), circumflex ($zl\tilde{a}_3to$), circumflex on half-length ($k\hat{o}_2lo$ ['wheel']), and rising stress on half-length ($j\grave{a}_1h\breve{o}d\breve{a}$, $l\ddot{i}p\breve{a}m\ddot{i}$ ['linden tree' (abl. pl.)]) existed only in the first syllable; in the others, the acute reigned supreme ($m\bar{u}k\tilde{a}_2$, $ru_1k\bar{a}_3v\tilde{a}_3$ $lo_1p\tilde{a}_3t\ddot{a}$, $svo_1b\acute{o}_3d\ddot{a}$ ['freedom']).

The changes were four in number. The first stage: a progressive shift in nonfinal syllables; that is, the falling part of stress moves to the next syllable, with only the rising part preserved where it had been: $zl\tilde{a}_3t\breve{o} > zl\grave{a}_1t\hat{o}_2$, $vr\tilde{a}_2n\ddot{a} > vr\acute{a}_2n\tilde{a}_1$, $lo_1p\tilde{a}_3t\ddot{a} > lo_1p\acute{a}_2t\ddot{a}_1$. But in final syllables both parts of old stress remain intact: $m\bar{u}_3k\tilde{a}_3$, $ru_1ka_3v\tilde{a}_3$. The second stage: shortening of nonshort vowels in noninitial syllables; half-long vowels become short ($zl\grave{a}_1t\hat{o}_2 > zl\grave{a}_1t\grave{o}_1$; $lo_1p\acute{a}_2t\ddot{a}_1 > lo_1p\grave{a}_1t\ddot{a}_1$), and long vowels become half-long ($mu_3k\tilde{a}_3 > mu_3k\hat{a}_2$; $ru_1ka_3v\tilde{a}_3 > ru_1ka_2v\hat{a}_2$). The third stage: the loss of quantitative distinctions in final syllables, which is tantamount to the shortening of half-long vowels in final syllables: in *lipa* 'linden tree' and *muka* 'flour,' final *a* (originally, $l\acute{i}p\grave{a}_1$ and $m\bar{u}k\hat{a}_2$) acquires similar length. The fourth stage: the rise of new long vowels as the result of contraction, compensatory lengthening, etc.

As you can see, the new scheme is different from the old one in only one point: earlier, I lumped together shortening of all noninitial long and half-long vowels, and now I break this process into two stages and distinguish between the complete shortening of half-long vowels and the incomplete shortening of long vowels. But both basic points remain: (1) the shift of musical stress and (2) the emphasis on the first syllable (during the second stage), pointing to its special role: it probably had expiratorial stress.

I now go even further and suggest that Polish also experienced the shift of musical stress. Polish went through the same four stages, and the difference between it and Czech consists in that in Polish shortening of half-long vowels, during the second stage, also occurred in noninitial syllables (i.e., in both $lo_1pá_2t\tilde{a}_1 > lo_1pà_1t\tilde{a}_1$ and $lí_2p\breve{a}_1 > lí_1p\breve{a}_1$). This shows that the cause of the shortening of noninitial long and half-long vowels in Old Czech was not the absence of (expiratorial) stress on them; in fact, this shortening was "free," and expiratorial stress only prevented shortening from spreading to initial syllables. I am also struggling with stress in Kashubian and Polabian; so far, I have had no success. [pp. 37–38]

25 January 1923

With regard to your objections to my formula for the evolution of stress in Czech, I have the following to say.

1) In Czech, nothing indicates that accents on long final syllables preserved both their parts. I assume their preservation only because the progressive shift of stress that I reconstruct in Czech is inseparable from the same process in Slovenian, and in Slovenian the preservation of both parts of the old accent must be assumed because otherwise it is impossible to explain why at a later time stressed syllables in Slovenian and Serbian were treated absolutely alike.

Remember that the phenomenon under consideration is not restricted to Czech: it spread to several Slavic languages. As I pointed out in my French article [Trubetzkoy 1921], the evolution of stress presupposes a measure of dialectal continuity in Slavic, and the processes caused by this evolution affected areas not overlapping with individual languages. It is not improbable that, although identical in nature in Czech and Slovenian, a change like the progressive shift of stress differed in details, but since we are dealing with an identical phenomenon, it is safer to suppose that its manifestations were also similar in both languages.

2) The statement that long vowels did not occur in antepenultimate syllables stands or falls with Trávníček's law. In as much as there are exceptions to this law, that is, words like *průhon* ['boundary furrow, ridge, balk'], *původ* ['origin, descent'], *národ* ['people, nation'], *návrat* ['coming back, return'], etc., half-long vowels should not be barred from antepenultimate syllables. According to Šaxmatov, such long vowels were permitted only in immediately pretonic syllables, so shortening in nonpenultimate syllables occurred only when such syllables were stressed or pre-pretonic. I would not dare set up iron-clad rules: the majority of the syllables in question are prepositions and prefixes, and one must reckon with the influence of analogy. In any case, this phenomenon has been attested in Polish and Serbian and is, at the least, "dialectal Common Slavic."

One can make do with the following formula: in the third, fourth, etc. syllable from the end, long vowels, for the most part, underwent shortening, and when they remained intact, the next syllable was, *for the most part,* stressed. This nonacceptance (or avoidance) of length in syllables situated far from the end of the word should not be connected with putative fixed stress in word-final position or with expiratorial stress on the penultimate syllable. Rather, we are dealing with the shortening of the total duration of polysyllabic words. There is an avoidance of more than one syllable after a long syllable within a word, and if the syllable following a long base is stressed, it is preferable that this syllable also be long. Let me repeat: I have not found an exact formula regulating the occurrence of length in the third (fourth, etc.) syllable from the end. But it is clear that not all the Slavic languages obeyed the same law (cf. Sloven. *jágoda* 'berry' with Czech *jahoda,* Serb. *jȁgoda*) and that Czech avoided length in the third (fourth, etc.) syllable from the end.

3) You call the system of quantity and accents that I reconstruct for my second period unwieldy. I cannot accept this criticism. I agree that the expiratorial reinforcement of the first syllable was a nonphonological fact. The falling accent always hit the syllable immediately following the rising accent, and in this position it was obligatory (precisely like *svarita* in Vedic); consequently, it was also nonphonological, and the speakers must have been unaware of it. Of phonological importance were only length, half-length, and shortness. All of them were permitted in both stressed and unstressed syllables; under stress, half-long and short vowels always had the rising accent, while long vowels (in final syllables) had the rising-falling accent (^). What is so unwieldy here? The system is reminiscent of the East Lithuanian one described by Bishop Baranov-skij [Baranauskas 1899], the only difference being that the Lithuanian system is *more complicated:* it also has stressed and unstressed short, half-long, and long vowels, but on long vowels the acute and circumflex alternate.

Nor does your statement about the tendency to "turn sense-differentiating musical distinctions into distinctions of quantity" satisfy me in the least. To begin with, when *vrána : vrāna* becomes *vrāna : vrăna,* both sense-differentiating musical distinctions and sense-differentiating distinctions of quantity change. Second, why did *ā* become *ă,* while *ā́* preserved its length? This is what I call the *absence of the causal link* between evolution and the inherent properties of changing sounds.

I recognize the replacement of the original musical distinctions by quantitative ones in Latvian. In this language, the original musical distinctions gave way to the distinctions in the *quality of length:* instead of the musically even accent, smooth length arose, and the musically broken accent was transformed into uneven length, which was broken the more abruptly the greater the old musical leap had been. Here, evolution is indeed an inevitable consequence of the nature of the changing sound. Nothing like this happens when *ā* becomes *ă*. This change can be likened only to the school scansion of Greek and Latin iambs and dactyls: it was agreed to substitute stress for length and consider short syllables unstressed. But such operations can be made only artificially. Therefore, I am not ready to give up my theory of the evolution of Czech stress. I think that it needs a single correction (from the point of view of Czech alone): we must assume that half-long vowels, rather than long ones, underwent shortening in noninitial syllables (as I said above, shortening in final syllables does not follow from the evidence of Czech). [pp. 43–45]

Metatonic Accents in Slavic

27 October 1923

I find it extremely probable that original -ъ in the genitive plural [of Russian *čelovek* 'man'] was stressed. But as far back as in Common Slavic this stressed final -ъ caused the metatony of the vowel in the preceding syllable, that is, the rise in it of new accents on long bases: the so-called new acute emerged on "uneven" [or "broken"] long vowels and the new circumflex on "smooth" [or "extended"] long vowels. I don't like these terms invented by the Poles (Rozwadowski and Lehr-Spławiński [Rozwadowski 1915]). In accordance with my general conception [Trubetzkoy 1924], I call the new acute the *inverse circumflex* and the new circumflex the *inverse acute.*

In my opinion, the difference between the new (inverse) accents and the old (regular) ones consisted in that the former were falling-rising and the latter were rising-falling. The relation between the phases remained intact, for the first phase of the acute on a long base was longer than the second while in the circumflex on long bases the first phase was shorter, as shown in the following picture:

	Regular accent	Inverse accent
Acute on a long base	⌒	⌣╱
Circumflex on a long base	╱⌢	⌣╱

The second peak in both inverse accents was higher than the first. Therefore, in Russian we have stress on the second syllable of forms with pleophony (*vorona* – g. pl. *vorón* ['crow'], *vólos* – g. pl. *volós* ['hair']), according to the principle:

╱ and ╲

So **čelvěkъ* lost stress on ъ in Common Slavic and acquired the inverse acute on *ě*. The syllable *čel-* was not pre-pretonic but pretonic, and according to Šaxmatov, its preservation makes sense only if the emergence of pleophony predated the metatony. But the genitive plural *volós* shows that pleophony took place later than the metatony. Šaxmatov's [1915, sec. 243] theory does not carry conviction. In *gornostaj* ['ermine' < **goronostaj*], *skorlupa* ['shell, nut-shell' < **skorolupa*], *gordovoj* ['policeman,' the allegro form of *gorodovoj*], pre-pretonic *o* was lost exactly as in *skovroda* ['frying pan,' the allegro form of *skovoroda*]: it is the weakest of all unstressed vowels [all these words are stressed on the last syllable].

As regards the difference between *čolovek* and *čolek* [the latter with nonpala-talized *l*] in northern Russian dialects, it will be best to ascribe it to the fact that the genitive plural is in most cases used with numerals; together, they make up a long phrase, and in such phrases shortening has to overcome fewer obstacles than in the "freestanding" nominative. [pp. 58–59]

Stress in Czech and Hungarian

30 March 1923

Recently, I have had some chance to listen to Hungarian speech, for I take the "direct Hungarian" train from Baden to Vienna. Quantitative distinctions in Hungarian are much weaker than in Czech. Noninitial stress has an unmis-takable musical character. The first syllable is considerably higher than the others; in emphatic speech, the difference in height becomes even greater, and stressed syllables make the impression of recurring whizzes. [p. 48]

Sievers's Schallanalyse *in Relation to Old Russian;*
Bubrix and Belić on Slavic Accentuation; the State of the Art

19 September 1926

Have you read Sievers's [1926] metrical analysis of *The Lay of Igor's Host?* The old man has positively gone crazy. I was about to write a review but then took pity on him. . . .

Bubrix's [1927] rejoinder has my wholehearted approval. Belić's theory is monstrous from the methodological point of view, like almost everything produced by this celebrity from Belgrade. But I must say that although Bubrix's theory is impressive looking and "constructive," it is not convincing. Slavic accentology is an absolutely hopeless enterprise. The "revival" that one could witness on this "front" in the course of the last fifteen years has had only one result: every Slavic scholar now has his own accentological system fundamentally different from everyone else's. [p. 91]

20 November 1926

In connection with my course in Old Church Slavonic, I have given a lot of thought to the *Kievan Fragments*. If they are Moravian, which is hardly in doubt, they may shed some light on an obscure question in the history of stress in Czech. It is odd that this monument designates stress while all the other Old Church Slavonic monuments written in Glagolitic do not. Doesn't this practice show that the Moravians *needed* to be told where stress fell in Church Slavonic words while the South Slavs did not? To put it differently, doesn't it all mean that Czech had already lost free stress but that in the language of the church it was still required to follow the rules of South Slavic free stress? Then we would obtain the *terminus ante quem* of fixed stress on the initial syllable (or, rather, of the loss of phonological stress). It can be objected that the *Kievan Fragments* were written before the fall of the weak *jer*'s, as indicated by the precise orthography and the metrics reconstructed by you. Fixed stress, as far as I understand, presupposed the loss of the weak *jer*'s. [p. 96]

Stress and Quantity in Polabian; the Concept of Half-Free Quantity

1 November 1927

When we met last, I told you that I could not unravel the relations between stress and quantity in Polabian [see Trubetzkoy 1929a, 77ff.]. After your departure, I again looked through my notes, and although I did not arrive at a final solution, I have formulated several new theses and would like to know your opinion.

In Polabian, as we know it from written monuments, all stressed vowels are long, all posttonic vowels are short, and in pretonic syllables, both long and short vowels are permitted. . . . Thus, quantity is free, while stress is not, and the place of stress is determined by a simple formula: stress falls on the last long syllable of an accentual unit.

This formula must be recognized only because in pretonic syllables (in identical phonetic contexts) both short and long syllables occur. But on closer examination, we observe that the first syllable of an accentual unit is always long regardless of stress (there is only one dubious exception). The second syllable, insofar as stress falls on the third, is usually short and has length only under the obvious influence of related forms with a different place of stress, that is, by analogy. . . . [Some of the prefixed verbal forms, plurals with final stress, adjectives derived from nouns, and nouns with productive suffixes] have regular short second syllables. It is hard to say anything definite about words with stress on the fourth syllable, for too few of them have been recorded. Probably, their second syllables were also short . . . , and deviations should be accounted for by analogy. . . .

It appears that in pretonic syllables quantity is free owing to analogy. From a phonetic point of view, before analogy set in, quantity in pretonic syllables was not free. Without analogy, the formula of stress in Polabian would have been different, namely, *Stress is free, the stressed syllable and the first syllable in a word are always long, posttonic syllables are always short, the second syllable of a word is long only under stress.*

And there is the main problem. Is it possible that analogy should have replaced the system free stress + bound quantity by the reverse system, namely, free quantity + fixed stress? Another question is whether quantity, as we know it in Polabian, is quite free. As stated above, the first syllable was always long in that language, while short syllables were never stressed. Consequently, not all theoretically possible combinations of long/short with stressed/unstressed and with the number of syllables were permitted. Polabian was not like Czech, in which any syllable in a word can be short or long, words can consist of short syllables only, and stress can fall on a long or on a short vowel.

The question arises whether it would be expedient to introduce the concept of half-free quantity. Among the Slavic languages, not only Polabian but also Slovenian has such half-free quantity. This concept may possess some pragmatic value. In languages with completely free quantity (such as Czech and Serbian), neither short nor unstressed vowels undergo qualitative reduction, whereas in Polabian and Slovenian, the reduction of unstressed short vowels is fully developed: for instance, in Polabian, in short unstressed syllables, all the old high vowels became ə, and all the old nonhigh vowels turned into ă. What do you think? [pp. 111–13]

n.d. (Summer 1928)

I have kept working on stress and quantity in Polabian. A curious thing! Where in Proto-Polabian, after the fall of weak vowels, the final syllable was *long,* in "Modern" Polabian, the final syllable is short, and stress falls on the penultimate syllable; and where in Proto-Polabian the final syllable was unstressed and short, we now have a long stressed final syllable. . . . Somewhat more complicated is the picture with short stressed final syllables: it seems that they were treated differently in disyllables and in polysyllables and that the decisive factor was the length of the final syllable. At one time, there seems to have arisen a tendency to level out the total energy of final syllables, so the expiratorial energy of long vowels was weakened and that of short vowels reinforced. Then lengthening of expiratorially strong vowels and shortening of expiratorially weak vowels set in. [pp. 115–16]

Allegro Speech and Apocope in Slavic

2 November 1929

It is a correct and fruitful idea [Jakobson 1929, 48ff.] that the fall of *jer*'s was the result of allegro speech. Perhaps this is why forms without *jer*'s originated in the south and spread north and east: southerners always speak faster. Yet the speech tempo cannot explain the fall of *jer*'s. I think that the main factor was that weak *jer*'s made up a third degree of quantity. It was possible to reduce this system of three degrees of quantity to the regular system with two degrees either by abolishing the "overshort" vowels (i.e., the weak *jer*'s) or by making short vowels equal to long ones (i.e., by abolishing quantitative distinctions). The first possibility was suggested to southerners by their fast rate of speaking, and from them it moved north and east. But the northeast (the Great Russian dialects) had already chosen the second possibility, and that is why the fall of *jer*'s established itself late there. [p. 145]

A Phonological Reconstruction of Slavic Accents

12 October 1930

Don't you agree that Common Slavic falling stress was nonexistent from a phonological point of view, as is the case in Serbian? If a word had no acute ("old" or "new"), reinforcement went to the initial syllable (rather, to the beginning of the first mora). This is why stress is shifted to the preposition and so forth. Then one would have to accept Šaxmatov-Bubrix's definition of the old acute as short stress and of the new acute as long stress [Šaxmatov 1903; Bubrix 1926a], and the result would be the prosodic system of Modern Štokavian. It is not difficult to deduce the systems of individual Slavic languages from it. For example, in Štokavian, old phonological stress on the initial syllable was lost. In Czech, in the initial syllable the correlation *stressed ~ unstressed* turned into *long ~ short,* and in the other syllables it disappeared, etc. For the end of the Proto-Slavic epoch, this prosodic system is likeliest. It is much more difficult to explain how it came about.[6] [pp. 178–79]

Stress, the Archiphoneme, and the Nature of Poetic Meters

11 November 1930

In the linguistic consciousness, the passive (unmarked) phoneme of the correlation serves as the symbol of the archiphoneme. For example, for a native speaker of Russian, the symbol of the correlation t/t' is t, not t'. For a native speaker of Czech, the symbol of the correlation $a/\bar{a}$ is a, not $\bar{a}$. If we look at strong and weak vowels in Russian from this point of view, we will see that the unmarked member of this correlation is the stressed rather than the unstressed vowel, for a native speaker of Russian considers stressed *ú, á, í* to be the symbols of the correlations *ú/u, á/a, í/i*. To put it differently, the correlation of vocalic strength is expressed in Russian not as the opposition *stressed / unstressed* but as the opposition *unreduced / reduced*. Consequently, in transcription, a special sign (˘) should be reserved not for stressed but for reduced vowels. This is more correct: the transcription *golaj* renders less precisely the phonological nature of the word *golyj* ['bare, naked'] than the transcription *golăj*. Note also that *golăj* and *starăj* [= *staryj* 'old'] represent the same prosodic type in writing and in the linguistic consciousness, whereas *golaj* and *stáraj* are artificially given different representations.

This understanding of vocalic stress in Russian will explain the fact that in Russian versification metrical schemes are based on the arrangement of unstressed (reduced) vowels: iambic is a meter in which all odd syllables are unstressed, trochaic is a meter in which all even syllables are unstressed, while in trisyllabic meters a pair of unstressed syllables recurs at an interval of one syllable. [p. 182]

Stress and ĕi/ēi *in Baltic; a Whole Word as the Locus of Stress;* Tert/Tort *in Slavic*

n.d. (ca. 20 December 1931)

Kuryłowicz's [1931] article is very interesting, but I am not quite satisfied with it either. As far as the Baltic languages are concerned, his constructions seem rather plausible. But the process should be described differently. I can offer something like this. Let us suppose that at the initial stage the distinction between the two types of diphthong (*ei̯* and *ēi̯*) under old stress was lost but survived in unstressed syllables. Then, once stress was shifted back under the influence of morphological factors, syllables with new (shifted) stress might end up having two types of quantity (*ei̯* and *ēi̯*) and different accents, one of which coincided with the type that existed in syllables with old (unshifted) stress. By analogy, this distinction of accents could have been transferred to monophthongs. All this is possible, but I do not know the Baltic data well enough to check whether my hypothesis is correct.

I did not begin by questioning the rise of accentual distinctions caused by a morphological process; it was Kuryłowicz's starting point, namely, the coexistence of free quantity and free stress, that made me feel uneasy. But then I realized that the stress could have been a musical one, which only by chance left no traces. The Japanese type of musical stress, whose locus is the entire word, is also possible. Kuryłowicz seems to suggest (perhaps unwittingly) just this type when he says that the opposition was between words with stress on the stem and words with stress on the ending. His explanation of Slavic is much worse. Here, everything rests on unverifiable hypotheses. Still, what he has to offer is interesting. Perhaps, if we follow this path, we will get to the heart of the matter.

In the same issue of *Rocznik sławistyczny*, Lehr-Spławiński [1931a] brought out an article on *tert, tort* etc. Some passages are hopelessly naive from the methodological point of view. He ascribes the difference in the treatment of North Slavic *oȓt* > *rot* versus *órt* > *rat* to the fact that northern Slavs allegedly shortened circumflected long bases, but he does not say that in other cases circumflected *a* yielded *a*, not *o!* [pp. 233–34]

The Relative Chronology of Accentual Changes in Slavic

15 February 1932

Length in such words as Czech *pás* 'belt,' Polish *pas*, Slovak *pás* shows that the loss of intervocalic *j* and contraction in West Slavic are later processes than the Common West Slavic shortening of circumflex. Otherwise, **pâs < pòjas* would have shared the fate of the old circumflex, and the result would have been the shortened form **pǎs*. But the shortening of circumflected bases must have been concurrent with the abolishment of the musical correlation, for otherwise an impossible combination of two distinct short accents and one long one (˵, ˴, ´) would have arisen in the system. Circumflected bases must originally have been half long (i.e., longer than ˵ but shorter than ´); when musical distinctions ceased to exist, the half long merged with the short. It follows that the loss of musical distinctions antedated the contraction of vowels and, consequently, the fall of weak *jer*'s.

On the other hand, the lengthening of vowels under the acute in the first syllables of disyllables in Czech (*lȉpa > lípa* 'linden tree') undoubtedly preceded the loss of the musical correlation, for after this loss no difference could have existed between the old acute and the old circumflex. Since lengthening of old acuted bases in this position spread to neither Slovak nor Polish, the musical correlation must have been abolished earlier in them than in Czech. What do you think? [pp. 238–39]

Stress in Serbo-Croatian

10 May 1933

I have gone rather deeply into the question of stress in Serbo-Croatian. Quite independent of you, I also discovered that in some Čakavian dialects accentual and quantitative distinctions go together. For the dialect of Novî, my formula is identical with yours. . . . I formulated the rule for Novî so: If no syllable in a word is short, stress falls on the last syllable with a rise; in the absence of a syllable with a rise, stress is assigned to the first syllable with a rising-falling accent.

But such formulas are valid for only part of the Čakavian dialects. Take, for instance, the dialect of Brucje (on the island of Hvar; described by Hraste [1926–27]). It has neither posttonic long vowels nor long vowels before ´; unstressed long vowels occur only before ˜ and ˆ (ˆ is a phonetic realization of ˜: it occurs only on *a* in nonfinal syllables, and *ȃ* occurs only in final syllables; you have to correct what you wrote about it in *Travaux* 4:168–69 [Jakobson 1931a]). I have discovered only one rule: If a word contains two adjacent long syllables, the second receives a falling accent. Words without such sequences do not lend themselves to any rule, for one cannot seriously offer the following: Stress is assigned to one of the short syllables; if no short syllable receives stress, it is assigned to a syllable with a rising long accent; in the absence of such a syllable, it is assigned to a syllable with a falling long accent. Such a formula is tantamount to the admission of free stress. . . .

In a classic Štokavian dialect, two types of words alternate: some have the rising-falling accent, the others the falling one. In a sense group, stress is assigned to the syllable that has the highest end phase in a word. Are we justified in speaking about the *Tonverlaufskorrelation* ['the correlation of tonal movement'] within a single vowel? Since all pretonic syllables have a rise, their *Tonverlauf* ['tonal movement'] is determined by the context; the same holds for posttonic syllables with a fall. Stressed vowels have a rise in all noninitial syllables, so they, too, are phonologically neutral with regard to accents; and the same holds for vowels in monosyllables, which always have a fall. Consequently, only the vowels of the first syllables in polysyllabic words can be discussed from a phonological point of view. But it is not clear which solution is better: *Tonstufenkorrelation* [the correlation of stress ~ no stress] (*vòda* ['water' (nom.)], the first syllable is stressed, *vȍdu* ['water' (acc.)], the first syllable is unstressed) or *Tonverlaufskorrelation*. [pp. 268–70]

The History of Serbo-Croatian Accentuation; the Role of Contraction in the Development of Slavic Prosody

10 June 1933

While thinking about the evolution of prosody in Serbo-Croatian, I have arrived at the following conclusions:

1) If it is true that the Proto-Slavic acute was a short rising accent and that all pretonic syllables were rising while posttonic syllables were falling, the entire evolution of (Central) Štokavian prosody can be reduced to one act: *in stressed syllables, the rise was replaced by the fall*. Retraction of stress as a special act never took place. To put it simply, as soon as the highest syllable of a word became

falling (instead of rising), the syllable that immediately preceded it became automatically the last rising one, which means stressed, for in Štokavian, as well as in Proto-Slavic, the last rising syllable (or, in the absence of such, the first falling one) was considered stressed. Consequently, it is not the classic (Hercegovina) Štokavian type but rather the Kosovo-Resava one and others like it that deviate from Proto-Slavic.

2) If this is true, then, before the Common Štokavian rising accent in stressed syllables gave way to the falling accent, Proto-Štokavian had only rising accents on noninitial syllables and did not have *kopâš ['you (sg.) dig'], *bosî ['barefoot'], *bosôgā ['the same' (g. sg., m. n.)], etc. It is quite possible that by that time *j* had been lost and the vowels mutually assimilated. But the real contraction had not yet taken place (one can suppose the pronunciations *kopàaš, *bosòoga, etc.). The contraction (i.e., the merger of two adjacent vowels into one long one) took place in Proto-Štokavian after the changes ´ > ˆ, ˇ > ˜.

3) Unlike the contraction in Štokavian (in words like *kopàaš > kopâš, *bosòoga > bosôgā), the Čakavian contraction must have happened very early. And this is the heart of the matter. As soon as *bosôga* sprang up alongside *gòlōga* ['bare, naked' (g. sg., m. n.)], the old rule about obligatory stress on the last rising syllable was violated, for it could not be applied to short syllables. This resulted in the accentual (tonal) differences in short vowels losing their significance, but by way of compensation, differences in expiratorial intensity emerged. The old rule ("stress on the last rising syllable or, in the absence of such, on the first falling one") retained its validity only for long syllables and only in words without a "strong" short syllable. This may have been the cause of the deep distinction between the Štokavian and the Čakavian types, which prevented the change in Štokavian from spreading to the Čakavian dialect. What do you think?

I also have an important theoretical question. In South Slavic dialectology, dialects have been attested with free quantity and exclusively falling accents. If such dialects really exist, they can be interpreted in two ways: either they combine free quantity with free expiratorial stress and are anomalous from the point of view of your law, or they have polytonic systems in which rising tones cannot occur after falling ones and in which stress within a sense group always hits the first of the falling syllables.

How would it be possible to prove or disprove either of these interpretations? If a speaker of such a dialect, knowing nothing about phonetics or phonology, invented a system of accentuation and chose to mark all pretonic syllables as rising and reserved the sign of the falling accent not only for stressed but also for posttonic syllables, it would of course follow that the second interpretation is correct and the first wrong. But such favorable conditions could have owed their existence only to chance. They cannot be created experimentally, for if we taught our informant even so much as Vuk's system of designating accents, we would instill into this person the idea that pretonic syllables have a special type of accentuation. What do you say? . . .

Have you seen Trager's [1933] work on the accentuation of the *Kievan Fragments?* A definitely rotten work. I think you should write a review of it. [pp. 275–77]

25 January 1935

The rise of new long contracted vowels had a great influence on the development of the prosodic system in individual Slavic languages. I think that I wrote you once that I ascribe the difference between the Štokavian and the Čakavian prosody to the fact that in Proto-Čakavian contraction happened earlier than it did in Štokavian. If we bear in mind that contraction in West Slavic preceded and in South Slavic followed the fall of weak *jer*'s and that it took place first in Čakavian and then in Štokavian, we can assume that this phenomenon spread from northwest to southeast (the same is true of the earlier shift of the syllable boundary). It must have reached the Bulgarians and East Slavs last, and by the time contraction could have occurred in Bulgarian and Russian both languages had acquired expiratorial stress. And this is what prevented contraction in them: since quantity had disappeared, contraction was no longer needed. It follows that, far from saving the correlation of quantity, contraction, owing to the fall of quantity, did not even take place. [p. 317]

Stress and Quantity in the History of Czech;
Metatony in Slavic

2 February 1935

In my course, I explained the lengthening of ` and the shortening of ˆ in Czech as follows: ceteris paribus, a tendency existed to replace the opposition rising ~ falling by the opposition intense (long) ~ weak (short). In the opposition ´ versus ˆ, only ˆ could be shortened, and in the opposition ` versus ˇ only ` could be lengthened. This explanation is not incompatible with yours.

As far as I can judge, prosodic systems were not identical in all the dialects of Proto-Slavic. However one may look at metatony, the phenomena covered by this term differed from place to place. For instance, some facts seem to indicate that in Slovenian the so-called new circumflex did not merge with the old circumflex and that the distinction between them was the same as that between the new and the old acute and rested on length. In Proto-Slovenian, the old circumflex was shortened as a reaction to the rise of the new long circumflex and merged with ˇ. Later, the new ´ and ˆ remained intact, whereas the old ` and ˇ (from ˇ as well as from ˆ) were shifted: the falling syllable after an initial syllable with ˇ and the rising syllable before a final syllable with ˋ were lengthened and attracted stress to themselves. [pp. 323–24]

Diacritics in the Kievan Fragments

24 September 1935

I think I have finally got on top of the diacritics in the *Kievan Fragments*. The main problem is that some of them have two functions. You discovered this with regard to the acute [Jakobson 1935]. (By the way, you questioned the stress in *vьse*[N] ['all'] and *vьsemogyî* ['almighty'], but they are absolutely correct: compare *vьse*[N] and Russian *vóvse* ['altogether, at all'], and you will see that stress fell originally on *jer; vьsemogyî* is not a compound but a combination of two words. It is much more difficult to explain the place of stress in *dóstoini* ['worthy'].) Circumflex has three functions: (1) to indicate that two letters belong to one word or one syllable; (2) to substitute for the acute and the grave in some words ending in two letters (in its function of stress, the acute is replaced by circumflex over *o*[N], and as a sign of two separately pronounced vowels, it is written over prevocalic *y;* the grave is replaced by circumflex before *e*[N] in polysyllabic words); (3) to distinguish the genitive plural from the nominative/accusative masculine singular.

All this can be understood only in the light of Greek orthography. Note that the grave occurs only on final syllables, circumflex on final and penultimate syllables, the acute on any syllable—exactly as in Greek! My statistics on the Greek Gospels show that in two-thirds of all cases circumflex occurs on "diphthongs," some of which never have the acute or the grave, while others display a marked tendency toward circumflex (e.g., οῦ occurs five times more often than οὐ, οὺ; εῖ occurs four times more often than εἰ, εὶ; and only on αι does the grave predominate (owing to the highly frequent word καὶ ['and']). Half the cases in which circumflex in this Greek text falls on the "nondiphthongal" vowel of the final syllable are endings of the genitive plural. Vondrák's [1904] artful profundities are a waste: in the *Kievan Fragments,* circumflex on ъ simply reproduced the Greek circumflex on the ending of the masculine genitive plural.

In Greek texts, the accusative singular of the *o* stem differed from the genitive plural in that (1) the accusative singular had *oν,* in contradistinction to the *ων* of the genitive plural, and (2) the accusative singular had the grave under stress, while the genitive plural had circumflex. The first feature (*oν* vs. *ων*) could not be matched in Slavic, which had only one letter corresponding to ъ. So there was no other choice but to reproduce the second feature and put circumflex over ъ in the genitive plural.

Only ˇ (the sign of length) cannot be deduced from Greek. Nor can it be deduced from Latin. Curiously enough, in South Slavic, this sign was lost in its old function, whereas the Czechs seem to have retained it until the fourteenth century; according to Gebauer, in the early fourteenth century [Czech] Apocrypha . . . length was designated by an arc (half circle) turned upside down. This might bear out your theory about the longevity of Cyril and Methodius's tradition in Bohemia. But, on the other hand, it seems quite improbable that a trace of the Glagolitic designation of length should have survived only in monuments with a typical secular German orthography. So it is better to seek the origin of this sign in German tradition. In the fourteenth century, Germans often designated vowel length by a superscript *e* (*ů, å,* etc.). In careless writing, this *e* could have developed into ˘. If it turns out that such a simplified variant of *e* as a sign of vowel length existed in German, I would prefer to trace Old Czech ˘ to German rather than to the Glagolitic of the *Kievan Fragments*. We will have to talk it over with specialists in German paleography. [pp. 347–49]

Slavic Metrics (Mainly the History of the Decasyllable)

19 September 1926

You asked me about the Slavic decasyllablic verse. There are two types of such verse; according to South Slavic terminology, masculine (with a caesura after the fourth syllable) and feminine (with a caesura after the fifth syllable). The South Slavs used the masculine decasyllable in long epic, "heroic" [*junack*] lays. If you are right in thinking that such masculine decasyllables as the words of St. Vladimir:

Rusi est'   / veselie piti
Ne možem / bezъ togo byti
['Russia's joy is in drinking; we cannot do without it']

or Svjatoslav's appeal to his retinue:

Uže nam   / někamo sia děti
['We have nowhere to go']

preserve the traces of syllabic metrics, it follows that the masculine decasyllablic verse was also used by the East Slavs as the meter of heroic poetry. Contrariwise, the feminine decasyllablic verse is used by the South Slavs as the meter of low epic and lyric epic songs. Note that the Mordvins have all types of South Slavic meters with the exception of the masculine decasyllable and that they have no heroic poetry of any kind, only lower epic and lyric epic songs.

All this seems to indicate that among the South and East Slavs the masculine decasyllable was formerly connected with the long heroic lay, which throws serious doubt on Korš's [1907a] hypothesis about the origin of this meter from the Byzantine *nonepic* verse. In Slavic, the masculine decasyllable could develop from the meter 4 + 3 + 3 after the fall of the second caesura. Like other meters having two caesuras, this meter (4 + 3 + 3) goes back to a meter with one caesura, with several (in this case, three) syllables inserted between its parts; the meter 4 + 3 is very popular in Slavic (and Mordvin) wedding and ritual songs (especially about fortune-telling). However, this is true only of folk poetry. The bookish decasyllables could have arisen in some other way, and among the Western Slavs bookish poetry exercised an extremely strong influence on folk poetry. So the West Slavic verse 4 + 6 may, after all, have no historical connection with its South Slavic counterpart, the more so because the West Slavs have not preserved any relics of the long heroic lay. [pp. 90–91]

20 September 1937

The Pushkin issue of *Slavia* [vol. 14, no. 3 (1937)] is horrible! Absolutely awful is an article about Pushkin's translations from Serbian, which you advised me to read [Berkopec 1937]. . . . Too bad one cannot say the truth about "The Songs of the West Slavs," namely, that it is one of Pushkin's works where he was at his most slapdash. [p. 401]

Morphology

The Origin of Active Participles in Slavic

1 May 1929

How should the forms *neѕА* ['carrying'], *živА* ['living'], *grАdА* ['coming'] be interpreted? The origin of the nominative case of participles is obscure. It has never been noted that in the nominative singular active participles do not distinguish the masculine from the neuter, yet this is a very important circumstance. The lack of this distinction has, I think, the following explanation: the nominative masculine of the active participle in the perfect ended in *-ōs* (Gk. *ϝειδώς* ['having seen']), which became *u* in Slavic, but the same *u* must have been the reflex of *-ōnts* in the nominative masculine of the active participle in the present. Consequently, the masculine nominative participle in the perfect and in the present must have merged.

Two paths were open to the language: it could preserve the distinction between the masculine and the neuter but give up the distinction between the perfect and the present participle, or it could save the distinction between the perfect and the present participle but sacrifice the distinction between the masculine and the neuter. The second path was of course more convenient: the distinction between the genders was always clear from the context, while the confusion between the present and the past could have caused constant misunderstanding. The past participle *nesъ* goes back to the neuter, but the present participle *nesы* is the form of the masculine.

However, this does not mean that all the forms of the present participle can be traced to old masculines: some may well be neuters. The Indo-European forms were as follows: the nominative masculine *bherōn(t)s, plākjōn(t)s, sōdīn(t)s*, the nominative neuter *bheront, plākjont, sodĭnt* ['carrying, weeping, sitting']. They must have yielded Slavic *bery, *plačě ~ plačę, *sadî; *berǫ, *plačǫ, sadę*. However, only *bery* and *sadę* are attested; South Slavic *plača* cannot be deduced from *plākjōnts*, for neither Russian nor Polish has *plačě*.

The attested forms (except for *bery* and *sadę*) are new; they are products of contamination. Only the contamination *plākjōnts ~ plākjont* is easy to understand. After the delabialization of long vowels, two competing forms must have arisen: *plāčjēⁿ* (the old masculine = *plākjōnts*) and *plāčjǫn* (the old neuter = *plākjont*); they naturally became *plāčjen > plačę*. But a similar process can be imagined in the pair *berȳⁿ* (< *bherōnts*) ~ *beron* (< *bheront*): the contaminated form was *berȳⁿ*. Hence *nesа, živа, grада*, for if *ŭn* became *ǫⁿ* and *ĭn* became *eⁿ*, *ȳⁿ* must have become *ɵⁿ* (where *ɵ* is a mid nonback, nonfront vowel).

The form *plačę* easily supplanted *plačě* and *plačǫ*, for it was supported by the form *sadę* (*sadę* superseded the rival form *sadi < *sōdĭnts*, for *sadi* was ambiguous: it coincided with the second and the third person of the imperative and with the second and the third person of the "aorist"); in addition, the phoneme *ę* existed in the system and occurred elsewhere. But *nesǫ, živǫ,* etc. had fewer chances for survival since the phoneme *ɵ* occurred only in this form. Therefore, *nesy* stayed in the language, while *plačě* disappeared without a trace. In some dialects (probably including that of the First Teachers), the form *nesǫ* may never have existed.

This is a difficult explanation, but I cannot think of a better one. Accents are better left alone. I remember the late V. N. Ščepkin's statement. Some complicated question of Slavic phonetics came up at his seminar, and I suggested that we first find out what accent was in the form: perhaps that might help. Ščepkin smiled sarcastically and said, "This is a cruel method unknown even to the medieval Inquisition." According to Lehr-Spławiński, final *-s* turned every acute into a circumflex. Be that as it may, the ending *-y* (< *ōns*) in the accusative plural did not attract stress by Fortunatov–de Saussure's law and is, from the Slavic point of view, circumflected. [pp. 129–30]

Gender in Russian and the Caucasian Languages

24 February 1925 (D)

I have read your article on the categories of gender in Russian [Durnovo 1924a] with great interest. Don't you think that in Russian the plural is a category of gender rather than of number? The term *plural* strikes me as misleading when applied to Russian. One can speak only about the animate plural and the inanimate plural *genders;* these terms are of course as conventional as the designations of the other genders: *vorota* ['gate,' lit. 'gates'] is a noun of the inanimate plural gender, and it is connected with the concept of plurality no more than the feminine noun *dver'* ['door'] is connected with the female sex. The pairs *stol : stoly* ['table' : 'tables'], *derevo : derev'ja* ['tree' : 'trees'], and so forth are chance occurrences, and so are the pairs *nemec : nemka* ['German man' : 'German woman'] and *durak : dura* ['male fool' : 'female fool']. In general, the plural in Russian is independent of the singular. [pp. 427–28]

3 March 1925 (D)

My ideas about the "plural gender" were inspired by the study of the East Caucasian languages, in which the category of gender (in Chechen, there are six genders; in most Lezghian languages, there are four) is more semasiological than in Indo-European and where nearly all the plurals and singulars belong to different genders. In Archi, the designations of adult men belong to the first gender, of adult women to the second, and "nonpeople" (animals, objects, abstract notions) are distributed between the third and the fourth. But in the plural all "people," irrespective of their sex, belong to the third and all "nonpeople" to the fourth gender. Words designating multitudes of animate objects, people and animals alike, such as 'army,' 'nation,' 'flock,' and 'herd,' belong to the third, while words designating multitudes of inanimate objects (e.g., 'forest,' 'village') belong to the fourth gender. The verb agrees with the subject only in gender, not in number. So here the plural is undoubtedly a category of gender. In Avar, with its simplified system of genders, four genders exist: the first (of adult men), the second (of adult women), the third (of adult and nonpeople), and the fourth (= plural). As you see, in the Caucasian languages this is usual.

In the Indo-European family, the Slavic languages have preserved the sense of gender like no others; they display a tendency toward the semanticization of distinctions between the genders and emphasize these distinctions by the forms of declension. In this respect, they come especially close to the Caucasian type, and I would say that they have come a long way in this direction. [pp. 429–30]

25 August 1932

Kuryłowicz came to visit me. . . . We talked about grammatical correlations. This question interests him most of all. Incidentally, he believes that in the Slavic languages there is no correlation of gender. The gender of adjectives and pronouns is determined syntactically, and, except for a small number of the designations of human beings and animal names, nouns lack the required opposition. A case like *učenik* : *učenica* ['male pupil' : 'female pupil'] is unique (cf. *mel'nik* 'miller' : *mel'nica* 'mill'), and for the neuter even such examples are absent. So, in his opinion, it is a moot question which gender is unmarked. He may be right. We are too spoiled by classical grammar. When one looks at languages like Avar, in which the category of gender really exists as a living factor, one begins to wonder whether we indeed have genders. [p. 252]

Historical Morphology and Morphological Reconstruction

25 February 1930

In the grammar of Old Church Slavonic, not only phonology and morpho-nology but also morphology must be rewritten. Because of the "historical" ap-proach, certain phenomena of Old Church Slavonic grammar have been sys-tematically distorted. For example, the nominal declension is usually treated in an absolutely fantastic way: it is based on the fictitious *o*-stem, *u*-stem, etc., all of which had been lost long before the emergence of Old Church Slavonic. In other chapters, the perspective is distorted owing to the orientation toward the modern state of the Slavic languages (Russian, Polish, Czech), which is combined with the absurd notions of school grammar. Such is the treatment of the conjugation, especially the classification of verbs, based on the infini-tive instead of the present and the aorist, these two pillars of Old Church Sla-vonic. Absurdities are everywhere. But the Slavicists are perfectly satisfied. . . . The situation is probably not better elsewhere in linguistics. [p. 154]

n.d. (after 10 March 1930)

The prehistory of morphology is a difficult matter. In phonetics, the starting point, that is, the sound system of Indo-European, is more or less clear. But this is not true of morphology. The Indo-European ancestor of a Slavic sound is rarely dubious or debatable, while in morphology one runs up against such difficulties at every step. This complicates research tremendously. Conjuga-tion is a case in point. Once we move from prehistory to history, we observe that the Slavic languages are of little interest to a student of the evolution of morphological systems. In the course of the historical period, the Slavic morphological *systems* have changed very little, and the differences between them are insignificant; they are much smaller than the differences between the phonological systems. The only exception is Bulgarian, but this is the most troublesome language with regard to history, for its monuments do not reveal the process of evolution. So I am afraid that your dream of producing a logical history of morphology, like the one you produced for phonology, cannot be realized on Slavic material. [p. 156]

28 January 1931

I keep thinking about structural morphology, and all kinds of ideas occur to me. It seems that in morphology, just as in phonology, certain phenomena can be projected onto one plane. For example, person, number, and gender belong together, in contradistinction to cases, on the one hand, and tenses and moods, on the other. Differentiation between disjunctive and correlative oppositions is as fruitful in morphology as in phonology. In a small way, I have started collecting data from the structural morphology of the languages with which I am familiar. By the way, geographic zones exist in morphology as well. Eurasia is characterized by a highly developed system of declension. In Europe, declension is on its way out and has disappeared in the periphery (Italy, Spain, France, England, Denmark); in Asia, and in northern Africa, it is gone. In America, it seems to be hanging on only in the extreme north bordering on the Kamchatka languages. But it has nowhere flourished as it has in the Caucasian and Finnic languages. Curiously enough, Russian has introduced new case forms (*stakan čaju* ['a glass of tea'], *v lesu* ['in the wood']). [p. 190]

The Nature of the Paradigm (Declension in Russian)

3 February 1933

I have noticed something in Russian declension. I think that the starting point should be paradigms with the most rudimentary oppositions. In Russian, these are the numerals. With regard to the gender, the numeral *oba/obe* ['both'] displays the most rudimentary opposition feminine ~ nonfeminine in all the cases (the numeral *dva/dve* ['two'] has this opposition only in the nominative and the accusative). With regard to the cases, the most rudimentary oppositions can be found in *sorok* ['forty'] and *sto* ['hundred']: here the opposition is between the common direct case (*sorok, sto*) and the common indirect case (*soroka, sta*). These rudimentary oppositions can, in other declinable forms, yield further oppositions: the nonfeminine gender can fall into masculine and neuter, the common direct case can fall into the nominative and the accusative, and the common indirect case yields as many as four cases. But all these secondary oppositions coexist in one paradigm. For example, regular pronouns and adjectives in the singular look like this [*tot/to/ta* 'that'] (see table 1).

Don't you think that, for the opposition to exist in the linguistic consciousness, it must be concretized in a rudimentary form? Or, to be more precise, that only then can such an opposition be said to exist? [pp. 266–67]

Table 1

	Nonfeminine		Feminine
Cases and Genders	Masculine	Neuter	
Direct nominative	tot	to	ta
accusative			tu
Indirect genitive	tavo		
dative	tamu		toj
prepositional	tom		
ablative	tem		

The Reception of Phonology

Karl Bühler

27 May 1930

There has recently been some awakening of interest in phonology in Vienna. I can especially mention Karl Bühler, who, if I am not mistaken (ask Čiževskij), has a reputation in modern psychology. I knew that he studied the psychology of language, and I sent him an offprint of my article about vowel systems [Trubetzkoy 1929c]. He was greatly excited [by my theory], discussed it in his lectures, and spoke about it at a meeting of the Austrian Phonetic Society. We are going to meet soon and talk about these matters in detail. So far, we have exchanged only a few words. He says that the psychological basis of my construction should be changed, for associative psychology has had its day. He assures me that the essence of the linguistic part will not be affected. At present, I am reading his book *Die Krise der Psychologie* [Bühler 1927] to get an idea of what it is all about. Linguists of the older generation have also shown interest in phonology but are confused and do not know how to approach the subject. Kretschmer reads and rereads my Polabian studies [Trubetzkoy 1929a] and talks about phonology when he sees me, but it is clear from what he says that he has not yet mastered the subject. [p. 158]

Jacobus Van Ginneken

17 August 1930

I began to correspond with Van Ginneken, who keeps asking me about the phonological systems of the Caucasian languages and in passing about some general problems of phonology. It follows from his questions that he is well versed in the main concepts—a great achievement for a linguist of his generation. [p. 169]

Edward Sapir

n.d. (postmarked 24 April 1930)
Sapir sent me a long letter with glowing reports of *TCLP* [1] and with some interesting comments on my theory of vowels. In Russia, some people would also like to read our works. [p. 157]

André Mazon

28 January 1931
I have just read Mazon's [1930] review [of Jakobson 1929]. It is indeed outrageous. First of all, it is ignorant. He does not seem to know that de Saussure denied the possibility of systemic evolution. Mazon should not be allowed to get away with murder. We should strike back and do it well. As for Meillet, I do not think that he is beating a retreat. His letters are full of such "kind words" that one cannot renege on them: although they are often illegible, they constitute a written document capable of being used. His review of volume 1 of *Travaux* [*TCLP*] in *Revue* [Meillet 1931] is on the whole favorable. He took us to task only for the preface, and he may have been right: it does pass off a lot of generalities and commonplaces as something original (in the sections that do not concern phonology). In his latest letter (written after the conference), Meillet informs me that in the next issue of the *Bulletin* [*BSL*] there will be a detailed review of our works and again emphasizes his positive attitude toward us. [p. 189]

Phonology in Vienna

6 April 1931
Just before the Easter holidays I gave a talk on phonology to the Sprachwissenschaftliche Gemeinschaft [Linguistic Society]. The success was great. All received it very warmly, and there was a lot of discussion. Luick spoke most approvingly about historical phonology and cited several examples from English (not all of them equally convincing). Among other things, he said that acquaintance with phonological theories had eased his conscience, for, in the past, when teleological explanations of sound change occurred to him, he rejected them as antiscientific, but now he saw that that was a prejudice. Someone added that phonology rehabilitates *Papierphilologie* [paper philology] against *Ohrenphilologie* [aural philology], which is very good, for the dismissal of *Papierphilologie* sight unseen prevented scholars from drawing valid conclusions and making generalizations. This statement and Luick's words can explain the puzzling fact that we sometimes find acceptance with very old linguists. Several days after my presentation it was still being talked about, as

I heard on the grapevine. So an impression was made: have no doubt about it. [p. 198]

n.d. (ca. 20 December 1931)

Phonology is taking root in Vienna. In Kretschmer's seminar, several participants have given reports on phonology. Students are reading volumes 1 and 4 of the *Travaux* [*TCLP*]. Our Germanic scholars are also showing interest. Pfalz and Steinhauser teach their students to describe dialects from a phonological point of view. [p. 230]

Eberhard Zwirner

17 May 1932

I have received a letter from a certain Dr. Eberhard Zwirner from Berlin. He is a psychiatrist and became interested in phonology in connection with aphasia; he says that phonology can explain many pathological phenomena and requests offprints. [p. 242]

Eduard Hermann

29 October 1932

Eduard Hermann has sent me an article [Hermann 1932] in which he attempts to prove that one and the same sound can be the realization of more than one phoneme. His proof rests on misunderstandings, but it is praiseworthy that he gives such problems thought and does so earnestly and carefully. He also has some terminological suggestions: *Ausführung* ['implementation, manifestation'] instead of *Realisierung* ['realization'] (because the phoneme is reality in and of itself and needs no realization) seems tenable, but *Lautgeltung* ['sound value'] instead of *Phonem* ['phoneme'] is impossible. I wrote him a letter in which I tried to explain why his conclusions about the phonological ambiguity of sounds [overlap] are wrong. As could be expected, he did not disavow his errors and sent me two letters within three days. I will answer him in a placating tone, to the effect of "think well, young man," and change the subject. [p. 260]

Phonology in Czechoslovakia

30 November 1932

The *Festschrift* [*CGM*] is quite good. . . . Ružičić's [1932] article is rather weak, but his attempt to deal with phonology despite Belić's unspoken veto deserves respect. Among the beginning phonologists, Vachek is undoubtedly a bright and resourceful man familiar with all problems, but the theme of his article [Vachek 1932] is unfortunate. First of all, a young scholar runs a serious risk when he chooses polemic with a recognized authority for his debut: he jeopardizes his own career. In addition, from the point of view of "phonological tactics," we should avoid steps that can irritate a well-disposed "general," the more so as this "general" ([Daniel] Jones) is a member of the presidium of the [Internationale Phonologische] Arbeitsgemeinschaft [International Association for Phonology]. It was certainly useful to point out the logical drawbacks of Jones's views, but he should have done it in some other way, without emphasizing his disagreement in the title.

Novák's [1932] article is interesting, but in such a compressed form it is not fully convincing. It displays a tendency toward broad formulas, which, when offered by young authors, usually sound like hurried generalizations. The very first paragraph of the article contains two factual errors, caused by this tendency. It is wrong that all the languages on the Mediterranean coast have phonological expiratorial stress (the languages of the southern coast, from Morocco to Syria, have only the correlation of quantity, and on the Adriatic coast one finds Serbo-Croatian and Slovenian dialects with so-called musical stress). It is also wrong that German has the correlation of quantity. So, in sum, the young phonologists from Czechoslovakia are good, but they still need a lot of guidance. [pp. 261–62]

Phonology in Paris

5 December 1933

I have just received a letter from Isačenko. He participated in a meeting of the Société de Linguistique [de Paris], at which M[arcel] Cohen gave a talk entitled "Essai phonologique sur l'amharique." According to Isačenko, it was a miserable performance that had nothing to do with phonology. The main conclusion consisted in that Abyssinians speak in a low voice and even cover their mouths with a handkerchief and thus save their breath, which allows them to construct very long sentences. Their stress falls "vers la fin du mot et de la phrase mais pas tout à fait à la fin" ['toward the end of the word and the sense group but not quite at the end'], etc. (Isačenko adds: "I have never heard such drivel before.") In the ensuing discussion, Benveniste attacked Cohen and stated blankly that this was not phonology. Cohen helplessly defended himself and turned to Isačenko and Novák as experts and asked them: "Is it phonology or not?" Sorry as both of them were for the old man, they had to say that this was not phonology. Finally, Benveniste cornered Cohen, who stammered embarrassedly: "Alors, c'est plutôt de la morphonologie! . . ." ['Well, it is rather morphonology']. Meillet saved the situation in his conciliatory remarks at the end.

At the next meeting, the program for 1934 was discussed. Meillet and Vendryes moved that the first meeting after the Christmas break be wholly devoted to phonology. They pointed out that a pupil of Trubetzkoy's happened to be in residence who, naturally, was competent to elucidate this interesting question. The motion carried. So at the next meeting my unfledged pupil will appear in the capacity of—I am not sure which—a bull or a toreador. He is ready for the battle (he writes: "It is high time we gave these French a good push") but is a bit scared (Novák, as it turns out, speaks poor French). The French expect sensations from this meeting. They said to Isačenko: "Il y aura des morts" ['There will be casualties']. Vaillant rubs his hands in malicious anticipation and calls Isačenko "doctor utriusque phonologiae, structuralis et functionalis" ['doctor of both phonologies, structural and functional']. [p. 294]

Phonology in England, the United States, and the Netherlands

n.d. (May 1934)

In London, everything went well. I did not see linguists as such there. They don't even seem to exist. There are only people who, with half-childlike curiosity (half-sportsmanlike, in the Anglo-Saxon way), examine linguistic phenomena and treat them as though they were something entertaining. Most such people are polyglots, and they are quite numerous, but serious linguists can hardly be found. Phonology enjoys the success of a clever toy: everyone is piqued to death that in some language two absolutely different sounds are perceived as one phoneme. Nothing goes deeper than that. I was rather impressed only by a certain Firth. But his essay [Firth 1934] on "function" in linguistics shows that he does not fully understand general problems. (It brings us some harm that we are identified with de Saussure's school; note that the English judge us not only by vols. 1, 2, and 4 of *Travaux* [*TCLP*] but also by vol. 3, which I, to tell the truth, have not read.) In general, the attitude of [Daniel] Jones and his entourage toward us is most friendly. But let me repeat: This is not what we mean by the word *linguist*.

Since in England nothing is as it is in other countries (registered letters are left at grocery shops, one is allowed to walk on the grass in city parks, the shilling is divided into twelve parts, etc.), real linguists can well be hidden elsewhere, for example, in anthropology. Incidentally, Firth is indeed in some way connected with anthropologists, and Alan Gardiner, whom I met in Rome and who made a very good impression on me, is the chairman of the linguistic section of the International Congress of Anthropological and Ethnological Sciences that is going to take place in London. [p. 299]

Have you read Meriggi's [1933] latest attack on phonology? But the Americans and the Dutch are trying hard. Van Ginneken leaves no stone unturned.

I have not yet read his articles in *Onze Taaltuin* [Van Ginneken 1934a, 1934b], but some of them seem to be wholly phonological. Van Wijk [1934] pays his respects to phonology in the (otherwise rather weak) article on the imperfect in Old Russian. [pp. 304–5]

On Trubetzkoy's Introduction to the Principles of
Phonological Descriptions; *Phonology in Poland*

25 January 1935

The booklet [Trubetzkoy 1935] is small, about two signatures and a half. The edition will cost relatively little, and I think that we can break even or make some profit. The question is in what language to publish it. Perhaps it would be best to publish this manual simultaneously in German, French, and English. Last year, in Paris, Meillet volunteered to bring it out in French at the expense of the Société de Linguistique [de Paris]. He is no longer active, but I hope Vendryes will also agree to do so, or M[arcel] Cohen, who has some money for publishing linguistic questionnaires and manuals. If such a plan is accepted, the translation should be done by French phonologists (by the way, Martinet is a Germanic scholar). With regard to the English version, I have in mind a certain [A. C.] Lawrenson, an Englishman. Jones sent him to me to study phonology, and he is ready to undertake the work. But I wonder who will underwrite the English edition. The German edition can be published by some commercial press in Vienna or in Czechoslovakia. Since the booklet is small, and since we want it to have as wide currency as possible, it is a good idea to bring it out simultaneously in three languages. But if you and Mathesius decide otherwise, I will not object. My only demand is that the words *authorized translation from the German manuscript* be printed on the English and French editions. . . .

At present, one of the members of my seminar is [W.] Kuraskiewicz, a *privatdocent* at Krakow University, a pupil of Lehr-Spławiński's. . . . The main reason he is here must be the circumstance that he got support for a year's stay abroad. But it is noteworthy that he has come to me. In the summer, he will probably attend your lectures. [pp. 315, 317]

J. von Laziczius; Phonetic Descriptions by English Scholars

14 March 1935

Laziczius sent me his paper written for the London congress, should he get there. It contains a critique of Doroszewski and some objections addressed to me: in his opinion, I keep clinging to the psychological view of the phoneme. Then he offers his own view. He believes that phonology should deal with phonemes, "emphatica" (= stylistic variants), and "variants" (combinatory and nonobligatory) since phonology studies the sign function of sounds and this function is not restricted to phonemes but is also present in emphatica and variants. The difference is only in the "number of functions": phonemes perform all three of Bühler's functions (*Darstellung, Appell, Ausdruck* [reference, appeal, expression]), emphatica only *Appell* and *Ausdruck,* and variants only *Ausdruck* (?). It is all nonsense, but *anregend* ['thought provoking'], and we examined this work in my phonological seminar with great interest. On Saturday, 16 March, Laziczius himself will come to Vienna for a couple of days. [pp. 330–31]

30 March 1935

Laziczius spent two days here. There is nothing wrong with him, but, when it comes to his theory, he won't budge. It is correct that stylistic variants perform a certain unique function and must be isolated. However, it is false that phonology should study all such phenomena, and I was unable to dissuade him. Also, he has his own views on the nature of the phoneme. He objects to the distinction between the phoneme and its realization; he seems to identify the phoneme with what you call the *main variant* and relegates the term *variant* to secondary variants. Here, we did not go into details. On the whole, he appears to gravitate toward positivism (and in this he finds common cause with Doroszewski), but, strangely enough, he combines positivism and universalism. His article will appear in *Ungarische Jahrbücher* [Laziczius 1936b]. He probably will not go to London.

Do you know Rogger's [1934] book? The author sent it to me with a letter in which he apologizes that when the book was in the making his knowledge of phonology did not go beyond what was published in the proceedings of the Geneva congress and so some of his statements about phonology were inaccurate. Since that time he has read my article in *Journal de psychologie* [Trubetzkoy 1933] and become a supporter of phonology. The book is not quite satisfactory, perhaps because it displays no familiarity with phonological literature. But it also has the other drawbacks of modern German linguistics: dependence on the Neogrammarian tradition, the inability to see any other ways outside this tradition except for Vossler's and Schuchardt's theoretical vapidity, and as a result sterile abstract theorizing.

But I am really happy with the English. I have recently read several English descriptions of all kinds of exotic languages and cannot praise them enough. To be sure, they have no theory. But they understand everything in a practical way, and it is the easiest thing in the world "to translate such descriptions into the language of phonology." This happened because the English (at least in what concerns Oriental linguistics and exotic languages) did not have a firm Neogrammarian tradition and the tradition of historicism. Too bad: if we were living in English-speaking countries, a phonological description of the world would have been ready by this time. [pp. 332–33]

W. Freeman Twaddell

17 May 1935

Twaddell's book [Twaddell 1935] is interesting but rather sterile. He attempts to give the phoneme a definition that would be free from metaphysics and ends up with the denial of phonological systems. In principle, he operates with our definition of the phoneme as *terme d'opposition* ['member of an opposition'] but draws an absurd conclusion: since in a given position only some, rather than all, phonemes are opposed, a special system has to be set up for each position (my *Teilsysteme!* ['partial systems']), but these systems are allegedly incompatible (it is not clear why); consequently, a unified system of phonemes does not exist in a language. An excellent illustration of phonology and atomism being at cross-purposes. However, some of his ideas are rather interesting and worthy of attention. Curiously enough, he gives very few references to real phonologists, among whom he lists us and also Sapir. Most of all, he discusses the definition and the use of the term *phoneme* in the book by Leonard Bloomfield (my fellow student at Leipzig). To tell the truth, I have not read Bloomfield's *Language* [1933]; it is hard to read without knowing the language, when every third word has to be looked up. It would be good to give it to someone reliable and get a summary: perhaps there is something useful in it. [pp. 334–35]

Impressions of the Second International Congress
of Phonetic Sciences

3–4 August 1935

The papers given by Sommerfelt [1936], Trnka [1936], and me [Trubetzkoy 1936c] were devoted to special questions and do not seem to have made an impression. Vachek [1936a] spoke too long and criticized Twaddell [1935], that is, discussed the relations between the concepts of the phoneme and the sound. Brøndal [1936] gave a paper on the relation of the sound and the phoneme (he spoke English, and I did not understand anything, but I heard that there had been no heresies). Laziczius [1936a] (who replaced you) expounded his theory; so he, too, offered a definition of the phoneme. Hjelmslev [1936] introduced his "new" science of "phonematics" and also gave a definition of the "phoneme."

This meeting was followed by a rather long break, and I had a chance to talk to a few "outsiders." I gathered that the four papers devoted to the subject *autour du phonème* ['concerning the phoneme'] had tired and irritated everybody. Most people understood nothing and saw only one thing: no progress had been made, specialists keep debating the definition of the main concepts, and "each offers his own definition." . . .

Vendryès's [1936] paper was rather colorless. By the way, in his introductory remarks, he touched on the meeting of the previous day and expressed his disappointment that no unity had been achieved with regard to the difference between the phoneme and the sound, phonology and phonetics. He attempted, on the spot, "to formulate in two words" his understanding of the difference between phonology and phonetics, but his formula was inane and incomprehensible. . . .

Very interesting was Stetson's [1936] paper on the phoneme from the point of view of instrumental phonetics. Stetson is a consistent behaviorist and believes that phonemes are hard but not impossible to register instrumentally and that the difficulties are of the same type one encounters in registering other socially significant movements, for instance, separate dance steps. Bühler objected vehemently. . . .

After the farewell banquet, all kinds of diversions were organized; that is, some members of the congress made jocular speeches, sang songs, and the like. Every time the word *phoneme* turned up, it aroused an outburst of universal laughter. Horn composed a poem in Middle English on the themes of the congress. It ended in the following couplet:

wat is phonemes, wat is sunds?
twelf men haf twelf difinitiuns.

This couplet was later quoted by all and was rewarded with loud applause.

So I can say that this congress did not contribute to the propaganda of phonology in the wide circles of phoneticians and linguists because (and this is the main reason) instead of a unified phonology numerous approaches prevailed; the debate on the concept of the phoneme—which is beyond most people's comprehension—makes the impression of some scholastic logomachy, with no practical conclusions. It may be our fault. We knew that Hjelmslev would present a theoretical paper and that Bühler would also touch on the meaning of the phoneme, so we should have given up other theoretical papers: we should have asked Brøndal and Vachek to choose some other topics (of course, we could not put pressure on Laziczius, for we did not know until the last moment whether he would come to the congress). This way we would have offered fewer theoretical papers and avoided the impression that phonology is all about the definition of the phoneme. Now it is too late to talk about such things. The lack of serious interest in phonology could also be seen in the fact that very few people came to the meeting of the Arbeitsgemeinschaft and in the poor sales of our editions. My brochure sold badly; almost no one bought the bulletin, which I gave out free.

Although we failed to recruit new supporters at the congress, several old ones showed up, and it was good to meet them. I liked Laziczius very much, and I can say the same about Martinet, who is quite "ours," despite Hjelmslev's efforts to "convert" him; he intends to write his *thèse de doctorat* on the phonology of Danish. Kurath, an American and a friend of Sapir's, told me about phonology in the United States. Sapir and his whole school are probably quite ours. But Bloomfield has his own ideas. Twaddell's book had no response, and Sapir's pupil Swadesh will criticize it in the next issue of *Language* [Swadesh 1935]. But in general the trend represented by Twaddell is rather strong in America, for it rests on behaviorism, which dominates there. I also liked Uldall, a young Danish scholar. At present, he is under very strong influence from Hjelmslev, but Brøndal assured me that this was a temporary phenomenon and that he was beginning to feel disappointed in Hjelmslev.

The avowed enemies of phonology were absent this time, or, not to put too fine a point on it, Doroszewski broke a leg and had to stay home. To a certain degree, Hjelmslev is an enemy. His approach is the opposite of Doroszewski's. I believe that Hjelmslev is trying to "out-Herod Herod," that is, us. His "phonematics" aims at studying phonemes in their sound function in total disregard of their realization. For example, he rejects classification. According to him, it is wrong to set up the correlation of voice, for "voiced" is an acoustic phenomenon that presupposes a certain realization. Phonemes can allegedly be classified only by function. Thus, some phonemes of Russian are not permitted word finally (voiced obstruents), while other phonemes (all the others) occur in this position, and so forth. Since this trend claims to be a science independent of phonology, it won't seduce anyone. Within the framework of phonology, we have used this "method" from the beginning, along with the analysis of phonemes as members of oppositions (which cannot be separated from realizations). [pp. 342, 344–45]

Impressions of the Fourth International
Congress of Linguists

5 October 1936
I am really pleased with the Congress—that is, not so much with the congress as with its atmosphere. The feeling of isolation that depresses me so much in Vienna and prevents me from working seems to have gone away. It turned out that we were many. I don't understand why it "turned out": I had known approximately who worked in what country, but I was unable to visualize the picture in its details, and here it suddenly "turned out." A leap has taken place

since Rome. Generations always advance by leaps. In Copenhagen, it became clear for the first time that we not only occupied commanding posts but that behind us stood younger people who had learned from our writings and who could do things themselves. . . .

In our talks with the Americans, we forgot to warn them against Doroszewski, who is going to spend a year in Wisconsin (at the university where Twaddell teaches) and will scheme against us as best he can. It will be harder to warn them in written form. [pp. 371, 373]

Phonology in Japan

2 November 1936

You must also have received *Études de linguistique japonaise* by Tanakadate, Pletner, and Frei (= *Bulletin de la Maison Franco-Japonaise*). Frei's essay "Monosyllabisme et polysyllabisme dans les emprunts linguistiques" is quite literate, even though in no way a stroke of genius. The chapters devoted to the phonemic inventories of the Peking and the Tokyo dialects are fine, and their drawbacks should be laid at my, not at his, door, for it was I who started the whole business of treating neutralized phonemes as separate entities. In the foreword, Frei says that in 1936 the Cercle Linguistique de Tokio was organized and that it "inscrit l'étude de la phonologie japonaise en tête de son programme" ['made the study of Japanese phonology its foremost priority']. On the other hand, Hisanosuke Izui, a professor at the Kyoto School of Foreign Languages, has translated my *Anleitung* [Trubetzkoy 1935] into Japanese and published in some Japanese linguistic journal several articles, apparently on phonology [Izui 1936, 1937; Kobayashi 1936]. I have the offprints, but, naturally, I cannot read them; judging by the footnotes, he feels at home in phonological literature.

So there is some interest in phonology among Japanese scholars, but certain difficulties with finding someone to head the Japanese branch of the Arbeitsgemeinschaft remain. Although Frei is, as they say in the Soviet Union, "our guy through and through," according to my recollection of him, and in Karcevskij's opinion, he is not quite the man to lead the branch. Besides that, he is a foreigner, and the Japanese are sensitive when it comes to the national question. The Cercle Linguistique de Tokio is connected with Maison Franco-Japonaise ['The French-Japanese House'], which, like all such French organizations abroad, must be connected with the French embassy and French politics—a reprehensible circumstance in the eyes of the Japanese, given the present international constellation.

On the other hand, I have no idea about Izui's weight in Japanese scholarship, and the fact that he does not live in the capital is very much against his leadership. Tanakadate does not seem to enjoy much prestige at home. In his foreword, Frei mentions a certain Hideo Kobayashi, "introducteur de la linguistique genevoise au Japon" ['who introduced Saussurean linguistics to Japan'], but it is not clear whether he is a professor. I am a bit at a loss. Don't you think that, after all, it would be best to write to Frei, explain everything to him, and ask his advice? He may not be worldly enough, but he will know better on the spot. [pp. 374–75]

Phonology in Hungary and Bulgaria

5 February, 1937

Laziczius informed me that the Linguistic Society of Hungary had entrusted a six-member phonological commission with contacting the council of the Arbeitsgemeinschaft. He suggests that this commission be considered the Hungarian phonological group, which, I think, is acceptable.

You must have received Lekov's [Lekov" 1937] brochure directed against Mladenov. The Bulgarians should be instructed what to do; otherwise, [S. M.] Romanski, Lekov, and others will start such phonology and structural linguistics there—God forbid. Nothing is worse than enthusiasts of undigested new ideas, especially in the provincial wilderness. [pp. 386–87]

Alfred Schmitt

6 October 1933

We have some trouble on the phonological front. Alfred Schmitt has suddenly rebelled. I sent him my offprints in the summer, but he did not respond. And now he has written that, being an honorable man, he considers it his duty to inform us that after a lot of soul searching he feels disenchanted with phonology, no longer shares our views, and intends to criticize them in print. He assures us that he has not been lured by destructive ambitions but only wants to get at the heart of the matter. Among other things, he asked me to convey his deepest respect to you.

He does not say what caused his disenchantment and writes only that he considers phonology "als eine Angelegenheit der Schrift, und nicht der Sprache" ['a matter of writing, not of language']. This must be a relapse into the old fear of "paper phonetics," and the source of this change of mood can be Panconcelli-Calzia: Schmitt is in close contact with him (I think so because the formula about phonology being a matter of writing, rather than of language, occurs in Meriggi [1933], and Meriggi is Panconcelli-Calzia's colleague in Hamburg).

I detected some doubts about phonology even in his previous letter, in

which he said that, when we perceive words, we do not divide them into phonemes but make do with recognition of two or three features of the sound
structure of *das Wortganze* ['the word's image as a whole'] (as if the same does
not happen when we read!!). I did not answer him at that time, but apparently that was a mistake. Now he has veered round, and it is probably too late
to do anything, for he must have written something; he has not published it
yet, but it is always more difficult to give up what one has written. . . . So "our
man" in Germany, the only one, has become a turncoat. [pp. 286–87]

1 January 1937

I have received and read A[lfred] Schmitt's [1936] article. There is no Hitlerism
in it; on the contrary, everything is quite decent. One can learn a lot from it.
But his objections to phonology are very weak. This is not merely naturalism
or a relapse into the Neogrammarian theory but rather a false attempt to be
an innovator à la Schuchardt, a senseless and useless attempt by definition.
Also, everything is based on a misunderstanding. Schmitt mainly objects to
the idea of phonemes as bricks from which words are built. But if we ever said
such things, we meant them figuratively. Sure enough, a rejoinder is called
for, and we must decide how to do it in the best way possible. I anticipate that
our position can be advantageous, for we will be supported not only by the
structuralists but also by the conservatives, who will not relish Schmitt's para-
doxes. In a word, it is possible to turn things around, as happened in Geneva
after Hermann's talk.[7] In any case, all the linguists in Vienna with whom I discussed Schmitt's article expressed their indignation. It is, however, important
not to make a tactical error. [pp. 383–84]

12 April 1937

I have had a long talk with Pfalz. After having published his work on the
phonology of an East Bavarian dialect [Pfalz 1936], he looks on himself as a
phonologist and takes the interests of phonology close to heart, although
he is familiar with phonological literature in a minimal way and does not
understand a lot of things. He is enraged by Schmitt and intends to respond
in *Zeitschrift für deutsche Mundartforschung* "from the viewpoint of German
dialectology." To tell the truth, I am really afraid of this defense, for Pfalz is
a man with a very elementary psychology; he has a most primitive notion
of phonology and can say a lot of nonsense. According to him, the German
dialectologists who rally around the Marburg *Sprachatlas* ['linguistic atlas of
German'] will be on Schmitt's side, for they are in principle against the cartography of phonetics and believe that the goal of dialectology is to study
the geography of *words* in connection with *Siedlungsgeschichte* ['the history of
settlement']. For "our purposes," they are, in his opinion, useless (inciden-

tally, he counts [Ernst] Schwarz among them). But he knows other dialectologists who can be attracted to our cause—indeed, not by theories but by concrete work. He sets high store by our questionnaire.

Unfortunately, this questionnaire cannot be given to a dialectologist who has had no exposure to phonology. But Pfalz is willing to make an abstract usable for the areas that can interest students of the "Bavarian" dialects (i.e., Bavaria, the western regions of Czechoslovakia, and Austria without Vorarlberg). This abstract will be copied in the office of the Bayerisch-Österreichisches Wörterbuch (headed by Pfalz) and sent to the most qualified colleagues—so far, only in Austria. When answers based on this abstract come in, the resulting report can be processed, printed, and sent to all dialectologists. In his estimation, all this work will take less than a year. He recommends [L.] Heger as a liaison for Czechoslovakia, but I am not quite sure of Heger's attitude toward phonology (you know better). . . .

Bühler has read Schmitt's article and sees the root of the error in misapplying *Gestalttheorie*. To deny separate elements on account of the *Gestalt* is as wrong as to insist that the whole is nothing other than the sum of its parts. Both are "monistic" mistakes. Animals and children in the preverbal stage have *Schallgebärden* ['acoustic gestures'] that cannot be analyzed into phonemes. Human language differs from the language of animals in that it has phonemes and grammar (the existence of vocabulary is a feature common to both). He is going to write about these things in Zwirner and Westermann's journal [*Archiv für vergleichende Phonetik*]; they asked him to submit something to their journal about phonemes from the psychological perspective. Bühler has also read my rejoinder to Schmitt and approved wholeheartedly but found fault with the conclusion from a tactical point of view: he would not tread on the opponent's pet corn. He may be right. I will try to change the end and will again show it to you.

It is unclear where to publish my rejoinder. [W.] Koppers [the editor of *Anthropos*], whom I sounded as to his reaction, gave an evasive answer. . . . Pfalz and Bühler suggest *Archiv für vergleichende Phonetik*, but I am seriously opposed to this idea. Yet where else? What is the situation with *Časopis pro moderní filologii?* Do they accept articles in German, and would they publish my rejoinder to Schmitt? Who is responsible for such decisions? [pp. 388–89, 390]

19 April 1937

Westermann wrote me a most gracious letter with the request that I submit a phonological article to his journal and left the choice of subject to me. It would be silly to refuse, and, as I already have an article waiting to be published (my rejoinder to Schmitt), this invitation may be looked on as the finger of fate, and the article should go to him. Naturally, something will have to be changed. I will have to delete my attack on Meriggi (for he is one of the main contributors to this journal) and rewrite the conclusion (it is not polite to cast stones at naturalism in the pages of a phonetic journal). I hope I will be able to do so without taking away the edge. What do you think? [p. 390]

20 September 1937

I sent Schmitt an offprint of my rejoinder [Trubetzkoy 1937], and he responded with a very gracious letter. He backs out but, in principle, repeats his nonsense; at the end of his letter, he says that the algebraicization of linguistics frightens him. To tell the truth, while reading Hjelmslev's [1937] work on Lithuanian phonology, I also experienced intense resentment at the algebraicization of linguistics. [p. 401]

Phonology in Poland

26 October 1937

At the congress in Łwiw, a resolution was adopted on 17 May 1937 to organize a phonological section of the Polskiego Towarzystwa Językoznawczego [Polish Linguistic Society]. Thirteen people joined it. [p. 406]

K. von Ettmayer

22 November 1937

Ettmayer [1937] has brought out a horrifying article on the phoneme. With friends like this, who needs enemies! [p. 409]

Contemporary Linguistics: Stray Thoughts on Old
and Contemporary Scholars

N. Ja. Marr

6 November 1924

Marr's [1924] article beats everything he has written until now. But it is hard to "pillory" him in a review. First, there is nowhere to publish it; second, I am fully convinced that his work should be reviewed by a psychiatrist rather than by a linguist. Unfortunately (for scholarship), although Marr is nuts, he is not sufficiently crazy to be institutionalized. . . . Even the form of his essay is typical of a lunatic. How awful that most people have not yet noticed it! . . . [p. 74]

D. V. Bubrix

10 March 1925

Bubrix's "The North Kashubian System of Accents" [1922] has obvious and unmistakable features of genius, even though his theories will perhaps have to be rejected. I also admire the fact that he does not waste his time on bibliography and on criticizing other people's views, and I like his "algebraic" approach. Who is he? What do you know about him? [p. 81]

Jacobus Van Ginneken

n.d. (Summer 1928)

Has Van Ginneken sent you his [1928] inaugural speech on medieval Dutch literature from an ethnological point of view? Simply Bazarov [the prototypical Russian nihilist, the hero of Turgenev's novel *Fathers and Children*] in a cassock! It has nothing in common with the Formal method. I cannot understand why De Groot decided that this was the Formal method. . . . But curious and talented, as is everything Van Ginneken does. [p. 116]

Structuralism and "Cultural-Historical Linguistics";
V. N. Vološinov, N. Ja. Marr, and Others

1 May 1929

I have not read Vološinov's [1929] book. What you say about it is interesting. Vossler's approach to language must naturally appeal to Marxists, just like [W.] Schmidt's [1921] *Kulturkreistheorie* ['theory of culture circles'], despite its "clerical" underpinnings. It is a pity that such a "cultural-historical" approach in modern Russian linguistics exists and that our "structural" linguistics is far from ruling the day. . . . Not too long ago I received a book entitled *Jazyk i kul'tura* ['Language and Culture'] from a certain Nemirovskij [1928], a professor at a Teachers' Training College in Vladikavkaz. Although he works in a provincial town, he is well read and is fully aware of the latest trends. And what is the result? In contemporary scholarly literature, only those authors who connect language and "culture" seem "modern" to him, that is, Marr, Vossler, Schmidt, "Wörter und Sachen," and—believe it or not—even Kretschmer. He pits this cultural-historical linguistics against old—mechanistic and naturalistic—views on language. The Marxist pressure is so strong that such tendencies may easily get the upper hand in linguistics, for structuralists will have to change color and adapt, and such mimicry often results in people's beginning to believe in what they preach against their will—a rather miserable prospect. [pp. 130–31]

Jost Winteler

28 January 1931

Quite by chance, I ran into an excellent book by Winteler [1876]. For his time, it is truly remarkable. He distinguishes with absolute clarity the phonetic nature of a sound and its place in the system. He also distinguishes between physiologically possible sounds and those actually used for word differentiation. In general, he constantly approaches phonology. His term *dynamisch verwendet* ['used dynamically'] corresponds exactly to our *phonological* or *relevant*. Very interesting are his comments on the difference between what we call *Dreiecksystem* ['triangular system'] and *Vierecksystem* ['quadrangular system']. But especially interesting is his long excursus on languages that juxtapose voiced and voiceless consonants and those that do not; High German dialects belong to the second group. People like us can hardly believe that voice in *b, d, g* in their relation to *p, t, k* is described as an odd peculiarity of "some languages": the High German linguistic consciousness regards the difference as one of intensity. A wonderful book! Apparently, it played an important role in the history of German dialectology. But many of the author's thoughts were far ahead of his time. In his career, he did not go beyond a high school teacher. [p. 191]

Ferdinand de Saussure, the Geneva School,
Jørgen Forchhammer, Roman Jakobson

17 May 1932

I am not yet going out but no longer stay in bed and have begun to work (I was ill for five weeks and a half). . . . I have not yet written the article for Meyerson [Trubetzkoy 1933]. I do not even know what it will be about. I tried to write in bed, but the result was poor. I feel bored: how long can one repeat commonplaces! . . . For inspiration, I have reread de Saussure, but on a second reading he impressed me much less. There is comparatively little in the book that is of value; most of it is the old rubbish. And what is valuable is awfully abstract, without details. One begins to understand the direction in which his pupils developed. They hold forth on the system, but, except for Karcevskij [1927], no one has described the system of a living language, not even of French.

In one of your latest letters, you asked me whether I knew any good synchronic grammar of French. I addressed the question to several Romance scholars, but no one had heard about anything like that. This is scandalous. It was the duty of de Saussure's pupils to produce such a grammar.

Forchhammer has written me another long letter. I don't know whether it deserves an answer. . . . His *Grundlage der Phonetik* [Forchhammer 1924] is full of useful information, and his criticism of other manuals of phonetics is certainly justified. But his treatment of the basic questions is so shallow that the book loses whatever value it might otherwise have had. This weakness of theory also spoils the practical part, so his system cannot be applied to any concrete issues. For example, his description of the sounds of Russian, let alone of the Caucasian or American languages, is incomprehensible. He is utterly helpless when it comes to *Mouillierung* ['palatalization']: apparently, he knows only palatal *l* and *n* in the Romance languages and has never heard about palatal[ized] labials, etc. . . .

I did not understand anything in your summary on the causes of morphological change. I am afraid you have again been carried away by abstract formulas, which not only the uninitiated but also the initiated cannot understand on a first reading.[8] If you are going to publish it, supply every statement with examples. (241–42)

Viktor Šklovskij; on Writing Reviews; Georges Dumézil

25 January 1935

I have also read Šklovskij [1933]. A few things are interesting, but the whole testifies to decay. Šklovskij is always shuttling from scholarship to journalism. In the past, it was the right thing to do, but now it is absurd. And he is no longer young. May others look and beware: this is what happens when a scholar embarks on journalism and then tries to return to scholarship. . . .

You want me to write reviews of Kořínek (1934) and Stanislav (1933). I have looked through Kořínek's book (to tell the truth, only the summary) and rather liked it. But I have no time to read the entire book, and under such circumstances it would be unethical to review his work. Stanislav is dull reading. My eyesight is poor, and I read Czech slowly. Why should I spend my time and make an effort to read a book that I already know to be bad and useless, only to destroy it and thus get involved with the Czech internecine strife? In general, I don't like to write reviews, especially bad ones.

I have indeed attacked Dumézil [Trubetzkoy 1934], but mainly because he . . . speaks disparagingly about Russian scholars, [N. F.] Jakovlev, [L. I.] Žirkov, and [A. N.] Genko, among others, to whom he cannot hold a candle. Also, his books can become a dangerous source of false information. As regards Stanislav, . . . his work is so miserably insignificant that it cannot do any harm. [p. 319]

Bohumil Trnka

17 May 1935

In Trnka's [1935b] book, the chapter on vocalism is not quite up to snuff, but English vocalism is indeed absurd! The (rather simple) system of consonants seems to be presented in an acceptable way, bar a few cases (e.g., *h* is assigned to the same "bundle" as *k* and *g,* which is a "Bohemianism" of sorts). The most valuable part of the book is naturally the one devoted to the combination of phonemes. The specialists who have read this part have noticed some drawbacks: they say that Trnka included many obviously foreign and obscure words in his lists and, conversely, classified some old and familiar words with recent borrowings. I cannot judge. My only objection to Trnka, or rather my only criticism of his book, is that one cannot see the forest for the trees in it. There is no synthesis. I understand that, without comparing English to other languages (as was done by Mathesius), no generalization or synthesis is possible in this area of English phonetics, but some general conclusions could perhaps have been obtained even from this material. On the whole, it is a useful work. Methodological shortcomings were inevitable, considering the novelty of the subject: so far, the *Kombinationslehre* ['phonotactics'] of no language has been studied in such detail. [p. 334]

André Martinet; Carl Hj. Borgstrøm

20 September 1937

Both works by Martinet [1937a, 1937b] are quite professional and rather interesting. His study of Germanic gemination is still partly dependent on the "phonetic outlook," which is natural. But it is good that he dares criticize even such authorities as Meillet. His criticism of Meillet's theory of the aristocratic and democratic strata in the Indo-European protolanguage is most apt. Borgstrøm's [1938] work on the phonology of Norwegian . . . is less mature. Where the author deviates from our models and attempts to offer his own solutions, he fails pitifully. [p. 400]

Alf Sommerfelt

n.d. (early April 1938)

Has Sommerfelt sent you his book on Aranta [1938b]? The phonological chapter is tolerable, but the rest is very weak and has the moth-eaten look pardonable in the people of Lévy-Bruhl's generation. [p. 424]

Notes

1. Phonological Systems Considered in Themselves and
in Relation to General Language Structure

"Les systèmes phonologiques envisagés en eux-mêmes et dans leurs rapports avec la structure générale de la langue: Réponses reçues: 1. Fürst N. Trubetzkoy, Vienne," in *Actes
du Deuxième Congrès International de Linguistes, Genève, 25–29 août 1931* (Paris: Librairie
d'Amérique et d'Orient Adrien Maisonneuve, 1933), 109–13. This is an untitled response to
the topic "Phonological Systems Considered in Themselves and in Relation to a General
Language Structure," which had been proposed to participants in the Second International Congress of Linguists.

2. Phonology versus Phonetics

"Bericht von Prof. Dr. N. Trubetzkoy," in *Actes du Deuxième Congrès International de Linguistes, Genève, 25–29 août 1931* (Paris: Librairie d'Amérique et d'Orient Adrien Maisonneuve, 1933), 120–25. This is a discussion of papers, including Trubetzkoy's own (see
chap. 1 in this volume), delivered in the Fifth Plenary Session of the Second International
Congress of Linguists; we have supplied the title.

3. The Systematic Phonological Representation of Languages

"Charakter und Methode der systematischen phonologischen Darstellung einer ge-
gebenen Sprache," *Archives Néerlandaises de phonétique expérimentale* 8–9 (1933): 262–65.
Pages 92–312 of the journal are the *Proceedings of the International Congress of Phonetic
Sciences: First Meeting of the Internationale Arbeitsgemeinschaft für Phonologie, Amsterdam,
3–8 July 1932*.

1   In Ancient Greek, stops participated in the oppositions of voice ($\tau : \delta, \pi : \beta, \kappa : \gamma$) and
aspiration ($\tau : \theta = \pi : \phi = \kappa : \chi$); both were phonologically relevant before vowels and sonorants. Combinations of two stops behaved like individual stops and displayed the same
oppositions ($\kappa\tau : \gamma\delta : \chi\theta = \pi\tau : \beta\delta : \phi\theta$). But before the spirant s (σ), both oppositions were
neutralized, and the stops were not distinguished by voice or aspiration. (Their phonetic
realization in this position will not concern us here.) These phonologically neutralized
stops were not identified with any of the three stop classes (*tenuis, media, aspirata*) but
were perceived as distinct phonemes that had to be represented by letters of their own.
But, since they occurred only before s, special characters were created for the sequence
"neutralized stop + s": namely, ξ and ψ. In the Avestan alphabet, the dental stop is represented word finally and before obstruents by a character distinct from both t and d; apparently, in this position the stop was phonologically neutralized with respect to voice,
while in other positions the opposition $t : d$ was phonologically relevant. The Sanskrit

Devanagari alphabet possesses a special sign (the so-called *anusvara*) for the nasal that is phonologically neutralized with respect to place of articulation.

2 Here are some examples. In *Polish*, the opposition of voice is relevant in word-initial and medial position before vowels and sonorants but neutralized word finally. A word-final obstruent before a word beginning with a vowel or sonorant is realized in one group of Polish dialects as voiceless, in the other group as voiced. Koneczna's experimental research has shown, however, that in the second group word-final obstruents do not display normal voice but are rather "half-voiced" (see Koneczna 1933, 262). In *Eskimo*, the phonological opposition between oral and nasal stops is relevant word initially and medially ($t : n = p : m = k : \eta = q : \underline{n}$). In the Greenlandic dialects this opposition is neutralized word finally; the resulting stops, which are phonologically neutralized with respect to nasality, are realized in one dialect group (West Greenland, Labrador) as voiceless oral sounds (t, p, k, q) and in the other (North and East Greenland) as nasals. Forchhammer (1924, 192–93), who interviewed a North Greenlandic informant, observed that his word-final stops were only "half-nasal": they began without nasalization and ended on a voiceless nasal. In *Russian*, where the opposition between palatalized and nonpalatalized consonants plays a significant role, it is neutralized before palatalized *r'*, *l'*, *n'*. At least in some speakers' pronunciation, labials and dentals in these positions are "half-palatalized." *Upper German* obstruents display the intensity opposition of lenis : fortis. In the Bavarian-Austrian dialects, this opposition is neutralized word initially, and the resulting sounds are realized as "half-fortis"; i.e., their intensity is between that of the lenes and that of the fortes. Such examples can easily be multiplied.

4. A Theory of Phonological Oppositions

"Essai d'une théorie des oppositions phonologiques," *Journal de psychologie normale et pathologique* 33 (1936): 5–18.

1 This distinction does not affect the "Projet" definitions of *phonological unit* and *phoneme* significantly. The phoneme remains a "phonological unit that cannot be reduced to smaller and simpler phonological units." The "phonological unit" must from now on be defined as a "term of a directly or indirectly distinctive opposition."

2 In morphology, one could cite the neutralization of gender oppositions in the plural in German, the neutralization of the opposition between the future and the present subjunctive in the first-person singular of first-conjugation verbs in Latin, etc.

3 This rule is violated only by foreign words, such as *Skandal* 'scandal,' *Szene* 'scene,' *Sphinx* 'sphinx,' *Smoking* 'tuxedo,' and *Snob* 'snob,' and by dialect words borrowed into the standard language that still retain the mark of their vulgar origin, such as *Wurstel* 'fool,' *Kasperl* 'fool' (both with *š*), etc.

4 I restrict myself to a few summary comments. A multilateral opposition is *homogeneous* if its terms can be considered as two links of a chain composed exclusively of terms of bilateral oppositions. It is *heterogeneous* if this condition is not met. Thus, in French, the opposition *u-ā* is homogeneous because its terms can be seen as members of a chain of bilateral oppositions (*u-o*, *o-ō*, *ō-ā*), while the opposition *t-a* is heterogeneous. Among homogeneous multilateral oppositions, we may distinguish further between *rectilinear* oppositions, which permit only one chain of intermediary bilateral oppositions (French

u-i = u-y, y-i), and *curvilinear* oppositions, which admit of more than one chain (French *u-e = u-o, o-œ, œ-e,* or *u-y, y-œ, œ-e,* or *u-y, y-i, i-e*).

5   Formerly, the term *correlation* designated a proportional privative opposition, while all other types of opposition were called *disjunctions.*

5. On a New Critique of the Concept of the Phoneme

"Über eine neue Kritik des Phonembegriffes," *Archiv für die vergleichende Phonetik* 1 (1937): 129–53.

1   For orientation, see Mathesius 1929b, Bühler 1931, 1936, Čyževskyj 1931, Jakobson 1931b, Bloomfield 1933, chaps. 5–8, Trubetzkoy 1933, 1935, 1936b, 1936c, Laziczius 1936b, and Twaddell 1935.

2   Sometimes a reviewer merely expressed his satisfaction that a book contained "little phonology" (Mazon 1935b, 277) or that a young scholar stayed away from phonology altogether (Mazon 1935a, 98).

3   *Translator's note:* The bibliographic reference given at this place in the original article is clearly wrong; we have omitted it without attempting to guess at a substitute.

4   See Vachek 1936b, 235–39.

5   See Laziczius 1936b. I do not agree with Laziczius completely, for I believe that among the linguistically relevant features of expression are those that mark the speaker as a member of a certain age group, sex, social class, and so on. Emotional coloring, however, belongs to the means of appeal. On the combinatory variants, see below.

6   In this example, the vowel can be separated from the preceding *l* by a hard vowel onset, but this is a nonobligatory phenomenon and does not occur in fast speech.

7   These are "situation indicators" in Bühler's (1931, 42ff.) sense (with the same German word *Morgen* as an example).

8   Cases in which a phonemic split arises by the loss of a feeling for certain optional variants or for the expressive function of certain sound distinctions are extremely rare and much less certain.

9   It is true that each word is a "Gestalt" and hence contains something more than the sum of its parts. This "something more," however, cannot be localized at any particular point in the word; it is a kind of rule or pattern that governs the arrangement of the word elements (i.e., phonemes). The same may be said of the sentence: it, too, is a "Gestalt" and contains more than the individual words, namely, a certain sentence pattern. And if the "Gestalt" nature of the sentence does not preclude the existence of the individual words, then the "Gestalt" character of the word is no argument against the reality of phonemes.

10 To avoid misunderstanding and misinterpretation, I should add the following clarification. The positivist-naturalistic viewpoint is fully justified in *phonetics,* which is concerned with the *phenomena of speech,* but must not be applied to *linguistic norms.* This follows from the sign nature of all linguistic norms and from the view of linguistics as a social science.

6. Phonology and Linguistic Geography

"Phonologie und Sprachgeographie," in *Réunion phonologique internationale tenue à Prague (18-21/XII 1930)*, Travaux du Cercle Linguistique de Prague 4 (Prague: Jednota Československých matematiků a fysiků, 1931; reprint, Nendeln: Kraus, 1968), 228–34.

7. Quantity as a Phonological Problem

"Die Quantität als phonologisches Problem," in *Actes du quatrième Congrès international de linguistes tenu à Copenhague du 17 août au 1er septembre 1936* (Copenhague: Einar Munksgaard, 1938), 117–22.

8. The Phonological Basis of Quantity in Various Languages

"Die phonologischen Grundlagen der sogenannten 'Quantität' in den verschiedenen Sprachen," in *Scritti in onore di Alfredo Trombetti* (Milan: Ulrico Hoepli, 1938), 155–74.

1   The terms *act of speech* [*Sprechhandlung*] and *language structure* [*Sprachgebilde*] were coined by Karl Bühler and are approximately equivalent to Saussure's *parole* and *langue* (see Bühler 1933).

2   On Estonian, for which the standard grammars give four degrees of quantity in the vowels, see Polivanov (1928, 197–202). A similar revision seems to be in order for North Albanian (the description in Lowman [1932] is unsatisfactory), as the evidence of linguistic geography also indicates (cf. Havránek 1933, 29).

3   Despite Lehr-Spławinski's (1932) objections, I stand by my old position (Trubetzkoy 1929a, 77; Trubetzkoy 1930-31, 56). It is impossible to make the presence of short vowels dependent on the position of secondary stress, because the secondary stress itself depends on the length of the neighboring syllables: if secondary stress falls on the first syllable in *jod'ăd̦i* 'berries' but on the second in *zilozü* 'iron,' this is due solely to the length of the second syllable. As for words with short vowels in both of the last two syllables, I believe that a word such as *mŭtkă* 'cap' has lost the status of a borrowing.

4   The law that free quantity and free expiratorial stress cannot coexist in the same system was first formulated by Roman Jakobson (1923) in his book on Czech metrics. Readers not fluent in Russian or Czech can have read about the law in my "The Phonetic Evolution of Russian" (1925 [chap. 17 in this volume]); later it was treated in the *Travaux du Cercle Linguistique de Prague* by Jakobson (1931a, 182) and me (Trubetzkoy 1929c, 42–43; Trubetzkoy 1931d, 102–3). The original formulation of the law was incorrect insofar as the term *quantity* is ambiguous from the phonological point of view.

5   The lack of consensus in phonetic descriptions of the two short tones shows that their tonal movement is nondistinctive. Courant (1914, 19) describes the second tone as rising, Karlgren (1915-26, 257) as falling; the fourth tone is level according to Courant but falling according to Karlgren. Both accounts were based on Peking pronunciation.

6   On other languages with phonological differences of tone movement in short syllabics, see Jakobson (1931a, 175ff.). Where the two kinds of short tone movement are not simply manifestations of emphasis vs. nonemphasis, one of them distinguishes meaning, while the other separates words. Thus, the language of Vuk Karadžić contains no genuine differences of tone movement but only the opposition between words with free stress and those without it (which always display word-separating falling stress on the initial syl-

lable). In speaking French, many Serbs systematically accentuate the first syllable of the word (with falling intonation). Jakobson's interpretation of the Serbian stress system provides a completely satisfactory explanation for this apparent paradox.

7 Jakobson (1931a, 180–81) has already pointed out the phonological similarity between the "correlation of tone interruption" and the correlation of tone movement.

8 For this reason, bimoric syllables do not have to be twice as long as monomoric ones. Instrumental research shows that, in languages with the analytic interpretation of quantity, differences in the duration of sounds are much smaller than in languages with the energetic interpretation. This can probably be explained by the fact that the "mora number" is sufficiently indicated by the tonal movement, among other things, and thus does not require further specification through length. In certain African languages with the correlation of register, observers have noted only pitch differences, no differences of quantity. It is very likely, however, that in such cases the opposition monomoric-bimoric does indeed exist in the phonological consciousness of native speakers, although it is expressed only through tone movement.

9 This designation has nothing to do with the metrics of the languages. The Latin hexameter is mora counting, even though Latin is a syllable-counting language in our terms, and Serbo-Croatian metrics is based on syllable counting, although most Serbo-Croatian dialects are mora counting. The relations between the metrics and the phonological system of a language constitute a problem area of their own and cannot be treated here.

10 According to Sapir (1933, 262–63), an average, phonetically untrained native speaker of English cannot conceive of a short vowel without a following consonant. American college students who hear isolated short open syllables spoken in a phonetics exercise think that they hear a glottal stop (i.e., the most "substanceless" of all consonants known to them) after the short vowel.

11 When German is sung, short vowels are often lengthened or spread over several notes. The opposition between etymologically long and short vowels is then sometimes expressed solely by the type of contact between the vowel and the following consonant ("loose" and "close" contact) or the method of articulation of the consonant. This circumstance, pointed out to me by Dr. Bruno Sonneck, shows that the syllable cut, not the duration of the sound, is decisive for quantity in German.

12 In Siamese, short bases are short vowels; long bases are long vowels, diphthongs, and combinations of vowel + nasal. My knowledge of Siamese is limited to Trittel (1930).

13 Trittel does not mention the existence of the glottal stop after long bases with falling or "suppressed" tone; he says only, "In falling tones the vowels are frequently shortened" (1930, 20 n. 1). This is probably an acoustic illusion that is easily explained if we are dealing with the sequence long base + glottal stop. Forchhammer (1924, 204) posits vocal closure in such cases and cites among other examples the word *mai* 'not', which Trittel records with falling tone. Syllable-final *k, t,* and *p* in Siamese have been described as implosive rather than explosive.

14 This link also manifests itself in the phonetic realization. Geminated consonants usually display the same kind of close contact with the preceding vowel as consonants after checked vowels do. In Italian, stressed vowels are pronounced short before geminated consonants, long before simple ones. If, however, only the correlation of consonant gemination, not the correlation of syllable cut, exists for the Italian phonological consciousness (in contrast to German, Dutch, or English), this is because the phonetic opposition

long, free vowel vs. short, checked vowel is permitted in Italian only medially (e.g., *pica* 'magpie' : *picca* 'pike, spear') but in German also finally (*Kahn* 'skiff' : *kann* '[I] can').

15 The objective duration of such consonantal morae is shorter than that of short (i.e., monomoric) vowels, which is why Sapir calls them *anacruses* instead of *morae;* but the difference is surely phonetic rather than phonological.

16 The differences of tone movement in the reinforced (emphatic) geminated consonants of Gweabo are expressed by varying expiratorial strength, whereas most languages with differences of tone movement in vowels express these through pitch distinctions. The reason for this lies not in the phonological but in the phonetic nature of consonants as opposed to vowels.

17 The excellent phonetic descriptions of Lapp dialects by Äimä, Lagercrantz, Nielsen, Qvigstad, Ravila, Collinder, and Itkonen all suffer from the same deficiency, which should not be held against these esteemed scholars, however, since neglect of the phonological perspective has characterized virtually the entire field of linguistics up to now. Quantitative relations in the Lapp vowels, too, have been presented in dialect descriptions in a way that is phonetically correct but phonologically unsatisfactory. Phonologically, Lapp possesses a correlation of vowel intensity; i.e., it distinguishes *only two* kinds of vowels, heavy and light. In most of the dialects that have been studied, both kinds of vowels occur before nongeminated consonants, light geminates, and heavy geminates. (There are also dialects that permit only light vowels before heavy geminates, such as the coastal dialect of Maattivuono.) In the phonetic realization, the duration of the vowel is inversely proportional to that of the following consonant. Therefore, if only the physical duration of the Lapp vowels is taken into account, some dialects yield at least six degrees of quantity. But this can be correct only from a phonetic standpoint, of course!

18 In Estonian, too, intensity and gemination form a bundle. Further investigation is necessary, however, to determine whether geminated consonants also reveal differences of tone movement.

19 Anyone who considers the strict distinction between these concepts to be a step backward (see, e.g., Meriggi 1934, 66) has obviously not yet understood the nature of linguistics and its relations to other social sciences.

9. How Should the Sound System of an Artificial International Language Be Structured?

"Wie soll das Lautsystem einer künstlichen internationalen Hilfssprache beschaffen sein?" *Travaux du Cercle Linguistique de Prague* 8 (1939): 5–21.

1 *Translator's note:* The figures given display various inconsistencies, which we have not tried to correct. It is not clear, e.g., why the sum from point 3*a* is not included in the total for point 3 and that from point 4*a* not included in the total for point 4. The article was published posthumously and, to judge by the large number of typographical errors in the rest of the text, may not have been proofread.

2 *Translator's note:* This figure was supplied by the editor to fill in a space left blank (by a mark of ellipsis) in the published article.

10. On Morphonology

"Sur la 'morphonologie,' " in *Mélanges linguistiques dédiés au Premier Congrès des Philologues Slaves*, Travaux du Cercle Linguistique de Prague 1 (Prague: Jednota Československých matematiků a fysiků, 1929; reprint, Nendeln: Kraus, 1979), 85–88. Trubetzkoy explained in a note, "This article pretends to no other purpose than to convey the author's greetings to the First Congress of Slavic Philologists in Prague."

11. Thoughts on Morphonology

"Gedanken über Morphonologie," in *Réunion phonologique internationale tenue à Prague (18–21/XII 1930)*, Travaux du Cercle Linguistique de Prague 4 (Prague: Jednota Československých matematiků a fysiků, 1931; reprint, Nendeln: Kraus, 1968), 160–63.

1   For languages without different types of *morphemes* (e.g., Chinese), the possible sound types of *words* must be established. As stated above, this is to be done under a separate division of phonology, not morphonology.

12. The Relation between the Modifier, the Modified, and the Definite

"Le rapport entre le déterminé, le déterminant et le défini," in *Mélanges de linguistique offerts à Charles Bally* (Genève: Georg, 1939), 75–82.

1   In Russian, a group of two nouns can represent all three classes of phrases. The difference in meaning is conveyed by the intonation: *čelovek-zvér'* 'the beast of a man' (modifying phrase) without a pause between the two terms or stress on the first; *čelovék zvèr'* 'man is a beast' (predicative phrase) with a short pause between the terms, a rising tone on the first, and a falling one on the second; *čelovèk, zvèr'* (. . . *ptìca*) 'man, beast, . . . bird' (associative phrase) with a fairly long pause between the terms and a "listing intonation" (falling tone) on each of them.

2   But in Old Church Slavonic, where the notion of definiteness was expressed by special adjective forms (procedure 3 above), the definite could be distinguished from the indefinite even in combination with a demonstrative pronoun. In Mordvin, nouns modified by demonstratives take sometimes the definite, sometimes the indefinite form, although it is difficult to say whether there is any distinction in meaning.

3   Circassian (or Lower Circassian), the closest relative of Kabardian, differs from the latter in that it recognizes the opposition definite-indefinite in both cases. But different definite articles are used in the two cases: *-r* (as in Kabardian) in the nonmodifying and *-m* (which in Kabardian serves as a case ending without marking definiteness) in the modifying case.

13. The Problem of Genetic Relations among the Great Language Families

"Il problema delle parentele tra i grandi gruppi linguistici: 4. Fürst N. Trubetzkoy, Vienna," in *Atti del III Congresso internazionale dei linguisti (Roma, 19–26 settembre 1933–XI)*, ed. Bruno Migliorini and Vittore Pisani (Florence: Felice Le Monnier, 1935), 326–27, 333. This is an untitled response to the topic "The Problem of Genetic Relations among the Great Language Families," which had been presented to participants in the Third International Congress of Linguists.

14. Thoughts on the Indo-European Problem

"Gedanken über das Indogermanenproblem," *Acta Linguistica* (Copenhagen) 1 (1939): 81–89. In 1958, Vyač. Ivanov obtained from Roman Jakobson the Russian original, which is much longer than the 1939 text; the complete version was published in *Voprosy jazykoznanija* 7 (1958): 65–77. We have restored the missing passages in brackets. Additional passage quoted by Jakobson [1975, 74] but suppressed in the Soviet edition:

> In this respect, Marr's "new linguistic doctrine" is not a bit different from so-called bourgeois linguistics. And, if the belief of "bourgeois linguists" that the agglutinating languages are more "primitive" than the inflecting ones can be ascribed to "the social order of world imperialism," the readiness of Marr and his followers to share this belief stems from their servility to European linguistics (learned most superficially, for that matter). To the extent that Marr's teachings went beyond a paranoiac's delusions (like his idea of "the four elements" *ber, sal, jon,* and *ruš*), they were a rehash of the old (and not always the best) theories of European scholars. With the help of the basest type of political fustian and a totally artificial appendage of Marxist phraseology (often absolutely inane), this hodgepodge of maniacal ravings and borrowed, cast-off theories was dished up as a new, truly Marxist theory of linguistics, and, under Soviet rule, where sabotage so often makes it to the top, it acquired a monopoly on the science of language. As a result, Soviet linguistics has been checked in its development for a long time. It has become the laughingstock of the civilized world, and, what is much worse, it has lost touch with the genuinely progressive and revolutionary trends that are fighting for recognition in Europe and America.

15. Thoughts on the Latin *ā*-Subjunctive

"Gedanken über das lateinische *a*-Konjunktiv," in *Festschrift für Univ.-Prof. Hofrat Dr. Paul Kretschmer: Beiträge zur griechischen und lateinischen Sprachforschung* (Berlin: Deutscher Verlag für Jugend und Volk, 1926), 267–74.

1 Schleicher himself did not take this step. He identified Lat. *agat* 'drive' (3d p. sg. pres. subj.) with the *subjunctive* Skt. *ajati,* Gk. ἄγῃ, but saw in Lat. *aget* (3d p. sg. fut.) an *optative* that he supposed to be identical with Skt. *ajēt,* Gk. ἄγοι (Schleicher 1871, 696, 704).

2 In the light of this conclusion, the widespread view that in Proto-Italic the Indo-European optative and subjunctive merged into a single mood must be abandoned. The theory of an injunctive origin of the *ā*-mood also falls since, as we have observed, an injunctive could yield a subjunctive but not an optative. In the form given it by Brugmann (1916, 529–30), this theory runs into other difficulties as well. According to Brugmann, in the dialects where the *ā*-subjunctive existed at all, it was formed, "not from individual tense stems, but from the general verb stem." The term *general verb stem* is puzzling in this context. In Indo-European, every verb form had to have a certain aspectual category (*Aktionsart*), which was expressed in part by the presence or absence of affixes, in part by root ablaut: all forms with the same aspect belonged as a rule to the same temporal (rather, aspectual) stem. If the *ā*-subjunctive was really formed, "not from individual tense stems, but from the general verb stem," how was the aspect of this modal form expressed? The form must have had some aspect; an Indo-European verb form without aspect is an impossibility. Or did this *ā*-subjunctive arise at a time when the system of aspects had not yet taken shape? Brugmann seems indeed to want to attribute the whole process to a period

in which noun and verb were not yet differentiated (p. 530). But that would be not only a Pre-Italic but also a Pre-Indo-European period, about which only unprofitable speculation is possible.

3   In this way, Thurneysen's statement that Old Irish subjunctives like *cria, genathar* "are clearly descended from the I[ndo-]E[uropean] aorist" (1909, 356 [1946, 380]) can be vindicated.

4   A different explanation, one based on *bhujeti,* was suggested by Osthoff (1881, 25–26).

5   *Tulat* has the sense 'ferat' (3d p. sg. pres. subj. of 'carry') and is thus linked with *tuli,* not *tollo.* It should be noted that this *tuli* was an Indo-European *perfect:* Old Latin attests *tetuli* a number of times.

6   In Germanic, Hirt (1892, 206) derived Goth. *bairau,* Old Norse *bera* 'carry' (1st p. sg. pres. subj.) from **bherām* (Lat. *feram*); others have looked for the *ā*-mood (= *ā*-optative) in the Gothic 3d-p. sg. pres. subj. *salbo* 'anoint' (e.g., Streitberg 1896, 346). These ideas will not concern us here. In any case, the remaining forms of the Germanic subjunctive are derived from the Indo-European optative; should certain Germanic subjunctives be shown to contain the formant **ā,* this would not contradict my theory of the optative meaning and function of the *ā* mood.

16. The Pronunciation of Greek χ in the Ninth Century A.D.

"Die Aussprache des griechischen χ im 9. Jahrhundert n. Chr.," *Glotta* 25 (1936): 248–56.

1   I consider the doubts recently expressed by Kul'bakin (1935, 70) to be unfounded. The Paris *Abecenarium Bulgaricum* is, in any case, completely independent of the alphabet poems.

2   The only exceptions are s and *t,* which have the same numerical value as in Greek (*s* = 200, *t* = 300), even though they do not meet the conditions given above. These exceptions are easily explained if we consider that only two places remained free between *r* (= 100) and *v* (= 400) and that the relative order of the letters of the Greek alphabet had to be followed unconditionally.

3   Professor Max Hermann Jellinek had the kindness to translate this entire passage for me, as I do not read Danish; I thank him most cordially.

4   Connections between the Glagolitic and the Coptic alphabets were pointed out especially by Fortunatov (1913), and the dependence of certain Glagolitic letters on the Armenian alphabet was suggested already by Šafařík (1853, 13). Recently, the connection between certain Glagolitic letters and the characters of the three alphabets mentioned above was acknowledged also by Nahtigal (1923, 166ff.).

5   Traces of the old usage of the second *x* character with the numerical value 6,000 and of the struggle between the older and the newer representations of the thousands can perhaps be discovered. Vaillant has shown very convincingly (Vaillant and Lascaris 1933, 6–8) that the mysterious word *etx'bex'ti,* which appears in a report of the baptism of the Bulgarian czar Boris in a Russian–Church Slavonic manuscript of the fifteenth century, was corrupted from a Glagolitic date. Boris was baptized in 864, which corresponds to the year 6372 in the Byzantine calendar. In Glagolitic letters, this number had to be expressed as *etnb* (*e* = 6, *t* = 300, *n* = 70, *b* = 2). According to Vaillant, the source text must have contained an error that was later corrected. But the first copyist wrote the incorrect and correct forms side by side and, to make matters worse, transcribed them into Cyrillic; the second copyist corrupted the passage further by replacing *n* with *i,* which is quite

understandable given the similarity of these letters in Cyrillic. Corruptions of this type occurred frequently in the transcription of Glagolitic manuscripts into Cyrillic. In this ingenious explanation, only one point remains unexplained, namely, the presence of *x* in *etx'bex'ti*. This puzzle may find its solution if we assume that in the earliest version the number 6,000 was originally expressed by the second *x* character (which would not necessarily have to stand at the beginning). We can imagine the successive "corrections" and errors more or less as follows: (1) first, we find *txb* (with *n* mistakenly omitted); (2) then *xtn* is written above this (perhaps by the same scribe); (3) next, *e* is preposed by another scribe familiar with the newer representation of the thousands (i.e., *etxb* and *extn* with erased *x*); (4) in the course of transcription into Cyrillic letters, *etx'bex'tn* is mechanically copied (the diacritical mark above *x* is probably a misunderstood trace of the erasure of *x*); and (5) *n* is replaced by *i*.

17. The Phonetic Evolution of Russian and the Disintegration of the Common Russian Linguistic Unity

"Einiges über die russische Lautentwicklung und die Auflösung der gemeinrussischen Spracheinheit," *Zeitschrift für slavische Philologie* 1 (1925): 287–319.

1   *Translator's note:* We use *Belorussian* for Trubetzkoy's *weißrussisch* (White Russian) and *Ukrainian* for his *kleinrussisch* (Small Russian). *Great Russian* (*großrussisch*) is 'Russian proper.'

2   I use this expression, like other designations for various periods in the development of Russian sounds, in a conventional way. By *preliterary period,* I mean a period the beginning of which is older than the beginning of writing in Russian and the end of which falls about the middle of the twelfth century.

3   Perhaps the "Central Slavic" change *g* > *γ* and the South Slavic change *tl, dl* > *l* operated simultaneously. Certain Slovenian dialects that change *g* to *h* and preserve the sound combinations *tl, dl* may have stood closer to Central Slavic than to South Slavic at the time of the operation of these two sound laws.

4   It is characteristic that the spelling и for ѣ appears in North Old Russian (e.g., in the *Novgorod Minei* of 1096: претьрьпилъ ѥси etc.) as well as in South Old Russian (e.g., in *Svjatoslav's First Anthology* of 1073: ниции, въ вѣри etc. besides вероѭ , неделю etc.) but that reverse spellings (ѣ for и) do not occur. In any case, the и in examples such as въ вѣри (*Svjatoslav's First Anthology* of 1073) cannot be identified with modern Ukrainian *i* (in *u viri*). The Ukrainian change *ě* > *i* did not become possible until old *i* had become *y:* otherwise, we would have **u vyry* today. There is, on the other hand, no trace of the confusion of the letters и and ы in South Old Russian texts before the 1160s.

5   For the sake of brevity, I subsume both phenomena under the name *transformation of the semivowels.*

6   I designate this whole period as *the period 1164–1282.* These dates are conventional and lay no claim to delimiting the period in question exactly. It may have begun about the 1150s and come to an end in the 1260s.

7   The only position in which *y, i* before *j* (*i̯?*) remained unchanged seems to have been the position before the combination *jě:* e.g., Russ. слѣпые больщие from **slěpyjě, *bolьšijě.* Apparently, **jě* (or **i̯ě*) became *jje* (or *i̯i̯e*), and *y, i* were treated differently before the long *jj* (or *i̯i̯*) that arose in this way than before normal, short *j* (or *i̯*).

8　Also, ъ that arose from *y* before *j* was not identical with old ъ in all Old East Russian dialects. The latter was a labialized back vowel (an *o*-colored *u*), while the ъ that arose from *y* was, at least in some dialects, an unrounded central vowel, whence the dialectal South Great Russian forms *mèju, möju,* etc.

9　Juret's (1922) discussion is instructive for the phonetic side of the problem (see also Ronjat 1924). Ukrainian breaking seems to have been unknown to both scholars.

10　See the list of these dialects and information on the sound value of *ω* in Durnovo (1918, vol. 1, pt. 2, p. 54n) and Vasil'ev (1917).

11　Czech deviates from the other languages in cases *c* and *d*. In the stressed antepenult, acute *o* appears in Czech as long in *můžeš*, dialectal *zxůceš*, Old Czech *kuoleš, hluozeš*, etc., while the other acute vowels are always short in this position (*jahoda*, etc.). However, since the metatony that transformed short *o* into acute *o* in these verb forms is a relatively young (late Proto-Slavic) phenomenon, we may assume that it occurred later than the shortening of stressed long vowels in the antepenult. In any case, the Czech situation *můžeš-jahoda* indicates that acute *o* was no shorter than the other acute vowels. In the nominative singular of the *o, jo,* and *i* stems with medial *o,* a short vowel won out (under the influence of the other cases) in Proto-Czech as in the other West Proto-Slavic dialects: thus, Czech *bob* 'bean,' *plod* 'fruit,' *skot* 'cattle,' *hvozd* 'nail,' etc. Only later did this *o* in West Proto-Slavic dialects undergo lengthening before voiced consonants. In Polish, the lengthening is systematic; in Czech, it is not regular, but it does not depend on the original intonation: thus, on the one hand, *dvůr* 'yard,' *kůň* 'horse,' *stůl* 'table,' *kůl* 'stake,' *vůl* 'ox,' *nůž* 'knife' (where Proto-Slavic had acute *o*), and, on the other hand, *hnůj* 'puss,' *důl* 'dale,' *sůl* 'salt,' *dům* 'house,' *vůz* 'cart,' *Bůh* 'God' (where Proto-Slavic had circumflex *o*).

12　I have tested this principle on non-Indo-European material as well—primarily East Asian and African (with the help of the Viennese Africanist Privatdozent Dr. W. Czermak, whom I cordially thank)—and have found no exception.

13　Great Russian *suxoj* 'dry,' *drugoj* '(an)other,' *takoj* 'such,' *Lukojan* (proper name) prove that the change *ky* > *k'i* did not reach Great Russian until after the completion of the change *yj* > ъ*j* (see Šaxmatov 1915, 351). Great Russian *kij* 'billiard cue' is puzzling insofar as here, for no apparent reason, the change *yj, ij* > ъ*j*, ь*j* has also failed to occur.

14　It is easy to show that the same opposition between conservative Ukrainian and Belorussian and individualistic Great Russian also existed in the area of morphology. We need only think of the peculiar and radical innovations in Great Russian declension, such as the creation of two syntactically distinct genitives (*stakan čaju* 'a glass of tea' ~ *vkus čaja* 'the taste of tea') and locatives (*v lěsu* 'in the woods' ~ *o lěsě* 'about the woods'), the elimination of the old gender distinctions in the plural, etc.

15　It is also possible to assume as the starting point the existence of two greater dialect groups, of which each is in turn divided in two: the southwestern, i.e., Ukrainian and Belorussian, and the northeastern, i.e., North and South Great Russian.

16　I cannot share the view of Šaxmatov and Durnovo that this phenomenon is much older, older at least than the loss of quantity. Rather, I see the reduction of the number of vowels in unstressed syllables as the direct consequence of the loss of quantity and the development of the expiratorial accent. Similar processes are often found in languages with a strong expiratorial accent even without free quantity: on Indo-European territory, cf. Modern Greek, Bulgarian, Vulgar Latin, Old Armenian. On Russian territory, it must in any case be later than the changes in the semivowels since *o, e* from strong ъ, ь (and from *y, i* before *j*) in unstressed syllables are treated exactly like original *o, e*. Šaxmatov's and Durnovo's theories rest on the unproved and improbable assumption that *ā* was shortened earlier than *ȳ, ū, ī*. Normally, as is well known, it is the close vowels that are especially prone to shortening, while open vowels tend to preserve their length.

17 As far as I know, this sound law was first formulated by Durnovo (see Durnovo 1924b, 195).

18 But *os'muška* with the meaning 'one-eighth of a pound' without *v*, evidently because the connection with *vosem'* 'eight' is not felt as clearly.

19 *Editor's note:* Also in *navostrit' uši*, lit. 'sharpen one's ears,' i.e., 'prick one's ears.'

20 It is difficult to decide whether this law, according to which *v-* was inserted between a preceding vowel and *ω*, did not also operate word medially. In the cases in which, according to the prevailing view, *v* replaces dialectal *g* (or *γ*), it generally stands before an old *ω: Gr. Russ. dial. *tovò* (*tovω beside *togo, togω*) 'of this,' *povost* (*povωst beside *pogost*) 'parish churchyard,' *xorovod* (*xorovωd beside *xorogod*) 'round dance.' We could, therefore, postulate *toω, *poωst, *xoroωd. But the question is then how to explain the loss of *g* (or *γ*). It is impossible to presume a regular loss of *g* (or *γ*) between *o* and *ω* because of such words as *rogòža* 'coarse packing cloth, bast mat' and *pogòda* 'weather,' which, as far as I know, preserve their *g* (or *γ*) in all Great Russian dialects.

21 This systematic *v*-prothesis must not be confused with the sporadic *v*-prothesis and *h*-prothesis before unbroken *o* (*voko, hoko* 'eye,' *vorix, horěx* 'nut,' etc.) and *u* (*vuž, huž* 'already,' *vuxo, huxo* 'ear,' etc.) that occur frequently in various Ukrainian and Belorussian dialects.

22 Earlier, in the eleventh century and the first half of the twelfth, *k'* appears to have existed only in the combination *sk'* before *ě*: e.g., чловѣчьскѣи 'male,' женьскѣи 'female' (*Sviatoslav's First Anthology*, 1073), and other similar forms. The form рабоу своꙕмоу Дъмъкѣ 'to his slave Dъmъko' (*Novgorod Minei*, 1096), which stands alone in terms of morphology as well, is all the more puzzling for the fact that the name *Dъmъko* occurs nowhere else. Can it be a scribal error?

23 The structural significance of the change *ky > k'i* for Old and later East Slavic must not be underestimated. It was not until palatalized *k', g', x'* were introduced into the sound system that Gr. Russ. *rukě* 'arm/hand,' *nogě* 'leg/foot,' *snoxě* 'daughter-in-law' (all dat. sg.), *v domikě* 'in a little house,' *peki* 'bake!' *pomogi* 'help!' (imper.), Gr. Russ. *tkët* '(he) weaves,' Beloruss. *pekëš'* '(you) bake' (sg.), etc. became possible. The texts show that such innovations did not gain ground until the fourteenth century, i.e., after the change *ky > k'i*.

18. On the Chronology of Some Common Slavic Sound Changes

"Essai sur la chronologie de certains faits phonétiques du slave commun," *Revue des études slaves* 2 (1922): 217–34.

1 Given that the majority of the changes of this period are common to Proto-Slavic and Proto-Baltic, it would be possible to call the period *Balto-Slavic*. But this name could give rise to misunderstandings that I would prefer to avoid.

2 I have accepted for the vowels the classification system proposed by Bell and developed by Sweet, but I have replaced the English phonetic terms *narrow* and *wide* by Passy's terms *tense* and *lax* [*voyelle tendue, voyelle relâchée*]. In my transcription of Common Slavic, *o, e, ö* are lax vowels and *ǫ, ę, ǫ̈* tense vowels; *a* is high-back-unround, *ɒ* is Bell and Sweet's mid-back-unround; the *jer*'s are designated by *ъ* and *ь*; and *ĭ* and *ŭ* are short lax *i* and *u* (*ĭ* is high-front-wide-unround, *ŭ* high-back-wide-round).

3 The Finnish data may admit of another explanation. West Finnic and Mordvin *a* corresponds regularly to labialized vowels in the other Finnic languages (Lapp *uö*, Cher. *ü, o*, Zyryan *o*, Votic *u* : W Finn. *kala*, Mordv. *kal* = Lapp *kúöllē*, Cher. *kol* 'fish'; W Finn. *sata*, Mordv. *s'ado* = Lapp *cúöhtē*, Cher. *šüdö*, Zyryan *s'o*, Votic *s'u* 'hundred'; W Finn. *askeli* 'footstep,' Mordv. *as'k'el'ams* 'walk' = Cher. *oškɒl*, Zyryan *vos'kol* 'footstep'; W Finn. *maksa*, Mordv. *makso* = Lapp *múöksē*, Votic *mus* 'liver,' etc.). Where Lapp has the corresponding long sound, West Finnic has not *ā* but rather *uo* from *ō̜* (Lapp *süötna*, Mordv. *san*, Cher. *šün* = W Finn. *suoni* 'vein'; Lapp *n'üölla*, Mordv. *nal* = W Finn. *nuoli* 'arrow'). Could not the *a* of West Finnic *kala, sata*, etc. go back to an originally labialized vowel (such as *a̜*)? This would explain the *uo* of West Finnic *suoni, nuoli* (vs. Mordv. *san, nal*) and would accord perfectly with the Lapp, Cheremis, and Permic data. If this supposition is admissible (which it is up to Finno-Ugric specialists to decide), then the *a* of West Finnic *pappu, akkuna*, etc. would be explained very simply: the West Finns would have rendered the open *o* of Proto-Russian by *a̜*, which later became *a* together with all other instances of Proto-Finnic *a̜*.

4 Mikkola (1894, 1.74) seems to have overlooked the fact that Slavic *-ŭ* is rendered by Finnish *-i* only after voiceless consonants: Finnish *pappi* (= Russ. *popъ* 'priest'), *sirppi* (= *sьrpъ* 'sickle'), *hurtti* (= *xъrtъ* 'greyhound, borzoi'), *hursti* (= *xъlstъ* 'canvas'), *risti* (= *krьstъ* 'cross'), *siisti* (= *čistъ* 'clean'). In this position, *-ŭ* seems to have become devoiced at a very early date (see Meillet 1913b, 236), and a whispered *-ŭ* will not have been reproduced by foreigners with the same precision as the more or less voiced *-ŭ* of *bobŭ* 'broad bean,' *lādŭ* '(good) order,' *tŭrgŭ* 'market.'

5 See Van Wijk 1916, 462n. This conclusion can also be reached in another way. We have seen that the change of *ō* to *ā* (delabialization of long vowels) occurred later than the dialectal lengthening of *e, o* in the groups *tert, *tort, *telt, *tolt. The change of *čē* to *čā* must have preceded this lengthening; otherwise, *čērdō* would have yielded *čārdā* > *črada* instead of *črěda* (OCS *črěda*, Czech *třída*).

6 This proves that Baudouin de Courtenay was wrong in supposing that *oi* and *ei* had been changed to *ě, i* before the progressive palatalization of the gutturals. Since *oi* became *ei* (> *ī*) after palatalized consonants, the change of *oi* to *e* must be later than that of *jo* to *je* and consequently also later than the progressive palatalization of gutturals.

7 This is the only defensible chronology. True, Brückner claims that, before it became *ě*, old *oi* was able to be monophthongized into another phoneme that after *j* yielded *i* and in all other positions *ě* (see, e.g., Brückner 1917, 76). But this claim collapses as soon as one tries to supply details. If the first result of the contraction of *oi* was a palatal vowel, it would have had no need to be palatalized to *i* after *j*; if *oi* contracted to a velar vowel, on the other hand, one can easily imagine its changing to *i* after *j*, but it is impossible to conceive of how or why this velar vowel could have ended up as *ě* in all other positions.

19. On the Original Value of the Common Slavic Accents

"De la valeur primitive des intonations du slave commun," *Revue des études slaves* 1 (1921): 171–87.

1 *Translator's note: Abrupt* and *smooth* are more or less literal translations of the French *rude* and *douce*, which correspond to *Stoßton* and *Schleifton* in German, *acute* and *circumflex* in English. As is evident from Trubetzkoy's discussion, the choice of terminology and the

precise meaning of these conventional names vary according to the language being described, and at the level of historical reconstruction there is little consensus even today. We have retained *abrupt* and *smooth* in certain places in the present article for historical reasons; but in Trubetzkoy's follow-up article of 1924 (chap. 20 in this volume) we have substituted *acute* and *circumflex* everywhere, for the parent as well as the daughter languages.

2 In what follows, I employ the sign ˜ for the smooth accent of Common Slavic, the sign ˝ for the abrupt accent, and ˆ for the accent of the so-called open short vowels (*e, o*) of Common Slavic. The other signs (ˆ ˜ ´ `) are used in the sense given them by Vuk Karadžić: thus ´ marks the short rising accent, in contrast to Valjavec's usage.

3 According to Šaxmatov, this change occurred in Common Slavic.

4 Stage 4 of the development in Slovenian (see above) is also a manifestation of this tendency, for it changes the nonhomogeneous monosyllabic contour into a homogeneous (falling) tonal movement.

5 *Translator's note:* We find this word attested only in Serbo-Croatian, not in Czech.

6 Mordv. *orta* = Russ. *voróta* 'gate' proves that the first Russian-Mordvin contacts must be dated before the change of the sound group *tort* to *torot*. At the time of this change, Russian stress was not yet purely expiratorial. The meter of Russian folk poetry, therefore, must have been different from what it is today.

20. On the Proto-Slavic Accents

"Zum urslavischen Intonationssystem," in *Streitberg-Festgabe*. Herausgegeben von der Direktion der Vereinigten Sprachwissenschaftlichen Institute an der Universität zu Leipzig. Leipzig: Market & Petters, 1924, 359–66.

1 *Translator's note:* Grave translates *Kurzton,* which Trubetzkoy also calls the *short accent* or the *accent of [short]* e *and* o. For *acute* and *circumflex*, see chap. 19, n. 1, above.

2 In the mountains between Jablunk and Zips, some Polish dialects have initial stress. On the other hand, there are Czech dialects in Silesia and Moravia with penultimate stress. In Czech, polysyllabic words have main stress on the first syllable and secondary stress on the penult; in Polish, such words have main stress on the penult and secondary stress on the first syllable. The difference between these types is one of degree, not of kind, whence the fluctuations in the border dialects.

3 Attempts have repeatedly been made to derive West Slavic fixed stress, which is always initial or penultimate, from Proto-Slavic conditions, by assuming either regular accent retractions (as in the Štokavian dialect of Serbo-Croatian) or analogical leveling. All such explanations, including Lehr-Spławiński's (1923), seem to me incorrect. The fact that quantitative relations in Czech are the exact opposite of those in Serbo-Croatian (Cz. *lípă* 'linden tree,' *zlătŏ* 'gold'; Serbo-Cr. *lípă, zlătŏ*) contradicts the assumption of a parallel development of the two languages. The free tonal stress of Proto-Slavic and the fixed expiratorial stress of West Slavic are completely different things; there need not be any genetic relation between them. From the speaker's perspective, a language with fixed stress (like Czech or Polish) has *no stress;* free stress, on the other hand, is psychologically real as it affects meaning. This opposition is so fundamental that it cannot be bridged by assuming partial accent shifts and analogical leveling. Accentuation of the Czech type can have arisen in only one way: the old tonal distinctions produced new distinctions of quantity

as a result of a regular linguistic change, and, when these new distinctions had become paramount in the speakers' consciousness and nuances of tone and expiratorial stress only secondary, the dynamic characteristics of individual syllables were reorganized according to the external requirements of rhythm. Polish went one step further and replaced distinctions of quantity with those of quality. For a Polish syllable, neither expiratorial stress nor quantity nor tonal movement is relevant; only the quality of the individual sounds matters.

4 I designate the inverse acute with spiritus lenis and the inverse circumflex with spiritus asper over the vowel: *gýnešь* 'perish, languish,' *mȁžešь* 'smear,' *pȋšešь* 'write,' *xvȁlišь* 'praise' (2d p. sg. pres.). Proto-Slavic short vowels underwent certain changes in the same forms in which the long ones were inverted. It is usually assumed that in such cases the short vowels (*e, o*) received a short rising tone. But, if we compare the reflexes of this short rising tone in all the Slavic languages, we will see that it was identical with the normal acute. I write, therefore, *kőža* 'skin,' *xődišь* 'walk' (2d p. sg. pres.), *bőbъ* 'bean,' etc., with the same symbol ˝ as for the normal acute.

5 Proto-Štokavian may also have transformed the inverse circumflex into a normal one under the same conditions (which are unknown to us). But this cannot be proved since after the regressive accent shift the reflexes of the inverse and the normal circumflex in Štokavian merged.

21. On the Development of the Gutturals in the Slavic Languages

"Die Entwicklung der Gutturale in den slavischen Sprachen," in *Sbornik" v" čest' na Prof. L. Miletič" za sedemdesetgodišninata ot" roždenieto mu (1863-1933)* (Sofia: Izdanie na Makedonskija naučen" institut", 1933), 267-79.

1 Novák (1930, 19-20) confirms this for Slovak, but there is no doubt that the situation is the same in Czech, Ukrainian, and Upper Sorbian as well.

2 Cf. Zubatý (1910, 106-7) and Trávníček (1927, 25-26), and see Novák (1930:14) on γ in Slovak (e.g., *boγ bi dal* for *Boh by dal* 'God would give'). In Czech, γ regularly appears not only for old *x* (as in *abiγ dal* for *abych dal* 'that I would give') but also for old final *h* (e.g., *būγ bi dal* for *Bůh by dal*). Medially, as well, I have frequently heard γ instead of *h* before voiced obstruents.

3 Even Ukrainian and Czech *x*, which are significantly more "close" than their Russian counterpart (see Broch 1911, 78-79, 91), display less audible friction than Upper German *ch*, to say nothing of Dutch.

4 A disruption of the regular structure of the sound system would be perceived here only by a foreign observer in whose mother tongue *x*, *γ* and *h* are three separate phonemes, as is indeed the case in Dutch. Although Van Wijk possesses an enviable gift for languages and an astonishingly precise command of several Slavic languages, he is not always able to free himself from a subconsciously Dutch perception of sounds. This is confirmed by another passage in his article (Van Wijk 1932, 75), in which he declares that he perceives palatalized consonants as "consonant + *j*," aspirates as "consonant + *h*," and affricates as "plosive + spirant" and wants to attribute objective validity to this perception. The explanation for this perception is the simple fact that Van Wijk's native language possesses none of the three phoneme types in question. For a Russian, the sound *c* is just as homogeneous as, say, *l*, and the relation *t : t′* is treated by a phonetically untrained Russian

no differently than the relation $t : d$. Only foreign phonemes with no equivalent in the observer's mother tongue will be perceived as phoneme combinations. Speakers of a language lacking the opposition tenuis – media or fortis – lenis would no doubt perceive our d, b, g as combinations of t, p, k with an indeterminate "opener." To study the phonological system of a foreign language, we must suppress our own perception of sounds and put ourselves as objectively as possible in the natives' shoes.

5 For East Slavic territory, a fricative pronunciation of the voiced guttural is confirmed already by the oldest sources (Constantine Porphyrogennetos).

6 It is true that Bavarian g is a voiceless stop, but Slavs treat this sound as voiced (this is regarded in Austria, for example, as a sign of Slavic accent).

7 Old Hungarian is thought to have preserved the voiced guttural fricative (from Finno-Ugric $*k \sim *\gamma$) into the twelfth century. But this sound occurred only intervocalically or finally after a vowel; its pronunciation in other positions will have been just as difficult for Hungarians of that time as the pronunciation of the guttural nasal η initially or after a consonant is for modern Germans. Moreover, the later development of this Old Hungarian sound—namely, its vocalization—shows that it was especially open, an articulation that does not have to be assumed for Old Slovak $*\gamma$ at the time of the Hungarian settlement. Therefore, the $*\gamma$ of Slovak place-names was originally reproduced in Old Hungarian not by the Old Hungarian voiced fricative but by the plosive g. I would like to take this opportunity to thank Dr. Julius von Laziczius for information on the current state of the γ problem in historical Hungarian linguistics.

8 Such *termini ante quos* for Czech are the regressive assimilation of voice (*kde* 'where,' pronounced *gde;* see Trubetzkoy 1925, 292 [see chap. 17, p. 112, in this volume]; and Jakobson 1926a, 812ff.) and the loss of reduced nasal vowels, a process usually referred to as the *denasalization of nasal vowels* (see Trubetzkoy 1927–28, 671).

9 On the terms *variant, stylistic variant,* and *principal variant,* see "Projet de terminologie phonologique standardisée" (1931, 319ff.) and Trubetzkoy (1929a, 116–17).

10 Bartek's (1931, 47) view that the Slovak change $\gamma > h$ was contemporaneous with the Old Hungarian epenthesis between two word-initial consonants is based on erroneous logic, as Novák pointed out (1930, 6–7). But Trávníček's (1927, 17ff.) idea (accepted by Novák) that the change $\gamma > h$ is later than the assimilation of voice cannot be supported either. The sound x in Czech *Bůh* 'God,' *lehký* 'light' (adj.) (pronounced *būx, lexkī*) shows only that finally and before obstruents γ had not yet become h at the time of the assimilation of voice; it in no way proves that in other positions (before vowels and sonorants) γ cannot have become h or acquired h as an optional variant by this time. Indeed, in cases such as *abych byl* 'that I would be' (pronounced *abiɣ bil*), the γ that arose from the assimilation of voice has still not become h even today.

11 Trávníček thinks that the letter h was the best available means of representing γ ("the roman alphabet, from which the Czech script was created, did not have a sign for γ, so the old scribes resorted to the letter h since it designated a similar sound" [1927, 27]), but it is difficult to accept this view. Languages that use the roman alphabet and possess the sound γ usually represent it with g or digraphs. Certain roman writing systems recently developed for languages of the Soviet Union do represent γ with h (e.g., the Ossetic roman writing system), but this stems from the traditional pronunciation of roman h as γ in Russian secondary schools. The designation of Old Hungarian γ by h in old texts is apparently linked to the very open quality of this sound (cf. n. 7 above).

12 The Czech glosses in the Hebrew alphabet cited by Mazon (1927) seem to prove that

around the middle of the thirteenth century velar γ had not yet succumbed to *h*. The orthography of these glosses could be the product of tradition, however, since Czech glosses are frequently found in Hebrew texts of the thirteenth century, as was pointed out to me by Roman Jakobson. If Zubatý's interpretation of forms like *chlupý* 'foolish' and *v chromadě* 'in a heap/crowd' in a manuscript of Kabátník's travelogue from the end of the fifteenth century is correct, *h* cannot be regarded as the principal variant for this period. But these forms can have other explanations.

13 In Proto-Slavic, the sound *dž* occurred only in the combination *ždž*, which linguistic intuition necessarily interpreted as *zž*. So *dž* was not an independent phoneme at this time but a combinatory variant of the phoneme *ž*.

14 The sounds *c* and *dz* were always palatalized and occurred only before front vowels; *s* and *z* were palatalized before front vowels, nonpalatalized before consonants and back vowels. At this time, however, palatalization had no phonological value but was simply a "natural pronunciation" for all labials and dentals before front vowels. Therefore, there is no need to designate it with diacritical marks here.

15 This was the case in the South Proto-Slavic dialects and in Pre-Slovak, in which the change *d', t' > dz, c* did not take place until later (see Trubetzkoy 1930, 385ff.).

16 This problem did not exist in the dialects that preserved *dz:* the coexistence of the pairs *k : x* and *k : g* was supported by the analogy of *c : s* and *c : dz*. It was not until *dž* became an independent phoneme in these dialects that the gutturals became isolated: *g : k : x* was not parallel to *dz : c : z : s, dž : č : ž : š*.

17 Later, this system underwent drastic changes in the individual dialects, the most important being the spread of the correlation of voice to all the obstruents. This innovation seems to have occurred first in Pre-Slovak, in which new *c, dz* arose from *t', d'* (= Proto-Slavic **tj, *dj*) soon after the change *g > γ* (see Trubetzkoy 1930, 387–88). Instead of the new *dz* being eliminated, a new *dž* was created for *č* and a new *g* for *k* after the model of *c : dz* (through various new coinages, expressive and onomatopoeic forms, and loans from other languages). The old three-member bundles were thus transformed into four-member bundles (*c : dz : s : z, č : dž : š : ž, k : g : x : γ*). Ukrainian seems to have acquired the phonemes *dz, dž, g* much later than Slovak and primarily under foreign influence. Today, however, they form part of the Ukrainian standard language and many dialects.

18 In an earlier article (Trubetzkoy 1925, 293 [see chap. 17, pp. 112–13, in this volume]), I suggested that the North Russian merger of *c* and *č* was perhaps due to the influence of West Finnic languages (since then I have found the same idea in Černyšev 1902, 117–18). The opposition between *č* and *c'*, which still exists today in Komi (Zyryan), Udmurt (Votic), and some dialects of Mari (Cheremis), was abandoned by the West Finns very early on, although the distinction *š : s'* was long retained. The assumption of West Finnic influence on North Russian is thus quite plausible in this case. Nevertheless, even if a West Finnic language did serve as model for the merger of *č* and *c* in North Russian, the motivation for following this model was the need to eliminate the correlation of constriction. Jakobson says correctly, "It is only from the point of view of the requirements of the phonological system that this isolated Finnic borrowing can be understood" (1929, 46).

19 These are the "North Russian dialects of the Volga group" and the "Central Russian dialects" according to the terminology of Durnovo, Sokolov, and Ušakov (1915).

20 Even in the dialects with plosive *g* and the opposition *č : c* (as in Standard Russian), the correlation of constriction no longer exists: *č* is "soft" (palatalized) and dorsal and therefore has no obvious affinity with consistently "hard" (nonpalatalized), apical *š*, while *x*

displays very weak velar friction and is produced much lower in the mouth than k, and the relation between k and x therefore appears very distant from both an acoustic and an articulatory point of view. Finally, c is one of the "unpalatalizable" consonants (i.e., it has no palatalized counterpart), while s is palatalizable.

21 I will not go into details of the dialectal development here. It should be emphasized, however, that all the dialectal evidence (including that cited in Bošković 1931) can easily be explained from the phonological standpoint.

22 For example, it is questionable whether the Pre-Bulgarian dialects that had preserved dz and therefore had no "guttural problem" participated in the laryngealization of x. The present geographic distribution of the reflexes of Proto-Slavic x can be due to later shifts.

23 Cf. Broch 1911, 40, 67, and the opinions of other scholars cited there.

24 The chronology of the weakening of the velar friction of North Russian x cannot be determined; the phenomenon appears to be relatively late. The fact that x is represented by k in Russian loanwords in Latvian indicates the strongly velar nature of the sound. But this does not take us very far since even today, despite the weakening of friction, North Russian x remains more velar than laryngeal.

25 The isolated position of x with respect to voice also weakened its affinity with k: the relation $x : k : g$ was not the same as $s : z : c : dz$ and $š : ž : č : dž$. The isolation of x led not only to the weakening of its friction but also to its failure to be palatalized before y and e (< ь, oje), whereas the palatalization of k and g in certain positions (especially before final e) was later even phonologized (e.g., pairs such as *Polskę* 'Poland' [acc.] : *polskie* 'Polish' [m. pl. inanimate, f. pl., nt. sg.], *drogę* 'road' [acc.] : *drogie* 'expensive' [m. pl. inanimate, f. pl., nt. sg.]). On palatal x in modern standard Polish, see Nitsch 1931.

26 Therefore, the noticeable laryngealization of x in South Slavic dialects cannot be explained by the influence of a so-called linguistic substrate. It is true that the change $x > h$ is also found in the neighboring non-Slavic languages: Albanian and Hungarian. But in these languages the change seems to be fairly recent, and it may well have been a product of Slavic influence! In any case, even if the laryngealization of x did have a foreign model, what was said in n. 18 above about the merger of c and $č$ in North Russian applies here as well: the motivation for imitating the foreign model was the striving for a solution to the problem of the gutturals.

22. Remarks on Some Iranian Words Borrowed by the North Caucasian Languages

"Remarques sur quelques mots iraniens empruntés par les langues du Caucase septentrional," *Mémoires de la Société de Linguistique de Paris* 22 (1922): 247–52.

1 The Adyghe have the bizarre custom of giving their children names that sound more like terms of abuse: *Çauaiə* 'ugly boy' is quite common, and one finds Circassians named *Çaunaš'ə* 'cross-eyed boy,' *Ḥat'at'* 'fat dog,' and so on. The Islamic clergy is fighting an uphill battle against the custom; names of this type remain more popular than Islamic ones, and I knew a Circassian woman who was named *Ḥabzəfiž* 'white bitch,' even though she was the daughter of a muezzin.

2 In Common Adyghe, stops (and affricates) could be voiced, voiceless-aspirated, or voiceless-glottalized; these remained unchanged in both Circassian and Kabardian. Common Adyghe also seems to have had a series of unaspirated, weak, voiceless stops that are represented in Kabardian by voiced stops and in Circassian by aspirated voiceless ones: Circ. *p'yt'ə* = Kab. *byde* 'solid,' Circ. *k'u* = Kab. *gu* 'wagon,' Circ. *k'jat'ə* = Kab. *ğat'e* 'saber,'

Circ. *c'ə* = Kab. *dze* 'tooth,' Circ. *č'ən* = Kab. *žen* 'run' (< *džen*: Kabardian does not permit *č*, *dž* and transforms them into spirants).

3 Certain details of the Adyghe version seem to be highly obscene, and I was unable to convince my Circassian informant—an ostentatiously pious centenarian—to enlighten me on the subject any further.

23. On the Prehistory of the East Caucasian Languages

"Zur Vorgeschichte der ostkaukasischen Sprachen," in *Mélanges de linguistique et de philologie offerts à Jacq. van Ginneken*. Paris: Klincksieck, 1937, 171–78.

1 The weakening of the closure of old **g*, **b*, **d* after vowels was necessary in order to differentiate these phonemes from old glottalized **ḵ*, **p̣*, **ṭ*, which had become voiced in the same position. Where voiced stops follow vowels in modern Chechen and Ingush, they go back not to old voiced stops but to old **ḵ*, **p̣*, **ṭ* (cf. Sommerfelt 1938a, 138ff.).

2 Examples can be found in Trubetzkoy 1922, 191ff. Compare further Ingush *tχə*, Bats *tχe* 'wool' = Agul *xej*; Chechen *-aχar*, Avar *-iλine* 'go'; and perhaps also Ingush *bårχ* 'multicolored,' Avar *boɲon* 'pig' (or Dargwa *birḥ* 'red-brown'?).

3 The nasal of the nasal conjugation originally constituted part of the verbal root and hence appears in certain derivations outside the conjugation paradigm proper. The verbal root **kᵒ* 'eat,' which belongs to the nasal conjugation, forms in Avar not only the verb *kuine* 'eat' but also the noun *koen* 'food' and the secondary iterative *koanaze*. This last form must be linked with Lak *kanan* 'eat,' probably an iterative of *-ukān* 'eat.' So the nasal roots must originally have inserted a nasal before endings and suffixes in Lak as well; the disappearance of the distinction between the nasal and the nonnasal conjugation is an innovation.

4 On the regular reflexes of Common Samurian **kk* (which is normally derived from the Common East Caucasian voiceless lateral affricate) in the individual Samurian languages, see Trubetzkoy 1922.

5 Its byform *halbilu-*, with the familiar extension *-lu* (cf. Andi *guržiolu* 'Georgian,' *ermenliolu* 'Armenian'), is the source of Andi *hajbulu* 'Avar' and Godoberi *habulu* 'Avar' via remote dissimilation and dissimilatory loss, respectively, of the first *l* sound in anticipation of the second.

24. The Universal Adoption of the Roman Alphabet: Peoples of the Caucasus

"Peuples du Caucase. Extrait d'une lettre du Prince N. Troubetzkoy," in *L'adoption universelle des caractères latins* (Paris: Institut International de Coopération Intellectuelle, 1934), 45–48.

25. The Phonological System of Mordvin Compared with That of Russian

"Das mordwinische phonologische System verglichen mit dem russischen," in *Charisteria Gvilelmo Mathesio qvinqvagenario a discipvlis et Circvli Lingvistici Pragensis sodalibvs oblata* (Prague: Pražský Lingvistický Kroužek/Cercle Linguistique de Prague, 1932), 21–24.

1 I will confine my remarks here to the Mordvin written language, which is based on the Erzya-Mordvin dialect of the village of Kozlovka. See the description of this language in Bubrix 1930, and cf. further Evsev'ev 1929.

2 For example, the opposition between dynamically strong ("stressed") and weak ("un-

stressed") vowels is phonologically relevant in Russian but not in Mordvin (see Bubrix 1930, p. 23, sec. 32). The same can be said of the opposition palatalized-nonpalatalized labials, which in Mordvin is the result of external conditions (labials are palatalized before and after *e, i*, otherwise nonpalatalized). Mordvin *v* is a combinatory variant of *u̯*, as *v* (or *v'* before *e, i*) appears only before vowels, *u̯* (or *u̯*̣ after *e, i*) only before consonants and word finally, so *v* may be considered a sonorant, whereas Russian *v/v'* is an obstruent (although of a special kind). Since, unlike Russian *č*, Mordvin *č* has the same place of articulation as *š/ž* and a palatalized counterpart, the Mordvin correspondence *s : c = s' : c' = š : č* is a constriction correlation (stops vs. fricatives), whereas in Russian *c* and *s* are disjunct phonemes. On the concepts *phonological value* and *disjunct* and *correlative phonemes*, see Trubetzkoy 1929a, 111ff. and Trubetzkoy 1931d.

3 Common archiphonemes are U, O, A, E, I, P, T, K, F, S, Š, X, R, L, M, N, J; in addition, Russian possesses Ŝ (Ш, ЗЖ), Ĉ (Ч), and C (Mordv. *c, c'* belong to the archiphoneme S) and Mordvin V (as sonorant; Russ. *v, v'* belong to the archiphoneme F). Common correlations are those of voice and of palatalization in consonants; in addition, Russian displays the correlation of intensity in vowels (*u : ŭ = a : ă = i : ĭ*) and Mordvin the constriction correlation (*s : c = s' : c' = š : č*).

4 In medial obstruent clusters in Russian, all obstruents are voiced or voiceless depending on the quality of the last one (*kăs'it'* 'mow' ~ *kăz'ba* 'mowing' [n.], *kălodă* 'large block of wood' ~ *kălotkă* 'small block of wood, cobbler's last'). In Mordvin, this occurs only if the following obstruent is voiceless (e.g., *kuz* 'fir tree' ~ *kustomo* 'without a fir tree'); if it is voiced, it becomes voiceless *after* voiceless obstruents (*kudo* 'house' ~ abl. *kudodo, kuz* 'fir tree' ~ abl. *kuzdo*, but *šokš* 'pot' ~ abl. *šokšto*). In Russian, *word-final* obstruents are neutralized with respect to voice and are realized as voiced *before* voiced obstruents, voiceless in other positions (*naž dom* 'our house' ~ *naš ăt'ec* 'our father,' *nož d'ad'ĭ* 'the uncle's knife,' *noš ătca* 'the father's knife'). In Mordvin, on the contrary, *word-initial* obstruents are neutralized with respect to voice and are realized as voiceless *after* a pause and *after* voiceless sounds but remain voiced in other positions (e.g., *panar* 'shirt,' *orčak panar* '[you (sg.)] put on a shirt!' ~ *ašo banar* 'white shirt,' *od banar* 'new shirt,' *c'oran' banarzo* 'the boy's shirt'). Only in polysyllabic words do word-final voiced consonants become voiceless in Mordvin, and then only before a pause, not in sandhi. This rule, whose area of operation is very narrow already, admits of exceptions: word-final *z'* remains voiced in polysyllabic verb forms even before a pause.

5 Russian consonants are phonologically neutralized with respect to palatalization in certain positions. All consonants *before* pretonic *ă*, all consonants except *l before* nonpalatalized dentals, and all labials *before* medial *u, ŭ* are nonpalatalized; all consonants *before* *e* are palatalized; *before v'* and *before* palatalized dentals, sibilants are palatalized, and all other consonants (except *l*) are non- or half-palatalized. In Mordvin, such a phonological neutralization occurs not before but *after* certain phonemes: all dentals except *s, z, c* are palatalized *after e, i* and *after* palatalized dentals but nonpalatalized *after* nonpalatalized dentals. Progressive assimilation occurs only before *l', s',* and *z'*.

6 After dentals, only the affricates *c, c', č* (or *dz, dz', dž*, which occur solely in this position) are pronounced. But they are perceived as *s, s', š* (or *z, z', ž*) since the fricatives are the unmarked members of the constriction correlation.

7 For the sake of completeness, it should be mentioned that Mordvin has a rule that is oriented in both directions: obstruents that are not in direct contact with a vowel are phono-

logically neutral with respect to voice and are realized as voiceless (e.g., *andoms* 'nourish' ~ frequentative *antnems*, etc.).

8   The vowel *o* may stand in a noninitial syllable only after nonpalatalized consonants and only following a syllable with *u, o, a*. On the other hand, *e* occurs after nonpalatalized consonants only if the preceding syllable contains *e* or *i*; after palatalized consonants, *e* may occur irrespective of the vowel of the preceding syllable. So the opposition between *o* and *e*, which in the initial syllable can differentiate meaning (e.g., *kov* 'moon' ~ *kev* 'stone'), is in noninitial syllables the result of external, phonetic conditioning. The vowel *u* occurs in noninitial syllables after nonpalatalized consonants between a syllable with *u, o, a* and one with *a, i* (e.g., *amul'ams* 'scoop' [v.], *kulcuni* 'he hears'). In the same position, *o*, too, but not *e*, is permitted (e.g., *kudoška* 'like a house') (see Trubetzkoy 1929c, esp. 58–59).

9   As mentioned in n. 4 above, initial obstruents are neutralized with respect to voice. The opposition between voiced and voiceless obstruents, which in initial and final position can differentiate meaning (e.g., *kozo* 'whither' ~ *koso* 'where,' *lugas'* 'meadow' ~ *lukas'* 'moved back and forth,' *ked'* 'hand' ~ *ket'* 'hands,' *noldaz'* 'left' [part.] ~ *noldas'* 'left' [v.]), is in initial position the result of external conditioning (e.g., *orčan banar* 'I put on a shirt' ~ *orčak panar* 'put on a shirt!'). Initial dentals except *s, z* are palatalized before *e*, whereas medially before *e* nonpalatalized dentals are possible as well (*s'este* 'thence').

10   These figures have been obtained from the Mordvin text and its Russian translation printed as an appendix to Bubrix 1930. Neither text is very extensive (the Mordvin contains approximately 1,120 phonemes, the Russian approximately 1,180), but the proportions in longer texts ought to be roughly the same. It would be interesting to perform a more precise statistical analysis of the functional load of Mordvin phonemes by means of Mathesius's method.

From Trubetzkoy's Letters to Roman Jakobson.

1   Apropos the dual. From the Slavic point of view, Meillet's thesis is absolutely untenable. In what sense are the modern Slovenians and Sorbians less civilized than the Serbians or Bulgarians? Why were seventeenth-century Polabians less civilized than their Russian contemporaries? Strange as it may seem, the dual has been preserved only by those Slavs who have experienced an especially strong German influence (except for the Czechs).

2   *Editor's note:* Page numbers in brackets after selections from the letters indicate placement in *N. S. Trubetzkoy's Letters and Notes* (Trubetzkoy 1975). The symbol "(D)" after the date designates letters written not to Jakobson but to Nikolai Durnovo.

3   *Roman Jakobson's note:* A. A. Gruška, professor of Latin at Moscow University, insisted on observing the traditional place of word stress in reciting Latin poetry.

4   *Editor's note:* The source of the latter statement is Kranzmayer's personal communication (see Trubetzkoy to Jakobson, n.d. [July 1936], in Trubetzkoy 1975, 361).

5   *Editor's note: ḍ* and *ṭ* designate palatalized plosives.

6   *Editor's note:* Jakobson commented, "Your observations on Slavic accentology are convincing. I believe that soon the historical phonology of prosodic elements in Slavic will be fully elucidated."

7   *Roman Jakobson's note:* When Thurneysen, Hermann's teacher, spoke out against him and defended phonologists as faithful adherents of the idea of sound law.

8   *Editor's note:* The theoretical foundations of Jakobson 1932 are meant.

Bibliography

Abbreviations

BSL	*Bulletin de la Société de Linguistique de Paris.*
CGM	*Charisteria Gvilelmo Mathesio qvinqvagenario a discipvlis et Circvli Lingvistici Pragensis sodalibvs oblata.* Prague: Pražský Linguistický Kroužek/ Cercle Linguistique de Prague, 1932.
IF	*Indogermanische Forschungen.*
IORJAS	*Izvestija Otdelenija russkogo jazyka i slovesnosti Rossijskoj* [later: *Imperatorskoj*] *Akademii nauk.*
MSL	*Mémoires de la Société de Linguistique de Paris.*
Proceedings Amsterdam	Proceedings of the International Congress of Phonetic Sciences: First Meeting of the Internationale Arbeitsgemeinschaft für Phonologie, Amsterdam, 3–8 July 1932. *Archives Néerlandaises de phonétique expérimentale* 8–9 (1933): 92–312.
Proceedings London	Daniel Jones and D. B. Fry, eds., *Proceedings of the Second International Congress of Phonetic Sciences . . . Held at University College, London, 22–26 July 1935.* Cambridge: Cambridge University Press, 1936.
RESl	*Revue des études slaves.*
SORJAS	*Sbornik Otdelenija russkogo jazyka i slovesnosti Rossijskoj* [later: *Imperatorskoj*] *Akademii nauk.*
TCLP 1	*Mélanges linguistiques dédiés au Premier Congrès des Philologues Slaves.* Travaux du Cercle Linguistique de Prague, 1. Prague: Jednota Československých matematiků a fysiků, 1929. Reprint, Nendeln: Kraus, 1979.
TCLP 4	*Réunion phonologique internationale tenue à Prague (18–21/XII 1930).* Travaux du Cercle Linguistique de Prague, 4. Prague: Jednota Československých matematiků a fysiků, 1931. Reprint, Nendeln: Kraus, 1968.
TCLP 6	*Études dédiés au quatrième congrès de linguistes.* Travaux du Cercle Linguistique de Prague, 6. Prague: n.p., 1936. Reprint, Nendeln: Kraus, 1968.

Association Internationale pour les Études Phonologiques/Internationale Phonologische Arbeitsgemeinschaft. 1932. *Bulletin d'information,* no. 1. Appeared in *Časopis pro moderní filologii* 19:51–64.

Association Internationale pour les Études Phonologiques/Internationale Phonologische Arbeitsgemeinschaft. 1935. *Bulletin d'information,* no. 2. Appeared as supplement to *Časopis pro moderní filologii,* vol. 22, no. 1.

Bally, Charles. 1933. "Spécimens de concordance entre la structure grammaticale et le système phonologique." In *Actes du Deuxième Congrès International de Linguistes, Genève, 25–29 août 1931.* Paris: Maisonneuve, 116–18.

Baranovskij [Baranauskas], Anton [Antanas]. 1899. "Zametki o litovskom jazyke i slovare I-VIII." *SORJAS* 65, no. 9:1–80.

Baranowski [Baranauskas], Anton [Antanas], and Hugo Weber. 1882. *Ostlitauische Texte mit Einleitungen und Anmerkungen.* Weimar: Böhlau.

Bartek, Henri. 1931. "Le passage de *g* à *h* en slovaque." *RESl* 11:40–49.

Baudouin de Courtenay, I. A. 1893. "Dva voprosa iz učenija o 'smjagčenii' ili palatalizacii v slovjanskix jazykax." *Učenyje zapiski Imperatorskogo Jur'evskogo Universiteta*, no. 2, unofficial section, pp. 1–30.

Baudouin de Courtenay, J. 1894. "Einiges über Palatalisierung (Palatalisation) und Entpalatalisierung (Dispalatalisation)." *IF* 4:45–57.

Bauer, Hans. 1933. Untitled response to the topic "Les systèmes phonologiques envisagés en eux-mêmes et dans leurs rapports avec la structure générale de la langue" proposed to congress participants. In *Actes du Deuxième Congrès International de Linguistes, Genève, 25–29 août 1931.* Paris: Maisonneuve, 114.

Belić, A. 1909. "Zametki po čakavskim govoram." *IORJAS* 14:180–265.

Belić, A. 1921. "Najmlaća (treća) promena zadn'enepčanix suglasnika *k, g* i *x* y praslovenskom jeziku." *Južnoslovenski filolog* 2:17–39.

Bergmann, Fr. 1921. "K chronologii některých staročeských zjevů mluvnických." *Listy filologické* 48:223–39.

Berkopec, O. 1937. "Puškinskie perevody serboxorvatskix narodnyx pesen." *Slavia* 14:416–40.

Bloomfield, Leonard. 1933. *Language.* New York: Holt.

Borgstrøm, Carl Hj. 1938. "Zur Phonologie der norwegischen Schriftsprache (nach der ostnorwegischen Aussprache)." *Norsk Tidsskrift for Sprogvidenskap* 9:250–73.

Bošković, R. 1931. "O prirodi, razvitku i zamenicima glasa *x* u govorima Crne Gore." *Južnoslovenski filolog* 11:179–97.

Broch, Olaf. 1895. "Zum Kleinrussischen in Ungarn." *Archiv für slavische Philologie* 17:320–416.

Broch, Olaf. 1900. *Ugrorusskoe narečie sela Ubli (Zemplinskogo komitata).* Issledovaniia po russkomu iazyku, vol. 2, pt. 1. St. Petersburg: Tipografija Imperatorskoj Akademii nauk.

Broch, Olaf. 1911. *Slavische Phonetik.* Sammlung slavischer Lehr- und Handbücher, ser. 2, col. 1. Heidelberg: Winter.

Brøndal, Viggo. 1936. "Sound and Phoneme." In *Proceedings London*, 40–45.

Bronisch, Gotthelf. 1896–98. *Kaschubische Dialektstudien: Die Sprache der Bëlöcë.* 2 vols. Leipzig: Harrassowitz.

Brückner, Alexander. 1917. "Slavisch-Litauisch." In *Slavisch-Litauisch, Albanisch* (Grundriß der indogermanischen Sprach- und Altertumskunde, 3), vol. 3 of *Die Erforschung der indogermanischen Sprachen*, sec. 2 of *Geschichte der indogermanischen Sprachwissenschaft* (ed. Wilhelm Streitberg). Strassburg: Trübner, 3–107.

Brugmann, Karl. 1916. *Vergleichende Laut-, Stammbildungs- und Flexionslehre nebst Lehre vom Gebrauch der Wortformen der indogermanischen Sprachen.* Vols. 1–2 of *Grundriß der vergleichenden Grammatik der indogermanischen Sprachen*, by Karl Brugmann and Berthold Delbrück. 2d ed. Strassburg: Trübner. Reprint, Berlin, 1967.

Bubrix, D. V. 1922. "Severokašubskaja sistema udarenij." *Izvestija Otdelenija russkogo jazyka i slovesnosti Rossijskoj Akademii nauk* 25:1–194.

Bubrix [Bubrich], D. 1926a. "Du système d'accentuation en slave commun." *RESl* 6:175–215.

Bubrix, D. V. 1926b. "O jazykovyx sledax finskix tevtonov-Čudi." *Jazyk i literatura* 1, nos. 1–2: 53–92.

Bubrix, D. V. 1927. "Nochmals über die Akzentlehre von A. Belić." *Zeitschrift für slavische Philologie* 4:369–75.

Bubrix, D. V. 1930. *Zvuki i formy erzjanskoj reči po govoru s. Kozlovki (Kozlovsk. r. Avt. Mord. obl.).* Moscow: Centr izd. narodov SSSR.

Bubrix, D. V. 1932. "O vzaimootnošenijax russkogo i finskix jazykov"/"Rapports de la langue russe et des langues finnoises." In *Sborník prací I. Sjezdu Slovanských Filologů v Praze 1929/ Recueil des travaux du Iᵉʳ congrès des philologues slaves à Praha en 1929*, vol. 2, *Přednášky/ Conférences*, ed. Jiří Horák et al., 454–57/969–72. Prague: n.p.

Bühler, Karl. 1927. *Die Krise der Psychologie.* Jena: Fischer. 2d ed., 1929.

Bühler, Karl. 1928. "Die Symbolik der Sprache." *Kant-Studien* 33:405–9.

Bühler, Karl. 1931. "Phonetik und Phonologie." In *TCLP* 4, 22–25.

Bühler, Karl. 1933. "Die Axiomatik der Sprachwissenschaften." *Kant-Studien* 38:19–90.

Bühler, Karl. 1934. *Sprachtheorie: Die Darstellungsfunktion der Sprache.* Jena: Fischer.

Bühler, K[arl]. 1936. "Psychologie der Phoneme." In *Proceedings London*, 162–69.

Černyšev, V. 1902. "Kak proizošla mena *c* i *č* v russkix govorax? (Vopros lingvistam)." *Russkij filologičeskij vestnik* 47:117–18.

Courant, Maurice A. L. M. 1914. *La langue chinoise parlée: Grammaire du kwan-hwa septentrional.* Paris: Leroux.

Čyževśky, D. 1931. "Phonologic und Psychologie." In *TCLP* 4, 3–22.

De Groot, A. W. 1933. Untitled response to the topic "Les systèmes phonologiques envisagés en eux-mêmes et dans leurs rapports avec la structure générale de la langue" proposed to congress participants. In *Actes du Deuxième Congrès International de Linguistes, Genève, 25–29 août 1931.* Paris: Maisonneuve, 112–14.

Dumézil, Georges. 1932. *Études comparatives sur les langues caucasiennes du nord-ouest (morphologie).* Paris: Maisonneuve.

Dumézil, Georges. 1933. *Recherches comparatives sur le verbe caucasien.* Paris: Champion.

Durnovo, Nikolai. 1918. *Dialektologičeskie razyskanija v oblasti velikorusskix govorov.* Pt. 1, *Iužnovelikorusskoe narečie.* No. 2. Trudy Moskovskoi Dialektologičeskoi Komissii, 7. [Moscow:] n.p.

Durnovo, Nicolas [Nikolai]. 1924a. "La catégorie du genre en russe moderne." *RESl* 4:208–21.

Durnovo, Nikolai. 1924b. *Očerk istorii russkogo jazyka.* Moscow and Leningrad: Gosudarstvennoe izdatel'stvo. Reprint (Slavistic Printings and Reprintings, 22), 's Gravenhage: Mouton, 1959.

Durnovo, Nicolas [Nikolai]. 1926. "Le traitement de *sk dans les langues slaves." *RESl* 6:216–23.

Durnovo, Nikolaj [Nikolai]. 1929. "Mysli i predpoloženija o proisxoždenii staroslavianskogo jazyka i slavianskix alfavitov." *Byzantinoslavica* 1:48–85. Includes a summary in French.

Durnovo, N. N., N. N. Sokolov, and D. N. Ušakov. 1915. *Opyt dialektologičeskoj karty russkogo jazyka.* Trudy Moskovskoj Dialektologičeskoj Komissii, 5. N.p.: n.p.

Endzelin [Endzelins], J. 1899. "Über den lettischen silbenaccent." *Beiträge zur Kunde der indogermanischen Sprachen* 25:259–77.

Endzelins, Janis. 1911. *Slavjano-baltijskie etjudy.* Xar'kov: Tipografija M. Zibergera.

Ettmayer, Karl von. 1937. "Das Phonem im Sprachunterricht." *Germanisch-Romanische Monatsschrift* 25:381–89.

Evsev'ev, M. E. 1929. *Osnovy mordovskoj grammatiki.* Moscow: Centrizdat narodov SSSR. Reprinted in vol. 4 of his *Izbrannye trudy* (Saransk: Mordovskoe knižnoe izdatel'stvo, 1963).

Firth, John R. 1934. "Linguistics and the Functional Point of View." *English Studies* 16:18–24.

Forchhammer, Jörgen [Jørgen]. 1924. *Die Grundlage der Phonetik: Ein Versuch, die phonetische Wissenschaft auf fester sprachphysiologischer Grundlage aufzubauen.* Indogermanische Bibliothek, sec. 3, vol. 6. Heidelberg: Winter.

Fortunatov, F. F. 1895. "Ob udarenii i dolgote v baltijskix jazykax." *Russkij filologičeskij vestnik* 33:252–97. Translated into German by Felix Solmsen as "Ueber accent und länge in den baltischen sprachen," *Beiträge zur Kunde der indogermanischen Sprachen* 22 (1897): 153–88. The announced continuation did not appear.

Fortunatov, F. F. 1913. "O proisxoždenii glagolicy." *IORJAS* 18, no. 1:221–56.

Gebauer, Jan. 1894–1929. *Historická mluvnice jazyka českého.* Prague and Vienna: Nákladem F. Temského.

Havránek, Boh[umil]. 1933. "Zur phonologischen Geographie (Das Vokalsystem des balkanischen Sprachbundes)." In *Proceedings Amsterdam,* 119–25.

Hermann, Eduard. 1932. "Phonologische Mehrdeutigkeit eines Lautes." *Philologische Wochenschrift* 52:115–18.

Hirt, Hermann. 1892. "Vom schleifenden und gestossenen Ton in den indogermanischen Sprachen." *I F* 1:1–42, 194–96.

Hjelmslev, Louis. 1936. "On the Principles of Phonematics." In *Proceedings London,* 49–54.

Hjelmslev, Louis. 1937. "Accent, intonation, quantité." *Studi Baltici* 6:1–57.

Hraste, M. 1926–27. "Crtice o bruškom dialektu." *Južnoslovenski filolog* 6:180–214.

Immisch, Otto. 1912. "Sprach- und stilgeschichtliche Parallelen zwischen Griechisch und Lateinisch." *Neue Jahrbücher für das Klassische Altertum, Geschichte und Deutsche Literatur und für Pädagogik* 29:27–49.

Ivšić, Stjepan. 1912. "Akcenat u gramatici Ignata Alojzije Brlića." *Rad Jugoslavenske Akademije Znanosti i Umjetnosti* 194:61–155. Reprinted in his *Izabrana djela iz slavenske akcentuacije (Gesammelte Schriften zum slavischen Akzent): Mit einer Einleitung sowie Berichtigungen und Ergänzungen des Verfassers herausgegeben von Christiaan Alphonsus van den Berk,* Slavische Propyläen, 96 (München: Fink, 1971), 545–64.

Jakobson, Roman. 1923. *O češskom stixe, preimuščestvenno v sopostavlenii s russkim.* Sborniki po teorii poetičeskogo iazyka, 5. Berlin: OPOIAZ-MLK. Translated in abridged and revised form into Czech as Jakobson 1926b. Reprinted, with an English translation of the 1926 foreword, in Jakobson 1979, 3–130.

Jakobson, Roman. 1926a. Review of František Trávníček 1924. *Slavia* 4:805–16. Translated into English as "Contributions to the Study of Czech Accent" in Jakobson 1971, 614–25.

Jakobson, Roman. 1926b. *Základy českého verše.* Praha: Odeon.

Jakobson, Roman. 1929. *Remarques sur l'evolution phonologique du russe, comparée à celle des autres langues slaves.* Travaux du Cercle Linguistique de Prague, 2. Prague: Jednota Československých matematiků a fysiků. Reprint, Nendeln: Kraus, 1968. Also reprinted in Jakobson 1962, 7–116.

Jakobson, Roman. 1931a. "Die Betonung und ihre Rolle in der Wort- und Syntagmaphonologie." In *TCLP* 4. Reprinted in Jakobson 1971, 117–36.

Jakobson, Roman. 1931b. "Prinzipien der historischen Phonologie." In *TCLP* 4, 247–67. Reprinted in French in Jakobson 1962, 202–20 and in English in Jakobson 1990, 184–201.

Jakobson, Roman. 1932. "Zur Struktur des russischen Verbums." In *CGM,* 74–84. Reprinted in Jakobson 1971, 3–15. Translated into English as "Structure of the Russian Verb," in his *Russian and Slavic Grammar: Studies, 1931–1981,* ed. Linda R. Waugh and Morris Halle (Berlin: Mouton, 1984), 1–14.

Jakobson, Roman. 1935. "Český verš před tisíci lety." *Slovo a slovesnost* 1:50–53. Translated into English as "Czech Verse of a Thousand Years Ago" in Jakobson 1985, 347–54.

Jakobson, Roman. 1936. "Beitrag zur allgemeinen Kasuslehre." In *TCLP* 6, 240–88.

Jakobson, Roman. 1937. "Spornyj vopros drevnerusskogo pravopisanija (*dъžg´, dъžč´*)." In *Zbornik lingvističkix i filološkix rasprava A. Beliću*. Belgrade: Mlada Srbija 39–45. Reprinted in Jakobson 1962, 247–53.

Jakobson, Roman. 1962. *Selected Writings*. Vol. 1, *Phonological Studies*. The Hague: Mouton. 2d, expanded ed., The Hague: Mouton, 1971.

Jakobson, Roman. 1971. *Selected Writings*. Vol. 2, *Word and Language*. The Hague, Paris: Mouton.

Jakobson, Roman. 1979. *Selected Writings*. Vol. 5, *On Verse, Its Masters and Explorers*. Prepared for publication by Stephen Rudy and Martha Taylor. The Hague: Mouton.

Jakobson, Roman. 1985. *Selected Writings*. Vol. 6, *Early Slavic Paths and Crossroads*. Edited, with a preface, by Stephen Rudy. 2 pts. The Hague: Mouton.

Jakobson, Roman. 1990. *On Language*. Edited by Linda R. Waugh and Monique Monville-Burston. Cambridge, Mass.: Harvard University Press.

Jakovlev, N. F. 1928a. "Matematičeskaja formula postroenija alfavita." In *Kul'tura i pis'mennost' Vostoka*, vol. 1. Moscow: Central'noe izdatel'stvo narodov SSSR, 41–64.

Jakovlev, N. F. 1928b. "Razvitie nacional'noj pis'mennosti u vostočnyx narodov Sovetskogo Sojuza i zaroždenie ix nacional'nyx alfavitov." *Revoljucionnyi Vostok* 3:206–34.

Jespersen, Otto. 1904. *Lehrbuch der Phonetik*. Leipzig: Teubner.

Jones, Daniel. 1931. "On Phonemes." In *TCLP* 4, 74–79.

Juret, [Abel]. 1922. "Essai d'explication de la transformation des voyelles latines accentuées *ẹ, ọ, a* en roman *ie, uo, é*." *BSL* 23:138–55.

Karcevski [Karcevskij], Serge. 1927. *Système du verbe russe: Essai de linguistique synchronique*. Prague: Plamja.

Karcevskij, Serge. 1931. "Sur la phonologie de la phrase." In *TCLP* 4, 188–227.

Karcevski [Karcevskij], Serge. 1933. Untitled response to the topic "Les systèmes phonologiques envisagés en eux-mêmes et dans leurs rapports avec la structure générale de la langue" proposed to congress participants. In *Actes du Deuxième Congrès International de Linguistes, Genève, 25–29 août 1931*. Paris: Maisonneuve, 114–16.

Karinskij, N. M. 1909. *Jazyk Pskova i ego oblasti v XV veke*. St. Petersburg: Tipografija M. A. Aleksandrova.

Karlgren, Bernhard. 1915–26. *Études sur la phonologie chinoise*. Archives d'études orientales, 15. Leiden: Brill; Stockholm: Norstedt. Pages 1–388 also issued as the author's thesis (Upsala: Appelberg, 1915).

Koneczna, Halina. 1933. "Einige Erscheinungen des Sandhi in der polnischen Sprache." In *Proceedings Amsterdam*, 262–65.

Kořínek, Jozef M. 1934. *Studie z oblasti onomatopoje: Příspěvek k otázce indoevropského ablautu (une contribution à l'étude des alternances vocaliques en indo-européen)*. Nákl. Filosofické fakulty University Karlovy. Práce z vědeckých ústavů, 36. Prague.

Korš, F. 1896–97. "O russkom narodnom stixosloženii." *IORJAS* 1, no. 1 (1896): 1–47; 2, no. 2 (1897): 429–504.

Korš, F. 1907a. "Proisxožděnie desjatisložnogo stixa južnyx i zapadnyx slavjan." In *Sbornik statei, posviaščennyx V. I. Lamanskomu*. St. Petersburg: n.p., 482–97.

Korš, F. 1907b. *Vvedenie v nauku o slavjanskom stixosloženii*. Otdel'nyj ottisk iz "Sbornika po slavjanovedeniju," 2. St. Petersburg: Tipografija Imperatorskoj Akademii nauk.

Kreinovič, E. A. 1934. "Nivxskij (giljackij) jazyk." In pt. 3 of *Jazyki i pis'mennost' narodov Severa* (Naučno-issledovatel'skaja associacija Instituta narodov Severa CIK SSSR: Trudy po lingvistike, vol. 3). Moscow and Leningrad: Gosudarstvennoe učebno-pedagogičeskoe izdatel'stvo, 181–228.

Kretschmer, Paul. 1896. *Einleitung in die Geschichte der griechischen Sprache.* Göttingen: Vandenhoeck & Ruprecht.

Kretschmer, Paul. 1905. "Die slavische Vertretung von indogerm. *o.*" *Archiv für slavische Philologie* 27:228–40.

Kul'bakin, S. M. 1921. "L'œuvre de A. A. Šachmatov." *RESl* 1:144–52.

Kul'bakin, St. M. 1935. "Beleške o Xrabrovoi apologiji." In *Srpska Kral'evska akademija nauk i umetnosti,* vol. 168. Filosofsko-filološke, društvene i istoriske nauke, vol. 86, no. 2. Belgrade, 43–77.

Kul'bakin, S. [M.] 1937. Review of "Die Aussprache des griechischen χ i[m] 9. Jahrhundert n. Chr.," by N. Trubetzkoy (*Glotta* 25 [1936]: 248–58). *Južnoslovenski filolog* 16:223–24.

Kuryłowicz, Jerzy. 1931. "Le problème des intonations balto-slaves." *Rocznik slawistyczny* 10: 1–80.

Laziczius, Julius von. 1936a. "A New Category in Phonology." In *Proceedings London* 57–60.

Laziczius, Julius von. 1936b. "Probleme der Phonologie: Zeichenlehre—Elementenlehre." *Ungarische Jahrbücher* 15:495–510.

Lehr [Lehr-Spławiński], Tadeusz. 1917. *Ze studjów nad akcentem słowiańskim.* Prace Komisji Językowej Akademji Umiejętności w Krakowie, 1. W Krakowie: Nakładem Akademji Umiejętności.

Lehr-Spławiński, Tadeusz. 1921–22. "Stosunki pokrewieństwa języków ruskich." *Rocznik slawistyczny* 9:23–71.

Lehr-Spławiński, Tadeusz. 1923. "De la stabilisation de l'accent dans les langues slaves de l'ouest." *RESl* 3:173–92.

Lehr-Spławiński, Tadeusz. 1931. "O t. zw. 'przestawce płynnych' w językach słowiańskich." *Rocznik sławistyczny* 10:116–37.

Lehr-Spławiński, Tadeusz. 1932. "Zur Betonung im Polabischen." In *Mélanges de philologie offerts à M. J. J. Mikkola à l'occasion de son soixante-cinquième anniversaire le 6 juillet 1931 par ses amis et ses élèves.* Suomalaisen Tiedeakatemian Toimituksia/Annales Academiæ Scientiarum Fennicæ, B.27. Helsinki: Suomalaisen Tiedeakatemia, 108–13.

Lehr-Spławiński, Tadeusz. 1933. *Gramatyka polabska.* Lwowska bibljoteka slawistyczna, vol. 8. Lwow: K. S. Jakubowski.

Lekov", Ivan". 1937. "Novi nasoki v" suvremennoto ezikoznanie." *Filosofski pregled"* 9:162–71.

Liewehr, Ferd[inand]. 1929. "Ein Beitrag zur tschech.-deutschen Lehnwörterkunde (im Anschlusse an Mayers Schrift "Die deutschen Lehnwörter im Tschechischen"). (Fortsetzung)." *Slawistische Schulblätter* 3:24–26.

Lowman, G. S. 1932. "The Phonetics of Albanian." *Language* 8:271–93.

Marr, N. [Ja.] 1924. "Ob jafetičeskoj teorii." *Novyj Vostok* 5:303–39.

Martinet, André. 1937a. *La gémination consonantique d'origine expressive dans les langues germaniques.* Copenhague: Levin & Munksgaard; Paris: Klincksieck.

Martinet, André. 1937b. "La phonologie du mot en danois." *BSL* 38:169–266.

Mathesius, Vilém. 1929a. "On the Phonological System of Modern English." In *Donum Natalicium Schrijnen 3. Mei 1929.* Nijmegen: Dekker & Van de Gegt, 46–53.

Mathesius, Vilém. 1929b. "Ziele und Aufgaben der vergleichenden Phonologie." In *Xenia pragensia Ernesto Kraus septuagenario et Josepho Janko sexagenario ab amicis collegis discipulis oblata.* Pragae: Sumptibus Societatis Neophilologorum apud Societatem Mathematicorum et Physicorum, 432–45.

Mathesius, Vilém. 1931. "Zum Problem der Belastungs- und Kombinationsfähigkeit der Phoneme." In *TCLP* 4, 148–52.

Mathesius, V[ilém]. 1933. "La place de la linguistique fonctionelle et structurale dans le développement général des études linguistiques." In *Actes du Deuxième Congrès International de Linguistes, Genève, 25–29 août 1931.* Paris: Maisonneuve, 145–46.

Mazon, A. 1927. "Le passage de *g* à *h* d'après quelques gloses judéo-tchèques." *RESl* 7:261–67.

Mazon, André. 1930. "Chronique: Publications: Russe." *RESl* 10:103–20.

Mazon, André. 1935a. "Chronique: Publications: Russe." *RESl* 15:97–122.

Mazon, André. 1935b. "Chronique: Publications: Slovaque." *RESl* 15:277–79.

Meillet, Antoine. 1896. "Varia." *MSL* 9:136–59.

Meillet, Antoine. 1902–5. *Études sur l'étymologie et le vocabulaire du vieux slave.* Bibliothèque de l'École des hautes études . . . , Sciences historiques et philologiques, 139. Paris: Bouillon.

Meillet, Antoine. 1908–9a. "Quelques formes verbales slaves." *MSL* 15:32–39.

Meillet, Antoine. 1908–9b. "Sur la quantité des voyelles fermées." *MSL* 15:265–68.

Meillet, Antoine. 1913a. *Aperçu d'une histoire de la langue grecque.* Paris: Hachette.

Meillet, Antoine. 1913b. "Le désinence -tŭ du vieux slave." *MSL* 18:232–38.

Meillet, Antoine. 1922a. "L'emploi du duel chez Homère et l'élimination du duel." *MSL* 22: 145–64.

Meillet, Antoine. 1922b. *Introduction à l'étude comparative des langues indo-européennes.* 5th ed. Paris: Hachette.

Meillet, Antoine. 1931. Review of *Travaux du Cercle Linguistique de Prague,* 1–2. *BSL* 31, no. 3: 18–20.

Meriggi, P. 1934. Review of *Proceedings Amsterdam. IF* 52:65–66.

Mikkola, J. J. 1894. *Berührungen zwischen den westfinnischen und slavischen Sprachen.* Suomalais Ugrilaisen Seuran Toimituksia/Mémoires de la Société Finno-Ougrienne, 8. Helsingfors: Druckerei der Finnischen Litteraturgesellschaft.

Mucke, Karl E. 1891. *Historische und vergleichende laut- und formenlehre der niedersorbischen (niederlausitzisch-wendischen) sprache, mit besonderer berücksichtigung der grenzdialecte und des obersorbischen.* Preisschriften gekrönt und herausgegeben von der Fürstlich Jablonowski'schen Gesellschaft zu Leipzig, Nr. 18 der historisch-nationalökonomischen Section. Leipzig: Hirzel. Reprint, Leipzig: Zentral-Antiquariat der Deutschen Demokratischen Republik, 1965.

Nahtigal, Raiko. 1923. "Doneski k vprašanju o postanku glagolice." *Znanstveno društvo za humanistične vede v Ljubljani* 1:135–76.

Nemirovskij, M. Ja. 1928. *Jazyk i kul'tura; k uvjazke lingvistiki s obščestvennymi naukami (Posvjaščaetsja N. Ja. Marru k 40-letiju ego naučnoj dejatel'nosti).* Izvestija Gorskogo Pedagogičeskogo Instituta, vol. 5, Otdel "pedagogičeskij i obščestvenno-istoričeskij." Vladikavkaz: n.p., 109–57

Nitsch, K. 1931. "Polskie 'chy, chi' i 'hy, hi'." *Sprawozdania z czynności i posiedzeń Polskiej Akademji Umiejętności* 36, no. 3:5–9.

Novák, L'udovít. 1930. "Zmena *g > h* v slovenčine." *Sborník matice slovenskej* 8:7–26.

Novák, L'udovit. 1932. "De la phonologie historique romane: La quantité et l'accent." In *CGM,* 45–47.

Osthoff, Hermann. 1881. *Die tiefstufe im indogermanischen vocalismus.* Pt. 4 of *Morphologische Untersuchungen auf dem Gebiete der indogermanischen Sprachen,* by Hermann Osthoff and Karl Brugmann. Leipzig: Hirzel.

Paasonen, H[eikki]. 1910. "Über den versbau des mordwinischen volksliedes." *Finnisch-Ugrische Forschungen* 10:153–92.

Paul, Hermann. 1960. *Prinzipien der Sprachgeschichte.* 6th unchanged edition. Tübingen: Niemeyer. Translated into English by Herbert August Strong as *Principles of the History of Language* (London: Longmans, Green, 1888; reprint, College Park, Md.: McGrath, 1970).

Pedersen, Holger. 1923. "Runernes oprindelse." *Aarbøger for Nordisk Oldkyndighed og Historie,* 3d ser., 13:37–82.

Pfalz, Anton. 1912. *Die Mundart des Marchfeldes.* Deutsche Mundarten, 4. Sitzungsberichte der Kais[erlichen] Akademie der Wissenschaften in Wien, Philosophisch-Historische Klasse, vol. 170, no. 6. Wien: Holder.

Pfalz, Anton. 1936. "Zur Phonologie der bairisch-österreichischen Mundart." In *Lebendiges Erbe—Festschrift aus dem Kreise der Mitarbeiter an der Monumentalsammlung "Deutsche Literatur" zum 60. Geburtstage ihres Verlegers Dr. Ernst Reclam.* Leipzig: Verlag von Philipp Reclam jun. 9–19.

Polivanov, E. D. 1928. *Vvedenie v jazykoznanie dlja vostokovednyx vuzov.* Vol. 1. Leningrad: Leningradskij vostokovednyi institut im. A. S. Enukidze.

Polivanov, E. D., and N. Popov-Tativa. 1928. *Posobie po kitajskoj transkripcii.* Moscow: Izd. Kommunističeskogo universiteta trudiaščixsia Vostoka.

Pos, H. J. 1933. "Quelques perspectives philosophiques de la phonologie." In *Proceedings Amsterdam,* 226–30.

"Projet de terminologie phonologique standardisée." 1931. In *TCLP* 4, 309–22.

Ravila, Paavo. 1932a. "Zum Einfluss des Russischen auf das Mordwinische." In *Mélanges de philologie offerts à M. J. J. Mikkola à l'occasion de son soixante-cinquième anniversaire le 6 juillet 1931 par ses amis et ses élèves.* Suomalaisen Tiedeakatemian Toimituksia/Annales Academiæ Scientiarum Fennicæ, B.27. Helsinki: Soumalaisen Tiedeakatemia, 252–62.

Ravila, Paavo. 1932b. *Das Quantitätssystem des seelappischen Dialekts von Maattivuono.* Helsinki: Suomalais-ugrilainen seura.

Rogger, Kaspar. 1934. *Vom Wesen des Lautwandels.* Leipziger romanistische Studien, 1. Sprachwissenschaftliche Reihe, 6. Leipzig: Selbstverlag des Romanischen Seminars.

Ronjat, Jules. 1924. "Accent, quantité et diphtongaison en roman et ailleurs." *BSL* 24:356–77.

Rozwadowski, Jan. 1915. *Historyczna fonetyka czyli głosownia języka polskiego. Język polski i jego historya, z uwzględnieniem innych języków na ziemiach polskich.* Vol. 1 (= *Encyklopedya polska,* vol. 2). Warsaw: Nakładem Akademii Umiejętności, 289–422.

Ružičić, G. 1932. "Le čakavo-kajkavien *j* pour le slave *dj.*" In *CGM,* 39–41.

Šafařík, Pavel Josef. 1853. *Památky hlaholského písemnictví.* Prague: Haase.

Sapir, Edward. 1921. *Language: An Introduction to the Study of Speech.* New York: Harcourt, Brace.

Sapir, Edward. 1931. "Notes on the Gweabo Language of Liberia." *Language* 7:30–41.

Sapir, Edward. 1933. "La réalité psychologique des phonèmes." *Journal de psychologie* 30:247–65.

Šaraf, G. 1927. "Paljatogrammy zvukov tatarskogo jazyka sravnitel'no s russkim." *Vestnik naučnogo obščestva tatarovedenija* (Kazan') 7:65–102.

Šaxmatov, A. A. 1903. Review of *Die serbokroatische Betonung südwestlicher Mundarten,* by M. Resetar. *IORJAS* 6, no. 1:339–53.

Šaxmatov, A. A. 1915. *Očerk drevnejšego perioda istorii russkogo jazyka.* Enciklopedija slavjanskoi filologii, vol. 11, pt. 1. Petrograd: Izdanie Otdelenija russkogo jazyka i slovesnosti Imperatorskoj Akademii nauk.

Schleicher, August. 1861–62. *Compendium der vergleichenden Grammatik der indogermanischen Sprachen.* Weimar: Böhlau. 2d ed., 1866; 3d ed., 1871; 4th ed. 1876 (Weimar: Böhlau). Translated into English by Herbert Bendall as *A Compendium of the Comparative Grammar of the Indo-European, Sanskrit, Greek, and Latin Languages* (London: Trübner, 1874–77).

Schmidt, Johannes. 1872. *Die Verwandtschaftsverhältnisse der indogermanischen Sprachen.* Weimar: Böhlau.

Schmidt, P. 1899. *Trojakaja dolgota v latyšskom jazyke. SORJAS,* vol. 67, no. 2. St. Petersburg: Tipografija Imperatorskoj Akademii nauk.

Schmidt, Wilhelm. 1921. *Die Sprachfamilien und Sprachkreise der Erde.* Heidelberg: Winter.

Schmidt-Wartenberg, H. 1899. "Phonetische Untersuchungen zum lettischen Akzent." *IF* 10: 117–44.

Schmitt, A[lfred]. 1936. "Die Schallgebärden der Sprache." *Wörter und Sachen* 17:57–98.

Schwab, E. 1925. "Zum Übergang von g zu h im Čechischen." *Archiv für slavische Philologie* 39: 293–96.

Schwarz, Ernst. 1934. "Jazyk německý na území ČSR." *Československá vlastivěda* 3:524–98.

Sechehaye, A. 1933. Untitled response to the topic "Les systèmes phonologiques envisagés en eux-mêmes et dans leurs rapports avec la structure générale de la langue" proposed to congress participants. In *Actes du Deuxième Congrès International de Linguistes, Genève, 25–29 août 1931.* Paris: Maisonneuve, 118–20.

Setälä, E. N. 1912. "Über Art, Umfang und Alter des Stufenwechsels im Finnisch-Ugrischen und Samojedischen." *Anzeiger der Finnisch-Ugrischen Forschungen* 12:1–128.

Sievers, Eduard. 1926. *Das Igorlied metrisch und sprachlich bearbeitet.* Berichte über die Verhandlungen der Sächsischen Akademie der Wissenschaften zu Leipzig, Philologisch-Historische Klasse, vol. 78, no. 1. Leipzig: Hirzel.

Šklovskij, V. B. 1933. *Čulkov i Levšin.* [Leningrad:] Izd[atel'st]vo pisatelej v Leningrade.

Sobolevskij, A. I. 1909. "Važnaja osobennost' starogo pskovskogo govora." *Russkij filologičeskij vestnik* 62:231–34.

Sommerfelt, Alf. 1936. "Can Syllable Divisions Have Phonological Importance?" In *Proceedings London,* 30–33.

Sommerfelt, Alf. 1938a. "Études comparatives sur le caucasique du Nord-Est." *Norsk Tidsskrift for Sprogvidenskap* 9:115–43.

Sommerfelt, Alf. 1938b. *La langue et la société: Caractères sociaux d'une langue de type archaïque.* Oslo: Aschehoug; Cambridge, Mass.: Harvard University Press.

Stanislav, Ján. 1933. "Datív absolutny v starej cirkevnej slovančine." *Byzantinoslavica* 5:1–112. A French summary, "Le datif absolu dans le vieux slave," appears on pp. 98–106.

Starčević, Šimo. 1812. *Nova ricsoslovica iliricska, vojnicskoj mladosti krajicsnoj poklonjena trúdom i nástojànijem Shime Starcsevicha xupnika od novoga u líci.* U Tarstu: Slovima Gaspara Weis.

Stetson, Raymond H. 1936. "The Relation of the Phoneme and the Syllable." In *Proceedings London,* 245–52.

Stevanović, Mixailo S. 1933–34. "Istočnocrnogorski dijalekat." *Južnoslovenski filolog* 13:1–129.

Streitberg, Wilhelm. 1896. *Urgermanische Grammatik: Einführung in das vergleichende Studium der altgermanischen Dialekte.* Sammlung von Elementarbüchern der altgermanischen Dialekte, 1. Heidelberg: Winter.

Swadesh, Morris. 1935. Review of *On Defining the Phoneme,* by W. Freeman Twaddell. *Language* 11:244–50.

Thurneysen, Rudolf. 1884. "Der italokeltische conjunctiv mit â." *Beiträge zur Kunde der indogermanischen Sprachen* 8:269–88.

Thurneysen, Rudolf. 1909. *Handbuch des Alt-Irischen.* Indogermanische Bibliothek, Sammlung indogermanischer Lehr- und Handbücher, ser. 1, vol. 6. Heidelberg: Winter. Translated into English by D. A. Binchy and Osborne Bergin as *A Grammar of Old Irish*, rev. and enlarged ed. (Dublin: Dublin Institute for Advanced Studies, 1946).

Trager, George L. 1933. *The Old Church Slavonic Kiev Fragment: Its Accents and Their Relation to Modern Slavonic Accentuation*. Language Monographs Published by the Linguistic Society of America, 13. Baltimore: Linguistic Society of America.

Trávníček, František. 1921. "De la quantité en tchèque." *RESl* 1:204-27.

Trávníček, František. 1924. *Příspěvky k nauce o českém přízvuku*. Spisy filosofické fakulty Masarykovy university v Brně, vol. 7. Brno: Alniv.

Trávníček, František. 1927. *Příspěvky k dějinám českého jazyka*. Spisy filosofické fakulty Masarykovy university v Brně, 19. Brno: Filosofická fakulta s podporou Ministerstva školství a národní osvěty v Komisi knihkupectví A. Píša.

Trittel, Walter. 1930. *Einführung in das Siamesische*. Lehrbücher des Seminars für Orientalische Sprachen zu Berlin, 34. Berlin: de Gruyter.

Trnka, Bohumil. 1930. *On the Syntax of the English Verb from Caxton to Dryden*. Travaux du Cercle Linguistique de Prague, 3. Prague: Jednota Československých matematiků a fysiků.

Trnka, Bohumil. 1935a. "O definici fonématu." *Slovo a slovesnost* 1:238-40.

Trnka, Bohumil. 1935b. *A Phonological Analysis of Standard English*. Příspěvky k dějinam řeči a literatury anglické od členů Anglického semináře při Universitě Karlově, 5. Filosofická fakulta University Kárlovy: Práce z vědeckých ústavů, 37. Prague. Rev. ed., ed. Tetsuya Kanekiyo and Tamotsu Koizumo (Tokyo: Hokuoku, 1966). Rev. ed. reprinted as Alabama Linguistic and Philological Series, 17 (University of Alabama Press, 1968).

Trnka, Bohumil. 1936. "On the Phonological Development of Spirants in English." In *Proceedings London*, 60-64.

Trubetzkoy, N. S. 1921. "De la valeur primitive des intonations du slave commun." *RESl* 1:171-87. Chapter 19 in this volume.

Trubetzkoy, N. S. 1922. "Les consonnes latérales des langues caucasiques-septentrionales." *BSL* 23:184-204.

Trubetzkoy, N. S. 1924. "Zum urslavischen Intonationssystem." In *Streitberg-Festgabe*. Herausgegeben von der Direktion der Vereinigten Sprachwissenschaftlichen Institute an der Universität zu Leipzig. Leipzig: Market & Petters, 359-66. Chapter 20 in this volume.

Trubetzkoy, N. S. 1925. "Einiges über die russische Lautentwicklung und die Auflösung der gemeinrussischen Spracheinheit." *Zeitschrift für slavische Philologie* 1:287-319. Chapter 17 in this volume.

Trubetzkoy, N. S. 1926. "Studien auf dem Gebiete der vergleichenden Lautlehre der nordkaukasischen Sprachen." *Caucasica* 3:7-36.

Trubetzkoy, N. S. 1927-28. "Ob otraženijax obščeslavjanskogo ę v češskom jazyke." *Slavia* 6: 661-84.

Trubetzkoy, N. S. 1929a. *Polabische Studien*. Sitzungsberichte der Akademie der Wissenschaften in Wien, philos.-hist. Klasse, vol. 211, no. 4. Wien: Hölder-Pichler-Tempsky.

Trubetzkoy, N. S. 1929b. "Sur la 'morphonologie.'" In *TCLP* 1, 85-88. Translated into Japanese by Hisanosuke Izui as "Keitai-on'ingaku ni tsuite," *Hōgen* 7 (1937): 242-46. Chapter 10 in this volume.

Trubetzkoy, N. S. 1929c. "Zur allgemeinen Theorie der phonologischen Vokalsysteme." In *TCLP* 1, 39-67.

Trubetzkoy, N. S. 1930. "Über die Entstehung der gemeinwestslawischen Eigentümlichkeiten auf dem Gebiete des Konsonantismus." *Zeitschrift für slavische Philologie* 7:383-406.

Trubetzkoy, N. S. 1930–31. Review of *Gramatyka polabska*, by T. Lehr-Spławiński. *Slavia* 9:154–64.

Trubetzkoy, N. S. 1931a. "Gedanken über Morphonologie." In *TCLP* 4, 160–63. Chapter 11 in this volume.

Trubetzkoy, N. S. 1931b. "Die Konsonantensysteme der ostkaukasischen Sprachen." *Caucasica* 8:1–52.

Trubetzkoy, N. S. 1931c. "Phonologie und Sprachgeographie." In *TCLP* 4, 228–34. Chapter 6 in this volume.

Trubetzkoy, N. S. 1931d. "Die phonologischen Systeme." In *TCLP* 4, 96–116.

Trubetzkoy, N. S. 1932. "Das mordwinische phonologische System verglichen mit dem russischen." In *CGM*, 21–24. Chapter 25 in this volume.

Trubetzkoy, N. S. 1933. "La phonologie actuelle." *Journal de psychologie normale et pathologique* 30:227–46. Translated into Japanese by Hideo Kobayashi as "Gendai no on'inron," *Onseigaku kyōkai kaihō* 43 (1936): 1–7; 44 (1936): 8–11.

Trubetzkoy, N. S. 1934. Review of *Études comparatives sur les langues caucasiennes du nord-ouest* and *Recherches comparatives sur le verbe caucasien*, both by Georges Dumézil. *Orientalistische Literaturzeitung* 37:629–35.

Trubetzkoy, N. [S.] 1935. *Anleitung zu phonologischen Beschreibungen*. Association internationale pour les études phonologiques. Brno: Édition du Cercle Linguistique de Prague. Reprinted as vol. 2 of the series Lautbibliothek der deutschen Mundarten (Göttingen: Vandenhoeck & Ruprecht, 1958). Translated into English by L. A. Murray as *Introduction to the Principles of Phonological Descriptions*, ed. H[ermann] Bluhme (The Hague: Nijhoff, 1968). Translated into Japanese by Hisanosuke Izui as "On'in wa ikani kijutsu subekika," *Hōgen* 6 (1936): 547–74.

Trubetzkoy, N. S. 1936a. "Die altkirchenslavische Vertretung der urslav. *tj, *dj.*" *Zeitschrift für slavische Philologie* 13:88–97.

Trubetzkoy, N. S. 1936b. "Essai d'une théorie des oppositions phonologiques." *Journal de psychologie normale et pathologique* 33:5–18. Chapter 4 in this volume.

Trubetzkoy, N. S. 1936c. "Die phonologischen Grenzsignale." In *Proceedings London* 45–49.

Trubetzkoy, N. S. 1936d. Review of *An Introduction to the Ibo Language*, by Ida C. Ward. *Anthropos* 31:978–80.

Trubetzkoy, N. S. 1937. "Über eine neue Kritik des Phonembegriffes." *Archiv für die vergleichende Phonetik* 1:129–47. Chapter 5 in this volume.

Trubetzkoy, N. S. 1938. "Die phonologischen Grundlagen der sogenannten 'Quantität' in den verschiedenen Sprachen." In *Scritti in onore di Alfredo Trombetti*. Milan: Hoepli, 155–74. Chapter 8 in this volume.

Trubetzkoy, N. S. 1939. *Grundzüge der Phonologie*. Travaux du Cercle Linguistique de Prague, 7. Prague: n.p. Reprint, Göttingen: Vandenhoeck & Ruprecht, 1958. Translated into English by Christiane A. M. Baltaxe as *Principles of Phonology*. Berkeley: University of California Press, 1969.

Trubetzkoy, N. S. 1950. *The Common Slavic Element in Russian Culture*. Edited by Leon Stilman. New York: Columbia University Department of Slavic Languages.

Trubetzkoy, N. S. 1954. *Altkirchenslavische Grammatik: Schrift-, Laut- und Formensystem*. Edited by Rudolf Jagoditsch. Sitzungsberichte der Österreichischen Akademie der Wissenschaften, Philosophisch-Historische Klasse, vol. 228, no. 4. Wien: Rohrer.

Trubetzkoy, N. S. 1956. *Die russischen Dichter des 18. und 19. Jahrhunderts: Abriß einer Entwick-*

lungsgeschichte. Edited by Rudolf Jagoditsch. Wiener Slavistisches Jahrbuch, additional vol. 3. Graz: Böhlau.

Trubetzkoy, N. S. 1964. *Dostoevskij als Künstler*. Slavistic Printings and Reprintings, 56. The Hague: Mouton.

Trubetzkoy, N. S. 1973. *Vorlesungen über die altrussische Literatur*. With an afterword by R. O. Jakobson. Studia historica et philologica, sectio slavica, 1. Firenze: Distr. Licosa—Commissionaria Sansoni.

Trubetzkoy, N. S. 1975. *N. S. Trubetzkoy's Letters and Notes*. Edited by Roman Jakobson et al. Janua linguarum: Series maior, 47. The Hague: Mouton.

Trubetzkoy, N. S. 1987. *Izbrannye trudy po filologii*. Moscow: Progress.

Trubetzkoy, N. S. 1988. *Opera slavica minora linguistica*. Sitzungsberichte der Österreichischen Akademie der Wissenschaften, Philosophisch-Historische Klasse, 509. Wien: Verlag der Österreichischen Akademie der Wissenschaften.

Trubetzkoy, N. S. 1990. *Writings on Literature*. Edited and translated by Anatoly Liberman. Theory and History of Literature, 72. Minneapolis: University of Minnesota Press.

Trubetzkoy, N. S. 1991. *The Legacy of Genghis-Khan and Other Essays on Russia's Identity*. Edited, and with a postscript, by Anatoly Liberman. Michigan Slavic Materials, 33. Ann Arbor: Michigan Slavic Publications.

Twaddell, W. Freeman. 1935. *On Defining the Phoneme*. Language Monographs Published by the Linguistic Society of America, 16. Baltimore: Waverly.

Uslar, P. K. 1890. *Etnografija Kavkaza. Jazykoznanie*. Vol. 4, *Lakskij Jazyk*. Izdanie Upravlenija Kavkazskogo Učebnogo Okruga. Tiflis: Tipografija Kanceljarii Glavnonačal'stvojuščego graždanskoij čast'ju na Kavkaze.

Vachek, Josef. 1932. "Daniel Jones and the Phoneme." In *CGM*, 25–33.

Vachek, Josef. 1933. "Über das phonologische Problem der Diphthonge mit besonderer Berücksichtigung des Englischen." *Práce z vědeckých ústavů filosof. fakulty Karlovy university* 33 (Studies in English by Members of the English Seminar of the Charles University, 4): 87–170.

Vachek, Josef. 1936a. "One Aspect of the Phoneme Theory." In *Proceedings London*, 33–40.

Vachek, Josef. 1936b. "Phonemes and Phonological Units." In *TCLP* 6, 235–39.

Vaillant, A., and M. Lascaris. 1933. "La date de la conversion des Bulgares." *RESl* 13:5–15.

Van Ginneken, Jacobus. 1928. *De geschiedenis der middelnederlandsche letterkunde in het licht der ethnologische literatuurwetenschap . . . : Rede, uitgesproken op den vierden geboortedag der Keizer Karel Universiteit te Nijmegen 31 Mei 1928 door den Rector-Magnificus Dr. Jac. van Ginneken S.J.* Nijmegen: N. V. Dekker & van de Vegt en J. W. van Leeuwen.

Van Ginneken, Jacobus. 1932. "La tendance labiale de la race méditerranéenne et la tendance laryngale de la race alpine." In *Proceedings Amsterdam*, 167–83.

Van Ginneken, Jacobus. 1934a. "De phonologie van het algemeen Nederlandsch." *Onze Taaltuin* 2:321–40.

Van Ginneken, Jacobus. 1934b. "Het phonologisch systeem van het algemeen Nederlandsch." *Onze Taaltuin* 2:353–65.

Van Wijk, Nicolaas. 1916. "-ę und -ě im Akk. Pl. der *jo*-Stämme und im Gen. Sg., Nom. Akk. Plur. der *jā*-Stämme." *Archiv für slavische Philologie* 36:460–64.

Van Wijk, Nicolaas. 1932. "De moderne phonologie en de omlijning van taalkategorieën." *De Nieuwe Taalgids* 26:65–75.

Van Wijk, Nicolaas. 1934. "Das altrussische Imperfekt und die russische Konsonantenerweichung." *IF* 52:32–44.

Vasil'ev, L. L. 1917. "O značenii kamory v nekotoryx drevnerusskix pamjatnikax XVI–XVII vekov (K voprosu o proiznošenii zvuka *o* v velikorusskom narečii)." *Russkij filologičeskij vestnik* 78, nos. 3–4:156–86.

Vasmer, Max. 1907. "Zwei kleine Abhandlungen." *Zeitschrift für vergleichende Sprachforschung* 41:154–64.

Vendryès, Joseph. 1902. *Recherches sur l'histoire et les effets de l'intensité initiale en latin.* Paris: Klincksieck.

Vendryès, Joseph. 1936. "Phonologie et langue poétique." In *Proceedings London,* 105–06.

Vološinov, V. N. 1929. *Marksizm i filosofija jazyka: Osnovnye problemy sociologičeskogo metoda v nauke o jazyke.* Leningrad: Priboj. 2d ed., Leningrad: Priboj, 1930. 2d ed. translated by Ladislav Matejka and I. R. Titunik as *Marxism and the Philosophy of Language* (New York: Seminar, 1973; Cambridge, Mass.: Harvard University Press, 1986).

Vondrák, Václav. 1904. *O původu Kijevských listů a Pražských zlomků a o bohemismech v starších církevněslovanských památkách vůbec.* Královská česká společnost náuk, Prague. Spisy poctěni jubilejní cenou, 15. Prague: n.p.

Vondrák, Wenzel [Václav]. 1906–8. *Vergleichende Slavische Grammatik.* Göttinger Sammlungen indogermanischer Grammatiken. 2 vols. Göttingen: Vandenhoeck & Ruprecht. 2d ed., 1924–28.

Walde, Alois. 1916. "Die italischen Sprachen." In *Griechisch, Italisch, Vulgärlatein, Keltisch.* Grundriß der indogermanischen Sprach- und Altertumskunde 1, vol. 1 of *Die Erforschung der indogermanischen Sprachen,* sec. 2 of *Geschichte der indogermanischen Sprachwissenschaft* (ed. Wilhelm Streitberg). Strassburg: Trübner, 127–230.

Ward, Ida C. 1936. *An Introduction to the Ibo Language.* Cambridge: Heffer.

Winteler, Jost. 1876. *Die Kerenzer Mundart des Kantons Glarus, in ihren Grundzügen dargestellt.* Leipzig and Heidelberg: Winter.

Žirkov, L. I. 1924. *Grammatika avarskogo jazyka.* Trudy Podrazrjada issledovanija sev[ero]-kavk[azskix] iazykov pri In[stitu]te vostokovedenija v Moskve, 3. Moscow: n.p.

Zubatý, Jos. 1910. "Výklady etymologické a lexkální." *Sborník filologický* 1:95–164.

Index

Vorarlberg, 252
Vossler, Karl, 245, 254

Walde, Alois, 201
Ward, Ida C., 78
Weber, Hugo, 51, 142
Westermann, S. D., 252
White Mountain, 185
Winteler, Jost, 254
Wisconsin, 249

Zips, 272 n.2
Žirkov, L. I., 171, 256
Žizdra, 217-18
Zubatý, Josef, 273 n.2, 275 n.12
Zwirner, Eberhard, 241, 252

Languages

Abkhaz, 81, 165-66, 176
Adyghe, 165-68, 176, 177, 276-77 nn.1-3
Africa: languages of, 54, 94, 238, 263 n.8;
    South, languages of, 66
Agul, 170-73, 176, 277 n.2
Aisorian, 186
Akhvakh, 176
Alan, 166. *See also* Ossetic
Albanian, 70, 80, 89, 131, 276 n.26; North,
    262 n.2
Aleut, 62, 63
Altaic, 85, 91-98. *See also* Uralo-Altaic
America: languages of. *See* North American
    languages
Andi, 47, 170, 173, 176, 277 n.5
Arabic, 7, 37, 45, 52, 65, 67, 80, 81, 175-77,
    195, 197
Archi, 93, 97, 170-73, 176, 236
Armenian, 64, 70, 95, 97, 106-07, 132, 165,
    168, 175, 176, 186, 207, 267 n.4; Old, 269
    n.16
Asia and Eurasia: languages of, 43, 238. *See
    also* East Asia: languages of
Asia Minor: languages of, 95
Australian aboriginal languages, 64
Avar, 45, 47, 53, 95-97, 170-73, 176, 236-37,
    277 nn.2-3
Avar-Ando, 171-74

Avestan, 149, 165-66, 168, 259 n.1. *See also*
    Iranian; Persian
Azeri, 169, 175-76, 188-89, 202. *See also* Tatar

Bagulal, 176
Balkar, 80, 166, 176
Baltic, 90, 129, 146-51, 206, 212, 227, 270 n.1
Balto-Slavic, 150-51, 270 n.1
Bantu, 67, 90, 94
Bantuoid languages, 94
Bashkir, 151
Basque, 95, 97
Bats, 170, 172-73, 176, 277 n.2
Batsbi. *See* Bats
Belorussian, 39-41, 110-11, 114-17, 119-21,
    123-24, 126, 158-59, 216-18, 269 n.14, 270
    nn.21, 23
Bengali, 64
Berber, 94-95
Bezhita, 176
Botlikh, 176
Budukh, 176
Bulgarian, 53, 70, 80-81, 90, 105-06, 120,
    122, 144, 146, 151, 158, 163, 194, 231, 237,
    269 n.16, 279 n.1; Pre-Bulgarian, 161, 276
    n.22. *See also* Church Slavonic
Burmese, 60, 64, 66-67, 69. *See also* Tibeto-
    Burmese
Buryat, 96, 202

Čakavian, 45, 53, 143, 154-55, 163, 209-10,
    228-31. *See also* Serbo-Croatian
Caucasian, 95-98, 107, 175-77, 186, 238, 239;
    East, 57, 76, 80, 85, 97-98, 168-69, 170-74,
    236, 277 n.4; North, 43, 79, 86, 92-93, 95-
    97, 165-69; South, 43, 95; [North-]West,
    176, 190
Caucasian-Mediterranean, 95
Caucasus: languages of, 43, 165-69, 175-77
Celtic, 88, 99-103, 132, 200-01
Chamalal, 176
Chechen, 45, 47, 52, 85, 92, 97, 165, 168,
    170-74, 176-77, 197, 236, 277 nn.1-2
Cheremis, 271 n.3, 275 n.18
Chinese, 53-54, 60-61, 63-68, 71, 95, 186,
    262 n.5, 265 n.1; North, 46, 54, 66-68;
    South, 60-61. *See also* Sino-Tibetan
Chukchi, 94, 186

Paleo-Siberian, 78, 94. *See also* Samoyed
Permic, 271 n.3
Persian, 52, 62, 67, 70, 96, 165, 169, 195, 197;
  Middle, 168; Old, 97, 168, 203. *See also*
  Avestan; Iranian
Polabian, 52, 187, 194, 197, 199, 215, 220,
  224-25, 262 n.3, 279 n.1
Polish, 33, 39, 40, 45, 70, 76, 122, 130-31,
  140, 145-46, 152-54, 163, 184, 187, 195,
  196, 207, 212-13, 220, 228, 260 n.2, 272-73
  nn.2-3, 276 n.25
Portuguese, 80
Posavina: dialects of, 154
Prakrit, 45, 47, 52, 197, 203
Prussian, Old, 90, 148-49

Romance, 60, 71, 88-89, 97, 207
Romanian, 53, 70, 80, 132
Russian, 28-29, 31-34, 39, 45, 53, 61, 65, 70,
  72-73, 76, 81, 82, 88, 92, 109-64, 176-77,
  178-79, 183, 189, 191, 194, 195, 199, 202,
  207, 209, 212-18, 222-23, 226-27, 231,
  235-37, 238-39, 260 n.2, 265 n.1, 267 n.5,
  268-76, 278-79 nn.2-10, 279 n.1; Old,
  109-28, 189, 210-11; pidgins, 210
Rutul, 172-73, 176, 190

Samoyed, 94, 96, 186, 202. *See also* Paleo-
  Siberian
Samurian, 170, 173-74, 277 n.4. *See also*
  Lezghian
Sanskrit, 76, 86, 97, 100, 101, 149, 166, 168,
  198, 259-60 n.1, 266 n.1; Vedic, 168, 204-5
Scythian. *See* Iranian
Semitic, 75-76, 79, 85-86, 90, 93-97, 186, 191
Serbian, 105-6, 141-46, 150, 151, 215, 220,
  225, 226, 263 n.6, 279 n.1
Serbo-Croatian, 48-49, 51, 53, 65, 70, 82,
  90, 118, 122, 152, 155-56, 158, 163, 209-
  10, 228-31, 242, 262-63 n.6. *See also*
  Čakavian; Kaikavian; Štokavian
Siamese, 55-56, 63, 263 nn.12-13
Sino-Tibetan, 95
Slavic, 33, 60, 72-74, 76, 80, 82, 87-90, 92,
  96, 103, 104-64, 183, 189-90, 198-200,
  208-9, 211-34, 236-37, 267-76
Slovak, 45, 52, 70, 112, 122, 133, 140, 152-53,

157-59, 189, 196-97, 215, 228, 273-75 nn.1,
  2, 10, 15, 17
Slovenian, 45, 53, 63, 65, 90-92, 96, 118, 122,
  141, 143-46, 153-56, 163-64, 206, 208,
  215, 225, 231-32, 242, 279 n.1
Slovincian, 152-53, 156. *See also* Kashubian
Sorbian, 122, 145-46, 162, 213, 215; Lower,
  161-62; Upper, 112, 157-59, 161-62, 273
  n.1, 279 n.1
Soviet Union: languages of, 175-77, 186, 274
  n.11
Spanish, 53, 65, 70, 80, 238
Štokavian, 143, 154-55, 205, 209-10, 226,
  229-31, 272-73 nn.3, 5. *See also* Serbo-
  Croatian
Sublekhitic, 91-92. *See also* Ukrainian
Sudanic, 60, 64, 78, 79, 94
Svan, 175
Swahili, 70
Swedish, 64, 70, 80

Tabasaran, 47, 170, 172-73, 176
Talysh, 176
Tamil, 45, 47, 62, 64, 67, 70
Tat, 176
Tatar, 63, 96, 151, 169. *See also* Azeri
Thai. *See* Siamese
Tibetan, 79
Tibeto-Burmese, 94
Tindi, 176
Tlingit, 62, 63
Tsakhur, 172-73, 176
Tungus, 45, 186
Tungusic, 94
Turanic, 85, 179, 196
Turkic, 28, 43, 67, 78-80, 82, 90, 94, 186, 188,
  202
Turkish, 37, 70, 82, 98, 158
Turkmen, 45
Tushian. *See* Bats

Ubykh, 165-66
Udi, 173-74, 176
Udmurt, 275 n.18. *See also* Votic
Ugric, 77, 96, 196, 202. *See also* Finno-Ugric
Ukrainian, 53, 70, 91-92, 96, 110-28, 133,
  151, 157-59, 215-16, 218, 273 nn.1-3, 275
  n.17

Linguistic Examples

1. SLAVIC

oko (Cz.), 142, 185
okó (Bulg.), 144
ȍko (Serb.), 142
okô (Sloven.), 144
olovo (Russ.), 125
ol'xa Russ.), 125, 135
*okuno, 130
onъ (Russ.), 125
ona (Russ.), 125
ono (Russ.), 125
os' (Russ.), 125
osen' (Russ.), 125
osina (Russ.), 125
osmě (OCS), 125
os'muška (Russ.), 270 n.18
ospa (Russ.), 126
ostro (Russ.), 125
ostryi (Russ.), 125
otъ (Russ.), 125
ot'ca (Russ.), 117, 125
otče (Russ.), 125
otčina (Russ.), 125
otčizna (Russ.), 125
otecъ (Russ.), 125
*otò, 125
otьcь (OCS), 136–37
ov'ca (Russ.), 125
ozero (Russ.), 125

pas (Pol.), 228
pás (Cz., Slovak), 228
p'eč (Russ.), 116–17, 121
pekëš' (Russ.), 270 n.23
peki (Russ.), 270 n.23
pěnędzь (OCS), 134–35
pered (Ukr.), 116
pervyj (Russ.), 138
pet' (Russ.), 92
pič (Ukr.), 116–17
pieč (Ukr., Beloruss.), 116–17, 121
pijate (OCS), 103
pijite (OCS), 103
*pijoite, 103
pip (Ukr.), 119
*pišešь, 273 n.4
pīt'i (Cz.), 61
pit'ī (Cz.), 61
plačate (OCS), 103
plačite (OCS), 103

plačѧ (OCS), 235
plod (Cz.), 269 n.11
*plōkjoite, 103
pó mъstu (Russ.), 132
pǫ uxu (Russ.), 132
pobryde (Ukr.), 115
po-dvidzati (OCS), 134
pogoda (Russ.), 270 n.20
pogost (Russ.), 270 n.20
poj (Russ.), 92
polьdza (OCS), 134
pol'ga (Russ.), 136
pol'is's'e (Ukr.), 121
polje (OCS), 132
polju (Russ.), 132
Polskę (Pol.), 276 n.25
polskie (Pol.), 276 n.25
*poltĭno, 130
pol'za (Russ.), 136
pomogi (Russ.), 270 n.23
popъ (OCS), 271 n.4
posěj (Russ.), 199
pos'ij (Russ.), 199
pǫti (OCS), 133
povilika (Russ.), 134
povost (Russ.), 270 n.20
pozolota (Russ.), 150
pretъrъpilъ jesi (ORuss.), 268 n.4
přin'is'it'i mn'e stakan vady (Russ.), 61
pr'ĭn'ik (Russ.), 28
prórok (Serb.), 150
prosyš (Ukr.), 119
průhon (Cz.), 220
prvý (Old Cz.), 199
*prѡs'išĭ, 118
ptáci (Cz.), 140
pták (Cz.), 140
ptica (Russ.), 265 n.1
půchod (Cz.), 150
puop (Ukr.), 119
původ (Cz.), 220
pup (Ukr.), 119
*pѡpъ, 118

rabu svojemu Dъmъkě (OCS), 270 n.22
raby (OCS), 133
rȁk (Serbo-Cr.), 118
ràk (Sloven.), 118
*rĭkǫ, 137

2. INDO-EUROPEAN EXCEPT SLAVIC

arguet (Lat.), 100
attulat (OLat.), 102
āusins (OPr.), 148
aūsys (Lith.), 148
Äxsärtäg (Ossetic), 167
Äxsnartˈ (Ossetic), 167

ba (OIr.), 102
baēvarə (Avestan), 166
bairau (Goth.), 276 n.6
baȓda (Latv.), 148
barzdà (Lith.), 148
bärzond (Ossetic), 169
Batˈraz (Ossetic), 167–68
Baum (Ger.), 29
beau (Fr.), 19
Bein (Ger.), 62
benust (Umbr.), 103
bera (OIr.), 102
bera (Old Norse), 276 n.6
*bere-, 102
berid (OIr.), 102
Berlin (Ger.), 67
bëurä (Ossetic), 166
*bhei-, 165
*bherām, 276 n.6
*bherois, 103
*bheroite, 103
*bherōn(t)s, 235
*bhū, 101, 102
*bhū-jē, 101
*bhū-jē-t, 101
*bhujeti, 267 n.4
*b(h)und(h)ānt, 103
*bh(u)we-, 102
*bh(u)weti, 103
bhūyāt (Skt.), 101
bibam (Lat.), 102
Biene (Ger.), 24
bière (Fr.), 62
Binder (Ger.), 29, 36
bindzä (Ossetic), 165, 166
Bohne (Ger.), 24
bon (Fr.), 19
boūt (OPr.), 148
brach (Ger.), 93
bräche (Ger.), 93
brālis (Latv.), 147
brechen (Ger.), 93

Bretschen (Ger.), 162
brich (Ger.), 93
brólis (Lith.), 147
Bruch (Ger.), 92
brüchig (Ger.), 93
Bruder (Ger.), 193
bun (Ossetic), 166
buna- (Avestan), 166
bunt (Ger.), 25, 36
búti (Lith.), 148
*bwā, 102

ça (Fr.), 19
cacher (Fr.), 19
campum (Lat.), 32
capiam (Lat.), 102
capiet (Lat.), 100
capsim (OLat.), 101
casser (Fr.), 19
cent (Fr.), 32
centum (Lat.), 32
champ (Fr.), 19, 32
Christ (Ger.), 67
col (Fr.), 32
collum (Lat.), 32
conuĕnat (OLat.), 102
crée (Fr.), 18
crenaid (OIr.), 102
cria (OIr.), 102, 267 n.3
crie (Fr.), 18

dagh (Skt.), 166
dah (Skt.), 166
*daγ, 166
*daikāti, 99
dem (Lat.), 100
det (Lat.), 100
devaja (Skt.), 168
dhārayišyāmahē (Skt.), 205
dicam (Lat.), 100, 102
dicat (Lat.), 99–100
dice (OLat.), 100
dices (Lat.), 100
dicet (Lat.), 99–101
dicit (Lat.), 99
diene (Ger.), 24
dixerim (Lat.), 101
doit (Fr.), 16
dos (Fr.), 63

3. NON-INDO-EUROPEAN

p'çi (Adyghe), 165
p'çᵘym (Abkhaz), 165
p'çy (Adyghe), 168
P'çyçan (Circ.), 165
*Pet'ɑrez, 167–68
p'yt'ə (Circ.), 276 n.2
pχa (Chechen), 172
pχar (Ingush), 172
pχī (Chechen), 172

Qujc'ykᵘo-qo (Kab.), 167
quz (Turkic), 28

Raipitsiçi (Japanese), 67
raman kudo (Mordv.), 81
ramasa kudont' (Mordv.), 81
ramasak kudont' (Mordv.), 81
ramat kudo (Mordv.), 81
riçam (Kuri), 172
riḳ (Lak), 172
risti (Finn.), 271 n.4

s'ado (Mordv.), 271 n.3
sag (Bats), 170
saj (Chechen), 170
san (Mordv.) 271 n.3
sata (WFinn.), 271 n.3
sēn (Chechen), 170
sëra (Mordv.), 204
s'este (Mordv.), 279 n.9
siisti (Finn.), 271 n.4
sipitaru (Japanese), 67
sirppi (Finn.), 271 n.4
s'o (Zyryan), 271 n.3
šokš (Mordv.), 278 n.4
ššar (Lak), 172
ššaran (Lak), 97
ššaraššar (Lak), 97
s'u (Votic), 271 n.3
šüdö (Cheremis), 271 n.3
šün (Cheremis), 271 n.3
suoni (WFinn.), 271 n.3
sūötna (Lapp), 271 n.3

ṭal (Kuri), 173
ṭar (Kuri), 172
tese (Avar), 97

tetese (Avar), 97
ttarḳ (Lak), 171
ttur (Agul), 172
tturčal (Lak), 171
turku (Finn.), 130
tχe (Bats), 277 n.2
tχə (Ingush), 277 n.2

ṵáịe (Adyghe), 166
-uçar (Bats), 172
-uçin (Lak), 172
'udə (Circ.), 166
ukān (Lak), 172, 277 n.3
-ukkin (Lak), 170
-ula (Avar), 173
-una (Avar), 173
unedexešir (Circ.), 81
uostɑγa (Circ.), 166
ur'i (Dargwa), 172
ut (Tsakhur), 173
üt (Agul), 173
üttan (Agul), 173
-uṭu (Tsakhur), 173
-uzar (Chechen), 172

vac vekerula (Avar), 95
vocas til bosula (Avar), 95
vos'kol (Zyryan), 271 n.3

war'a (Dargwa), 173
wiç (Dargwa, Udi), 172, 173
wiça (Archi), 172
wirt (Kuri), 173

Xamyš' (Circ.), 167
xej (Agul), 277 n.2
xir (Agul), 172
xodé (Kab.), 166
*xṵede, 166
xuras (Archi), 97
xuraxu (Archi), 97
xxa (Lak), 172

yüz (Turkic), 28

žaɣn (Bats), 170
žajna (Chechen), 170
žen (Kab.), 277 n.2

χᵛar (Kuri), 172
χχ̀undericca (Avar), 171
χχ̀unzaqew (Avar), 171

Subjects

Merger. *See* Sound change: phonemic merger

Metatony in Slavic, 153–56, 222–23

Metrics, 263 n.9; Balto-Slavic, 151; Latin, 263 n.9; and the prosodic system of a language, 194–95; Serbo-Croatian, 263 n.9; Russian, 227, 233; Slavic, 233–34

Modifier and modified, 78–82

Monosyllabicity. *See* Sound change

Monophthongization in Old Russian, 123

Moods in Indo-European, 99–103, 266 n.2, 267 n.6

Mora: in Danish, 207; and duration, 263 n.8; in Gweabo, 54. *See also* Mora-counting languages

Mora-counting languages, 55, 263 n.9

Morphology: intensity, 195–96; object of, 3, 11; opposition, 238; paradigm, 238–39; structural history of, 237. *See also* Case; Morphonology; Phonology: and grammar

Morphonology, 72–77

n lost between a vowel and *s*, 133

Name giving by Adyghe and Circassians, 276 n.1

Nasality, 197; in Eskimo and Greenlandic, 260 n.2

Naturalism in phonetic sciences. *See* Positivism in phonetic sciences

Neogrammarian linguistics, 40, 245

Neutralization in morphology, 81, 260 n.2

Neutralization in phonology. *See* Phonemic opposition

Opposition. *See* Phonemic opposition; Morphology: opposition

Optative in Indo-European. *See* Moods in Indo-European

Palatalization, 194; in Chechen and Lak, 171; in Mordvin, 178; in Old Russian, 114, 133, 137–38, 160; in Polabian, 194; in Polish, 184; in Russian, 178, 191, 260 n.2; in Serbo-Croatian, 209; terms for, 190

Phoneme: concept of 15, 23–24, 245, 246–47, 251, 260 n.1; and letter, 37; overlapping variants, 241; reality of, 29, 37; as sound

and intention, 3–4, 6; variants, 27, 191–92, 241, 245

Phonemic merger. *See* Sound change

Phonemic opposition: as basis of phonological analysis, 15, 29; binary vs. nonbinary, 186–87; classification, 14–21, 23, 186–87, 260–61 n.4; neutralization, 12, 18, 20

Phonemic split. *See* Sound change

Phonological analysis: concepts and procedures. *See* Archiphoneme; Correlation vs. disjunction; Markedness; Phoneme; Phonemic opposition; Phonological rules; Phonological system; Phonological units; Rhyme in phonological analysis; Symmetry in phonological analysis; Vocalic features; Vocalic Systems

Phonological rules, 11–13

Phonological system, 3, 189. *See also* Phonology: ethnically restricted laws

Phonological units, 23–24, 34–35, 244–45. *See also* Emphatica

Phonologization. *See* Sound change

Phonology: in Bulgaria, 250; in Czechoslovakia, 241–42; in England, 243; ethnically restricted laws, 189–90; forerunner of, 255; in France, 242–43; in Germany, 245, 250–53; and grammar, 8–9, 13, 37–38, 178, 190; in Hungary, 250; in Japan, 249–50; and linguistic geography, 39–43; in the Netherlands, 244; object of, 3, 6, 11, 245; organization of, 5, 10; and philosophy, 14; and phonetics 6–10, 59, 188–89, 194, 247–48; in Poland, 244; and psychology, 14; reception of, 22–38, 239–53; and reconstruction, 4; and sociolinguistics, 4; subdivisions, 3, 11; and typology, 10, 178–79; in the United States 243; and writing 4, 7. *See also* Historical phonology: Phonological analysis

Phonotactics in English, 257

Pleophony 116, 152, 154, 155, 216, 222

Positivism in phonetic sciences, 253, 261 n.10

Prosody. *See* Accents; Metrics: and prosody; Mora; Mora-counting languages; Quantity; Stress; Syllabicity; Syllable-counting languages

Protheses: *j* in Russian, 207; *v* in Russian, 125–27, 270 nn.17–21
Protolanguage: concept of, 129; disintegration, 109, 128, 129, 212. *See also* Language history: convergences and divergences
Purism in Czech, 184–85

Quantity: in Common Slavic, 152–53; in Czech, 218–22; concept of, 44–59; degrees of, 52, 204, 226; and diphthong, 198–99; and the divisibility of geminates, 45, 56–57; and the divisibility of the syllabic, 45–46, 48, 53–55; and extendibility, 44–46, 52–53; in Finno-Ugric, 203–04; half-free, 225; homologous with stress, 187–88; as intensity, 45, 52, 56–57; in Lapp, 264 n.17; in Old Russian, 119, 122, 127; point vs. line, 20, 44, 51–52; as strength, 58; and syllable cut, 46, 55–56, 204, 263 nn.10, 11, 14; and tone movement, 46, 51, 53–55, 263 n.8; as weight, 58. *See also* Stress: free stress and free quantity

Reconstruction: family tree theory 110; and history, 214; wave theory, 94, 111. *See also* Language history: convergences and divergences; Disintegration; Phonology: and reconstruction; Relative chronology; Substrate
Reduction of vowels in Old Russian, 116, 269 n.16
Relative chronology, 114–17, 119, 121, 133, 135, 137–38, 209, 212, 228, 230, 268 n. 4, 271 n. 6, 274 n.10
Rhyme, 28
Romance languages: origin, 88–89
Root structure in various languages, 85

Schallanalyse, 223
Semivowels, 198–99; in Old Russian, 113–14, 117, 122, 126
Sibilants: in German, 21; in Japanese, 20; in Old Russian, 123
Slavic languages: overview of their history, 211–18
Sociolinguistics. *See* Artificial language: as a social problem; Language union; Purism in Czech

Sound change: and binary oppositions, 187; and biology, 209; change in the realization without change in the status of the phoneme, 159, 163; contrasting reinforcement in a diphthong, 136; degrees of a distinctive feature, 136, 138; ease of articulation, 131; and functional yield, 32–33; as a generational phenomenon, 31–33; as a goal-oriented process 4, 157, 207–8, 240; and inherent properties of sounds, 219, 221; long vowels and the degree of opening, 207; and markedness, 208; and a new image of words, 127; and "paper philology," 240; parallelism in the development of sounds, 117–18, 130–31, 219; phonemic merger, 32; phonemic split, 32, 210–11; phonological and grammatical structures interdependent, 190; phonologization, 27, 32, 126–27; rephonologization, 172; and speech tempo, 207; strength of, 127; as a structural change 4; and syntax, 207; as tendency, 138; unity of, 138. *See also* Historical phonology; Language change
Speech and music. *See* Language and music
Split. *See* Sound change: phonemic split
Stød. *See* Glottal stop
Stress: absent in some languages, 70–71; in Chinese, 262 n.5; and consonantal timbre 189; in Czech, 223; degrees of, 153; fixed and redundant, 45; in Finno-Ugric, 201–4; free stress and free quantity, 53, 119, 195–97, 230, 262 n.4; homologous with quantity, 187–88; in Hungarian, 223; in Indo-European, 201; as intensity 45, 52; in Japanese, 227; and morphological intensity, 195–96; musical, 197, 205; not purely expiratorial, 272 n.6; in Polabian, 224–25, 262 n.3; whole words as the locus of, 227–28. *See also* Accents
Structural linguistics, 38
Stufenwechsel in Finno-Ugric, 203–4
Subject predicate relations, 78–79
Subjunctive. *See* *ā*-Subjunctive in Latin; Moods in Indo-European
Substrate, 43, 276 n.20
Syllable-counting languages, 55
Syllabicity, 198–99

Syllable cut. *See* Quantity and syllable cut

Symmetry in phonological analysis, 187

Syntax. *See* Modifier and modified; Sound change: and syntax

System. *See* Artificial phonemic system; Phonological system

Tone languages. *See* Stress: musical; Quantity: and tone movement

Typology. *See* Phonology: and typology

Universals, 187. *See also* Phonology: ethnically restricted laws

Utterance, aspects of, 26, 30, 261 n.5. *See also* Emphatica

Versification in Latin, 200–2

Vocalic features, 196

Vocalic systems, 187–88

Voice, correlation of, 20, 160, 204, 259 n.1, 260 n.1

Vowel harmony, 91–92, 196

Wave theory. *See* Reconstruction

Weakening of vowels in Old Russian. *See* Reduction of vowels in Old Russian

Anatoly Liberman is Professor of Germanic Philology at the
University of Minnesota.
Marvin Taylor is Instructor in Scandinavian at
the University of Bochum, Germany.

Library of Congress Cataloging-in-Publication Data
Trubetzkoy, N. S. Studies in general linguistics and language
structure / N. S. Trubetzkoy; edited by Anatoly Liberman ;
translated by Anatoly Liberman and Marvin Taylor.
p.   cm. — (Sound and meaning) (Includes bibliographical
references and index.)
ISBN 0-8223-2280-3 (alk. paper).
ISBN 0-8223-2299-4 (pbk. : alk. paper)
1. Trubetskoĭ, Nikolai Sergeevich, kniãz', 1890–1938.   2. Grammar,
Comparative and general—Phonology.   3. Language and languages.
4. Linguistics.   I. Liberman, Anatoly.   II. Trubetskoĭ Nikolai Sergeevich,
kniãz', 1890–1938.   III. Series.   IV. Series: Includes bibliographical
references and index.
P85.T75N19   1999   414'.092—dc21   2001-18338   CIP